THAILAND
FOR COUPLES

DAVID NGUYEN

ISBN: 978-0-646-83621-8

Author: David Nguyen

Co-Author: Rona Gindin

Editor: Emma Gibbs

Book Cover Designer: Liliana Guia

Map Designer: Velly Yuliani Goenawan

TABLE OF CONTENT

HOW TO USE THIS GUIDE

DISCLAIMER

This book has all you need to know to plan a romantic trip to Thailand: We gathered the information from repeated visits, followed by countless hours of research and fact-checking. But, despite this, there is one thing to bear in mind throughout: things change. Businesses close; others open. Chefs revamp menus, change focus, or move on. Prices fluctuate. Train lines and flight routes expand or are curtailed. What's more, due to the worldwide Covid-19 pandemic, many of the places featured here will have shuttered—many just temporarily but others permanently—or reduced their operating hours and changed their prices. Unfortunately, no amount of painstaking research can preclude the fact that things may well have changed once you hit the ground yourselves. In other words, use our suggestions as a launching point, but check the specifics before you travel. Websites, Facebook pages (which are frequently more up-to-date), emails, and phone calls will lead you to the most current situation. *Thailand for Couples*, its authors, and its publisher are not responsible for any decision you make, nor any damage, loss, cost, or error that's the result of those decisions, based on our suggestions. Check your facts, travel safely, and have yourselves a sensational vacation.

CURRENCY

Thailand uses the baht. You'll see it written as ฿ and THB. One baht is made up of 100 satang. At press time, one United States dollar equaled 30.13 baht, meaning prices can look ridiculously high even when they're low. For example, a $100 hotel room will cost ฿3,012.80. Throughout this book, we list prices in United States dollars, calculated at the rate given above: This is to give you a general idea of what to expect, but it's important to always check for current prices yourself.

DOLLAR RATING SYSTEM

Throughout this guide a dollar figure is assigned to each accommodation and restaurant. For accommodations it represents the approximate cost for a 2-bedroom hotel and for restaurants, it represents the estimated cost for a main meal per person.

ACCOMMODATION

$ - Budget under $100
$$ - Mid Range $100 - $250
$$$ - Expensive $250+

RESTAURANT

$ - Budget under $30
$$ - Mid Range $30 - $100
$$$ - Expensive $100+

MAPS

We've designed and included maps to help you get oriented easily. For each chapter, the yellow drawing represents the entire destination. Within, you'll find black dots; each is the approximate midpoint of the neighborhood, town, or city named. Airports are marked by dots with airplanes inside. Each chapter also has a blue drawing representing the whole area of Thailand and specific to each chapter, there is a yellow highlighted area representing the city/island being discussed.

MAP OF THAILAND

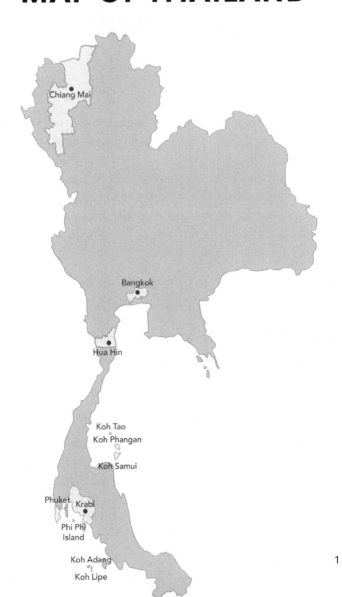

WELCOME TO THAILAND

Sitting at the heart of Southeast Asia and blessed with not one but three coasts, Thailand is an undoubtedly beguiling destination. To the visitor, what's on offer can at times seems like an embarrassment of contradictions—history and modernity, idyllic islands and vibrant cities, ultimate luxury and bare-bones economy—but the result is a country that provides much more than you could ever hope to squeeze into one trip, and one that will leave you hankering to return.

Visiting as a couple, you'll be spoiled for choice when it comes to romance, whether it's sipping cocktails in a chic rooftop bar or digging your toes into the sand while you eat dinner at a plastic table, whether indulging in a luxurious spa treatment or paddling your way through mangroves in a kayak. And, even if your ideas of a romantic vacation don't quite align, you'll find it easy to mix and match experiences.

In fact, one of the hardest things about planning a vacation to Thailand is narrowing down the list of places to visit—though, on a romantic holiday in particular, it's worth focusing on only a handful of places so you don't have to travel at a breakneck speed. If sunbathing is a priority, head to one of the coasts or islands where your choices are as simple as white or golden sands, bare or busy, sunny or tree-lined. Whatever you choose, chances are that a picturesque string of longboats awaits, their owners ready to whisk you away for a short voyage. If you love sand and sea but are more action-minded, you'll find opportunities for world-class snorkeling and diving around coral reefs, not to mention kayaking, paddle boarding, and other water and boat-based adventures.

If you're happiest exploring natural landscapes, drive or hike to waterfalls and scenic outlooks, and venture into cave systems and jungles. To really immerse yourself, camp or rent a bungalow in a national park, or—for the ultimate luxury—choose a resort room on a remote island. (The weddings at these secluded outposts? Second to none.) For miniature doses of nature immersion, you can spend a day with elephants at a sanctuary or, seek out serene botanical gardens abloom with indigenous flowers.

Wherever you end up, you won't want to miss out on experiencing Thai culture, whether it's strolling through a night market to sample the food and pick-up artisanal crafts, or taking a front seat at a Muay Thai boxing match. Then there's that other stand-out local activity: Thai massage. Unlike the Swedish and deep-tissue versions common in the States, Thai massages are less sedentary. Your masseuse will bend and lift your limbs and arch your entire back in a gymnastic feat. In the end, your muscles will be loose in a whole new way. Take that, jet lag! Perhaps best of all, you'll find an abundance of couples' treatments at tranquil spas throughout the country, allowing you to dial up the romance.

For many couples, one of the country's major drawcards is its food—aromatic, lemongrass-laced, and utterly delicious. You'll be spoiled for choice, with everything on offer from sizzling snacks from a street hawker to multi-course gourmet meals.

Even the less adventurous will find ample to please their palates, whether it's in the familiar and ubiquitous noodle dish of pad Thai, a modern coffee bar, or an international restaurant serving up familiar Western staples.

Nightlife can be as little or as much as you want. If you're a pair of party animals, you'll probably want to time your visit to coincide with one of the raucous full moon parties. For something altogether more sophisticated, let a bartender pour you chilled champagne from a rooftop bar that appears to float above its location. At its heart, though, Thailand is a place to relax: Sip a beer while watching a soccer game in a sports bar, or sway barefoot on the sand to live music at a hut along the shoreline.

The accommodations on offer throughout Thailand will wow you. The only thing likely to hold you back is how much your money can stretch. Take your pick from familiar, multi-national chains and luxurious beachfront resorts with infinity pools and cocktail bars to rustic yet atmospheric motels and bamboo huts on the sand. We've chosen the most alluring options for every budget.

Here's the take-away: Thailand is a gloriously romantic destination, no matter what kind of vacation you enjoy. Book your ticket. And appreciate every moment you have together in this welcoming country.

Romantic dinner on a beach in Thailand

WHEN TO GO

Thailand's climate can be split into three seasons: cool (November through February); hot (March through May); and rainy (June through early November). Don't be fooled by the name—cool season is, with the exception of the far north, only comparatively cool and at most you'll only need a sweater after dinner. This is the best time to visit, with less threat of rain and many of the nation's fascinating festivals taking place—but, unsurprisingly, this is also high season. Low season is hot season. You'll see higher temperatures and find the air a lot more humid. In exchange you get lower prices on hotels. If you really want to keep your budget low, visit during the rainy—or value—season, although be aware you may experience rain like you've never seen it before—the monsoon. That said, what better, more romantic reason to hole up together in your hotel? And rain rarely means all-day rain. If you get a downpour in the morning, it may well be dry enough for beach time in the afternoon, or vice versa. The prices for flights and lodging are rock-bottom during this stretch of time.

Note that Thailand is long and it has three coastlines. There are significant regional variations. For example, the Gulf Coast tends to have slightly different seasons, with rain between October and January. Before booking your flight, be sure to research the weather in the locations you've chosen.

Temperature-wise, in Bangkok (roughly in the middle of the country) temperatures rarely vary much from 90°F (32°C) in winter, but climb to 100°F (38°F) in March. Chiang Mai is in the north, so the sun is a little weaker. Still, you'll be sweating in the 91°F (33°C) heat in February, which rises to over 100°F (40°C) in the spring. The temps do cool to as low as 40°F (5°C) at night around Christmas time.

Thailand's beach destinations lie to the south of Bangkok where, fortunately, breezes help compensate for a fiery sun. Destinations on the east coast fronting the Gulf of Thailand enjoy temperatures year-round that range from the high 70s to the low 90s Fahrenheit (mid 20s to low 30s Celsius), while west-coast locales along the Andaman Sea, including the Phi Phi Islands and Krabi, are just a tad cooler.

BANGKOK

WHY GO

Bangkok—a metropolis loaded with personality—is meant for romance. Here you'll find everything from age-old temples and sunset river cruises to indulgent spa treatments, romantic rooftop bars, and sizzling nightclubs—not to mention treehouse accommodations and some of the best food in the region. It's no exaggeration to say we could go on for pages describing what's on offer.

Better yet, the American dollar goes far here, especially for a major metropolis. You can cuddle up in a motel for next to nothing, or live grandly in a sleek all-suite hotel for what a Holiday Inn would cost you back home. You can feast extravagantly on aromatic street food for pocket change, or enter a chef-driven fine dining restaurant for a sensual multi-course experience. You can pick up inexpensive souvenirs at street markets or load up on international designer goods at splashy malls. Whatever brings you together, Bangkok has it, big time.

You'll never cover the entire 606 square miles (1,569 km²) in one trip, whether you explore the neighborhoods by MRT underground, overhead Skytrain, open-sided tuk-tuk, river ferry, bus, taxi, or private tour guide. That's for the best. No matter where you explore, whom you meet, and what new experiences you try, Bangkok will always have more for you to discover. That's surely one reason why Bangkok is ranked the world's most visited city, with as many as 22 million visitors a year.

Known in Thai as Krung Thep, this sophisticated city is Thailand's capital and its metropolitan region is home to 14 million residents—more than a fifth of the country's population. Today's city began as a trading post back in the 1400s and, by the 19th century, was known as Siam. You might remember that from Rodgers and Hammerstein's musical The King and I, which was based on the semi-autobiographical novel Anna and the King of Siam. (Cue Whistle a Happy Tune, or, more appropriately, the duller Hello, Young Lovers.)

Nowadays you'll know Siam mainly as a stop on the Skytrain (pronounced "see-AHM"), with no Yul Brynner in sight. Bangkok benefited from an Asian investment boom in the years before 2000, which brought mega-money and, ultimately, extra sophistication. Meanwhile, the world-famous red-light districts continue to draw those looking to add a little edge after dark, just as a diverse club scene entertains party-happy adults after hours.

TRAVELING FROM THE AIRPORT

If you're flying in from another country, you'll arrive at the main airport, Suvarnabhumi Airport (BKK, suvarnabhumi. airportthai.co.th), aka New Bangkok Airport, or—if you're on a lower-fare flight—possibly Mueang International Airport (DMK, donmueangairport.com). Many hotels will arrange for a car to meet you. That's easiest but you'll save money by hailing a taxi at the official stands. Bring the name of your hotel written in Thai, as not all drivers understand English. Alternatively, from BKK the Airport Rail Link City Line will get you into the city proper in half an hour for only a couple of dollars, though you'll need a taxi for the last leg of your trip. You'll land at the Phaya Thai Station, which is near government offices in the Ratchathewi District. At the Phaya Thai Station, you can also hop on the BTS Skytrain's Sukhumvit Line, which in turn connects with the Silom Line via Siam Station. These two routes might move you closer to your hotel for a low price, and quickly. At the DMK airport, a metered taxi will take between 45 minutes and two hours to reach the center, depending on traffic, and cost around about $7, or you can take Bus No. 29 for less than $1.

GETTING AROUND

Unfortunately for a city this size, both the underground and overhead rail systems cover only parts of the metropolis. So many extensions are planned that by 2025 the system may be as big a London's Underground—but that won't help you now. Taxis are cheap but the traffic is so dense that, honestly, sometimes there is no best way to get somewhere. We suggest you plot your days wisely: Cluster attractions that are geographically close together into a single outing when possible. At the very least, maybe start thinking of taxi journeys as another chance to spend time together.

Overall, you are likely to find that public transport is the easiest and fastest way to get around the city, assuming there are overhead or underground trains going in your direction. The website transitbangkok.com will tell you the best route. If you have the budget, you can also hire a private driver. Walk when you can, of course. That's best for dipping into unexpected finds. Bangkok is so large, however, and so hot and humid, that even the hardiest trekkers often need alternatives with wheels or tracks.

Where possible, we give the approximate price from central Siam to the Grand Palace.

BTS Skytrain (bts.co.th/eng) Clean, reliable trains with easy-to-follow maps. Buy your ticket at the station then jump on a train. A trip from the central Siam station to the Grand Palace costs $1.25.

MRT subway (transitbangkok.com/mrt.html) Also clean and reliable. The only snag is that you need to buy a new ticket when transferring to/from the Skytrain. A single ride is $1.25.

River taxi A little hard to navigate, but once you do, you'll find that zooming along the river from one point to another is a fun and scenic way to get around. Prices vary, beginning at under $1.

Grab (grab.com/th/en/locations) Bangkok's answer to Uber and Lyft. Assuming you have internet access, you can order your rides via smartphone app. Cost $2.85

Tuk-tuk These open-air taxis are a hoot in rural areas but can be uncomfortable with Bangkok's smoggy air.

Tuk-tuk in Bangkok

Bus (bmta.co.th/en/bus-lines) Public buses connect the entire city, and they're cheap. "Normal" and express options are available. The main issue, of course, is traffic. Cost $0.50.

Motorbike taxi Quick and easy, but not so great for two of you together.

Taxi Traditional taxis work here as they do in New York. Hail one what's available. Make sure the driver turns on the meter. Then sit back and rest until you reach your destination. Cost $4.

WHERE TO STAY

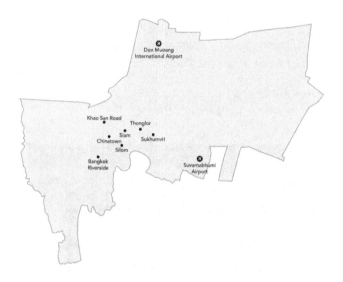

Bangkok area map

Bangkok is divided into 50 districts. Below are the popular areas and streets to stay in the city.

Bangkok Riverside ริมแม่น้ำกรุงเทพ

If you're the types who'll arrive with a checklist of major tourist sites and an itinerary to help you to see them efficiently, Bangkok Riverside is the neighborhood for you. The major hotels here offer Western and Thai amenities so after each expedition you'll be able to kick up your road-weary feet in comfort—maybe even at an in-hotel spa for a side-by-side massage. Here you'll also find old homes that have been transformed into one-of-a-kind boutique hotels, offering a more personable lodging experience. And, as the name says, you'll be by the Chao Phraya River, giving great access to water transportation.

The main perk of a Bangkok Riverside stay is convenience: you'll have easy access to the city's prime sightseeing destinations, including the mystical Royal Palace and all the temples and other treasures surrounding it. You'll be able to arrive early, beating the heat and the crowds, and making your tours more enjoyable. In this part of town, the Asiatique Market is an easy stop for dinner and souvenir shopping, the flower market a quick place to grab a bouquet for the hotel room, and Icon Siam an air-conditioned mall loaded with stores and eateries.

Chinatown ไชน่าทาวน์

If you've been to a Chinatown in any major metropolis, you'll know what to expect in Bangkok's: bustling sidewalks, steaming aromatic street foods, and storefronts loaded with trinkets of every imaginable kind. Bangkok's Chinatown began in the 1780s so it has had time to get it right. The main artery is Yaowarat Road, and twisting side streets add to the intrigue. The vibrant area is a great escape from the city's more polished neighborhoods. It's also a destination for buying gold, both bars and, ahem, jewelry—hint, hint! You can shop for goods at the other end of the price range at Sampeng Market. The Golden Buddha and Wat Traimit Temple are worth a detour. In terms of lodging, this used to be a good choice only for budget travelers. Now it has a funky edge: old buildings have been updated and transformed into one-of-a-kind hotels with unusual, even playful, decors.

Khao San Road ถนนข้าวสาร

If you're on a roughing-it kind of budget, you'll find your kind on Khao San Road. This is a backpackers' hub, a world of young travelers, with modestly priced lodging, inexpensive food and drink—especially the street vendors near Democracy Monument, and a party atmosphere every night. Pick a hotel on a side street as Khao San Road itself is noisy after dark. There's no Skytrain stop, which is a downside, so you may have to become an expert at navigating the river ferry system. On the upside, you'll be walking distance from the Grand Palace, the Golden Mount Temple, and The Bangkok National Museum, the city's largest, so it'll be easy to see those main sites. You'll be within the non-touristy Banglamphu district, which is a great place to take in the restaurants and temples that locals prefer.

Siam สยาม

If you're the type of twosome that makes time for the local take on Madame Tussaud's in every city, then Siam is the spot for you. This part of Bangkok is a clutch of shopping malls, each bigger and more packed with attractions, stores, and places to eat than the next. Locals congregate in the area to shop. Tourists head here for go-to's like the wax museum and the SEA LIFE Bangkok Ocean World aquarium, not to mention an ice-skating rink (CentralWorld) and high-tech movie theaters showing the latest blockbusters. Then take a break from sale racks and bins for a tour of Jim Thompson's House, where the eponymous silk trader once lived. Also, in Siam the Bangkok Art and Culture Centre has visual art exhibits.

Silom สีลม

Silom is two worlds in one. By day, it's similar to New York's Wall Street—a financial district with high-rises, bank headquarters, and law firms. The hotels here may have been designed for business travelers, but that's a boon for you as the lodging tends to be high-end. If you want some culture, visit the Bangkok Folk Museum. Fresh air? Head for Lumphini Park, a large green expanse with jogging trails and workout equipment.

Once the white- and pink-collar workers head home, Silom gives over its streets to recreation. You can enjoy authentic Thai meals in restaurants that have been in the same family for years or get a buzz on at a sky bar (there's something innately aphrodisiacal about such settings). You can shop for fun, if overpriced, goods at the Patpong Night Market.

Sukhumvit สุขุมวิท

Sukhumvit has *everything* you'll need for your romantic vacation—except, essentially, tourist sites. Centered around the hubbub of busy Sukhumvit Road—you'll want to walk or use the easily accessible public transportation because the traffic here is daunting—this is an amenity-rich quarter of the city. You'll find both mid-priced hotels and indulgent ones with lovely perks, not to mention an array of glitzy shopping malls loaded with tempting retail goods. Here too is fine Thai food, excellent street food and, for those who tire of tamarind and galangal, everything else from American grocery stores and Irish pubs to German sausage.

It's a chicken-and-egg situation, but Sukhumvit is where expats tend to settle—from the U.S., though you'll also find sub-neighborhoods populated with folks from Japan, India, and Arab countries. High-rise apartment and condo buildings abound. To see the locals living their daily lives, stop into the Khlong Toei Market, stocked with fresh foods. If nightlife is part of your romance routine, you needn't go far. Sukhumvit is so large that it has it all: intimate lounges, lively dance clubs, and a range of red-light districts. In particular, the side streets Soi 11 and Soi 55 are party hubs.

Thonglor ทองหล่อ

Thonglor is small potatoes compared to the larger neighborhoods featured here—in fact, it's is technically part of Sukhumvit, but the vibe is more polished. The area is such a charmer that we're including it anyway. This slim part of town runs around Thonglor

Road—always congested, and with no traffic lights so crossing by foot is a challenge. Still, it's a wonderful choice if you enjoy the types of activities Bangkok's young professionals do: It's a relatively quiet urban enclave filled with wine bars and barista bars, yoga studios, and boutiques. Thonglor still has its touristy offerings, like an indoor surf studio and an escape room. But mostly it's a nice place to spread out in an all-suite hotel, grab a $10 Thai massage, or unwind over a lemongrass martini or a chilled glass of Chablis. The nightlife options are known to be cool, whether it's a gaming bar, craft beer outlet, or sleek dance club.

ACCOMMODATIONS

Bangkok Loft Inn บางกอกลอฟท์อินน์ $

(bangkokloftinn.com; 02862-0300; 55, Somdet Phra Chao Tak Sin Rd, Bang Yi Ruea, Thonburi)

You'll have all the essentials, in a stylish space, at Thonburi's Bangkok Loft Inn. Teak floors give a luxe yet light look to each of the 32 accommodations within the hotel's four stories. In addition to one or two smartly attired beds, you'll have a sleeper sofa, a desk, a bathrobe, a coffeemaker, and even daily maid service. The Executive Suites also have a living room area. The whole place comes across as peaceful, and a lobby lounge, restaurant, airport pick-up, and room service keep things easy. A Skytrain station is nearby.

Bangkok Tree House บ้านต้นไม้กรุงเทพ $$

(bangkoktreehouse.com; 082995-1150; 60 Moo 1, Petch Cha Hueng Rd, Phra Pradaeng)

And now for something completely different. Bangkok Tree House is a funky out-of-the-way eco-hotel whose design was inspired by Henry David Thoreau's *Walden*. If a love of nature is what you two have in common, it might be an Eden for you. You'll stay in a three-level "nest" that's notable for its outdoor bamboo shower and rooftop sunbed, with lush foliage and native bamboo seemingly everywhere and digital detox discounts for Thai residents. The hotel can be reached only by boat, bike, or foot; once you're there, free bike rentals are a great way to tour the property. In addition, it's dog-friendly, grows much of its own produce on the premises, uses energy-efficient lightbulbs and carbon-free cooking equipment, composts natural waste, hang-dries laundry, and has no air-conditioning outside the nests, ensuring a real eco experience. It also embraces whatever creatures of nature visit naturally, whether butterflies or lizards. You can also sleep under stars in a two-person "View with a Room" offering 360-degree views. Hint: The Tree House offers proposal and green wedding packages.

Lebua At State Tower เลอบัวแอทสเตททาวเวอร์ $$

(lebua.com/hotels/lebua-at-state-tower; 02624-9999; 1055 Silom Rd, Bangrak)

Boutique hotels offer a more intimate environment for couples, and the pampering Lebua has only 136 accommodations. Each unit is a suite with a top-quality bed, separate living room, balcony, and kitchenette—a great place to store your bubbly. Wake up to views of the Chao Phraya River and take some time in the pool, fitness center, or sauna before heading out to explore. You'll be right near Michelin-starred restaurants, or—better yet—you can head straight up to the building's 63rd floor to hang out together sipping Hangovertinis made with 18-year-old Chivas Regal at the Original Sky Bar Bangkok. The bar is seemingly suspended in mid-air above the metropolis, so get your camera phone ready. Speaking of hangovers, the hotel's restaurants played a part in the 2011 film *The Hangover Part II*. Hopefully you'll have better mornings.

Novotel Bangkok Ploenchit Sukhumvit โนโวเทลกรุงเทพ เพลินจิตสุขุมวิท $

(novotelbangkokploenchit.com; 02305-6000; 566 Phloen Chit Rd, Khwaeng Lumphini, Pathum Wan District)

Centrally located in Ploenchit, which offers easy access to many other parts of Bangkok, this Novotel is a modern hotel with all you'll need. Choose from 370 rooms and suites, then head over to the restaurant, bar, outdoor pool. and fitness center. You'll have a desk if you need, a day bed and, best of all, natural light pouring into your glass-walled bathroom. Ooh-la-la.

Shanghai Mansion Bangkok เซียงไฮ้แมนชันกรุงเทพฯ $

(shanghaimansion.com; 02221-2121; 479 481 Yaowarat Rd, Samphanthawong)

Cross the red bridge into the Shanghai Mansion Bangkok and you'll begin a Chinese-Thai experience you'll recall for years to come. The hotel has the sexy look of 1930s Shanghai, a style that carries into the decor and live jazz of the Red Rose restaurant. The interiors honor the building's storied past as a trading house (1892), Chinese opera house (1908), stock exchange, textile trading center, and department store. Today, art-deco touches, rich fabrics, and imperial furniture—plus delightful bits of whimsy—make this a one-of-a-kind place to pucker up. Even the most basic rooms are suite-like with brocades and other playful takes on the styles of yore. All are reasonably priced and therefore offer true value. Be sure to book an *omakase*-style (design-your-own) spa pampering package with Spa Burasari Treatments before exploring Chinatown right outside your door.

Shangri-La Hotel, Bangkok โรงแรมแชงกรีลากรุงเทพฯ $$-$$$

(shangri-la.com/en/bangkok/shangrila/; 02236-7777; 89 Soi Wat Suan Plu, New Rd, Bangrak)

The Shangri-La has not only Western comforts and sweeping

Chao Phraya River views, but way more—several restaurants, spa treatments, tennis courts, and two swimming pools, for starters. The 802-room hotel is also centrally located with easy access to the Skytrain, buses, and ferries. Choose the style that speaks romance for you: a modern Thai groove via handicrafts and accessories in the Shangri-La wing, or a western luxe look in the Khrung Thep section. Oh, and before a day of sightseeing, get sweaty together in a boxing or yoga class.

BREAKFASTS

Crepes & Co. เครปแอนด์โค $

Crepes, French
(crepesand.co; 02015-3388; 59/4 Langsuan Soi 1, Ploenchit Rd, Lumpini Subdistrict; daily 9am-11pm)
When you know you have a big day ahead of you and want to start out on full bellies, step onto Crepes & Co. You'll feel so satisfied that you won't even think about hunger until dinner time. The specialty is the eponymous thin French pancakes known as crepes, of course. You can get those savory, perhaps with chicken, coriander, and Béchamel sauce, or sweet, such as the version flambéed with Calvados. Oversized plates of egg dishes, multi-part breakfast "sets," salads, pastas, and Mediterranean specialties will fuel you up morning, noon, or night. The setting is a shingled house with a cozy yet open dining room.

Kay's Boutique Breakfast อาหารเช้าแบบบูติกของ Kay $

European
(kaysboutiques.com; 02245-1953; 116/55-57 Rangnam Rd, Phayathai, Ratchatewi, another unit in Central Embassy; Wed-Mon 6:30am-4pm, Tue 6:30am-noon)
Light, bright and airy—maybe it's the New York connection, but something about Kay's is absolutely refreshing, and that's before

you get to the food. Since 2016, the Kobkulsuwan family has been plating up elegant breakfasts in a dining room that is chic and all-white with recessed lighting and an open kitchen. It's not the brunch pasta carbonara, the Oh My Omelet, or the Hangover French Toast that will merit your Instagram minutes, nor even the homemade granola with mango, coconut, and yogurt. You'll be in selfie-heaven in the flower-covered corridor leading into the restaurant.

Simple. เรียบง่าย $

International

(simplenaturalkitchen.com; 02662-2510; 31 Soi Sawatdi, Phra Khanong Nuea, Watthana; Tue-Fri 9am-6pm, Sat-Sun 8am-6pm) The folks at Simple. keep it simple. They buy seasonal ingredients when they can, locally produced ones too, and organic whenever possible with the help of the Thai Green Market Group. They transform those foodstuffs into hearty breakfasts, from an American-style French toast to a full English breakfast and a Middle-Eastern eggplant shakshuka. Cold-pressed juices, smoothies, salads, entrées (plenty of with quinoa): It's all about being natural and healthful. The Simple. staff serves it all up in an eclectic casual space that feels as much like a home dining room as a restaurant.

Snooze Coffee House $

European

(snooze-coffee-house.business.site; 098268-2940; 170/4 Samsen Rd, Opposite to Samsen Soi 5; daily 7:30am-4pm) It's all about breakfast at Snooze, whatever that means to you. Wake up with 100 percent Arabic coffee, stuff yourselves with a home-cooked traditional Western breakfast, or go light with a salad, smoothie, or sandwich, even a vegetarian choice. Snooze covers the morning basics—whatever "morning" means to you, from pancakes to spinach quesadillas, since it's open past lunchtime.

The Coffee Club คอฟฟีคลับ $

Australian, Thai

(thecoffeeclub.co.th; 092248-6901; 21 Sukhumvit 61 North Klongtan, Watthana; daily 6:30am-8pm)

The Coffee Club has been serving Australians java, breakfast, and lunch since 1989, and now Thailand is among the nine countries to have the concept. In Bangkok, the all-day restaurant is located right near the Mariamman Temple. Like its siblings (there are over 400 of them), the restaurant plates up eggs, burgers, sandwiches, entrées, and iced drinks throughout the day. To keep the quality consistent, the company carefully sources ingredients like quinoa, avocado and baby rocket.

LUNCHES AND DINNERS

Blue Elephant ช้างสีน้าเงิน $$

Thai

(blueelephant.com/bangkok; 02673-9353; 233 Thanon Sathon Tai, Yannawa BTS Surasak; Mon-Fri 11am-2:30pm and 5pm-9:30pm, Sat-Sun 11am-9:30pm)

The Blue Elephant has all the makings of a tourist trap, yet its consistently good food—self-described "Royal Thai Cuisine"—keeps the place in the critics' good stead, and it's even rated by Michelin. The menu is under the direction of Chef Nooror Somany Steppe, who started the concept in Europe and now oversees the kitchens of branches in several cities worldwide. The Bangkok version is located in a historic mansion and decorated in colonial style, and it also has a cooking school and sells branded packaged foods. Many of the ingredients used are grown on a northern Thai mountain. Pick and choose classics like steamed black-truffle dumplings, or sweet basil and chili sea bass, or live it up with your love by ordering the four-course chef's tasting menu, which has many influences from Belgium, where the chef once lived.

Dine in the Dark รับประทานอาหารในความมืด $$

European, Asian

(dineinthedarkbangkok.com; 02649-8358; 250 Sukhumvit Rd, Khwaeng Khlong Toei, Khet Khlong Toei Sheraton Grande Sukhumvit)

If a candlelight dinner sounds romantic, how about a meal in absolute darkness? That's what you'll find at Dining in the Dark, a four-course repast meant to help diners experience vision impairment while raising funds for Thailand's Foundation for the Blind. Nuzzle leg to leg while sampling a Western, Asian, or vegetarian meal, or a "surprise" mix, in absolute blackness ("Is that shrimp, sweetie?" "Maybe there's a hint of orange in the sauce?"), along with add-on wine or cocktail pairings. Giggle over the big reveal once you're done, when a staffer shares details of what you consumed. Dress for date night; a light dress code is enforced.

Ethos Vegetarian and Vegan Restaurant ร้านอาหารมังสวิรัติ และมังสวิรัติ Ethos $$

Vegetarian, Thai, International

(ethosbangkok.com; 02280-7549; 85/2 Tanao Rd, Banglumpoo)

Ethos takes healthy food to the nth extreme. This meat-free restaurant serves organic rice, takes three days to make its own tempeh, and home-ferments its kombucha tea and vinegar. You'll find Eastern, Indian, Thai, and Western specialties here, from spaghetti with vegan meatballs to falafel, lassis, fruit juices, and house-baked vegan pastries. Even the muesli is created in-house; have it with homemade yogurt or with coconut milk.

Govinda Vegetarian Restaurant in Bangkok ร้านโกวินดา มังสวิรัติในกรุงเทพมหานคร $

Vegetarian, Italian

(govindarestaurantbkk.com; 02663-4970; 6 5 -6/6 Sukhumvit Rd, Khlong Toei; Wed-Mon 12pm-2:30pm and 6pm-12:30pm)

Vegans can fuel up worry-free at this light and bright meat-free Italian establishment that is so committed to quality that it makes its own dairy-free cheese. The menu provides a taste of Europe minus the animal proteins, turning out the likes of pasta puttanesca, pizza, lasagna, gnocchi, risotto, and carpaccio—even (faux) chicken Milanese, all with plant-based products. Gluten-free options are available.

Il Bolognese $$

Pizza, Seafood, Steakhouse, Italian

(ilbolognesebangkok.com; 02286-8805; 139/3 Sathon Soi 7, South Sathon Rd, Thung Maha Mek; daily 11:30am-2:30pm and 5pm-11pm)

Rustic, flavorful pastas, pizzas, meats, and seafood dishes enchant in the city of Bologna, and those menu items are recreated in Bangkok at Ristorante Il Bolognese. The homey, casual glass-walled dining room—with a pizza oven in the center, where you can see the chefs at work—uses some imported foods in its kitchen. Expect the likes of pizza with speck and gorgonzola, tortellini in broth, savory meatballs, and a welcome shot of limoncello.

Insects in the Backyard แมลงในสวนหลังบ้าน $$

Mediterranean

(insectsinthebackyard.com; 02035-7000; 460/8 Sirindhom Rd, Bang Phlat; Tue-Sun 11:30am-10pm)

If either of you has ever watched *Survivor* and fancied joining in when contestants eat bugs, now's your chance. A restaurant called

Insects in the Backyard, inside Thonburi's hipster Chang Chui Art Hub, specializes in bug cuisine. Bigger and better than the bags of crunchy dried grasshoppers popular at night markets, this is food art. Not only does executive chef Mai Thitiwait carefully source and artfully cook these creatures; his restaurant's website touts insects' good-for-you qualities, calling the edibles "high-protein superfoods." The bugs are couched into bigger, better dishes such as cream of chestnut soup with creamy tomato sauce and white cricket. Another is nachos with silkworms, cherry tomato salsa, and sour cream. The decor plays with the bug theme, so stop in at least to see the plastic insects and such.

Lord Jim's ลอร์ดจิม $$

Asian, Seafood, International

(mandarinoriental.com/bangkok/chao-phraya-river/fine-dining/restaurants/seafood-cuisine/lord-jims; 02659-9000; 48 Oriental Avenue Mandarin Oriental Bangkok; Tues-Sun hours vary)

You'll see business deals being made around you as while lunching at Lord Jim's, a bustling river-view hotel restaurant with an all-you-can-eat midday meal. Fill up your plate again and again with grilled seafood, sea bass in a salt crust, filet mignon, pan-seared duck breast, and signature items like pan-fried fois gras and banana prawns with three peppers. For the grand finale, indulge in a Crepe Suzette. For a special dinner, dress up (no shorts, closed footwear) and dine a la carte on raw oysters, a sashimi platter, or wood-grilled Australian steaks.

May Veggie Home อาจ Veggie Home $

Vegetarian, Asian

(mayveggiehome.com; 02118-2967; 8/3 Sukhumvit 16, Ratchadapisek Rd, Klongtoei; daily 10:30am-9pm)

May Veggie Home has been serving plant-based hearty meals since 2011. The mother and daughter who run the restaurant have moved it to a bright new spot, and now serve baked goods and ice cream too—every bit of it vegan-friendly. Load up on soup with cucumber and glass noodles, fried faux fish with a sweet-and-sour mango salad, green curry with tofu, and stir-fried vegetarian chicken in basil sauce. Or go American with a meat-free burger and fries. But leave room for the sweets because a Thai iced tea or passionfruit dairy-free ice cream, or a vegan dark chocolate cake, will bring a kiss of bliss to any meal.

New York Style Steak & Burger สเต็กและเบอร์เกอร์สไตล์ นิวยอร์ก $$

American, Burger, Steakhouse

(nysteakandburger.com; 02262-0920; 28 Soi Sukhumvit 22, Khlong Toei; daily 11:30am-midnight)

When you crave a big ol' American-style burger or steak, this modern establishment with bricks and woods will transport you straight to Manhattan. The owner may be one-time Thai model Khun "Lina" Naalinlat, yet this Asian entrepreneur knows her USA beef: she uses only USDA-certified Angus, which means the quality is ensured. Choose from four cuts of steak, all charcoal-grilled; the chateaubriand is a natural for sharing. There's also a choice of five sauces, plus sides of grilled veggies or fried, roasted, or baked potatoes. Alternatively, go more casual with a burger: the beef is ground in-house and the toppings are outrageous. The Manhattan Monster has bacon, cheddar cheese, a fried egg, chili, onion rings, lettuce, tomato, and housemade pickles between the buns along with the half-pound (220g) patty. Not big on beef? Salads, soups, lamb chops, and a salmon entrée round out the menu. And hey, you're dipping into The Big Apple for this meal, so end with a creamy slice of cheesecake. Dine indoors or out.

Patara Fine Thai Cuisine ภัทราอาหารไทยรสเลิศ $$

Vegetarian, Asian, Thai

(patarathailand.com; 021852-9601; 375 Soi Thonglor 19, Sukhumvit 55 Rd, Khlongtan Nuea, Wattana; daily 11:30am-2:30pm and 5:30pm-10pm)

Patara means "gracious lady" and refers to this international chain's founder, Khun Patara Sila–On, who opened the original in London back in 1990. Today vegetarians (and meat eaters) in the UK, Geneva, Singapore, Vienna, and Bangkok's own Thonglor neighborhood gather for a creative and upscale culinary experience. It's a date-night must. Indoors or out, try vegetarian specialties such as vegetable curry or sautéed mock duck with garlic chili and basil. The chefs are big on serving vegetables and fruits that are unfamiliar to most visitors. More adventurous couples should splurge on one of three Gastro menus, which are multicourse feasts. Wines and cocktails are available.

Raan Jay Fai ระนาดเอก $$

Thai

(02223-9384; 327 Mahachai Rd, Samranras Subdistrict, Phra Nakon; Wed-Sun 10am-10pm)

Raan Jay Fai may look like any other street food vendor with seats, but you may well have to wait hours to eat here. Once the Michelin guide awarded roadside hawker Supinya Junsuta's humble spot a coveted star (a first for Bangkok), and Netflix followed by featuring the specialties on *Street Food*, this no-frills place became a bucket-list destination. Prepare to share with your honey, because once you get your turn to taste foods from the chef—she'll be clad in her signature ski goggles, beanie, and black apron—you'll want the crab omelet *and* the hot-and-spicy drunken noodles *and* the tart *and* the aromatic tom yum soup. Junsuta may be in her 70s, yet she continues to work magic at her charcoal-fired stove. Show up early to get your name on the waiting list.

sala rattanakosin eatery and bar ศาลารัตนโกสินทร์ร้านอาหาร และบาร์ $$

Romantic, Asian, International

(salahospitality.com/rattanakosin/dine/eatery-and-bar; 02622-1388; 39 Maharat Rd, Rattanakosin Island, Tha Tian Pier sala rattanakosi; daily 7am-10:30am; 11am-4:30pm; 5:30pm-10:30pm) Waterfront restaurants are meant for romance, and the warm, modern restaurant within sala rattanakosin boutique hotel embraces its perch overlooking Chao Phraya River and Wat Arun, the Buddhist Temple of Dawn. Begin with craft beers or cocktails (try a Sala Sunset garnished with fresh mango) at the rooftop bar, then head indoors for creative dishes with global flavors. Start your meal with one of the oyster dishes, whether you prefer your edible aphrodisiac in a salad with lemongrass and kaffir lime leaves or Japanese-style in tempura batter. The flavors burst from there—perhaps Tasmanian salmon with tikka spices, banana blossom salad with Thai chili jam, or twice-cooked pork belly with pumpkin puree and young ginger marmalade.

Tealicious $

Thai

(tealiciousbangkok.asia; 02630-7710; 492 Trok To, Soi Charoen Krung 49 Bangrak; Thu-Tue noon-11pm)

At Tealicious, the noodle-wrapped prawns, tom yum soup, and red curry with duck breast and lychees are prepared to order, from scratch. If you're wary about allergic reactions, say, the kitchen will adjust a dish for you. It'll also spice to your level. Western Spicy is the middle choice, with Not Spicy at one end Volcano Spicy! at the other. The simple spot's large menu also includes smoothies, spirits, teas, and coffees.

Thipsamai ทิพย์สมัย $

Thai

(thipsamai.com; 02226-6666; 313-315 Maha Chai Rd, Samran Rat, Phra Nakhon; daily 10am-9pm)

The noodle dish pad Thai was developed during World War II, and Thipsamai claims to have served it longer than any restaurant in Bangkok. Today the restaurant attracts not only locals and tourists but also international media (CNN Travel, BBC), not to mention a Bib Gourmand recognition in the Bangkok Michelin Guide. The original unit on Mahachai Road is the real deal and, in addition to several varieties of pad Thai, offers fun round-booth seating in an imitation river setting. Still, you can see what the fuss is about at a handful of smaller branches located in tourist hubs around town. Those are likely to have a shorter wait for service. Thipsamai sells its own retail line of branded Thai foods such as pouches of rice noodles and boxes of ready-to-cook pad Thai ingredients.

Veganerie มังสวิรัติ $

Vegetarian, Asian

(veganerie.co.th; 02258-8489; multiple branches)

If you have a yen for a meat-free meal any time of day, grab one to go, or dine in, depending on the location. Veganerie has six units, each enticingly contemporary. Best yet, it has just about anything you're keen to eat, as its 150+ menu offerings cover the gamut from spring rolls to apple-berry-almond-crumb pie, from vegan dumpling soup to massaman curry with baked roti, from chocolate-banana waffles to avocado toast with crispy imitation bacon. No wonder the chain has racked up so many awards since its 1995 debut, among them the Good Food Award (Gold Seal) 2017 and The Great British & Egyptian Food Award (2016). The entire menu is free of dairy, eggs, preservatives, and trans-fat.

Yaowarat at Night (Chinatown) เยาวราชยามค่ำคืน $

Chinese immigrants started setting up shop in Bangkok in 1782, and now the city's Chinatown is one of the world's largest. It's a bustling area filled with shops, street vendors, and of course restaurant after restaurant and street food hawker after street food hawker, all based around Yaowarat Road. You can eat gloriously here for very little money, as meals from soy-sauce chicken to stir-fries to shark-fin soup are served in extremely modest digs. Time your visit for a meal, but pad your schedule so you'll be here long enough to also feel hungry for a Chinese sweet with a cup of tea. Chinese desserts tend to be way less sweet than western desserts. The area is especially enticing after dark. At that time, the temps are lower so it's more comfortable to walk around, yet the crowds—and people-watching—are colorful, just as they are during the day. Chinatown was all but immune to the city's effort to close down street food vendors, so you'll still have access to noodles with crabs cooked on the spot, shrimp dumplings, and for the more Instagram-oriented among you, soft-boiled blood cockles.

DESSERTS AND COFFEES

Audrey—Cafe de Fleurs $

European, Asian
(audreygroup.com/AudreyDesFleurs; 02003-6244; 1357 Sukhumvit 35 Alley, Khlong Tan Nuea; daily 11am-10pm)
If your partner likes sugar and spice and everything nice, this is where to woo her. Audrey—Café de Fleurs is one of several Audrey cafes around Bangkok. With Provençal-style light woods and neutral tones plus flowers and plants dangling overhead, this is a girly-girl's nirvana. Dip spoons au deux into the Flower Pot Cake that looks like a potted plant yet is really a pudding cake

and chocolate crumbles; 16 varieties are available. Savories such as unusual pizzas are also on the menu.

Cher Cheeva เฌอชีวา $

Thai

(facebook.com/chercheeva; 062445-5565; 342/3 Phayathai Rd, Thanon Phetchaburi; weekends noon-7pm)

Sweet treats are as pretty as they are tasty at Cher Cheeva, a café and teahouse that offers cooking lessons. Your dessert might arrive in the form of purple flowers or hand-painted candies, accompanied by a dusty pink tea garnished with rose petals. Nimman Naruedee is a must: Translated as Fifth Level Paradise, it's a platter of several treats including some made with coconut milk or mango along with a hot regular or herbal tea; specifics vary so repeat guests always taste something new. The café's name refers to trees and life, and the interior features greenery and flowers around a modern Thai sensibility.

CODE Cafe of Dessert Enthusiasts CODE Cafe ของผู้ชื่นชอบ ของหวาน $

Asian

(facebook.com/codedesserts; multiple locations)

CODE stands for Café of Dessert Enthusiasts, and this small chain of sweeteries is all about being on-trend. Some of its treats are black, an au courant hue. Many are layers of assorted colors inside clear plastic cups. And all are gussied up to garner likes on your Facebook feed. No selfie needed; the food alone will get a following. You can't go wrong with the Lava Toast: Insert your fork into the cake and a Thai-tea flavored orange liquid oozes out to join the ice cream and whipped topping on the plate. Share this and you'll both be up all night. The Salted Egg Lava Croissant is also unusual. It, too, has a surprise liquid filling. You'll be filming; just sayin'.

Gallery Drip Coffee แกลลอรีดริปกาแฟ $

Coffee

(facebook.com/GalleryDripCoffee; 081989-5244; 107 Rama 1 Rd, Wang Mai, Pathum Wan; Tue-Sun 10:30am-7pm)

Most people visit the Bangkok Art and Culture Centre for a dose of modern art, yet coffee aficionados show up just for a cup of java. Beneath a freeform beehive-esque ceiling, the baristas here make hot and cold drinks with beans grown in the mountains of northern Thailand (and elsewhere). Those single-source beans are roasted in a former school house, then ground and placed in filters, ready for hot water to be poured over them. The price varies widely depending on the bean you choose. Some regulars are so enchanted with the pick-me-ups here that they keep their own mugs on the premises. Teas and desserts are also on offer.

Kyo Bar เคียวบาร์ $

Japan

(kyorollen.com/kyobar; 02610-7583; 991 Rama I Rd, Pathum Wan; daily 10am-10pm)

The café chain Kyo Roll En has been wowing Bangkok with artful Japanese desserts for years, yet nothing has been as show-stopping and creative as what's going on at Kyo Bar, the same company's 13-seat haute dessert destination. Run by Thai-born chef Dej Kewkacha, this ode to original sugar creations does things its own way. The selections change regularly in *omakase* style, meaning the pastry chef creates at whim based on seasonal ingredients. You'll watch your dessert being plated and then the chef who makes your order will explain the components to you. Each presentation is like a painting, whether it's Cacao Story, a miniature island complete with trees comprised of chocolate, hazelnut, and miso, or a nearly all-white exotic "ravioli" of pear, risotto, and black pepper.

Make Me Mango ทำมะม่วงให้ฉัน $

Asian, Mango

(makememango.business.site; 085199-1314; 67 Maharat Rd, Phra Borom Maha Ratchawang, Phra Nakhon; daily 11am-9pm)

What a luscious little spot to dig into a refreshing mango dessert, your legs twirled together—especially on the second-floor hammock. Make Me Mango is a bright little café specializing in sweets and smoothies made with the eponymous tropical fruit. You can never go wrong with the iconic mango with sticky rice, but why stop there? The Make Me Mango specialty adds mango ice cream, mango pudding, and Thai custard with that rice. Check out mango bingsu, made with azuki beans, a mango ice cream sundae, and mango pureed with sago.

Mo & Moshi โม & โมชิ $

Ice Cream

(moandmoshi.com; 02252-2688; 979 Siam Center Building, Rama 1 Rd, Rm 408 & 433 2nd floor, Prathumwan; hours vary)

Enticingly modern and bright, Mo & Moshi has a lot going for it—but you'll always hear first about the 22-scoop ice cream sundae. The two of you may need to bring along friends for this indulgent specialty, a design-your-own affair involving up to 14 flavors and wooden paddles instead of mere spoons. If you're sticking to your time-for-two routine, you can still go a little wild with the smaller yet artfully layered Candy Celebration or Delicious Dozen. Maybe a neighboring table will let you snap a quick photo of its oversized Strawberry Supreme for your Snapchat feed. The 22 balls of sweetness, the waffles, the cake layers, the Pocky sticks... they are wow-worthy together in a giant pedestaled glass bowl. Then again, imagine the witty captions you can use with a pic of a single-serving ice-cream burger. The "buns" are pastel thanks to foods like beetroot or green tea.

Pancake House บ้านแพนเค้ก $

Pancake

(pancakecafedesserthouse.com; 02722-2370; multiple units; 11am-10pm)

Thailand missed out on America's whole IHOP era, but Bangkok's Pancake Café makes up for the loss. Today, visitors and residents can flip over the flavor, texture, and aroma of these scratch-made flapjacks—on their own with whipped butter, served with savories like ham and eggs, or as a dessert. Toppings include apple crumble and Nutella.

Phil Coffee Company บริษัท ฟิลคอฟฟี่ $

Coffee

(philscoffeecompany.com; 097125-4204; 21 Sukhumvit 61 North Klongtan, Watthana; Mon-Fri 8am-5pm, Sat-Sun 9am-5pm)

Phil means love in Greek, and it is love—of excellent coffee—that led the three siblings whose initials spell out P.H.I.L to develop this coffee roasting and coffee bar concept. The minimalist space pours coffee drinks made from small-batch beans collected from around the globe. In 2018, Phil Coffee Company earned the 1st Runner Up award by the Thailand National Coffee Roasting Championship. Order a blend of the day, a pour-over, a cold brew, or maybe a latte, then settle into one of the 20 or so seats, and watch out of the window-wall as Bangkok rushes by. Many local restaurants and cafes also serve Phil coffees.

Theera Healthy Bake Room $

Bakery, European

(theerahealthybakeroom.com; 090506-2222; 67/9-10 Sukhumvit 42 Alley, Khwaeng Phra Khanong; weekdays 8am-6pm, weekends 8:30am-6pm)

This Bangkok mini-chain bills itself as "The original healthy bake room," by which owner Theeta 'Uang' Hotrakity is referring to worry-free indulgence: You can sweeten your day of sightseeing with baked goods that are gluten-free and vegan. Count on no dairy, eggs, soy, or nuts in most items. Hotrakity, trained at Le Cordon Bleu, started developing these recipes after she saw her autistic son thrive when she cut gluten from his diet. Now she serves pasta, smoothies, lattes, pancakes, omelets, breads, and pastas as well. Order a day in advance and Theera will deliver to your hotel room.

FOOD TOUR

Bangkok Food Tours ทัวร์อาหารกรุงเทพ

(bangkokfoodtours.com/tours; 095943-9222; 14/9 Soi Mooban Wandee Samsen Nai, Phaya Thai; hours vary)

With all the neighborhoods, outposts, street vendors, and restaurants on offer, where does one start to eat? Worry not: Bangkok Food Tours makes those decisions for you. Since 2011, the locally owned company has been bringing visitors on curated food tours that involve tasting specialties while meeting owners and chefs. It even won an award in 2013 for its Historic Bangrak Food Tasting and Culture Tour. Today the company operates a wide variety of options, such as: midnight food tour by tuk-tuk, all desserts, street food at the Chatuchak weekend market, vegetarian, nighttime street foods in Yaowarat (Chinatown), and the Offbeat Floating Markets food tour. The guides talk about culture and history along with edibles. Prices start at about $50 and include whatever you'll taste. Wear comfortable shoes, and dress respectfully on tours involving bars or Buddhist temples.

COOKING CLASSES

Baipai Thai Cooking School ใบไผ่โรงเรียนสอนทำอาหารไทย

(baipai.com; 089660-6535; 8/91 Soi Ngamwongwan 54 Ngamwongwan Rd, Ladyao Chatuchak; Mon-Sat 8:30am-5:30pm)

Once you've become enchanted with chicken satay, red curry pork, or mango with coconut sticky rice, learn how to make it. This accredited, two-story, open-air cooking school a half-hour from downtown (free transportation is provided from several parts of Bangkok) offers various half-day cooking classes six days a week. Choose a class based on the dishes that will be taught, then go to work as instructed at a fully equipped personal kitchen station. You'll be shown an organic herb garden or taken on a market tour to see how coconut cream is made. What fun you'll have recreating this meal back home, just the two of you.

Chef LeeZ Thai Cooking Class เชฟลีซเรียนทำอาหารไทย

(chefleez.com; 086568-1311; 4/488 Seri Thai Rd, Soi 57, Alley 19; daily 10am-2pm)
Hidden away in a gated neighborhood near Ramkhamhaeng Road (explicit directions are provided), Chef Lee teaches one class a day, each time featuring a dozen classic Thai dishes. Sessions begin with a market tour, then proceed to the air-conditioned kitchen. Eight or fewer students of all ages learn to make tom yum paste, pad Thai, massaman curry chicken and more, with vegans and other dietary concerns also being accommodated. Customers receive access to an online recipe book and cooking videos.

ENTERTAINMENTS

Calypso Cabaret คาลิปโซ่คาบาเร่ต์

(calypsocabaret.com; 02688-1415; 194 Charoen Krung Rd, Wat Phraya Krai, Bang Kho Laem; daily 7:30pm and 9pm)
Indulgently attired with feathers, sequins, and other bold costuming props, a crew of cross-dressing performers lip-sync their way through 16 choreographed acts in 70 minutes during this twice-nightly show. You'll be beguiled by the Broadway-style

opening. That's followed by Elvis, Misty, and other entertaining sets, just as Calypso Cabaret has offered since 1988. A Thai dinner add-on is available.

Geisha performance at Calypso Cabaret

Movie Theatres

Bangkok may be gloriously cultural and cosmopolitan but it's also hot, humid, and crowded. When you want to escape it all, duck into a nice air-conditioned movie theater. Choose a regular one or, better yet, one of the newer upscale facilities. Be sure to check whether your movie choice is in the original English, dubbed into English, or has English subtitles. You'll be away from itineraries, rain, shopping and, for an hour or three, the realities of life. Plus you can smooch in the dark. The location—finding a cinema nearby—may outrank your desire for 4DX, a big screen, a stocked bar, or exceptional service, but you can find whatever perks you prefer.

Embassy Diplomat Screens by AIS (embassycineplex.com;) at Central Embassy goes by the tag "The Cinematic Residence" because the seating is so comfortable. The five theaters have REAL-D-XL projection and cozy sofas-for-two, plus daybeds and other seats ideal for snuggling. There is also a full-service lounge with free nibbles and wine, and butler service. At **Enigma at Paragon Cineplex** (majorcineplex.com/en/cinema/paragon-cineplex) in Siam Paragon Shopping Center, your experience begins with massage chairs in a dimly lit lounge and proceeds to include craft cocktails and sofa-bed seating plus a meal and beverages. There's also a 4D screen. **SF World Cinema** (sfcinemacity.com) at Pathum Wan District and several other locations, there is several luxury theaters and the World Max Screen, together offering four projection systems. Depending on the theater, you can choose from a variety of seats, including beanbags, daybeds, lazy chairs, moon beds, and sun benches. Film festivals have been held here.

Muay Thai

Muay Thai, also known as Thai Boxing, is the national sport of Thailand. Known as "The Art of Eight Limbs" since fists, knees, elbows, and shins are permitted for use—in other words, your whole body is a weapon—it dates back to the mid-1700s and has grown in popularity in recent decades. Its heyday was the 1980-1990s, yet the sport continues to be admitted into international competitions and is said to have 3,800 dedicated gyms worldwide. In Bangkok, you can watch this sport in action at **The Lumpinee Boxing Stadium** (lumpineemuaythai.com), the largest such stadium in the country and the one known for having the most respected fighters compete. This stadium is used to train Royal Thai Army troops as well as individuals. You can also experience the sport at **Rajadamnern Stadium** (rajadamnern.com), the other major stadium in town, which is easier to reach. Both hold fights several times a week.

Siam Niramit สยามนิรมิต

(siamniramit.com; 02649-9222; 19 Thiam Ruam Mit Rd, Huai Khwang; Wed-Mon 5:30pm-10pm)

Siam Niramit is an hour-and-a-half extravaganza that celebrates Thailand's 700-year history and rich culture in three acts. Arrive early for a buffet dinner, pre-show entertainment, and experiences of a recreated rural Thai village, and you can make a full evening out of your visit. Billed as a "Journey to the Enchanted Kingdom of Siam," Siam Niramit's main show is an indoor theater event featuring 100 performers who wear 500 costumes during the time they're on stage. Act I is "Journey Back to History," Act II a tribute to diversity and karma, and Act III a focus on Buddhist festivals. Before the show, you can fill up at an all-you-can-eat dinner at Sawasdee Restaurant, then watch costumed entertainers outdoors. Make time for the recreated village honoring Thailand's four regions, watching demos of craftspeople making silk, painting batik, and pounding rice. Do be aware that there have been claims of animal cruelty against the elephants and other animals featured before and during the show. There is a second Siam Niramit in Phuket, and in January 2020 its theater was named in the *Guinness Book of World Records* as having the tallest proscenium arch at 57ft 7 inches (17.6m).

> ## Bangkok's Real Name Is Looooooong
>
> The name *Bangkok* is simple, if a little too easy a launch point for adolescent humor. It's also not the city's real name. Officially, the Thai capital is the 168-letter mouthful **กรุงเทพมหานคร อมรรัตนโกสินทร์ มหินทรายุธยามหาดิลก ภพนพรัตน์ ราชธานีบุรีรมย์ อุดมราชนิเวศน์ มหาสถาน อมรพิมาน อวตารสถิต สักกะทัตติยะ วิษณุกรรมประสิทธิ์**, transliterated as Krung Thep Mahanakhon Amon Rattanakosin Mahinthara Ayuthaya Mahadilok Phop Noppharat Ratchathani Burirom Udomratchaniwet Mahasathan Amon Piman Awatan Sathit Sakkathattiya Witsanukam Prasit. No other city on the planet has a moniker that size. Perhaps unsurprisingly, even the residents don't call it that: They say Krung Thep, which means "city of angels," or Krung Thep Maka Nakhon, "the great city of angels. In fact, the latter is often used on official documents. The long name also means magnificent city, nine gems, royal palaces, good incarnate, and more. Bangkok is the official English-language version.

NIGHTLIFE

Co-Co Walk

If you're staying in Ratchathewi or Pratunam and don't feel like traveling to get wild with a few drinks, or if you just want a bar scene small enough to cover in one night, give Co-Co Walk a try. It's a tasteful, if unexciting, nightlife alley-style mall, more or less, where pool tables and skate ramps replace go-go bars and hustlers. Grab a beer tower at one bar, hear live music in another, and gaze into each other's eyes over a game of Eight-Ball before returning to your hotel.

Khao San Road

The U.S./Thai exchange rate makes the whole country a bargain for travelers; in Bangkok, your dollar will go farthest of all in the

Khao San Road area, less than a mile (1km) north of the Grand Palace. Instead of the "milled rice" for which the neighborhood is named and that was sold here until a few decades ago, today the big seller is affordability: We're talking about modestly priced hotel rooms, inexpensive Western and Thai street foods (not to mention grilled insects and other local treats), approachably priced apparel at market stalls, and questionable items like fake IDs, illegal DVDs, and used books. And so, it's not surprising that backpackers, gap-year travelers, and others on tight budgets congregate here. By night, you'll find them in an array of clubs and such that, in Khao San style, are priced for the frugal population. All those young people = FUN. Khao San Road has a global reputation as a place to party hearty and dance, dance, dance. Just step into the street and follow the neon signs—or use your ears. Pounding music floods the area, drifting out of door after door. Reggae? Classic rock? The sounds could be any range of music, so take your pick. Tight on cash? Pick up a six-pack at the grocery store and have your own party on the sidewalk. You won't be alone. Revelers regularly design festivities in this neighborhood. Or go part-way: Buy a budget-priced bucket from any number of bars. Alternatively, park your butts at a not-fancy street front bar—the seats might be flimsy plastic, but what will you care?—and order a round or three of cheap cocktails. Chances are you'll drink-hop among several places before stumbling pack to your hotel.

RCA (Royal City Avenue)

Call it RCA, Royal City Avenue, Ratchadaphisek, or Ratchada, this part of town north of Sukhumvit is Party City for the 20-something set. Take a cab or the metro to Phetchaburi, Ratchadaphisek, or Thailand Cultural Centre and you're in for a night of revelry—until 1am, which is late for Bangkok. RCA is known for its non-sleazy pick-up scene as well as its more than 50 clubs, bars, restaurants, and cafes, especially near Ratchada Soi 4. Dress up in the spiffier clothes you packed and head over, any night of the week, for dancing to international DJs, letting loose with hip-hop, taking in mash-ups between unrelated music genres, and, mostly, trying out new bars all night long. If there's a cover charge, it probably comes with free drinks.

Red Light Districts

Whether your voyeurs or looking for extra action, Bangkok has plenty of places with abundant opportunities. Expect flashy neon, seductive performances with and without poles, and enough thundering music and cheap booze to crush one's inhibitions. **Nana Plaza**, known as "The World's Largest Adult Playground," is a three-floor complex with go-go clubs—scantily clad or naked women dancing for an open audience—as well as "ladyboy" bars and rent-by-the-hour hotel rooms; plenty of folks will be happy to join you in those rooms for a price. You'll find it near the Skytrain's Nana Station in Khlong Toei. Tourists often prefer **Soi Cowboy**, where a few dozen go-go bars line the street. From 7pm on, whether you're privately sipping a beer or on the prowl, you'll be surrounded by glowing lights and a party atmosphere. Take the Skytrain to Asok Station or the MRT to Sukhumvit and walk between Sois 21 and 23. Visitors from abroad also frequent **Patpong**, two streets with a variety of bars, some crassly named, some heterosexual, others gay, a few for kinkier activities. Beware of scams in the upstairs venues with sex shows. When you've had enough entertainment, head over to the adjacent night market. Patpong is near the Skytrain's Sala Daeng station and the MRT's Si Lom.

Silom สีลม

By day, Silom is Bangkok's financial hub. Save your visit to the Bangrak subdistrict within Silom until after dinner and you can have any kind of experience you want. Really, *any* kind. Take the

Skytrain to Saphan Taksi or Surasak so you can sip craft cocktails at a rooftop bar, cozy up in a cute pub, rock out to live music of just about any post-1970 genre, or shop for bargains at a bustling night market. The Patpong quarter within Bangrak beyond the retail stalls is a whole other experience, and one not for prudes. You'll find so-called go-go bars, meaning barely dressed women are available for gawking and (ahem) more, plus an array of gay clubs, lounges, and bars—those are mostly in Soi 2 and Soi 4. Head over to Soi Thaniya for Japanese food, drinks, and nightlife, as well as massage parlors aimed at Japanese visitors; this area is called Little Tokyo. Among these streets, you can get your vocals on with karaoke, get skunk drunk for a pittance and, best of all, have colorful tales to tell your friends back home. Unless you want what happens in Patpong to stay in Patpong...

LIVE MUSIC

Brick Bar บริคบาร์

(brickbarkhaosan.com; 02629-4556; 265 1st Floor, Buddy Lodge Hotel, Khaosan Rd, Takad Yod Subdistrict; daily 7pm-1:30am)
Get your Caribbean on at Brick Bar, a spacious red-brick basement hideaway where several house bands play reggae, Jamaican ska, and rock 'n' roll nightly. You'll be among the few tourists in this hotspot frequented by young locals, who know that once midnight strikes dancing on the tables is all the rage. Benches and dance floors abound.

Saxophone Pub แซ็กโซโฟนผับ

(saxophonepub.com; 02246-5472; 3, 8 Ratchawithi 11 Alley, Thanon Phaya Thai, Ratchathewi; daily 6pm-2am)
Clasp hands and stroll into Saxophone Pub for an evening of live music. Jazz, blues, acoustic guitar—something on the mellow side is always going on up on stage. Open since 1987, the two-story

space has the warmth of a British pub. Grab a beer or colorful cocktails, snack on Thai foods, or shoot some pool upstairs.

The Rock Pub ผับร็อค

(therockpub-bangkok.com; 02251-9980; 93/26-28 Hollywood Street Building, Payathai Rd, Ratchatewi; Thu-Sun 7pm-1am)

Self-described as Bangkok's Classic House of Rock, this music hangout with a 1987 pedigree has been hosting bands from around the world for more than three decades. Metalheads and grunge-lovers gather for loud performances in a dark, not-fancy space, just as they have since the beginning.

Wanderlust Rooftop Bar

(facebook.com/wanderlust.rooftop; 088696-9445; 4/1, 44/2 Soi Akaphat, Thong Lo 13 Alley, Khlong Tan Nuea, Watthana; daily 5pm-midnight)

Woods and plants are fitting for this outdoor music emporium, a garden-like rooftop bar with regular live music. Head here on a night when you don't feel like dressing up. Simply wander over, find the elevator in the back hidden near the Little Beast restaurant, ride to the fifth floor, and settle down with reasonably priced drinks and Western-style burgers. Unwind under the stars or smog. You might hear electro-pop, or it might be classic rock—whatever it is, just chill.

BARS

CRU Champagne Bar บาร์แชมเปญ cru

(champagnecru.com; 02100-6255; Centara Grand at CentralWorld, 999/99 Rama 1 Rd, Phatumwan; daily 5pm-midnight)

Nothing sets the tone for togetherness like a bottle of brut, and at CRU Champagne Bar you can sip flute after flute with 360-degree panoramic views. High above the city, with chic white seating and a dramatic arch over the round bar that changes hues regularly, this oh-so-romantic destination is the place for special moments. Fuss a bit with your wardrobe before showing up to indulge and toast your love with the Pink Mumm No. 1 only available here. Not into fizz? Cocktails, including some made with Chinese tea, are also on the menu. Caviar? Oh yes, add it on, along with trendy Western snacks like sweet potato fries and Wagyu sliders.

Octave Rooftop Lounge and Bar Octave Rooftop Lounge และบาร์

(marriott.com; 02797-0000; 2 Soi Sukhumvit 57, Sukhumvit Rd, Watthana; daily 5pm-2am)
Slow dance, go wild, or simply sip your cocktails and gaze into one another's eyes—plus at the amazing city view—on the top floor of Octave, with its round bar and DJ entertainment. This seductive spot is the top level of a three-story hotel bar that rises from the 45th floor to the 47th. A lounge and private meeting area are also part of the complex. Arrive at 5pm to get happy hour prices on signature items.

Sky Bar สกายบาร์

(lebua.com/restaurants/sky-bar; 02624-9555; Lebue Bangkok, 63rd Floor, Lebua at State Tower, 1055 Silom Rd, Bangrak; daily 4pm-1am)
Will you go to the ends of the earth for each other? Sure, if the definition is a bar that juts over a rooftop 820 feet (250m) in the air. That's the setting for the swanky Sky Bar, a cocktail-attire hub where mixologists prepare beverages that smoke and foam, with greater Bangkok views in the distance. A regular on global "best rooftop bar" lists since 2013, this elegant river-view sanctuary is best forgotten for its role in *The Hangover Part II* movie. If you arrive before it opens, watch the city skyline from the same building's more casual Distil Bar, which has comfy sofa seating.

NIGHTCLUBS

DJ Station สถานีดีเจ

(facebook.com/djstationbangkok; 02266-4029; Silom Soi 2 Suriya Wong, Bangrak; daily 9pm-2am)
Colorful and crazy fun, DJ Station is an uber-popular nightclub for Bangkok's LGBTQ community. With inexpensive drinks in hand and an array of enticing music in the background, a night here involves lip-syncing drag queens, DJ-curated dance tunes, and a whole lot of shakin' going on.

Levels Club & Lounge เลเวลคลับแอนด์เลานจ์

(levelsclub.com; 082308-3246; Aloft Hotel, 6th floor, No.35, Sukhumvit Soi 11, Sukhumvit Rd)
Party like you're in London or New York at Levels, a three-part club on the 6th floor of a hotel. We're talking dim lighting with vibrant beams of color, sizzling music, and drinkers out to paaartaaay. Grab hands and head to the clubbing room, the bar, or the classier lounge, all of them connected for an ever-changing experience each evening. Entrance is free except for special events.

Sing Sing Theater ซิงซิงเธียเตอร์

(singsing-bangkok.com; 063225-1331; 45 Sukhumvit 45 Alley, Khlong Tan Nuea; Wed-Sat 9pm-2am)
The beautiful people—the ones who like to party, anyhow—congregate at Sing Sing, a sexy bar and nightclub with regular live music. Eastern touches define the sultry look, kind of Chinese-brothel-chic, which involves a dance floor-slash-stage with two bars and a mezzanine hanging over it. Canoodle just the two of you in tucked-away corners.

Sugar Club สโมสรน้ำตาล

(sugarclub-bangkok.com; 061391-3111; 37 Soi Sukhumvit 11, Khlong Toei Nuea)

Put on your party clothes and head to Sugar Club, the unofficial home of hip-hop and rap music in Bangkok. The crowd goes wild nightly, dancing freely in the two-story space, led by professional dancers hired to get the vibe vrooming. The people-watching is perfect from the veranda overlooking the dance floor. Drink discounts are offered regularly.

SHOPPING

Asiatique Riverfront เอเชียทีคริเวอร์ฟร้อนท์

(asiatiquethailand.com; 02108-4488; Charoen Krung Rd, Wat Phraya Krai, Bang Kho Laem; daily 4pm-midnight)
This open-air nighttime mall is themed into four "districts," each designed to represent the area from 1907 to 1947. After taking the BTS to Saphan Taksin, then the free shuttle or boat, you'll have access to all kinds of stores (1,500 total) and 40 food purveyors, plus entertainment. Asiatique Riverfront, opened in 2012, features Thai puppet shows, archaeological finds, concerts, Muay Thai matches, calypso, and a giant wheel ride. Be sure to seek out the Juliet Love Garden, where you can secure a padlock and toss the key into a fountain.

ICONSIAM ไอคอนสยาม

(iconsiam.com/th; 02495-7000; 299, Soi Charoen Nakhon 5, Charoen Nakhon Road Khlong Ton Sai, Khlong San; daily 10am-10pm)
ICONSIAM's slogan is "The Icon of Eternal Prosperity," and the mall—opened in 2018—does drip money. Located along the Chao Phraya River, it's part of a massive complex that will ultimately include two shopping malls, two condo towers, hotels, and a heritage museum, multiplex, fitness center, and way more. The six-story ICONSIAM itself has the SOOK Siam floating market on the first floor, plus 500 stores and 100 restaurants. Need iPhone help? Thailand's first Apple store is here.

MBK Center มาบุญครอง

(mbk-center.co.th; 02853-9000; 444 Phayathai Rd, Pathum Wan; daily 10am-10pm)

Ritz and glitz are so much fun to see, but when you're ready to actually buy something practical, MBK Center may be your best bet. The largest shopping mall in Asia when it opened in 1985, today the facility is a hub for young shoppers and tourists on moderate budgets. Its eight stories hold over 2,000 stores and restaurants, among them the anchor Tokyu department store. Various areas specialize in Thai handicrafts, electronics, furniture, and apparel. Food courts, a hotel, a movie theater, and a play zone add to the diversity.

Pantip Plaza พันธุ์ทิพย์พลาซ่า

(pantipplaza.com; 02254-9797; 604/3 Petchaburi Rd, Thanon Phetchaburi, Ratchathewi; daily from 10am)

Whether you want a spiffy new laptop, a knock-off DVD movie, or just a mousepad, this multilevel electronics mall will hook you up. The retailer's IT City and Hardware House are straightforward electronics anchor stores. In between are the used desktops, counterfeit software, vintage printers, and cameras waiting for a new home. Prices are low and negotiations often reap further discounts or add-ons.

Siam Paragon สยามพารากอน

(siamparagon.co.th; 02610-8000; 991 Rama I Rd, Pathum Wan; daily 10am-10pm)

Mega-mall Siam Paragon calls itself "The Pride of Bangkok," and it sure has a lot to offer. Its Paragon Department Store is among Asia's grandest retailers, and it shares the mall with about 350 other brands. The SEA LIFE Bangkok Ocean World aquarium resides here, along with a bowling alley, karaoke venue, events venue, and 15-screen movie theater.

Terminal 21 เทอร์มินอล 21

(terminal21.co.th/asok; 02108-0888; 88 Soi Sukhumvit 19, Sukhumvit Rd, Khlong Toei Nuea, Watthana; daily 1am-10pm)

Terminal 21 is a small award-winning chain of shopping malls, and the Bangkok version, known as Asok, offers way more than 600 stores, a cineplex, and places to eat. Various parts of the nine-floor complex are geographically themed, so while you're scouting for lipstick or a cute clubbing outfit you may feel as if you're at Paris' Champs-Élysées, California's Fisherman's Wharf, or a tropical Caribbean island. The exterior, however, resembles an airport.

MARKETS

Amphawa Floating Market ตลาดน้ำอัมพวา

(tourismthailand.org/Attraction/amphawa-floating-market; 02475-1351; Amphawa, Amphawa District, Samut Songkhram; Fri-Sun 9am-8pm)

Arrive early, and hungry, to best enjoy your time at this weekend floating market that's a little over an hour from Bangkok. Whether you tour around the canal and rivers on a longboat, walk the crowded areas by the wooden shops that line the canal, or ride rental bicycles side by side to explore, you'll want to eat: grilled seafood is the big draw, and a vast variety of sweets beckon too. One cup of Thai iced coffee (share it; trust us, if you value your sleep) and you'll be wide awake. The souvenir shopping is only so-so, but the nearby Wat Bang Koong temple is worth your time. During the May-October rainy season, a nighttime tour of fireflies flitting around cork trees definitely makes for a special time for two.

Chatuchak Weekend Market ตลาดนัดจตุจักร

(chatuchakmarket.org; 083956-3656; Kamphaeng Phet Rd, Lat Yao, Chatuchak; Sat-Sun 9am-6pm)

Hop on the Skytrain to Mo Chit Station and follow the crowds. The next thing you'll know you'll be two of the 200,000 people who spend hours upon hours each weekend wandering the 15,000 stalls at the 35-acre (14 hectares) Chatuchak Weekend Market—and you'll still never see it all. Said to be the country's largest market, and possibly the world's, this expansive retail arena has art and clothing, sneakers and souvenirs, plants and antiques, and even a section with small animals, some of them endangered. Not to mention all kinds of varieties of pad Thai.

Damnoen Saduak Floating Market ตลาดน้ำดำเนินสะดวก
(tourismthailand.org/Attraction/damnoen-saduak-floating-market; 089161-0909; Damnoen Saduak, Ratchaburi; daily 7am-5pm)

Damnoen Saduak may be the most touristy of Thailand's floating markets, but don't let that stop you from visiting. Whether you hire a driver or take a tour to get here—about an hour outside of Bangkok—you'll be immersed in a long-ago world. Exploration is done by longtail boat, stopping upon request to haggle with vendors on their own small boats or above you in stalls perched at the side of the canal. The entire area is a maze of three smaller markets, all picturesque with vendors wearing conical hats, foods steaming as it's cooked to order, and any number of possibly overpriced clothing and souvenirs to buy. Roger Moore, as James Bond, shot an action scene here for *The Man with the Golden Gun*, and Nicolas Cage filmed *Bangkok Dangerous* here. Bring your camera.

Damnoen Saduak Floating Market

Khlong Lat Mayom Floating Market ตลาดน้ำคลองลัดมะยม

(facebook.com/KlongLadMayom; 02422-4270; 30/1 Moo 15 Bang Ramat Rd, Bang Ramat, Taling Chan; Sat-Sun 7am-5pm)

It's unthinkable to go to Thailand and not experience a floating market, so if you can't make it to one of the bigger ones, head to Khlong Lat Mayom just outside the city. Take the Skytrain to Wongwian Yai, then hop in a taxi. You'll find yourselves surrounded by locals, being served pad Thai or an oyster omelet from a boat, then maybe picking up some tropical fruits and fresh flowers to bring back to the hotel.

Pak Khlong Talad ปากคลองตลาด

(Pak Klong, Talat Son Palace, Bangkok; open 24 hours)

Wake up crazy-early, or better yet stay up after a night at the clubs, to arrive at Pak Khlong Talad, Bangkok's flower market, between 2 and 3am. Here, near the Memorial Bridge and the Temple of the Reclining Buddha, you'll see a petal-laced floral wonderland at work. Vendors sell bulk orders of flowers wholesale, making this a real slice-of-life destination for tourists. The sheer quantities of petals being exchanged in the bustle is a phenomenon. It's also possible to go during the day, as the market never closes, but the real action happens in the wee hours before the city awakens.

Patpong Night Market ตลาดนัดกลางคืนพัฒน์พงษ์

(facebook.com/taradrodfi; Thanon Patpong 1, Suriya Wong, Bangrak; daily 5pm-1am)

For sure, you won't be the only tourists at the Patpong Night Market, but don't let that stop you. This Silom retail hub is a fine way to spend an evening perusing trendy T-shirts, bowls made of decorated coconut shells, knock-offs of designer watches, and all kinds of elephant souvenirs, taking breaks to sample exotic Thai flavors from foodservice stalls. It's surrounded by the kinds of bars you wouldn't take your parents to, but you can ignore the drinking holes entirely if you're more into night shopping than nudity.

Pratunam Market ตลาดประตูน้ำ

(Ratchaprarop Rd, Phayathai, Ratchathewi; hours vary)

Pratunam Market offers a different experience depending on what time of day you arrive, and each is worth a trip. The market is actually a mix-up of several markets: indoor mall stores, storefront wholesalers, and of course street vendors of all types. Together it's a beehive of consumers looking for a deal on outfits and business shoppers seeking large orders, all in a crowded area of alleyways around Ratchathewi's Phetburi and Ratchaprarop roads. Whether you want casual elephant-themed pants or formal wear, seek out stores selling them wholesale-style—three on one hanger for a single price. You won't be allowed to try them on, but the prices are so low it's worth the risk. Added together, Pratunum's mélange of markets is Thailand's largest clothing market.

Srinakarin Train Market (Rod Fai Market) ตลาดนัดรถไฟ ศรีนครินทร์ (ตลาดรถไฟ)

(081827-5885; 1 4 Srinagarindra Rd, Nong Bon, Prawet; Thu-Sun 5pm-midnight)

Known as Talad Rod Fair Train Night Market, Rod Fai Market, and Srinakarin Train Market, and combinations of the three, this low-key after-dark destination is more about wandering than shopping with a list. Within its three sections, vendors pawn everything from old kitchenware to vintage cars, from shoes seeking a new home to antiques. Like all markets, this one, whatever the name, has plenty of food vendors too.

MASSAGES

Feel Good Massage นวดรู้สึกดี

(facebook.com/feelgoodmassagebkk; 151 Kamphaeng Phet 2 Rd, Chatuchak; Sat-Sun 11am-6pm)

Take a break from bargain hunting at the Chatuchak Weekend Market by getting a foot, shoulder, or combo massage at this friendly and low-price shop. You'll reap not only soothed muscles but also air conditioning and free Wi-Fi. Walk-ins are welcome.

The Lavender Massage by Arunda The Lavender Massage โดยอรุณดา

(facebook.com/The-Lavender-Massage-1806125272957122; 02653-9396; 1, 3 Phetchaburi 15 Alley, Thanon Phaya Thai, Ratchathewi; daily 10am-1am)

Luckily in Bangkok you don't need a big budget to get a great massage. On street after street you'll find Thai massage parlors providing services in small spaces, separated by a cloth or other light divider. One of our favorites is The Lavender Massage by Arunda, which has nice touches like decorative mattress coverings and a variety of treatments—among them aromatherapy. Private rooms are available. End your visit with warm cups of tea in the shop's garden.

The Opium Spa at The Siam The Opium Spa ที่ The Siam

(thesiamhotel.com/spa; 02206-6999; The Siam Hotel, 3/2 Khao Rd, Wachira Phayaban, Dusit; daily 10am-10pm)

Designed to be intimate yet sophisticated and urban, The Siam's spa covers the whole gamut, from scalp treatments to manicures, all in a tranquil Zen setting. Start your vacation off right by booking time-for-two jet lag recovery, rejuvenation, or serenity packages. Your skin, your muscles, and even your faces will be relaxed and ready to take on the best of Bangkok. Book a yoga session for just the two of you, or have a private lesson to learn the basics of the local martial art Muay Thai.

The Oriental Spa at Mandarin Oriental

(mandarinoriental.com/bangkok/chao-phraya-river/luxury-spa; 02659-9000; 48 Oriental Ave, Khwaeng Khlong Ton Sai, Bangrak; daily 10am-8pm)

Bangkok's first spa and the only one to date that has been awarded five stars by Forbes, the Oriental is a posh and pampering experience even before the treatments begin. Guests arrive at the facility, across the river from its namesake hotel, and sip tea during an initial consultation. Then it's on to one of the treatment rooms, each with its own shower or steam room, the facial rooms, the specialty suites, some with vitality pools, or the relaxation lounge. The Oriental Signature lasts 90 minutes and involves six essential oils as well as Thai and European massage techniques. It concludes with a Thai herb spine and shoulder compress. Indulge together in a couple's suite, where you'll share a relaxation area, steam shower, and whirlpool tub. Be sure to request a marine salt bath or a rose milk one to enjoy, along with light snacks.

Yunomori Onsen ยูโนะโมริออนเซ็น

(yunomorionsen.com/sukhumvit; 02259-5778; Soi Sukhumvit 26 Khlong Tan, Khlong Toei, A Square; daily 9am-midnight)

Talk about the best of both worlds. Yunomori melds Thai massage with Japanese onsen bathing, in this case in mineral water from thermal springs. Soak in a thermal tub side by side as the steam rises around you. Japanese and Thai elements are interspersed throughout the unusual facility, which also has a Happy Rice restaurant on-site. Whether you go for the signature treatments or opt for an aromatherapy massage, an herbal compress, or a body scrub, you'll end your visit by rehydrating with a bottle of milk.

TOURS

Bridge on the River Kwai and Thailand-Burma Railway Tour สะพานข้ามแม่น้ำแควและรถไฟไทย – พม่า

(toureast.net; 02267-1400; 18-19th Floor, Charn Issara Tower 1, 942/157-159 Rama 4 Rd; hours vary)

TourEast is a Japanese company that shows visitors the sites around Asia. In Bangkok, the 10-hour group tour excursion out to the countryside is the best bet, enabling you to learn about the country's war history en route. From Bangkok, you'll travel in an air-conditioned bus to the Death Railway and so-called Bridge Over the River Kwai, as well as to Kanchaanburi's war cemetery and a war museum. Pineapple plantations and rice paddies provide picturesque scenery on the road, and an English-speaking guide will share insights. Prices start at $76 per person.

Chaophraya River Cruise ล่องเรือแม่น้ำเจ้าพระยา

(chaophrayacruise.com/en; 02541-5599; River City Pier Soi Charoenkrung 24, Talat Noi, Samphanthawong; daily 7pm-9pm)

We're not big on typical touristy endeavors overall, yet even the most cynical couples will get a kick out of a dinner cruise along the Chao Phraya River. Book passage on the 290-passenger Chaophraya or the larger 500-passenger Grand Chaophraya. You'll have access to a large buffet stocked with Thai and international dishes, plus a traditional Thai greeting dance and live entertainment throughout. The highlight is the scenery: as you dine, you'll glide past wow-worthy icons like the Grand Palace and Wat Arun, illuminated if it's dark outside. If there's a promotion on, prices can begin at about $30 per person.

Maeklong Railway Market and Damnoensaduak Floating Market with Small Group ตลาดรถไฟแม่กลองและตลาดน้ำ ดำเนินสะดวกกับกลุ่มเล็ก

(bigcountryvacation.com; 02234-7212; 550 Si Pharaya Rd, Mahapruktaram, Bangrak; hours vary)

Bigcountry Vacation will take you for matching "holy tattoos," also called *sak yants*, permanent Buddhist symbols of luck that are administered by monks. It's a centuries-old tradition. Be sure to hit up this licensed outfit for other small group tours too, such as a trip to two fabulous markets. You'll be escorted to the Maeklong Railway Market, with a train cutting through it, and the water based Damnoen Saduak Floating Market, where you'll shop while seated in a longtail boat. You'll feel like a pro with your guide's instructions, haggling like the locals do while learning appropriate bargaining etiquette. The six-hour trip is about $33 per person.

Private Ayutthaya Day Tour from Bangkok ทัวร์อยุธยาส่วนตัว จากกรุงเทพฯ

(tasteofthailand.org)

The city of Ayutthaya, an hour north of Bangkok, was established in 1350, the second Siamese city ever built. A cosmopolitan city-island, it was demolished in 1767 by the Burmese. Today the Ayutthaya Historical Park is a UNESCO World Heritage Site.

Let Taste of Thailand take you on a private day tour so you can explore the picturesque ruins at your own pace. You'll see statues, temples, palaces, and monasteries. You'll learn about a famous duel that was fought here, each participant atop an elephant. In one telling, one of the duelers was sliced in half by the other. One king was part of an elephant duel here. In addition to time at the ruins, your tour will include a stop at the Hua Ro market, a chance to see how the spun sugar dessert *roti sai mai* is made, a dye-craft lesson, and a meal on a floating rice barge. Yes, you'll get to sweeten your day with the treat translated as "silk rope"; it is likened to cotton candy. About $200 per person.

Private Guide in and Around Bangkok: Custom Tour ไกด์ส่วนตัวในและรอบ ๆ กรุงเทพ: Custom Tour

(yourthaiguide.com; 087528-8723; 46/3 Soi Soonvijai 4, New Petchburi Rd, Bang Kapi, Huai Khwang; hours vary)

Are you a history buff? A shopper? A culture vulture? Just interested in knocking all the major sites off your to-see list? Your Thai Guide is a licensed private-tour company that will, after getting an idea of your interests, match you with a guide who has similar interests so you can see, do, and learn more of what you care about. Your guide will prepare an itinerary just for the two of you and adapt as you go along. A full eight-hour tour of Bangkok's highlights such as the Grand Palace and Wat Pho begins at about $57 per person, and prices vary based on what you see in the urban area or beyond it. Your Thai Guide gets consistent excellent ratings from TripAdvisor.

Small Teak Boat Canal Adventure เรือลำเล็กผจญภัยคลอง

(thaicanaltours.com; 087109-8873; 780/488 Charoen Krung Rd, Bang Kho Laem; Mon-Fri 8:30am-3pm)

Spend a day immersed in Old Thailand, rural style. Thai Canal Tours will take just the two of you (or a small group) on an excursion through canals on a small teak boat. An English-speaking guide will help you explore local scenery and see locals going about their daily lives. Water, soft drinks, snacks, and a Thai meal are included during the 6½ hours. About $160 per couple for a private tour, less if you travel with others.

TEMPLES

Emerald Buddha (Wat Phra Kaew) วัดพระแก้ว

(emerald-buddha.com/; 02224-3290; Na Phra Lan Rd, Phra Borom Maha Ratchawang; daily 8:30am-3:30pm)

A highlight within the Grand Palace is the Emerald Buddha Temple, at the center of which is a cross-legged seated Gautama Buddha sculpture made of jasper and draped with gold clothing. The 26-inch-tall (66cm) idol dates to at least the 1400s and traveled Asia and other parts of Thailand before coming to the palace in 1784. Its headpiece and cloak are changed three times a year. Religious and other ceremonies take place here regularly. The Buddha, allegedly in meditation stance, has a special serenity about it that can be emotionally bonding for couples visiting side by side.

Flexi Walking Temple Tour: Grand Palace, Wat Pho, Wat Arun
Flexi Walking Temple Tour: พระบรมมหาราชวังวัดโพธิ์วัดอรุณ

(Explore Asia Tour; 098869-6819)

You could spend a year in Bangkok and not see all the wonderful highlights, yet the Grand Palace and surrounding gems are the number one priority for any visit here, no question. You can show up and walk around yourselves, or hire a private guide on the spot, but why stress? Book a guided tour with an established outfit like Explore Asia and you'll be guaranteed to see the highlights and get a solid education without the hassle of figuring out the details yourselves. Prices start at about $72 per person. Here are the biggies.

Grand Palace พระบรมมหาราชวัง

(royalgrandpalace.th/en/home; 02623-5500; Na Phra Lan Rd, Phra Borom Maha Ratchawang, Phra Nakhon; daily 8:30am-3:30pm)

The Grand Palace is a stunning complex that opened in 1782 and has been the official home of Thailand's kings since 1782, although royals have technically lived elsewhere since 1925. Official events still take place here, and government offices are contained within. Spires, sculptures, and buddhas abound, along with throne halls, courtyards, gardens, and a Hall of Justice. Dress appropriately for a house of worship to gain entrance and expect crowds. The rectangular area is about 54 acres (22 hectares), so wear comfy shoes.

Wat Arun วัดอรุณราชวราราม ราชวรมหาวิหาร

(watarun1.com/th; 02891-2185; 158 Wang Doem Rd, Wat Arun Subdistrict, Bangkok Yai; daily 8am-6pm)

With the English name "Temple of Dawn," Wat Arun is inherently romantic. Its inspiration is thought to personify the glowing red rays of the rising sun via its namesake, the Hindu god Aruna. Located near the river, this temple is a meld of colors in glass and porcelain that spire upward about 230 feet (70m) toward the sky, with a Khmer-style bell tower. You'll also see several large statues are there. Wat Arun's lore is sentimentally inspiring. According to the story, back in 1768 King Taksin had just completed battling the Burmese in Ayutthaya. He left and happened upon the site of Wat Arun as the sun was rising over the temple that was there at the time (then called Wat Makok) and had a vision of a grander structure. He later enhanced the temple to create that grander structure. Wat Arun was revamped thrice more, once during the late 1800s/early 1900s, and again in 1980 and the 2013-2017 period. The Emerald Buddha resided here until 1785.

Wat Pho วัดโพธิ์

(tourismthailand.org/Attraction/wat-pho; 02226-0335; 2 Sanam Chai Rd, Phra Nakhon; daily 8:30am-5pm)

The oldest and largest temple complex of the bunch is Wat Pho. It's the site of the most Buddhas in one place in the country and, most importantly, home of the Temple of the Reclining Buddha—a 150ft (46m) long, 49ft (15m) tall Buddha encased in gold leaf. The statue's feet alone are exquisite: 16ft (5m) long with a mother of pearl inlay dotted with religious symbols. The complex, started in the 16th century, is home to another 394 gilded Buddhas, plus a school for Thai massage, of all things, so head over after your visit for a shoulder massage. Wat Pho was Thailand's first public university and its educational offerings have evolved since. Other highlights include 108 bronze bowls that symbolize Buddha's characteristics; drop in a few coins to bring on good luck.

Temple of the Reclining Buddha, Wat Pho

ATTRACTIONS

Ancient City เมืองโบราณ

(muangboranmuseum.com/en/; 02709-1644; 296/1 Moo 7 Sukhumvit Road, Bangpoo Subdistrict; Sat-Sun 9am-7pm)

If you want to get all the Thailand basics out of the way in one swoop, consider taking the phony version. About an hour south of the city, Ancient City, also known as Siam City and Muang Boran Museum, is a massive outdoor museum filled with life-size and scaled-down replicas of Thai buildings from prehistoric times through the 1930s. More than 100 structures are here, all built with the help of the National Museum so that they're true to the originals. So, want to see Thailand's Phimai Sanctuary and the now-gone Grand Palace of Ayutthaya? Stroll over. The Prang of Wat Chulamanee? The Fortified Wall around Kamphaeng Phet? Hop on a complimentary bicycle. The faux landmarks are arranged geographically to align with their location within Thailand. To get here, take the Skytrain to Khaha and hop on the No. 36 shuttle bus, which will drive you the final 15 minutes for a small fee.

Bangkok National Museum พิพิธภัณฑสถานแห่งชาติพระนคร

(virtualmuseum.finearts.go.th/bangkoknationalmuseums/index.php/en/; 02224-1370; Na Phra That Alley, Phra Borom Maha Ratchawang, Phra Nakhon; Wed-Sun 9am-4pm)

The Bangkok National Museum will give you a full immersion into Thailand's history, its archaeology, and its arts. Dating back to 1989, it's housed in an 18th-century palace near the Grand Palace and has a dozen or so halls loaded with permanent and visiting exhibits—most with new multimedia displays and descriptions in English. Stones, weapons, fabrics, masks... you'll find it all here. The permanent displays focus on Thai history, archaeology and art history, and the Decorative Arts and Ethnological Collection, which includes costumes and royal emblems.

King Power Mahanakhon คิงเพาเวอร์มหานคร

(kingpowermahanakhon.co.th; 02677-8721; 114 Narathiwas Rd, Silom, Bangrak; daily 10am-midnight)

Bangkok's tallest building from 2016 through most of 2018, the King Power Mahanakhon in the city's central district is a multi-use skyscraper featuring condos, hotel rooms, duty-free shopping, and incredible views. It's a striking piece of architecture that looks like cubes have been cut out of the structure, almost pixilated or like a Jenga game in progress. Take the speedy video-show elevator up 70+ flights floor in under a minute, then clink two flutes of bubbly two floors higher at the Mahanakhon Bangkok SkyBar to get up energy for the SkyWalk, an adventure on its own. The Mahanakhon SkyWalk & Rooftop package will enable you to take a hydraulic glass elevator to the 78th-floor SkyDeck, with its 360-degree view from 1,017ft (310m) above the ground. If that champagne has kicked in, you might feel up to grasping hands and entering a glass standing area that offers views underfoot. Want to keep it mellow? Sit side by side at the first-floor Mahanakhon SkyRides virtual reality attraction. You'll don special goggles that will make it feel as if you're high up, and you can choose your preferred scenery, since the experience is digital.

Museum of Contemporary Art (MOCA) พิพิธภัณฑ์ศิลปะร่วมสมัย

(mocabangkok.com; 02016-5666; 499 Kamphaengpet 6th Rd, Lad Yao, Chatuchak; Tue-Sun 10am-6pm)

Bright and open, MOCA is five-story modern art museum owned by businessman Boonchai Bencharongkul, and most of the pieces showcased here since its 2012 opening are his. Nudity and creative takes on animals are notable parts of this vast array of portraits and paintings, which features Thai artists including Chalermchai Kositpipat and Hem Vejakorn, among others. Works of European, Chinese, and Vietnamese artists are also on display.

PAPAYA Design Furniture & Studio

(papaya55.com; 084528-7067; 306/1 Soi Lat Phrao 55/2 Lat Phrao Rd, Phlabphla, Khet Wang Thonglang; daily 9am-6pm)

If you like shopping, especially for old stuff, PAPAYA is your kind of place: it's a massive vintage store. Out in the suburb of Wang Thonglang, it covers more than three floors of warehouse space—here you'll find fussy furniture and oversized clocks, age-old toys, life-size superhero mannequins, and bicycles that have seen better days. The amount of *stuff* is just incredible.

PB Valley Khao Yai Winery

(khaoyaiwinery.com; 081733-8783; 102/2 Moo 5, Mitraparp Rd, Payayen Pakchong Nakhon Ratchasima; daily 9am-6pm)

The original producer of Thailand's New Latitude Wines, award-winning PB offers wine-tasting tours to visitors willing to drive or take a tour two hours beyond city limits. The 79-acre (32-hectare) plantation is lush and lovely, located near the Khao Yai National Park. Be sure to sample the tempranillo, chenin blanc, and other specialties.

ADVENTURES

Bike Tours

Why deal with bumper-to-bumper traffic when you can move faster on a bicycle? Plus, you can easily stop to see the sites. Three tour companies are especially geared for two-wheeler fans. **Follow Me Bangkok Tours** (followmebiketour.com) will lead you through the streets on several half-day tours such as sunrise by the temples, a riverside adventure, or even a night tour to a shrine, Chinatown, and a diner. Your guide will take pictures of you together. **Grasshopper Adventures** (grasshopperadventures. com) has single-day and multiday bike tours. In Bangkok, their stash of 100 cycles is ready for a canal boat and bike tour, peaceful bicycle trails, and Historic Bangkok, for starters. **Co Van Kessel Bangkok Bike and Boat Tours** (covankessel.com) is big on off-the-beaten-path itineraries—starting with alleyways and footpaths. Boats, trains, and bikes are part of a nine-hour excursion, while a variety of neighborhoods are the crux of a three-hour option.

Shark Dive ดำน้ำฉลาม

(sharkdive.org; 02261-4412; B1-B2 Floor, Siam Paragon 911 Rama 1 Rd, Pathumwan; daily 10:30am-6pm)

A little thrill goes a long way to firing up a romance, so dive right in and, well, dive with sharks. Via Planet Scuba, instructors will bring you face to face with blacktip, leopard, guitar, tawny nurse, and gray nurse sharks, as well as southern stingrays and other aquatic friends. Your adventure will take place at the SEA LIFE Bangkok Ocean World aquarium, located inside the Siam Paragon mall. Diving experience isn't necessary. Couples under 55 can participate. Prices start at $187 per person.

MUAY THAI CLASSES

When in Rome, right? Muay Thai, sometimes called Thai boxing, is integral to the country. You can buy tickets to watch a match or burn off some calories taking lessons yourselves. ("Hi Honey, let me punch you with this padded glove. XO") Learn the basics of the "art of eight limbs" with a specialist. **Master Toddy's Muay Thai** (mastertoddy.com) has been in the education game for five decades. If you're in town for a while, commit to a 25-hour one-week course and master the ABCs quickly. If not, take the two-hour Fundamentals class; you'll leave with a certificate signed by the Grand Master. **Attachai Muay Thai Gym** (attachaimuaythai. com/sport-gym) is named for owner Attachai Fairtex, a champion known as the "Left hand from god" for his successes. The studio offers daily training and private lessons, a good option if you're short on time. Walk-ins can take an introductory class from 8am to 3pm. If you can't find time for a class, stop by to purchase a couple of pairs of shiny logoed shorts. They'll be great on your next joint jogging session. **Luktupfah Muay Thai & Muay Boran** (luktupfah.com) is a family-run gym beyond city limits that offers training daily, whether you want to become a competitor or merely stay in shape.

YOGA'S

You can find yoga classes throughout Bangkok, and many instructors teach in English. **Yogatique Bangkok** (yogatiquebangkok.com) is an all-English studio with fan-cooled open-air sessions and air-conditioned yin ones. Vinyasa, hatha, and Relax and Renew are among the options, and workshops are held periodically. **Prem Yoga & Prana Ayurveda Center** (premyogprana.com) specializes in both its namesake practices and holistic therapies. Gentle, dynamic, and vinyasa flows are all on the schedule. Private classes for infertility and chronic ailments are available upon request. Courses like Shirodhara and Aryuvedic body oil are also often offered, while herbal tea is always free for the taking. At **Yoga Elements** (yogaelements.com), breath-focused yoga is a priority. The studio was founded by Adrian Cox, renowned for her BreathYoga method.

PHUKET

Phuket

WHY GO

If you only have time for one taste of Thailand, choose Phuket. The country's largest island offers a blend of Thailand's best elements all in one destination. Gloriously gorgeous beaches strung like pearls beckon along the Andaman Sea. In addition, you'll find historical buildings, a meld of cultures, glitzy shopping malls, interesting museums, and exotic street food—and that's just for starters.

Couples will find so many ways to spend time together here. Share a ridiculously romantic dinner—encased in a transparent air-conditioned bubble—while soaking up panoramic vistas, or party hard long into the night at a sizzling club. Parasail in tandem above a crowded beach, or sit for hours on a nearly deserted stretch of sand. Splurge on designer goods in a glitzy boutique, or pick-up matching ankle bracelets for a dollar or two apiece. Learn about trompe-l'oeil art in a dedicated museum, or shower an elephant. Get quickie massages for a few bucks apiece, or spend all day in a pampering spa.

The contrasts on Phuket are stark, and they're part of the reason this island is so beloved by travelers from around the world. It can be classy or raucous, cheap or expensive, fun or finessed. Explore it together and you're bound to have fun.

TRAVELING FROM THE AIRPORT

Phuket has one airport, Phuket International Airport (HKT; phuket.airportthai.co.th). It's one of the busiest in all of Thailand, with 16 million passengers passing through in a regular year. The airport is on the northern end of the island's western side and has two main terminals—one for domestic flights and the other for international flights.

The airport has a variety of transportation options for getting to your accommodations, so choose based on your budget. Many of the beach areas are about a 40-minute drive away: you can get there by metered taxi (meaning you can trust the price), which might be $30 to $60, depending on where you're going. You can also reserve a standard or executive taxi, or a van, in advance via the transport page on phuketairportonline.com. You can also reserve a limo online beforehand, which is a good way to lock in the price.

Airport buses run hourly to the tourist corridors such as Phuket Town and Patong Beach, and cost about a tenth of a taxi. The orange busses go to Phuket Town; buy tickets at the counter near the exit of Terminal 1. The cream-colored buses head to Karon, Kata, and Patong, and leave near the airport's north doors. You'll need to pay onboard; there are cash machines inside the airport should you need one. Minivans are another option: They'll take a bunch of passengers to their hotels' doors for just a few dollars apiece, but the driver might try to hard-sell you tours at a travel agency along the way.

Many car-rental options are available. It's best to reserve online in advance, but you can always walk up to any counter upon arrival. Familiar brands are located inside the terminal and others can be found just beyond airport premises.

Should you choose to use public transportation to reach Phuket from Bangkok, expect a long ride. The train trip takes. A train/bus combo takes nearly 14 hours; prices range from $15 to $60 per person, one way. Bus alone is a 12+ hour endeavor (some routes take 16 hours) and comes in at $20 to $30 per person. Want to drive? It'll take 11 hours minimum.

GETTING AROUND

Driving is on the left side of the road here and traffic tends to flare up, so it's worth considering other modes of transportation for getting around the island.

Bus Busses are called *songtaew*; they're blue, open-sided vehicles in which passengers sit on wooden benches. Slow but inexpensive, you can hop on them to and from Phuket Town and the beaches. Don't look for a bus stop though: you simply flag down a *songtaew* when you see one. Phuket's Ranong Road bus terminal is a hub.

Taxi If you have the budget, taxis are a good choice. They have meters, so you needn't haggle, and they're inexpensive. Generally yellow or red, taxis can be hailed, or you can ask your hotel or restaurant to call one for you. A quick trip will be about $3.50, a longer one maybe $15.

Tuk-tuk Tuk-tuks are open-sided taxis, essentially rickshaws with a small-car motor. Most are red in Phuket. They're used just like taxis except they do not have meters, so you'll need to negotiate the price in advance. The rates are similar to taxis—about $3.50 for a short trip, $15 and up for a longer one. They're fun in theory, but on a hot day you'll crave a/c.

Grab Thailand's answer to Uber and Lyft, Grab is an app-based taxi-like service. It's quick and easy – as long as you have internet access. You can choose from a regular car, limousine, or SUV limousine.

Motorbike Even if you're not a biker back home, you might find motorbikes an easy way to get around the island. You can rent your own at specialty shops all around the island, and they tend to be located near budget-priced hotels. Ask for a trustworthy recommendation at your accommodation's front desk. You're most likely to find motorbikes in use in abundance in the busiest resort areas such as Patong. If you're not keen to drive a motorbike yourselves, choose motorbike taxis, called **motosai** here.

Boat If you want to bop from beach to beach, or visit outlying islands, you can charter a longtail boat. You'll find them lined up at nearly every beach just waiting for customers, offering jaunts from $30 and up depending on distance. In Patong, look for your water ride at the southern tip of Patong Beach. The boatperson will usually speak English and will happily act as tour guide too.

WHERE TO STAY

Phuket area map

Bangtao

Long and lovely Bangtao—with the second-longest beach on the island—was a series of tin mines from the 1700s through the 20th century, when the land was abandoned. In the early 1990s company known as Laguna developed the once-barren expanse into an eco-friendly resort area. It is leafy and green, filled with high-end hotels and all kinds of activities for those lodging within. Luxury villas, moderately priced accommodations, and a few beach clubs are also located here. This is a place to relax: Sit on the beach, go water skiing, read a book, have a dinner out... that's the excitement. No dance clubs with music thumping 'til the wee hours. You'll find deep-pocketed travelers and families beside you in the boutiques and at dinner.

Kamala

Kamala is a somewhat gentler neighborhood, with restaurants on the beach, hawkers selling Thai foods, nightspots designed more for unwinding than partying, some better hotels, and full-service spas. Some beach clubs (sleek hubs for lounging, drinking, and socializing), however, are opening here. The place feels almost like a community since it runs at a more leisurely pace, which may be why retirees tend to congregate in the area. Longtail boats parked in one section are a scenic addition to the clear pretty water, so wedding couples often stage shots in Kamala, but you can also hire them to take you to other beaches. There's good snorkeling right offshore and surfing is ace at some times of the year. You can rent mats and umbrellas for the beach.

Karon

If the thought of an isolated beach puts you to sleep but too much action is a turn-off, Karon might be the compromise. The hotels here —many of them spread out—give you access a white-sand beach, one end of which is quiet; the other filled with restaurants, bars, and stores. So, you can buy a sarong at a market, grab a bite to eat, and visit a couple of attractions, like a Buddhist temple, but you'll still be in a beach-vibe part of town. The windsurfing is good here.

Kata

Kata is another not-too-busy, not-too-quiet part of Phuket. Other than a Club Med resort that takes up much of the beachfront, the area has modest hotels and guesthouses, and enough restaurants, bars, shops, and massage parlors to keep you satisfied. The beach has soft white sand and clear blue water, which is calm for swimming in winter. In summer, though, the currents and waves will keep you on dry land. The south end, however, is a surfing hub in summer. Trees provide shade, and you can rent loungers and umbrellas. It's fun to watch locals' fish for dinner from rocks off the beach.

Patong

If you're the types who are always up for day of fun and a night out, Patong might be the area to choose. The crux of the neighborhood is a 1.7mi (2,736m) golden-sand beach; from here it's easy to rent personal motor craft or take a parasail ride. Patong's second hub is Bangla Road, home to more nightclubs, bars, and restaurants than you'll get to drink in over the course of your stay. The LBGTQ crowd tends to congregate at the nearby Paradise Complex. Patong accommodations tend to be on the less expensive side, whether hostels or boutique hotels, and the crowd is largely European.

Phuket Town

If you're seeking a beach vacation, then Phuket Town isn't for you. But it is worth finding your way here at some point. The province's colorful capital, this mini city will give you a real taste of Thailand in general and the country's multicultural heritage in particular. You can wander narrow streets, visit shrines, tour museums, and be awed by Sino-Portuguese architecture. History buffs have endless sites to see, especially in the historic Old Town, while foodies can try all types of cuisines, and at reasonable prices. Meanwhile shoppers will be thrilled with local markets; they are crowded, vibrant pop-ups (temporary shops) filled with items you never knew you wanted. You'll deal with traffic here, and you'll need to trek to the beach, but you'll definitely have an authentic Thai experience.

Surin

In addition to enticing sand and sea—a west coast staple on Phuket—Surin has stars. In the sky, of course, but also on land. Ultra-wealthy folks have holiday homes here, so celebrities are often in town. If you get a kick out of spotting an A-lister across the restaurant dining room, you'll enjoy Surin: Book a stay in a luxury resort and settle in. Of course, there's much more to this area: soft white sand; calm swimming in summer; surfing rollers in winter; and beach chairs and umbrellas for rent; designer goods in boutiques; and street food from vendors. The snorkeling is fine in two distinct areas and, if you can get to elusive Pansea Beach, just north past a rocky divider; entry is through a hotel, the kayaking is special.

ACCOMMODATIONS

Amici Miei $

(amicimieihotelphuket.com; 098014-4611; 171/8 Soi Sansabai, Patong)

When the basics are more than enough for the two of you, Amici Miei will do just fine. This modest inn has air-conditioned guestrooms with balconies, private bathrooms, internet access,

TVs, and beach towels. The mountain views are just a big ol' plus. The rooms, which have Thai touches, are surprisingly attractive for the price point. You can get everything from croissants and pasta carbonara to pad Thai at the on-site café-bar. When you want more, head right outside: you're a short walk from a mall and upbeat Soi Bangla, and five minutes from Patong Beach.

Andaman Cannacia Resort & Spa อันดามันแคนนาเซียรีสอร์ท แอนด์สปา $

(phuket-cannacia.com; 076333-4324; 212 Kok Tanod Rd, Kata Beach)

You'll have a sensational stay at this hillside hotel, no matter what room you choose. But if you can swing the Honeymoon Suite, give it a go: At this hideaway you can take Jacuzzi soaks on your balcony with mountain and beach views. You can even sunbathe in your birthday suits, it's that private. This Asian-esque hotel is rich with silk fabrics and handicrafts, and offers interesting relaxation spots such as beanbags on a garden lawn, and there's a tri-level cascading pool. It's just a short walk to Kata Beach. On-site you'll find a coffee shop, an open-air restaurant, and a poolside bar.

Deevana Patong Resort & Spa ดีวาน่าปาตองรีสอร์ทแอนด์สปา $

(deevanapatong.com; 07631-7179; 43/2 Raj-U Thid 200 Pee Rd, Patong beach)

You'll find everything you need, from 235 clean-line, air-conditioned accommodations with an Asian sensibility to three restaurants—including a swim-up café!—at Deevana. Located right near happening Patong, you can party in town or unwind by the rectangular pool, with the help of a chilled coconut cut to order or a refreshing cocktail. Or splash in the quieter free-form pool. Some deluxe rooms and junior suites have their own hot tubs. The Orientala Spa offers couples packages such as one with a gold body scrub, a milk/bubble bath. and an aromatherapy cream massage; the couples' treatment rooms feature spa tubs for two. Thinking of tying the knot? Request a Thai ceremony where you'll be blessed by a Buddhist monk, or have a Western-style shebang with all your loved ones.

Summer Breeze Inn Hotel $

(summerbreezehotel.com; 07634-0464; 171/12 Soi San Sabai, Patong)

If you're headed to paradisiacal Phuket on a budget, this is a good bet. Summer Breeze has air-conditioned rooms and suites with TVs and pillow-top mattresses; the penthouse even has a sofa and kitchenette. A casual restaurant and bar are located in the lobby. You'll be on a quiet street right near the hopping clubs of Soi Bangla and Patong Beach, or you can head to the nearby Jungceylon Shopping Center for souvenirs.

The Boathouse, Phuket เดอะโบ๊ทเฮาส์ภูเก็ต $$

(boathouse-phuket.com; 076330-0157; 182 Koktanode Rd, Kata Beach)

Oh, lovebirds, it's worth staying at The Boathouse for the dining venues alone. The beachfront hotel's Thai and Western restaurant will give you a choice of the water-view dining room, terrace, or arched pool deck, or, for even more romance, you could arrange for a private chef and host to serve your meal right in a private beachfront villa. Romance packages at this modern 39-room and suite Kata Beach property often include touches like rose petal baths and cocktail classes for two. The reds and whites flow freely at the Friday three-course wine-pairing lunches. The hotel will beat any room rate found online within 24 hours of booking.

The Surin Phuket เดอะสุรินทร์ภูเก็ต $$

(thesurinphuket.com; 07631-6400; 118 Moo 3, Choeng Thale)
Bathrobes and slippers, a spa, and three restaurants—even

his-and-her beach hats greeting you upon arrival. The Surin is romantic indeed, and located on quiet Pansea Beach to boot. With 103 cottages and suites surrounded by swaying palms, this pampering hotel even provides Bluetooth speakers in the room so you can get that music going. As if the setting isn't special enough, you can book a candlelit four-course dinner on the sand; it comes with a bottle of bubbly. Free morning yoga on the beach is held three times a week.

BREAKFASTS

Café Kantary คาเฟแคนทารี $
International
(cafekantary.com; 07639-1514; 31/11 Moo 8 Sakdidej Rd, Phuket; daily 8am-11pm)
Café Kantary is a small, polished chain of coffee houses, and the Phuket outlet serves up a whole lot of fancy coffee drinks. From espressos to frappés to ice teas—plus the brand's own bottled cold brew—you will definitely wake up here. The concept is a little of everything: barista joint, gelateria, wine bar, breakfast spot and lunch place, offering paninis (bacon and egg, grilled pesto chicken), crepes, tuna melts, and spaghetti carbonara.

Campus Coffee Roaster โรงคั่วกาแฟแคมปัส $
Thai
(facebook.com/campuscoffeeroaster; 092218-9292; 6 Krabi Road, Talat Yai, Phuket Town; daily 8am-6pm)
This is the place for serious coffee. Campus Coffee Roaster gets its beans from northern Thailand, roasts the beans itself, then transforms them into hot and cold beverages, often single-origin creations. No wonder this place enters and places in competitions. Owner Khun Golf and his well-trained team prepare these drinks for you at this hip joint in Old Town. You'll sip surrounded by

brickwork, no-frills tables, and lots of plants. Stop by for a small-batch treat like drip coffee or jelly coffee, along with a slice of cake.

Mr. Coffee มิสเตอร์คอฟฟี่ $

European

(facebook.com/Mr.coffephuket; 061225-3671; Luca's Resort, 434/14 Patak Rd, Ban Karon; daily 8am-4pm)

Freshly baked breads and sweets are the crux of Mr. Coffee, along with a mighty cup of Italian coffee. Whether you're going for a day-starter meal of eggs and sausage, or a lunchtime sandwich on a fresh baguette, Mr. Coffee has got you covered.

Rose Espresso โรสเอสเปรสโซ $

European

(facebook.com/Rose-Espresso-164754713589677; 089774-5321; 13 Krabi Rd, Talad Nua, Muang; daily 8am-6pm)

With its flowered china cups and teapots, and old-time English decor, you'll wonder if you're in Stratford-upon-Avon, not Phuket. Breakfast amid the flowered wallpaper and ruffled sconces is a must here, although you may prefer to trade in eggs Benedict or granola for a house-made banana cake or chocolate brownie cheesecake.

The Breakfast Hut กระท่อมอาหารเช้า $

International

(facebook.com/thebreakfasthut; 089173-0878; 31/33 Moo 1, Rawai; daily 8am-4pm)

Rawai is home to loads of expats, and The Breakfast Hut serves them the morning meals they grew up with—whether that was North America or Europe. The warm, friendly spot dishes out crepes, pancakes, and big hearty plates loaded with eggs, bacon, sausage, tomatoes, baked beans (for the Brits), and toast. Muesli, omelets, sandwiches... you won't starve, that's for sure.

The Coffee Club เดอะคอฟฟีคลับ $

Australian, Thai

(thecoffeeclub.co.th; multiple locations)

Australians have started their days at The Coffee Club regularly since 1989, and this chain now has several outlets on Phuket, including at the airport. Expect strong lattes, chilled frappés, fruity cold brews (*that's* something you can't get at home) plus Western, Australian, and Thai-influenced breakfasts and lunches. We're looking at you, coconut pancakes with caramelized banana and candied cashews.

Thai Food

Chances are that you'll have already been introduced to the exotica of Thai cuisine at restaurants back home: tart and aromatic—thanks to lemongrass and kaffir lime leaves—tom yum soup; chicken satay served with a peanut sauce with so much more flavor than your pantry jar of Skippy; and the ubiquitous pad Thai, with subtle flavoring from tamarind paste and fish sauce. Imagine how much more you can try in Thailand.

When CNN Travel did a feature about the world's 50 best foods in 2020, several of those featured were Thai. *Som tum* was one—it's a salad of spiralized green papaya, sometimes with crab, doused in a sauce made with dried shrimp, lime juice, chilis, and garlic. Massaman curry, made with creamy coconut and vibrant spices, was another. You'll find both wherever you go in Thailand.

Unsurprisingly, Thai cuisine differs regionally. In the south, you'll find lots of gentle coconut cream and cashews, while northeastern dishes tend to be bolder and spicier. Central Thailand is big on food as artistry; that's said to be because the preparation done for the Thai royals seeped out into the community. The differences are due to climate, soil, and which foreigners spent time in each area over time, from Dutch and Portuguese to Burmese and Chinese. As a whole, though, the offerings fall under four categories: curries—the main types are red, green, yellow, orange, panang, and massaman; pounded foods, mainly referring to chile pastes; spicy salads; and boiled dishes, namely soups—not to mention stir-fried noodle and rice dishes. Each savory dish tends to meld sweet and sour along with bitterness and salt, and, in most cases unless you request otherwise, a dose of spice. For dessert, you can never go wrong with the iconic mango with sticky rice.

You'll come across the dishes best known to westerners on menus throughout Thailand; we recommend you seek out restaurants that specialize in local dishes in each place you visit. When you've had enough exotica, worry not. "Western" foods like burgers, smoothies, and sandwiches are easy to find.

Som Tum aka Papaya Salad

LUNCHES AND DINNERS

Black Ginger ขิงดำ $$

Thai

(theslatephuket.com/dine/black-ginger.html; 07632-7006; 116 Moo 1 The Slate Phuket, Nai Yang; daily 6:30pm-10pm)

This is why you packed your little black dress, your heels, that sports coat: Black Ginger is an experience worth the lipstick (ladies) and a close shave (gentlemen). This Thai-cuisine restaurant is located within the Chi-Chi Nai Yang Beach resort. Each dinner begins with a short raft ride across a small lagoon to what looks like a mansion. You'll start with cocktails at the bar—we recommend the Salted Guava Lips, which mixes gin, lemongrass, and guava flavors, and has a salty plum rim. Then you'll dine within one of several over-the-top indulgent rooms, or maybe at a candlelit table on the terrace. The Michelin-recognized menu features specialties such as crispy prawns with battered cha-plu "wild pepper" leaves and sweet chili sauce. Treat yourselves to the three-course tasting menu for 1,500 baht (under $50): This is a once-in-a-lifetime meal, after all.

EAT. bar & grill กิน. บาร์แอนด์กริล $$

Steakhouse

(eatbargrill.com; 085292-5652; 250/1 Patak Rd, Karon Beach)

If you're missing steakhouse meals from back home, get your fix at EAT. Split an appetizer of pan-fried foie gras with mango chutney and ciabatta, and maybe a tomato bruschetta. Then make your entrée the Black Angus filet mignon; it comes with truffled red wine sauce and fried potatoes. Another option: Chateaubriand. Swedish chef Christer Larsson and his Thai culinary team seek out fresh seasonal ingredients and prepare them in the cozy restaurant's open kitchen. Finish up with house-made pecan ice cream or Oreo cheesecake.

Kan Eang @ Pier คันเอียง @ ท่าเรี $

Seafood, Thai

(kaneang-pier.com; 083173-1187; 44/1 Moo 5, Viset Rd, Chalong; daily 7am-11pm)

Serving fresh fish and shellfish at simple wooden tables with views of Chalong Pier, Kan Eang has grown to be a Phuket staple since its 1973 debut. Choose to have your fresh seafood grilled or prepared with Asian or Western flavors while you enjoy the views: there's nothing basic about steamed curry mackerel mousse prepared with freshly pressed coconut milk and wrapped in a banana leaf, prawns with baked glass noodles, or steamed squid eggs with lime sauce. Finish off with a tiramisu-inspired tiramartini. The name means "easy going," which is a vibe that founder Chamnan Prachantabur set out for.

La Gritta Italian Restaurant ร้านอาหารอิตาเลียน La Gritta $$

Romantic, Italian

(lagritta.com; 07634-0112; 2 Muen-ngern Rd., Beach Kathu, Tambon Patong; daily 5pm-midnight)

Is this Milan, or is it Phuket? You'll get the best of two worlds at La Gritta, an elegant Italian restaurant with a suave indoor dining room and a spacious outdoor terrace with scenic bay views. Chef de Cuisine Patrizia Battolu serves up special meals such as snapper saltimbocca and hearty osso buco as well as risotto, pizza, and pasta. The wine list features many bottles from Italy and France. End your meal with a lovely digestif.

Macrobiotic World แมคโครไบโอติกส์เวิล $

Vegan, Healthy, European

(macrobioticworld.com; 07639-0301; 14/93-94 Moo 1 Highway 4233, Rawai; daily 9am-9pm)

If you shun white flour or food grown with pesticides, or follow a macrobiotic or vegan diet, Macrobiotic World has you covered.

This restaurant takes its version of healthful eating so seriously that it uses cold-pressed olive oil and unwashed sea salt. The space is also a grocery for nutritional supplements and organic ingredients, as well as a resource for culinary instruction. The chocolate cooking class sounds especially romantic to us. Ask about vegan and weekend buffets.

One Chun Cafe and Restaurant วันชุนคาเฟแอนด์เรสเตอรอง $

Thai

(facebook.com/OneChunPhuket; 094275-8924; 48/1 Thepkrasattri Rd, Talat Yai; daily 10am-9pm)

Khun Prang features family recipes at her restaurant One Chun, and the authentic Thai flavors have earned the restaurant a Michelin Bib Gourmand recognition. You'll dine in a casual yet special atmosphere within what may look suspiciously like a grandma's house—ruffly curtains and knick-knacks everywhere. In fact, the colonial-era building is well over a century old—yet it has Wi-Fi. Try deep-fried crispy tuna with spicy mango salad, stir-fried crab with lime sauce, or maybe yellow curry with coconut milk and crab. The prices are quite low.

O-OH Farm Suanluang O-OH ฟาร์มสวนหลวง $

Vegetarian, Asian

(oohfarmphuket.com; 099312-5552; 1/1 Virach Hongyok Rd, Between Chaofa Rd East & West, Talat Nuea; daily 9am-10pm)

Sit yourselves down at a long communal table and dig into an organic plant-based meal at the Phuket branch of O-Oh. Whether it's smoked salmon pizza, a salad from the hydroponic bar, green curry, or a vegan cookie and coffee, this place will fill you up.

Pad Thai Shop ร้านผัดไทย $

Thai

(padthaishop.restaurantwebexperts.com; 07635-5909; Patak Rd, Karon; Mon-Sat 8am-6pm)

When you want to slum it and fuel up on big plates and bowls full of local food, head out to the Pad Thai Shop. It's nothin' fancy, for sure, yet Phuket residents tend to fill it up fast, and tourists are starting to follow. The specialty is the namesake pad Thai, a noodle dish, and loads of other options are available. Be careful or you may wind up with chicken feet on your table. Your meal will cost under $10.

Pure Vegan Heaven สวรรค์ของมังสวิรัติบริสุทธิ์ $

Vegan, Healthy, International

(pureveganheaven.com; 064014-4068; 45/28 Moo 1, Soi Ta-ied Evolve Health Club Phuket, Chalong; daily 9am-11pm)

The Phuket outlet of this four-unit vegan chain is all about plant-based dining. Options include Greek salad, pasta, and loaded nachos. Owner Pure Raksapan, a wellness guru, also owns an acai farm and a fitness center chain. Delivered meals are available via Grab.

Salute Italian Restaurant

Pizza, Italian

(ristosalute.com; 08004-0414; 58/5 Soi Patong Resort, Patong; daily 2pm-11pm)

Italian-American classics will lead to chianti-infused tête-à-têtes at this trattoria. Start with garlic bread, then get more garlic in your clams with white wine sauce or spaghetti with olive oil and chili peppers. The gnocchi, ravioli, fettuccini, and tortellini are made on the premises. Design your own pizza to share—enjoy it here or take it back to your hotel. Toppings range from gooey mozzarella and Italian sausage to hot dogs, tuna, and blue cheese; about two dozen specialty pies are available. With brick walls and red table coverings the place looks like it could be in Brooklyn circa 1970.

The Vegan Table ตารางมังสวิรัติ $

Vegetarian, Healthy, International
(vegan-restaurant-227.business.site/; 07622-3677; 106 Ratsada Rd, Talat Yai; daily 11am-8pm)

Whether you want a breakfast wrap, bangers and mash, or a spicy meatball pizza—all entirely meat-free—this is the place to go. This warm narrow restaurant on a busy street takes its plant-based menu seriously. Here they bake the breads, secure fresh vegetables, and cook each item from scratch. As for the vegan cheesecake? It pairs well with a soy-milk latte. The Vegan Table also sells its own bottled sauces and pickles.

DESSERTS

After You Dessert Café $

Japanese
(afteryoudessertcafe.com/en/; 07660-3204; Central Patong Mall, Rat Uthit 200 Pee Rd, Patong, Kathu; daily 11am-10pm)

Tucked away on the first floor of the Central Patong Mall, After You is a small, sleek, Japanese-style dessert shop, one of a chain with a couple dozen shops throughout Southeast Asia. Try an unusual sweet such as the Shibuya Honey Toast, made with loads of butter; other options include figgy pudding, crepe cakes, and chocolate lava cakes. Drinks, too, are noteworthy here—maybe you'll play googly eyes over a hot Horlick (it's malty) or a chilled plum soda.

Crepe is Crepe เครปคือเครป $

Crepe
(facebook.com/Crepeiscrepe.phuket; 07668-9599; No. 69 Yaowarat Rd, T. Talard-Yai Amphoe Muang; weekdays 10am-10pm)

Sweet and savory crepes are yours for the asking in Old Town, where Crepe is Crepe serves up its specialty to adoring couples and others. Some of the concoctions are oversized and perfect for sharing. The Parma Please is a well-portioned mix of Parma ham, cheddar cheese, and poached egg in a crepe. Honey I'm Home is topped with strawberries, bananas, vanilla ice cream, and honey in a special crispy crepe. The dining room is bright and cheerful.

Napoleon Bakery & Café นโปเลียนเบเกอรี & คาเฟ $

Bakery, French

(napoleonphuket.com; 084098-1985; 19 Lagoon Rd, Cherngtalay, Thalang; Wed-Mon 8am-5pm)

Since 2017, Napolean has treated Phuket locals and visitors to European pastries and meals. The croissants are made with imported French butter, and all breads and pastries are baked on the premises. This small-batch baker also serves egg dishes and bistro-style lunches in a spiffy, woodsy dining room. A newer, bigger restaurant is in the works; chefs have been hired to create a dinner menu for it.

Neko Cat Café Phuket

Cake, Ice Cream

(facebook.com/nekocatcafephuket; 093584-8355; 39/57 Soi Saiyuan, Rawai; Wed-Mon 10am-7pm)

You'd think Neko is a Barbie doll shop with its hot pink exterior and soft pink walls inside. But nope, it's a place where you sit on beanbags or chairs and play with cute cats while drinking your smoothie or coffee. Place your slice of cake on a low Japanese table and let the animal interactions commence.

Samero's $

Ice Cream, Italian

(sameros.com; Sainamyen Road 92, Patong; hours vary)

Whether you grab a simple house-made cone filled with hazelnut gelato on Patong's beach, or have a whole sundae served by employees in French maid uniforms near Patong's hospital, you'll be getting a taste of Samero's. This local trio of gelato chains has three very different outlets on Phuket. That said, at each you'll have hand-crafted cold treats, including vegan sorbets, made with natural and high-quality ingredients: Sicilian pistachios, Piedmont hazelnuts, Belgian cocoa powder, and Thai mangos, for instance. Samero's has entered and placed in the Gelato World Cup competitions. Coffees and some other sweets are also available.

Torry's Ice Cream ไอศกรีม Torry's $
Ice Cream
(torrysicecream.com; 07651-0888; 16 Soi Rommanee, Thalang Rd, Tumbon Taladnue, Aumpher Muang; Tue-Fri 11am-6pm, weekends 11am-9.30pm)
Artisan ice cream is the calling card of this light and bright spot. Located inside a Sino-Portuguese house, this café has vintage decor accents. The main attraction is the ice cream—maybe corn milk flavor or durian (in season), Thai milk tea, sweet potato or, if you must stick with what you know, chocolate, vanilla or bubble gum. Vegan options are available too. Have yours in a cup or cone, or sandwiched between two macaron cookies. Boozy versions might be spiked with Jack Daniels or Baileys Irish Cream.

COOKING CLASSES

Blue Elephant Cooking School โรงเรียนสอนทำอาหาร Blue Elephant
(blueelephant.com/cooking-school-phuket; 07635-4355; P 6 Krabi Rd, Talad Nuea; daily 9:30am-1pm, 1:30pm-5pm; Sunday morning only)

Learn to make four or five Thai dishes at a half-day culinary session produced by the owners of the Blue Elephant restaurant. Classes have either 12 or 36 students; morning ones begin with a market tour to understand Thai ingredients. You'll taste your creations at the end of the class.

Organic Thai Cooking การทำอาหารไทยอินทรีย์

(organicthaicooking.com; 07628-8258; 76/3 Moo 2, Rawai)
No more than two other people will be learning alongside you at Organic Thai Cooking, which instructs in traditional, vegetarian, and vegan meal preparation in an open kitchen surrounded by tropical garden. Once you master the basics of preparing traditional Thai dishes, you'll venture to a market where the teacher will introduce you to unfamiliar ingredients.

Phuket Thai Cooking Class by VJ สอนทำอาหารไทยภูเก็ตโดยวีเจ

(phuketthaicooking.com; 081710-5250; 83/1 Moo 2, Patak Soi 5, Patak Rd, Muang, Kata Beach; daily 10am-6pm)
Learning to prepare Thai cuisine—including curry paste with a mortar and pestle—couldn't be easier. The instructor, Chef VJ, speaks English fluently, and he'll provide free transportation from several island locales, plus bottled water throughout each session. Together with no more than a dozen others, you'll either attend a morning market and cook three dishes, or settle in for an evening of educational fun. You'll have your own cooking station, can adjust spice levels, and will be given gluten-free options if requested.

Positive Kitchen—Cooking with Chef Noi ครัวบวก – ทำอาหาร กับเชฟน้อย

(positive-kitchen.com/classes; 081797-4135; Perm Trub Villa 19/168, Si Sunthon, Thalang District; select days 1pm-4pm)
Chef-owner Tammasak "Noi" Chootong, of Phuket's three modern

Asian-cuisine Suay restaurants, is renowned for his stint on *Iron Chef Thailand*. Along long tables in his professional kitchen, Chef Noi gets students involved in cooking three dishes. Yours might be pomelo salad with grilled sea scallops, Tom Yum lobster bisque, and grilled lemongrass-marinated lamb chops with papaya salsa. Enjoy a tasting at the end of class.

ENTERTAINMENTS

Muay Thai

Thai boxing, or Muay Thai, is the national sport. You can watch pros go at this form of self-defense at two stadiums. **Patong Boxing Stadium** (boxingstadiumpatong.com) has matches Mondays, Thursdays, and Saturdays starting at 9pm; ask about free transportation, and book online for 10 percent off. **Bangla Boxing Stadium** (banglathaiboxingstadiumpatong.com) near Patong Beach hosts "super fights" with competitors from around the world. Grab a beer from one of four bars, take your seat on either level, and then watch the fighters go at one another. Fights start at 8pm.

Phuket Simon Cabaret ภูเก็ตไซม่อนคาบาเร่ต์

(phuket-simoncabaret.com; 087888-6888; 83/1 Moo 2, Patak Soi 5, Patak Rd, Muang, Kata Beach; daily at 6pm, 7:30pm and 9pm) Three times a night, this small but attractive theater puts on a transvestite stage show that goes all out with feathers and tiaras, and, of course, lip-syncing to music. Once the show is over, scurry out of your seat to greet the performers, who will happily pose for photos with you in exchange for a tip.

NIGHTLIFE

Bangla Road

If you think of beach destinations as all cut-off shorts and flip-flops, mellow days, and mellower nights, you haven't been to Bangla Road. Party Central is too modest of a description: This street—vehicle-free during evening hours—is lined with bars, and provocatively dressed women are likely to try to lure you in. The venues vary widely, from dance clubs to jazz bars. Want to watch pole dancers? You'll find them. Watch a soccer match on TV? You'll meet your tribe. See live bands? That too. Dance to hip-hop from a talented DC? Of course. Few of the venues have cover charges, so you can effectively stroll in, buy his-and-her cocktails, and get in the groove. If you're stumped as to where to even begin, hire a local guide; then you can beeline to the spots best for your tastes. Overall, the low-key bars are nearest the beach in the Soi Freedom hub, the girly bars in the center, and the dance clubs furthest inland in Soi Bangla.

Bangla Road

LIVE MUSIC

Bebop Live Music Bar

(f a c e b o o k . c o m / B e b o p - L i v e - M u s i c - B a r - Restaurant-714269582045888; 089591-4611; Takuapa Rd, Phuket; Tue-Sun 6pm-midnight)

At 9:30pm six nights a week, a band fires up and the party begins. Bebop may get your evening grooving with soul tunes, or it might be sensuous Latin songs, edgy jazz, or familiar pop. Whatever the genre, it'll be just the thing for a relaxed night out. Grab a drink and a light meal or snack, and watch the show.

Hard Rock Café Phuket ฮาร์ดร็อคคาเฟภูเก็ต

(hardrockcafe.com/location/phuket; 07636-6381; 48/1 Ruamjai Rd, Patong, Kathu; daily 11am-2am)

You can rock out to a Hard Rock night in so many destinations around the world, and it's fun to rack them up. Even if it's your first time, the two-level Phuket concert venue is a winner. The talent tends to be above par for the island, and the food and drinks consistent, if a little expensive. You'll find the Hard Rock on the edge of Patong. The bands entertain outdoors under the stars. You might as well have an iconic burger or hardwood-smoked ribs while you hang out.

Redhot Club Phuket เรดฮอทคลับภูเก็ต

(facebook.com/redhotpatong; 07634-0519; 86 Bangla Rd, Patong; daily 11:30am-2pm)

The party lasts for hours every night at Redhot. At this popular club at the far end of Bangla Road, live bands play back-to-back throughout the evening, maybe rock, maybe pop, or even reggae. The room is dark, and vibrant colored lighting illuminates the stage. Grab a beer, join hands, and watch the show.

Rockin' Angels Blues Café

(facebook.com/RockinAngelsCafe; 089654-9654; 55 Yaowarat Rd, T. Taladyai, A. Muang; Tue-Sun 6pm-1am)

It's all about Old Skool Blues at Rockin' Angels, an Old Town establishment where the house band won an award at a blues festival, and other blues artists from around the world find their ways to the stage. A dark, cluttered space where guitars hang from the wall behind the stage, it has a welcoming chill vibe. Sip one of the many whiskies or imported lagers, and let the evening roll along.

Roots Rock Reggae Bar & Shop

(phuketreggae.com; 087271-4656; 140/21 Nanai Rd, Patong Beach; daily 1pm-2:30am)

Roots is everything other Phuket bars aren't: It's on Patong Beach's Nanai Road, away from the club scene. It specializes in live music—always two nights a week, often more. And it stirs up 40 different cocktails. Plus, you're likely to depart having made new friends, as the indoor-outdoor club is so friendly. You might also leave with a leather satchel or wire-work bracelet hand-crafted by the owner, a man named Boy. It's a sliver of Jamaica in a Thai paradise.

BARS

Baba Nest บาบารัง

(babaphuket.com/baba-nest-exclusive-rooftop-bar/; 07637-1000; 88 Moo 8, Sakdidej Rd, Sri Panwa; daily 5pm-8pm)

Baba Nest is a rooftop bar in an elevated spot, designed for cocktails as the sun sets. You'll have 360-degree views around you and an infinity pool surrounding you as you sit on deck pillows and share exotically flavored cocktails or a bottle of bubbly. You can even get Mexican-style tapas like nachos. The setting is so romantic that this small bar with limited hours has been recognized by international media. No wonder you need to reserve your spot way in advance. A minimum purchase is required, but as the prices are steep this is a place to head to for a splurge.

Kee Sky Lounge

(thekeeresort.com/sky-bar-seaview-patong-beach.php; 07633-5888; 152/1 Thaveewong Rd, Patong; daily 5:30pm-midnight)
You'll fall in love all over again while having a cocktail or mocktail at the Modern Sino-Portuguese Kee Resort's Sky Lounge. Set on the sixth and seventh floors, it has 360-degree Andaman Sea views. The lounge resembles a sleek yacht: Sip at ease while on the wooden deck, in a lounge chair at the round bar, or atop a cushy couch. You can also eat while you drink, on the likes of grilled tiger prawns or a Wagyu ribeye. Alternatively, the two of you can dine in solitude encased in a giant bubble: The Bubble Me Up experience means you get that same excellent view, but also air conditioning, no bugs or rain, and a special dinner. Proposals and vow renewals happen here all the time.

BEACH CLUBS AND BARS

Bodega Phuket Pub Crawl

(bodegahostels.com/tickets/phuket-pub-crawl; 191/3 Rat-u-thit 200 Pee Rd, Patong; Mon, Wed, Fri from 7pm)
The crux: You'll get sloshed on this pub crawl with a bunch of strangers, mostly backpacking types. Starting at the Bodega Phuket hostel about 7pm, you'll receive a brightly colored vest and a "bucket of booze." Drinking games—beer pong, Cards Against Humanity—are played here until 10pm. Then you all proceed together to three Bangla Road bars. You'll receive a free shot at each bar during your 45 to 60 minutes inside.

Café del Mar Phuket คาเฟเดลมาร์ภูเก็ต

(cafedelmarphuket.com; 061359-5500; 118/19 Moo 3, Kamala Beach; daily 11am-2pm)

Take in the sun or the stars from a beach bed, high-top table or sofa between palm trees and under twinkly string lights. For the price of a couple of drinks (that's what it takes to get seated in a lounger) or a meal (the requirement to occupy a cabana), you can snuggle up just the two of you or mingle with new friends at Café del Mar, an offshoot of an Ibiza beach club that's just as cool as the original. Top DJs keep the music coming while you unwind. There is also a pool with a swim-up bar.

Catch Beach Club จับบีชคลับ

(catchbeachclub.com; 065348-2017; 12/88 Moo 2 Cherng Talay, Phuket; daily 10am-midnight)

This open-air establishment on sandy white Bangtao Beach has all the makings of a Jet Set gathering spot, like an infinity-edge pool, sunbeds, a dance floor, and cabanas, plus a DJ pumping out music day and night. And it gets better: You can receive a massage or skin treatment on your sun lounger. Drinks and meals are available.

Dream Beach Club ดรีมบีชคลับ

(facebook.com/dreambeachphuket; 084744-4330; Soi 2 Layan Beach, Cherngtalay Phuket; daily 11am-8pm)

Sand and sophistication aren't natural partners, yet Dream Beach Club melds the two seamlessly. The huge two-level oceanfront establishment on Layan Beach has a cool Hamptons vibe thanks to swimming pools, daybeds, loungers, four bars, and DJ-curated music, much of it jazzy. It also hosts parties featuring global talent and has a smaller mini-club called Level One that only opens later at night.

KUDO Beach Club คูโดบีชคลับ

(kudophuket.com/beachclub.html; 07660-9401; 150 Thawewong Rd, Patong; daily 10am-midnight)

You could easily just park yourselves at the KUDO Beach Club all day every day and make that your vacation. This establishment is located right on the sand of Patong Beach, and it has *everything*: two bars, a pool, and a restaurant. At KUDO, you'll find beach beds, two-top tables, bar stools, and lounge chairs. All are lovely spots for enjoying cocktails, food—including sunset dinners, and music, which is on the soft side during the day and morphs into party mode as the night goes on.

NIGHTCLUBS

Illuzion Phuket อิลลูชันภูเก็ต

(illuzionphuket.com; 07668-3030; 31 Bangla Rd, Patong; daily from 10pm)

Let loose with 5,000 of your fellow vacationers at Illuzion, at giant three-room nightclub with live music, hip-hop shows, and DJs, plus VIP tables and an all-you-can-drink-for-one-price option.

Sugar Club Phuket ชูการ์คลับภูเก็ต

(sugarclub-phuket.com; 098889-8590; 70/3 Bangla Rd, Patong, Kathu; Tu-Sun 9:30pm-midnight)

It's all about hip-hop at Sugar Club, a Bangkok offshoot with a sleek decor and daring lighting touches, booths, and high-top tables, and a mezzanine. B-boys and dancers get the party going nightly, along with musicians, DJs, and MCs, all with the promise of "nonstop entertainment."

TaiPan Disco ไทปันดิสโก้(

(taipandisco.com; 083647-5159; 165 Rat-U-Thit 200 Pee Rd, Patong; daily)

There's no cover charge at TaiPan, so you might find yourselves repeat guests if the upbeat vibe is right for you. A mix of imbibers gather here, young and old, residents and tourists—as long as they enjoy loud music, glaring lights, and congeniality. Coyote dancers—pro dancers hired to get guests moving and grooving—are keen to lead the way.

White Room Nightclub ไวท์รูมไนท์คลับ

(whiteroom-phuket.com; 081582-1756; Bangla Rd, Patong; daily 10pm-3am)

Music, lights, dancing, crowds, drinks... White Room is a lively choice for a night on the town. Buy a bottle to get your own VIP table, or just saunter onto the dance floor and get your moves on at one of the chicer hotspots in town. The sounds vary—maybe hip-hop, R&B, or whatever the house decides the trendsetting younger crowd may want. The white interior serves as a canvas for creative lighting.

SHOPPING

Central Festival Phuket เซ็นทรัลเฟสติวัลภูเก็ต

(centralphuket.com; 07660-3333; 199 Moo 4 Vichitsongkram Rd, Wichit; daily 10:30am-10pm)

A bright and bustling mall, Central Festival brings you retail satisfaction if you're homesick for designer and craft consumer goods. Linked by moving sidewalk to the Floresta Mall, this high-end complex has hues reminiscent of island waters, while Floresta tends toward Thai nature and art decor touches. You'll find great shopping, for sure, yet also an aquarium, an underwater dining experience, a 3D theme-park experience, and spa services. Add on a shrine and photo venues plus a pseudo floating market, and you may spend a whole day here.

Central Patong เซ็นทรัลปาตอง

(central.co.th; 183 Rat-u-thit 200 Pee Rd, Patong; daily 10:30am-10:30pm)

Food and shopping—that's what you'll find at the Phuket branch of the Central shopping mall, opened in 2019. The bottom floor is set up as a food hall selling grocery-style gourmet foods, surrounded by restaurants—and not the chains so common in competitor malls. The main floor has cosmetics and accessories, the second floor is women's fashion, the third apparel for men, plus luggage.

Jungceylon Shopping Center ศูนย์การค้าจังซีลอน

(jungceylon.com; 02663-7593; 181, Rat-U-Thit 200 Pee Rd, Patong; daily 11am-8pm)

Is this a Thai beach destination, or is it Mall of America? It's hard to tell at Jungceylon, a massive shopping center in Patong Beach. You'll find stores from 7-Eleven and Crocs to Levi's, along with a spas and massage parlors, banks, restaurants, an escape room, a bowling alley, and SF Cinema City, a multiplex with five screens.

MARKETS

Chillva Market ตลาดชิลวา

(facebook.com/Chillvamarket; 099152-1919; 141/2 Yaowarat Rd, Rassada; Mon-Sat 5pm-11pm)

A hip night market constructed of shipping containers (it's a trend worldwide), Chillva has an anything-goes feel—in a good way. Visit on a weekend when the flea market section is up and running: you can buy shoes or necklaces. Six nights a week, it's a great place for snacking on sausages, mango with sticky rice, or maybe dried grasshoppers. There are a couple of bars here that are ideal for chilling with a beer. You'll be surrounded by more residents than tourists, so be prepared to use your translation app if you need to communicate.

Naka Market (Phuket Weekend Market) ตลาดนัดนาคา (ตลาดนัดสุดสัปดาห์ภูเก็ต)

(086943-1140; Chao Fa West Rd, Phuket; Sat-Sun 4pm-11pm)

If you're wowed by size alone, make Naka your priority. This weekend night market is the place to pick up a woven handbag, papayas, a fun souvenir shirt, or a tasty street-food dinner. You can always get a bag of insects to eat here, and a (perhaps more appealing) refreshing ale. Buy vintage items in the covered area and new merchandise where it's open-air. And start early if crowds aren't part of your vacation plans. Near the Wat Nakha Ram temple.

Phuket Walking Street ถนนคนเดินภูเก็ต

(Thalang Rd, Tambon Talat Yai, Mueang; Sun 4pm-9pm)

Once a week, Phuket Old Town's Thalang Road transforms into the vibrant Phuket Walking Street, a night market. Maybe it's the music, perhaps the historical backdrop (colored lights are projected onto the buildings; they add a real pop), the cheerful toys, or just the weekend time slot, but families will be browsing alongside you here. Walk through the entry gate and stock up on gifts for friends back home—crafts, T-shirts, knick-knacks. Be sure to buy coordinating his-and-her flip-flops from a stall that makes the footwear to order. And arrive hungry, because a massive selection of intriguing street foods will beckon.

MASSAGES

Anantara อนันตรา

(anantara.com/en/mai-khao-phuket/spa; 07633-6120; 888 Moo 3, Tumbon Mai Khao; daily 10am-10pm)

Think a couple's massage sounds good? How about a couple's massage inside a treatment hut hidden behind lush greenery beside a serene lagoon? Or a bath for two under the open sky? Anatara is a couples' spa within an indulgent resort. All six treatment rooms are couples' suites, and the offerings will be as healing for your relationship as for your bodies. Think about a bamboo massage, chakra crystal balancing, or a rejuvenation package.

Banyan Tree Spa บันยันทรีสปา

(banyantreespa.com/find-a-spa/banyan-tree-spa-phuket; 07637-2400; 33, 33/27 Moo 4, Srisoonthorn Rd, Cherngtalay, Amphur Talang; daily 10am-10pm)

The flagship location of an international chain, Phuket's award-winning Banyan Tree Spa has taken a holistic approach since its 1994 opening. A personal touch, and natural herbs and spices, are the basis for treatment. Within pods made to resemble royal Thai shalas, you can be pampered with, say, a 90-minute Master Therapist Experience that's customized to your body's needs, or an Indonesian Traditions option with a Balinese massage and Lulur purifier, or a kaffir lime face mask. Ask about couple's treatments.

Kata Rocks Infinite Luxury Spa

(katarocks.com/phuket-luxury-spa; 07637-0777; 186/22 Kok Tanode Rd, Kata; daily 10am-8pm)

Kata Rocks is a luxury resort with villas, and its World Luxury Spa Awards-winning Infinite Luxury spa aims to meet the elevated expectations of upscale travelers. It has eight treatment rooms, each designed for a specific type of process. The two couples' rooms, for example, have his-and-her tubs in which to soak in bliss. Get color-light therapy in the chromotherapy room, spinal integration on a waterbed, or a Metronap rest pod in the sleeping pod room.

Let's Relax Spa

(letsrelaxspa.com/cities/phuket; eight Phuket locations)

Let's Relax has been providing budget-friendly spa services since

1998, and now the chain has several Phuket outlets—each with a one-of-a-kind decor. Custom spa music plays in a loop as you're greeted with a treat like coconut cookies and while you receive an aromatic hot stone massage, a four hands Thai massage, or maybe soak in a floral bath.

Original One Massage & Spa
(facebook.com/OriginalOneMassagePhuket; 07668-9559; 108/11 Taweewong Rd, Patong; daily 9:30am-11pm)
For more than a decade, the simple street front Original has been providing Thai massages and more on a pedestrians-only side street in Phuket. Stop by for a Thai herbal massage, a mani-pedi, or maybe a post-beach-day aloe-vera treatment.

So Thai Spa สปาไทย
(sothaispa.com/phuket; 34/125 Building 3, The Ashlee Plaza Hotel, Prachanukroh Rd, Patong)
So Thai's two Phuket spas look different, yet they'll tempt you with similar services. Book a couples' room and live it up with a four- or five-hour package. The So Thai Gold will de-stress you both with a foot massage, body scrub, body mask and wrap, hot oil massage, spa facial, and head and shoulder massage. Of course, you can hand-pick any one of those treatments too.

Sweet Lemongrass Massage นวดตะไคร้หวาน
(facebook.com/sweetlemongrassmassage; 081537-9099; 162/5 Nanai Soi 8, Patong; daily 10am-10pm)
Phuket's twin Sweet Lemongrass spas try to add a bit of luxury to a budget-friendly experience. With more than 10 beds apiece, they'll soothe your muscles with a sweet lemongrass rejuvenation, oriental foot massage, sports massage, or traditional Thai massage.

TOURS

John Gray's Hong by Starlight with Sea Cave Kayaking and Loy Krathong Floating John Gray's Hong by Starlight พร้อม พายเรือคายัคถ้ำทะเลและลอยกระทง

(facebook.com/tripstorekrabi; 084067-9979)

If you're going to take one day trip, this 12-hour powerboat excursion that ends at midnight is the one to choose. The focus is Phang Nga Bay, also known as Ao Phang Nga National Park, where small islands wow with cliffs, mango forest, lagoons, caves, and reefs. You'll see a raptor show while onboard, kayak through sea caves and monkey-populated lagoons on Panak Island, make a flower garland, and participate in a Loi Krathong ceremony involving bioluminescent waters. You'll enjoy a seafood/vegan dinner with three types of rice before heading back. From $130 per person.

Phi Phi Sunrise

(simbaseatrips.com; 081787-7702; Royal Phuket Marina, Thepkrasattri Rd)

On the Phi Phi Sunrise tour, you'll bop around the Phi Phi Islands on a speedboat for swimming, snorkeling, and taking in beautiful sites. You'll start at 6am to see the eponymous sunrise, and you won't regret it. Over eight hours, you'll have experiences like eating breakfast on a beach on Bamboo Island, swimming in an emerald Pileh Bay lagoon surrounded by limestone cliffs, snorkeling around Viking Cave, watching macaque monkeys, snorkeling off Nui Beach, and eating a restaurant lunch on Rang Yai. You'll also stop by Maya Bay, where *The Beach* was filmed. From $150 per person

Phuket City Tour: Karon View Point, Big Buddha & Wat Chalong (Multi Languages) ทัวร์ชมเมืองภูเก็ต: จุดชมวิวกะรน พระใหญ่และวัดฉลอง (หลายภาษา)

(viator.com/en-AU/tours/Phuket/Half-Day-Phuket-City-Tour-including-Karon-View-Point-Big-Buddha-and-Wat-Chalong/d349-146991P9)

Couples visit Phuket to relax, sure, yet the island is so rich in cultural sites that it's a shame to miss them. This tour lets you see three biggies in one air-conditioned excursion, so you can get the job done nicely before heading back to the beach. A guide will pick you up in an air-conditioned vehicle and take you to Karon View Point, or Three Beaches Hill, for a birds'-eye look at Karon beaches and the islands Kaya Noi and Kata Yai. Next up is Big Buddha Phuket, where a 148ft (45m) likeness of Maravija Buddha sits atop a grand stairway on Nakkerd Hill, with dharma music and bells adding to the serenity. With a concrete base inside a marble exterior, it's the third-tallest statue in the country. Your third stop will be the 19th-century Chaithararam Temple (Wat Chalong), a Buddhist monastery at which worshippers pay respect to a pair of monks who led an 1876 fight against the Chinese and also were herbal healers. There are also murals and statues of Buddha. Many claim this is a place of miracles. Your final stop will be Old Phuket Town to learn about Baba culture. From $22 per person.

Maravija Buddha in Phuket

Racha Noi & Racha Yai Dive Tour

(phuketdivetours.com; 087922-5536)

Whether you're a beginner diver or advanced, you'll have a chance to see the coral, fish, and wrecks at Racha Yai. Even newcomers with basic training can join the excursion to Rachel Yai, about an hour south of Phuket. Sloping walls, two reefs, and a snorkeling area in shallow water are all part of the day, and so is lunch. With the right up-to-date certification, you can also book a longer trip on a larger boat and head to the emptier waters of Racha Noi, two hours away, for your first two dives, dipping into Racha Yai on the way back. You'll likely see manta rays, barracuda, moray eels, and bannerfish. Breakfast and lunch are cooked on the boat.

Similan Islands Early Bird Day Trip from Phuket/Khaolak ทัวร์หมู่เกาะสิมิลันแบบเต็มวันจากภูเก็ต / เขาหลัก

(getyourguide.co.uk/activity/phuket-l32123/similan-islands-early-bird-day-trip-from-phuketkhaolak-t176829?utm_force=0)

The nine Similan Islands are renowned for their sea turtles living freely along sandy white-sand beaches with glass-clear waters, and this eight-hour tour will show you the best of this destination that's 90 minutes from Phuket. You'll be picked up at your hotel and brought via speedboat to a national park on this guided tour, which includes fruit, lunch, snorkeling equipment, and soft drinks. Highlights include walking to Sail Rock for the view, two snorkeling stops where those turtles are as fun to watch as the fish, and swimming in pristine Princess Bay. From $120 per person.

ATTRACTIONS

Chalong Bay Rum Distillery โรงกลั่นฉลองเบย์รัม

(chalongbayrum.com/en/home; 093575-1119; 14/2 Moo 2, Pa Lai Soi 2, Chalong; daily 11am-11pm)

Phuket is more about making memories—and tans—than making

spirits, yet the island's Chalong Bay distillery creates an award-winning signature rum from sugar cane raised without pesticides. The beverage is sold in many parts of the world. You can visit the distillery for a 30-minute guided tour any afternoon. At the end, you'll taste a mojito. Yes, that's Cuban, so clink glasses, say "¡Salud!" and go with it. Expect to pay around $10. The facility also has a tapas restaurant with homemade ice cream.

Gibbon Rehabilitation Project โครงการฟื้นฟูชะนี
(gibbonproject.org; 088590-9714; 104/3 Moo 3, Paklock, Talang)
Not only are these tree-swinging gibbons adorable, they're romantic: Mates sing to each other almost the way birds do. They're also a diminishing species, which is why since 1992 the Gibbon Rehabilitation Project has rescued, rehabilitated, and, when appropriate, released these miniature apes back into the wild. Hunters, pet stores, and tourist sites have led to a huge decrease in the population throughout Southeast Asia. You can visit, for free, although you'll need to pay about $7 to enter the National Park Wildlife and Plant Conservation Department first.

Green Elephant Sanctuary Park
(green-elephantsanctuarypark.com/en; 096651-3888; Green Elephant Sanctuary Park; daily 9am-4:30pm)
Spend half a day with elephants at this sanctuary park, where half a dozen adult and baby elephants wander freely and safely. You will feed these creatures with a trainer at your side, swim in a mud spa pool (pack a bathing suit, towel, and clean flip-flops), wash the animals in fresh water, and see them take a shower.

Monkey Hill
Many macaques make their home on Phuket, and you can monkey around with them—though don't touch them, they could bite—in an area, appropriately, known as Monkey Hill. The site is

really called Toh Sae Hill, and it's an elevated area of Phuket Town with nice views plus around 400 of these cutie-pie primates. A man going by Uncle Hog often puts on little shows with them. It's a hike of an hour each way or drive up a steep hill near the Green Forest restaurant in Rassada, Muang. Note that the road is closed to cars from 5pm to 8pm. Along your way, you'll see a little shrine, large faux tigers, and an exercise park.

ADVENTURES

Flying Hanuman ฟลายอิงหนุมาน

(flyinghanuman.com; 07654-0767; 89/16 Soi Kathu Waterfall, Kathu; dally 8am-5pm)

Zoom and climb over the top of untouched rainforest with Flying Hanuman, an ecotourism operator offering thrill experiences. Depending on which package you choose, you'll zip over much of the 20 acres (80,000m²) property (where locals still harvest rubber trees) on one of the 16 zip lines. Abseil points, spiral stairways, and dual zip lines are also on offer. All guests receive free rides to and from their accommodations, a wilderness walk, and fresh fruit; some packages include a meal.

Jungle Bungy Jump จังเกิลบันจีจัมพ์

(phuketbungy.com; 07632-1351; 61/3 Wichitsongkram, Kathu; daily 9am-6pm)

Book a tandem experience and the two of you can bounce and dangle from 165ft (50m) in the air, wrapped around one another, possibly screaming. You can also bungy jump solo, or backwards from the ground up. Whatever your choice, you'll have views of pristine lagoon and dense forest. Free transportation from five Phuket neighborhoods.

BEACHES

All of Phuket's resort areas are along the western shore of the island. They tend to be backed by trees and carved into crescents or strips of various sizes, so each seems like its own special destination. The Andaman Sea is always clear, although the hues differ. It may be calm in some places, rough in others, and that balance often changes from one season to another. The sand is as idyllic as you'd think it would be in such an exotic beach destination. Each strand has a distinct vibe. Choose the one that suits you best as a couple, but be sure to check out some of the others during your stay. Since the airport is at the northern end of the western strip, you'll be glad to know the beaches featured below are further south.

Freedom Beach

If small and intimate is more your beach style, try Freedom Beach. At less than a fifth of a mile long with powdery white sand and few crowds, it couldn't be more different from Patong. Located in a little cove, just south of Patong Beach, this secluded spot can only be reached by boat or via a half-hour downhill walk-through jungle. Most people pay the $35-or-so round-trip for the longtail boat experience, which is available during high season only. Once you're there, soaking up the picture-perfect sand and sea, not to mention the thin, towering palm trees, you'll feel as if you have *really* got away from it all. The snorkeling is mighty fine (bring your own gear), and you might join an impromptu soccer or volleyball match, but that's as wild as it gets. In season there are a couple of small restaurants here.

Kata Beach

Kata Beach, a 15-minute drive south of Freedom Beach is entirely different to the previous three beaches. It's neither wild nor secluded. Instead, it's a 0.9mi (1.5km) strip of sand with a Club Med and the chance to see yachts, especially in December when a regatta is in town. Families like it here because it's middle-of-the-roads vibe-wise, and many couples do too. You can rent water-sports gear from vendors, dine well in local restaurants, and surf when the wind is right. You can rent lounge chairs and umbrellas instead of sitting on the sand—although you'll also find plenty of shade trees. Masseuses will give you a Thai massage in the shade. You can see Pu Island from your perch.

Kata Noi Beach

At the southern end of Kata Beach, you'll find Kata Noi Beach, a small little subset of sand and surf; resorts cover most of the beachfront. The white-sand beach is perhaps best known for tsunamis that struck it in December 2004, though the beach is once again healthy. Kata Noi is not a crowd magnet, so you can spend gloriously quiet time here, swimming, sunning, having a casual lunch, and getting a massage. It's worth climbing to Karon Viewpoint to see the Kata Noi, Kata, and Karon beach at once. Some bars are on land directly above Kata Noi Beach and the view is terrific.

Paradise Beach

Jutting out into the sea at the southern top of Patong Beach, Paradise Beach is less than a mile long (150m) and you can only get to it by paying a fee of about $7. The Paradise Beach Phuket Club is the main attraction, along with non-motorized water sports. Stones on either end of the shoreline keep the jet skis away. You're most likely to seek out this remote spot at night, and once a month at that, when the Full Moon Festival turns the place into a thumping, jumping, bikini-clad after-dark zoo. The festivities are organized by a Bangla Road bar and require an admission fee. The prices vary by package and tend to include freebies like beer or T-shirts, which will help you advertise the event to the next month's crowd.

Patong Beach

Oh will you be busy at Patong Beach. Or, at least, you'll be busy seeing what's going on. A little under 2mi (3km) long and crescent-shaped, Patong Beach has golden sand and is quite the scene. Bring a mat or rent a lounger and umbrella, and set out to relax. It may not last long, because you'll be tempted by restaurants, beach massages and, hey, is that vendor selling a sarong? By day, you can get out on the water by boat, windsurf, or kayak. Beach Road, behind the palms, is either a comfort or a turn-off with McDonald's and other American chains. You'll find plenty of homegrown businesses too. Right nearby is Bangla Road, Phuket's center for late-night partying. It's lined with bars, cabarets, and nightclubs; barely dressed women will often stand under the doors' neon lights urging you to walk inside. Patong Beach is the most northern of the strands featured, and due west of Phuket City.

MUAY THAI CLASSES

Muay Thai is fun to try out, plus it's a great way to keep in shape: you can give it a shot at a local training camp. **Sinbi Muay Thai Training Camp** (sinbi-muaythai.com), set up by champion Khun Sing, is staffed entirely by trainers who have fought at a high level. Students have access to three rings and 22 bags, plus weights and more. The complex even has apartments for those interested in extensive study. Located near Nai Harn Beach, Sinbi welcomes walk-ins for group classes, held twice a day (Monday through Saturday), and also offers one-on-one beginner training. **Tiger Muay Thai and Mixed Martial Arts** (tigermuaythai.com) claims to be the largest such training facility in the country. So-called "holiday makers" are welcomed to its training program as warmly as serious students. Beginner classes have no more than eight people, and private classes are also available. Choose Kru Nai's **Rattachai Muay Thai Gym** (rattachaimuaythai.com) for group or private instruction for a day or longer. Like the others, **AKA Thailand** (akathailand.com) has fitness facilities and more. Co-owner Mike "Quick" Swick opens the facility to the public with group classes, training programs, and other sports like yoga.

YOGA'S

Beloved Yoga Rooftop Studio สตูดิโอโยคะบนดาดฟ้าอันเป็น ที่รัก

(ccshideaway.com/wellness/yoga-classes.htm; 07633-3222; 84/21 Patak Soi 10 at CC's Hideaway Hotel, Kata Beach)

If you're going to practice couples' yoga, you might as well do it in a special location—like a rooftop. Beloved has its mats atop a wooden floor that's itself atop the CC's Hideaway Hotel. It's covered to keep you cool, and trees and flowers join you up in the sky. Beloved offers several types of yoga including aerial, plus a Muay Thai boxing class. You can also book a session for just the two of you. Equipment, face towels, and water are included, plus you're treated to green tea when your yoga class is done. Ask about transportation.

Santosa Detox & Wellness Center

(santosaphuket.com; 07633-0600; 3 Soi Plak, Che2, Patak Rd, Kata Beach)

Santosa is the place to go for a three- to 21-day wellness or detox retreat, but its focus on health leads to yoga programs too. It offers traditional yoga and an "active cleanse" retreat. The yoga retreat experience is tailored to the guest: You'll work with your instructor to get the personal coaching you need. A private practice session including talk about yoga philosophy is also part of what is otherwise a group experience. You can just take a regular class for an hour, breathwork, yoga for the back, slow flow, Yin, aerial, and even hot yoga. The jungle walk sounds mighty tempting too.

Sumalee Yoga สุมาลีโยคะ

(sumaleeboxinggym.com; 088017-3018; 234/3 Moo 3, Soi Hua Tha, Si Sunthon)
Sumalee is primarily a Muay Thai boxing gym, but the facility hosts yoga experiences regularly. The yoga studio is an open-sided pavilion in the style of a Balinese shala. Take group or private Vinyasa classes, or opt for Hatha yoga or the calmer Yin. Aerial yoga was added in 2020. Weekend workshops can be a fun couples' activity.

The Yoga Shala Phuket เดอะโยคะชาลาภูเก็ต

(taysp.com; 80698-0813; Clubhouse at Land & House Park, 26/8 Moo 8, Chalong)
The Yoga Shala is a wellness center that blends tried-and-true yoga forms with current health trends. It's best known for Ashtanga instruction, and even hosts retreats and teacher training. Adjustment, water fasting, hip opening, anti-aging, and other subjects are also covered in classes and programs.

CHIANG MAI

WHY GO

While it's is the largest city in the north and has all the chic boutique hotels, raucous nightspots, and craft coffees of any urban center, Chiang Mai wears its rich culture on its proverbial sleeve. The downtown is a walled ancient city, albeit with hip new businesses alongside historic temples in the Lanna style, flaunting the region's signature style pointy, layered-roof style. Tribal cultures live on in the rural areas surrounding the city, home to gloriously lush and mountainous landscapes. The Rose of the North, as Chiang Mai is known, offers a vacation far, far different than any you'd find in America, and that's the appeal.

This is the place to buy handicrafts made in the same way by the same tribes for generations. To learn to prepare Thai meals quite different from the strip mall pad Thais you know. To tour not only legendary old temples but also outrageously artistic new ones.

You'll find plenty of opportunities for romance here. Waterfalls are easy to find, and you can picnic by their side, while hot-air balloons will take you soaring in the skies. Rooftop bars are the pucker-perfect place for a kiss with a cocktail, or you can board a dinner cruise, splash around with elephants, and bravely bite into piping hot street foods whose names you'll never know.

Lanna Culture

You'll hear "Lanna" (or La Na) referred to in northern Thailand, especially Chiang Mai and its surrounds. The word refers to cultural disciplines like dance and cooking styles, as well as the design of things such as architecture, temples, textiles, and wood and stone carvings. The Lanna composition began in the ninth century and evolved in the geographic areas around what is now Chiang Mai for a millennium. Indigenous Thai people, Burmese, Sri Lankans, the Chinese sect known as Yuan, and others contributed elements over time. The official Lanna Kingdom ran from the late 13th century through the mid-16th century, with elements remaining as late as the mid-19th century. "Lanna" is sometimes translated as "kingdom of a million rice fields."

For today's traveler, the Lanna influence is noteworthy for its history, its buildings, and of course its souvenirs. The distinctive look is most noticeable in the natural elements like flowers and birds, carved into wooden panels on buildings. These panels are also called *kalae*, and they're found everywhere from modest homes to sprawling retail complexes. Lanna temples have multi-tier roofs at a sharp angle, with small doors and windows.

You'll encounter Lanna references throughout your stay. If you place an illuminated basket in the river? That's a Lanna tradition with religious significance. It's often done during festivals, but a tour guide might give you the opportunity at any time. If you eat a spicy rice-based dish? It might have Lanna origins, if local chiles are used. The coconut-curry noodle dish *khao soi* has its roots here. Lanna Handicraft Tourism (handicrafttourism.com/en) can lead you to villages that specialize in certain crafts, such as "smiling" clay products at Par Tarn and naturally died, hand-woven cotton goods at Nong Arb Chang. In addition, day and multi-day Lanna cultural tours are available, some starting and ending in Chiang Mai.

HOW TO GET TO CHIANG MAI

Besides plane, you can also travel to Chiang Mai by bus, train, or car. From Bangkok, you can book a bus ride with a number of companies. Most busses leave from the Mo Chit station and take nine to 12 hours. See which has the amenities that matter to you at the best price. Prices range from $13 to $30 per person. busonlineticket.co.thai is a starting place. Thai Railways has a train from the Hua Lamphong station in Bangkok to Chiang Mai. The ride takes 11 to 15 hours. The scenery is special, although you'll miss much of it if you book a bunker and sleep onboard. Prices range from $15 to $40 per person. Begin at 12go.asia.com. If you want to drive and sightsee along the way, rent a car. But beware: This is like England, where you'll drive on the left, not the right, side of the road. Signs are in Thai and English.

You can also reach Chiang Mai from other Thai destinations such as Phuket and Koh Samui. Rome2rio.com has air, train, and plane details.

TRAVELING FROM THE AIRPORT

Once you arrive at Chiang Mai Airport (chiangmai.airportthai. co.th; CNX), you'll be in either the international or domestic terminal; they're in the same building. You'll be only 10 to 20 minutes from the city no matter how you travel, so no method will wipe out your cash supply.

Bus A modern large RTC Chiang Mai Smart Bus runs from the airport's International terminal to the city's Warroro Market and the Arcade bus terminal throughout the day from 6am to 6pm. It's the R3 Bus. Take the red route to get to Nimman Road, or the Suan Dok or Chang Phuek gates, the yellow route for the Chiang Mai or Thapae Gate, or the Night Bazaar. It's about $1 per person. Details are on the CM Transit smartphone app.

Grab Grab is like Uber and Lyft are at home; you can order a ride on the app. The app determines the price, so you will not have to haggle.

Private car If you'd prefer a nicer private vehicle, arrange in advance for a van or executive car. You can do that online at chiangmaiairportonline.com/chiang-mai-airport-transportation.

Public van/airport shuttle bus A van leaves for the city every half hour, ending in the city center. You can find the counter by Gate 9 on the first floor of the International Terminal. The journey will cost under $1 per person, and then you can walk to your hotel, or pick up a taxi or tuk-tuk from the drop-off point.

Rental car Several options are available, including Avis, Budget, Hertz, Chic, Drive, ASAP and Thai Rent A Car, all on the first floor of the Domestic Terminal in the Public Zone.

Songthaew These red, open-sided buses usually cost under $1.50 per person most of the time and will take you to or near your hotel; the routes are fluid based on what passengers need. They can be found outside most of the airport's exits. Prices are negotiable if you're the only ones boarding.

A Songthaew in Chiang Mai

Taxi Metered and airport taxis can be found on the first floor of the International Terminal. Metered taxis cost about $5 (including the airport surcharge), and the airport taxi comes to about the same, but it's a flat rate.

Tuk-tuk Tuk-tuks are small, open-sided vehicles; they're slow, but you'll get door-to-door service for about $4 total—probably with suitcases on your laps.

GETTING AROUND

The Old City is walkable, and the urban sprawl beyond that is still manageable on foot. If you don't have a rental car, consider renting a motorbike, hailing a taxi or tuk-tuk, or jumping onto an open-sided songthaew to get around the city. You can also use the Grab and Uber mobile apps if you have internet access.

Chiang Mai has recently expanded its public bus route. It now has eight bus lines comprised of spiffy big busses that make a total of 100 stops within the city. The Municipality Bus (chiangmaitransitredline.com) vehicles are red, the Smart Bus by RTC (facebook.com/rtccmcitybus/photos/706670026540428) blue.

These big, modern buses are only $1 a ride and have free Wi-Fi and disabled seating. If you think you'll ride this bus often, instead of using coins you can get a RABBIT or tourist card at an RTC counter at the airport or the Promenada or Central Festival malls. You can also use the CM Transit by RTC mobile app, which also gives real-time info on bus statuses.

WHERE TO STAY

Chiang Mai area map

Night Bazaar

On the other side of the Old City, Night Bazaar is just that—a night bazaar, in this case a daily market covering many, many streets that transform into a hangout after dark. You can buy all kinds of everything here, or wander the streets into pubs, girly bars, and cabarets. Adventurous eaters will never run out of new foods to try.

Nimmanhemin

Call it Nimman Road, as most Americans do, and enjoy the polished ambiance of this neighborhood. University students live here, along with young professionals, all of whom seemingly live within the hipster artisan coffee cafes and trendy restaurants. Spend your time perusing art in galleries, listening to interesting music, and smooching at happening nightclubs or rooftop bars.

Riverside

If you want a more polished place to stay, Riverside may be your best bet. This neighborhood by the Ping River is stocked with Chiang Mai's more upscale hotels, along with the chef-driven restaurants that serve those who lodge in that type of facility. It's on the quiet side here, with lovely views and waterfront dining. You can also combine dining and views by booking a dinner cruise. The Flower Market is a fine diversion, and spas abound.

The Old City

The ancient and the all-new meld seamlessly in the Old City, Chiang Mai's historic center. You'll find 700-year-old walls, a moat, and a couple hundred temples within this walkable square mile (2½km²). Along the way, you can eat fine meals, tour museums, buy stylish apparel, and get an aromatherapy facial. You'll also be within walking distance to nightlife and markets.

ACCOMMODATIONS

Akyra Manor Chiang Mai Hotel โรงแรมอคีราแมเนอร์เชียงใหม่ $$

(theakyra.com/chiang-mai; 05321-6219; 22/2 Nimmana Haeminda Rd, Lane 9, Mueang Chiang Mai)

Bring an urban edge to your Chiang Mai vacation by lodging at the Akyra. Both the rooms and suites at this Nimman District hottie have upscale extras such as Egyptian cotton sheets and natural cotton bathrobes, as well as design elements that give the spaces have an indoor-outdoor living feel. There's an infinity pool on the roof surrounded by daybeds and near the RISE bar. The suave and contemporary Italics Innovative Italian restaurant is a destination in its own right.

Bodhi Serene โพธิสงบ $

(bodhiserene.com; 05390-3900; 110 Ratchapakhinai Rd, Tambon Phra Sing)

The word "serene" is tempting in a city center, and Bodhi delivers. The first part of the name, Bodhi, is derived from the word describing the "tree of wisdom" under which Buddha became enlightened; a similar tree is on the premises. This gracious property, located near historic temples, has 12 New Wing rooms and 39 Old Wing rooms and suites, all outfitted with traditional Lanna woven fabric designs yet with modern amenities. The rooftop is the place to be: There you'll find a swimming pool, and a restaurant and bar overlooking the pool. You can also rent a bicycle or receive a Thai massage on the premises.

imm Hotel Thaphae Chiang Mai $

(immhotel.com; 05328-3999; 17/1 Kotchasarn Rd, Tambon Chang Moi)

Sweet and snazzy, the imm is a light, bright budget hotel in a city-center location, right next to Thapthae Gate. The rooms are crisp with natural colors and bold accents. The Grab & Go restaurant serves local and international breakfast foods every morning, while an entertainment room has a TV, games, and beanbag chairs. Also on-site are a washing machine, spa services, a tour desk, ping-pong, and foosball. Book directly to receive 15% off, a welcome drink, early check-in, and late check-out.

Ping Nakara Boutique Hotel & Spa ปิงนคราบูติคโฮเทลแอนด์สปา $

(pingnakara.com; 05325-2999; 135/9 Charoen Prathet Rd, Mueang Chiang Mai District)

Designed to honor Chiang Mai's past as a colonial center for teak production, the award-winning Ping Nakara is a visually noteworthy hotel: Its white exterior beckons with hand-carved fretwork and gingerbread characteristics. This boutique property, in the heart of the city near the Night Bazaar, has only 19 spacious rooms, each with one-of-a-kind furnishings and Persian carpets. You'll have access to a swimming pool surrounded by shaded loungers; The Library, with Asian travel resources; bars; a wine cellar; a spa; and a restaurant serving free breakfast, afternoon tea, and Thai dinners. The hotel will match any low rate posted elsewhere if you book directly.

Raminglodge Hotel & Spa ระมิงลอดจ์โฮเทลแอนด์สปา $

(raminglodge.com; 05327-1777; 17-19 Loi Kroh Rd, Tambon Chang Moi)

You'll find lots of indulgent extras at this city-center hotel with a wallet-friendly price. Lanna styling defines this 84-room property near the Sunday Market. In addition to a guest room with a/c, TV, Wi-Fi, bathrobes, free minibar, and slippers, you'll have access to free daily breakfast with indoor and garden seating, the Rock Me Burger lunch/dinner restaurant, on-site parking, spa services, and even a free-form outdoor swimming pool. A staffer will book tours for you.

Sukantara Cascade Resort & Spa สุกันทราแคสเคดรีสอร์ท แอนด์สปา $$$

(sukantara.com; 081881-1444; 12/2 M.8, T.Maeram, A.Maerim)
If you're in search of Brownie Points for booking the most romantic hotel of the vacation, choose Sukantara. This family-owned hotel has only 16 rooms, suites, and cottages, all of them luxe. Yours might have a whirlpool tub, plunge pool, or outdoor shower. All are air conditioned with Wi-Fi, plush bathrobes, cotton bed sheets, and slippers in traditional Lanna designs. Best of all, the accommodations are lined up along the way to a waterfall. The swimming pool faces the waterfall too, and a river. Peacocks roam the property, exotic birds fly freely, and the spa offers soothing treatments. Book what might be the most romantic dinner of your lives: At a Khan Toke meal, you'll share northern Thai specialties featuring tropical foods (Western options are available) while facing the waterfall, candles illuminating the table.

Thannatee Boutique Hotel ธารนทีบูติคโฮเทล $

(facebook.com/ThannateeHotelChiangmai; 05327-4500; 2 3-7 Rat Chiang Saen Rd, Tambon Hai Ya)
You'll feel like you're lodging in a historical novel at Thannatee, a 22-room boutique hotel in a teak building that emits true local flavor. The guestrooms are small yet each has rich Lanna accents along with antiques and wood furnishings made in the local style. In addition to modern basics like TVs, the Thannatee has a small charming pool surrounded by a stone wall and palm trees. Also available: a restaurant, rental bicycles, a free breakfast buffet, and free shuttles to the Old City and the airport.

Wealth Boutique Hotel $

(wealthboutiquehotel.com; 05390-3703; 60 Ratchapakhinai Rd, Tambon Phra Sing)

The Wealth gets an A for effort. With only 13 rooms and suites, this modern downtown hotel tries to meet every need the two of you will have—at a low price. Essentials are standard: a/c, minibar, safe, Wi-Fi, and cable. You'll also have 24/7 reception help, a coffee shop/restaurant, a swimming pool with a bar, laundry services, and room service. There are even computers for you to use in the lobby.

BREAKFASTS

Blue Diamond - The Breakfast Club บลูไดมอนด์ - The Breakfast Club $

International, Asian

(facebook.com/BlueDiamondTheBreakfastClubCmTh; 05321-7120; 35/1 Moon Muang Rd, Soi 9, Si Phum; Mon-Sat 7am-8:30pm)

Baguettes, croissants, and muffins hot out of the oven may greet you at Blue Diamond, along with rice bread for the gluten-intolerant. Walk up for a plate full of eggs, potatoes, and bacon, or get a vegan tofu scramble, choose an omelet, or opt for a pancake.

Butter is Better Diner & Bakery เนยดีกว่า $

American

(butterisbetterbakery.com; 05382-0761; 183 8-9 Changklan Rd, Tambon Chang Khlan; Wed-Mon 8am-5pm)

This restaurant is so into being America-away-from-home that it even sells a full Thanksgiving dinner to-go in November. In the morning, stop in for "Real American Food" made from scratch: house-made pastrami, jams, and bagels. Buttermilk pancakes, with gluten or without, waffles, and eggs Benedicts are typical choices.

Chiang Mai Breakfast World เชียงใหม่เบรกฟาสต์เวิลด์ $
International
(chiangmaibreakfastworld.com; 05327-8209; 24 1 MoonMuang Rd, Lane 2, Tambon Phra Sing; daily from 9am)

You might get distracted by the words "German Beer Garden" under the sign, or by the Thai menu items pictured on Facebook. But make no mistake: You'll get good breakfasts here, albeit in a beer-garden setting. Starting at 9am every day, the kitchen plates up hearty day-starter meals—120 versions, in fact. One option includes eggs, potatoes, bacon, sausage, ham, baked beans, and toast. If that's not your thing, look for baked goods, salamis, and cheeses.

Overstand ทน $
International
(overstand.co.th; 094626-8311; 19/3 Soi Ratchamanka 2, Phra Sing; Sat-Sun 8am-3pm)

"No progress without struggle" is on the Overstand logo, which may make you question your choice to breakfast there. Worry not. This coffee hangout is known for Western-style breakfasts, both plant-based variations and the kinds heavy on meat and eggs. Most take the form of breakfast sourdough sandwiches or breakfast pizzas. Locally raised and roasted coffee is key to the concept, as are smoothies. Local artists' works on the walls are a bonus.

LUNCHES AND DINNERS

Anchan Restaurant ร้านอาหารอัญชัญ $
Vegetarian, Asian, International
(anchanvegetarian.com; 090705-9971; 13/30-13/31 Petchkasem Rd, Khao Lak; daily 11:30am-8:15pm)

Chef-driven plant-based dining embraces local flavors at Anchan, a second-floor restaurant with a bakery below. The restaurant makes unusual dishes but none with meat alternatives, fish sauce, MSG, or produce grown with pesticides. The ever-evolving menu has a few staples, among them mushroom pad Thai, miso eggplant, and massaman vegetarian curry made with cardamom. Be sure to try the banana flower tom yum soup. Chef Aye offers a different featured dish each week.

AUM Vegetarian Restaurant ร้านอาหมังสวิรัติ. $
Vegetarian, Asian, American
(aum-vegetarian-restaurant.business.site;   05327-8315;   1,   4 Suriyawong Alley, Haiya Sub-district; daily 10:30am-8:30pm)
A rustic restaurant serving vegetarian food since 1982, AUM is near the Thapae Gate. At this second-floor spot, you'll find Asian and American flavors, all served in a cheerful, simple dining room. Pictures of several offerings are posted on the wall. Smoothies and juices are also available.

Boutique della Pasta บูติกพาสต้าเดลล่า $
Italian
(facebook.com/Boutique.della.Pasta;   086117-5387;   127/6 Ratchapakhinai Rd, Sri phum; Mon-Sat 3pm-10:30pm)
In a charming outdoor garden, covered or uncovered, and inside an Old-World dining room with dark woods and red linens, Boutique della Pasta serves a tempting array of Italian foods, many of the dishes created from imported ingredients. Ravioli and other pastas are made in-house, and so are the sauces and the dough for the thin-crust pizzas.

Chang Puak Gate Market ตลาดประตูช้างเผือก $
Thai
(248/70 Manee Nopparat Rd, Tambon Si Phum; daily 5pm-midnight)
No need to plan for this meal. Simply step out of the Old City's northern gate, and from 5pm each evening you'll be presented with a thrilling array of food options. This market has plenty of

choices designed for locals. That gives you the chance to sample stir-fries, rice dishes, and soups that might scare you a bit. At such low prices, it's not a big risk to order them. The vendors are regulars and provide plenty of seating. Between bites, you can shop for trinkets and apparel, and maybe catch a street show.

Chez Marco Restaurant & Bar $$

Steak, French, Asian

(facebook.com/chezmarcocnx; 081696-9508; 15/7 Loi Kroh Rd, Tambon Chang Moi; daily 12:30pm-9:30pm)

Oranges and yellows dominate this bistro, which would feel like a coffee shop if not for the fine plates of food and wine bottles throughout. It's essentially a French restaurant yet its steaks are known to be among the best in town. Then there's the rack of lamb, the chicken cacciatore, the beef marrow, the pasta... and the lobster tom yum, upon request. Chef Marco Arigo always has interesting combos coming out of the kitchen.

David's Kitchen $$

Fine Dining, Asian, European

(davidskitchen.co.th; 091068-1744; 113 Bumrungrad Rd, Wat Kate Subdistrict; Mon-Sat 11:30am-11pm)

Here's your date-night restaurant. Subdued lighting and music will greet you at David's, an owner-operated establishment with a friendly style and an ambitious menu offering food that transcends geographic boundaries. That means you might start with a soup transported from Spain, France, or Thailand, before moving onto house-made gnocchi, foie gras with mango chutney, braised lamb shanks... Whatever its origins, the food is special. Care is taken with details such as flatware, which is heavy, and linens, which are crisp. Ask about the four-course prix fixe dinner.

Khaomao-Khaofang Restaurant ร้านข้าวเม่า – ข้าวฟาง $$
Romantic, Thai
(khaomaokhaofang.com; 063665-5838; 181 Moo 7 Ratchaphruek Rd, Hang Dong; daily 11am-3pm, 5pm-9:30pm)
Khaomao-Khaofang serves northern Thai cuisine in a remarkable setting of rainforest and lake. Your table might be under trees or overlooking a pond. Talk about romantic. The ambiance is thrillingly other-worldly, with waterfalls and sculpted wood tabletops. The owners, he's a horticulturalist, she's a culinary instructor, carry through their attention to detail to the kitchen. You might fall head over heels with the watermelon topped with dried fish flakes, the chili-roasted duck, garlic-seafood fried rice, or stir-fried squid with salted egg. Finish your experience with black sesame dumplings in ginger tea.

Huen Muan Jai เฮือนม่วนใจ๋ $
Thai
(huenmuanjai2554.com/; 098261-8029; 24 Ratchaphuek Alley, Tambon Chang Phueak; Thu-Tue 11am-3pm, 5pm-10pm)
You're in Chiang Mai, so eat as the locals do. This is the place: Huen Muan Jai is in a Lanna-style Chang Phueak teak building with loads of plants and trees. Its name translates as "happy home," and Chef Charan Thipeung's foods are renowned for resulting in happy guests. Even Michelin recognizes this casual enterprise, where the culinary leader has been on TV shows. Experience the soup with jackfruit, the red pork curry with northern Thailand herbs, and the dip known as nam phrik num; it's made with grilled chile peppers.

Mae Ping Dinner Cruise ล่องเรือแม่ปิงดินเนอร์ $$
Romantic, Thai
(maepingrivercruise.com; 05327-4822; 133 Charoen Prathet Rd, Tambon Chang Khlan; daily 6:30pm-8pm)

Dine as you drift by Chiang Mai illuminated at night on the Mae Ping Dinner Cruise. During the 90-minute expedition aboard a 48-seat floating dining room, you'll see Ping River highlights while eating northern Thai foods. Free pick-up is available from nearby hotels.

Paak Dang Restaurant ร้านป้าแดง $$

Seafood, Thai

(paakdang.com; 082685-7249; 46, 1 Wang Sing Kam Rd, Tambon Pa Tan)

The food here is out of the ordinary, yet that's just the start of it. Paak Dang is a riverside restaurant in a teak building of Lanna design. It's run by Singaporean siblings who opened the restaurant as a way to give back to society. As such, they hire employees from the neighborhood and give lessons in English and Mandarin. For you, expect a Michelin-rated seafood meal set to live music in the evenings—and Ping River views if you dine outside. The food is a la minute, meaning each dish is cooked right before it's served. The specialty is live mud crabs in yellow curry sauce. If that's too authentic for you, go for the duck curry or jumbo river prawns instead, or even grilled rib-eye with a mint-cilantro-lime sauce.

Pun Pun Vegetarian & Organic Restaurant $

Vegetarian, Thai

(facebook.com/punpunlearningcenter; 084365-6581; 6/1 Moo 1, Suthep Rd, Wat Suan Dok; Thu-Tue 9am-4pm)

Take a break from touring to cool off with a chilled coconut juice or warm up with a vegetarian noodle soup with tofu, beet, and lime sauce at Pun Pun, located inside the Wat Suan Dok temple. A second unit is in the Santitham neighborhood a bit north of Old City, and both are related to an organic farm that promotes biodiversity. The temple restaurant has Isaan-style food, which includes herbs and vegetables you may not have encountered before. Those greens might be in curries, fusion wraps, salads, or soups. Seating is at communal rectangular tables.

Rock Me Burgers & Bar $

Burger, American

(facebook.com/Rockmeburger; 063895-2456; Nimmana Haeminda Rd Lane 15, Suthep; daily 11:30am-midnight)

The American gourmet burger trend surfaced in Chiang Mai in 2014 as Rock Me and the concept continues to rock this city. The casual restaurant has a wide variety of burgers: You can go traditional with ground beef and cheddar, or vegetarian with a veggie patty topped with sweet chile mayonnaise. Pork and fish options are equally fine. Be sure to indulge in the thick-cut onion rings and golden steak fries. Watching your weight? The menu has a few salads too.

Thajene Chomchan ธาเจนชมจันทร์ $

Seafood, Asian

(thajenechomchan.com; 081797-8790; 104/8 Moo 2, Soi Photaram 2, Photaram Rd, Chang Phueak; daily 5pm-midnight)

Sit outdoors for night air or indoors for air conditioning at this seafood restaurant with live musical entertainment, where the grilled river prawns and deep-fried sea bass with fish sauce are game-changers. The menu is huge, so you're bound to find something that suits you.

Tong Restaurant and Bar (TongTemToh) ต่องเรสเตอรองท์ แอนด์บาร์ (TongTemToh) $

Thai

(facebook.com/TongTemToh; 05389-4701; 1113 Nimmanahaeminda Rd, Suthep; daily 11am-9pm)

Ferns hanging from the ceiling, a big tree in the center, picnic-style tables, and shade umbrellas make Tong feel like an outdoor restaurant. That's fitting, as the specialty is grilled foods—although fire-seared items are only offered in the evening. Nab your spot in line and wait an hour if necessary, to sample Thai-style barbecue and a host of northern Thai specialties. That might mean chicken curry or a snake head creation, depending on whether you're as bold as the spices at this Nimman hot spot.

Why Ribs & Rumps ทำไมต้อง Ribs & Rumps $

Steakhouse

(why-ribs-rumps.business.site; 088267-2659; 50 Wiang Kaew Rd, Si Phum; Thu-Tue 4:30pm-9:30pm)

Australian steaks and tender pork ribs are served in bounty at Why, a Sriphoom spot with arched throughways and rudimentary art painted directly onto the wall. Meals are complete, whether beef, salmon, fish, or chicken, as proteins are served with mashed potatoes and vegetables. A few pastas are another option.

World Buffet Dinner at Le Crystal Restaurant บุฟเฟต์มื้อค่ำ ระดับโลกที่ห้องอาหารเลอคริสตัล $$

Buffet, French

(lecrystalrestaurant.com/world-buffet; 084177-6599; 74/2 Patan Rd, Pa Tan; Last Saturday of every month, 6:30pm-10pm)

Fresh oysters from France! Caviar! Foie gras! World Buffet begs for exclamation points. This extravaganza of luxury foods comes to Chiang Mai once a month. Sushi, cheeses, grilled meats, a chocolate fountain... they're all up for grabs at this somewhat formal restaurant—French the rest of the month—with river-view garden seating. As if the food isn't enough, musicians play jazz from 7:30pm onwards. $50 per person, $75 per person with wine.

DESSERTS AND COFFEES

Cheevit Cheeva ชีวจิตซีวา $

Bingsu, Korean

(cheevitcheevacafe.com; 087727-8880; 6 Siri Mangkalajarn Rd, Tambon Su Thep; daily 11am-9pm)

Calling itself "Chiang Mai's Premier Bingsu Café," the concept specializes in bingsu—Korean-style shaved-ice desserts. Each of the four local units is polished and upscale, yet with one-of-a-kind looks. Here the ice flakes are made from milk. They're flavored with all kinds of combos: mango and sticky rice, golden injeolmi (Korean rice cake), and melon mascarpone are among the concoctions. Regular desserts like dark chocolate fudge cake and matcha cheesecake are also available.

Dhara Dhevi Cake Shop ดาราเทวีเค้กช็อป $

Cake

(haradhevi.co.th/dining/cake-shop; 05388-8532; 51/4 Moo 1 San Kamphaeng Rd, Mueang Chiang Mai)

At the Dhara Dhevi resort, you can court like Victorian lovers in a frilly tea salon serving classic cakes, some with a British bent. Perhaps during your visit you'll find a white chocolate and butterfly pea cake, or an Alexandra cake. The menu is always full of sweet surprises. Dhara Dhevi also has pop-up macaron shops around Chiang Mai.

Fruiturday ผลไม้วันเสาร์ $

Fruit

(facebook.com/fruiturdaycnx; 094643-2643; Nimmana Haeminda Rd, Lane 11, Tambon Su Thep; daily 10:30am-11pm)

Fruiturday dishes out light, fruity desserts to be eaten in its narrow and bright dining room. Fresh fruit abounds in the shop, and the produce is used to make nearly every offering. That might be a freshly squeezed passion-fruit juice, a pudding made with young coconuts and topped with Japanese melon, or a mango pudding with coconut juice and whipped cream.

Here Is Snow นี่คือหิมะ $

Ice Cream

(facebook.com/hereissnow; 090330-1923; 176 Loi Kroh Rd, Tambon Chang Khlan; daily 7:30am-11:30pm)

This corner store has food such as Caesar salad, yet it's the ice cream that gets the attention. Triangular-shaped desserts including Banana Choco, watermelon, and Oreo are layers of sweet flavors, and they look as tempting as they taste.

Ice Cream 100 Flavors: Chiang Mai Exotic Ice Cream ไอติม100รส: Chiang Mai Exotic Ice Cream $

Ice Cream

(facebook.com/Iceloveyou; 093590-7172; 25 Suthep Rd, Srivichai Soi Suthep; daily noon-8pm)

A plantation-style little white building with lots of windows scoops up 100 choices a day of ice cream, both regular and vegan. As for flavors? It's always a good gamble to strut right in and see. Wild honey and bee pollen might be available, or Peach Love Classic, Funny Christmas, lychee yogurt, mango sticky rice, apple mint... just expect to try a new flavor every time you visit.

Jardin d'été Gelato and Dessert Café ชีวจิตชีวา $

Gelato

(facebook.com/jardin.dete.chiangmai; 095860-6262; 61 Airport Rd, T. Suthep; daily 9am-7pm)

This oddly shaped building in a deep gold hue somewhat resembles a honeycomb. Airy inside with light woods and plants on the walls, the establishment specializes in gelato and desserts. Go for a scoop of, say, strawberry gelato, or choose a chocolate layer cake or crème brûlée instead.

Love At First Bite รักแรกกัด $

Cake

(facebook.com/loveatfirstbitecnx; 05324-2731; 28 Charoen Muang Rd, Tambon Chang Moi; Tue-Sun 10:30am-6pm)

Green tea cheesecake, rhubarb pie, brownie sundae, cinnamon roll: a wide variety of sweet treats, along with hot and cold beverages, are the output of this ode to "Homebaked Cakes & Pies," as its sign says. Settle into a seat in the garden setting and dig into the sugar fix of your choice.

The Giant ยักษ์ $

Cake, International

(thegiantchiangmai.com/coffeeshop.html; 086776-2946; Ban Pok Huay Kaew Village, Mae On; Tue-Sun 8:30am-5pm)

It's hard to even explain The Giant. It's a five-room inn that has a casual coffee shop built around an enormous tree, which itself is surrounded by woods. Settle into your little fenced-off seating area perched above wildlife and share a couple of slices of layer cake, along with hot or cold coffee beverages. Pizzas, steaks, pastas, and Thai foods are also available.

Coffees

Ristr8to (ristr8to.com) owner Arnon Thitiprasert has won latte art championships, and his four barista bars are heavily into coffee culture. Influenced by Australia's bean scene, Thtiprasert has put together such serious shops that his team carefully chooses even the cups to best showcase the brew, with double shot ristretto the standard pour. **Ma-chill** (machillespressochiangmaithailand. wordpress.com) is an independently owned coffee bar and roaster. Ask for the house blend or a single-origin pour. You can also buy bagged cold brew to take back to your hotel. **Graph Café** and **Graph One Nimman**, under the **Graph Coffee Co.** (graphcoffeeco.com) umbrella, have urban panache. The company roasts its own beans and uses those to pour exceptional coffee drinks.

FOOD TOURS

Chiang Mai Foodie Tours เชียงใหม่ฟู้ดดีทัวร์

(cm.chiangmaifoodietours.com; 080494-8080; 192 Lumphang Rd, Muang Chiang Mai)

Spend half a day tasting local foods with The Original Foodie Tour by a company with the slogan, "Go where the locals go, Eat what the locals eat!" You'll meet up in the morning and head to a restaurant that has been making pork satay and the boiled chicken specialty kao man gai since 1957. From there, you'll proceed to a temple, a place to eat khao soi noodles, a museum, a destination for two desserts, and then a market. Too much for a morning? An evening tour is also available and is slightly different. $45 per person.

Evening Market Tour ทัวร์ตลาดยามเย็น

(chiangmaistreetfoodtours.com; 12 Ratchapakhinai Rd, Tambon Phra Sing)

You came to Thailand hearing about the amazing street foods. Yet it's intimidating. What tastes good? What's safe to eat? What's the etiquette involved in buying street food? Chiang Mai Street Food Tours solves the mysteries for you. Join this evening tour for no more than eight people, and let the culinary exploration begin. You'll head to a night market with a knowledgeable guide and try up to 10 dishes. The rice noodle specialty kanom jeen is one. Coconut dumplings and stewed pork legs are other favorites during the 2½ hour jaunt. Hotel transportation is available. $33 per person, $100 for a private tour for two people.

Northern Flavours Chiang Mai Food Tour ทัวร์ชิมอาหารเหนือ จังหวัดเชียงใหม่

(achefstour.com)

Hop on a songthaew truck and expect to feast. A Chef's Tour shares food history as well as best bites. This four-hour street food tour by an expert named Moui will introduce you to flavors you haven't yet tried. Expect maybe minced lamb salad and a curry called gaeng hang lae, rather than the ubiquitous pad Thai. You'll also get to meet some of the food purveyors and hear their stories. Day and nighttime tours are available, each going to about half a dozen spots and involving at least 15 foods. Eight people total. $59 per person.

COOKING CLASSES

Thai Akha Cooking School โรงเรียนสอนทำอาหารไทยอาข่า

(thaiakhakitchen.com; 061325-4611; 15/1 Soi Arrag 4, Si Phum; daily 9am-3pm, 5pm-9pm)

At Thai Akha, you'll learn to make the foods of Thailand's Akha community. They comprise a mountain culture descended from Chinese, Lao, and Myanmar immigrants a century ago, and their cuisine involves just about every living thing. You'll learn about the sub-culture of 800,000 people as you follow steps to prepare 11 dishes at your own station. The school is within the Old City. $35 per person.

Cooking class at Thai Akha Cooking School

Thai Cookery School โรงเรียนสอนทำอาหารไทย

(thaicookeryschool.com; 05320-6388; 47/2 Moon Muang Rd, Mueang Chiang Mai; daily 8:30am-5pm)

Sompon Nabnian became a Master Chef after traveling Thailand as a monk trainee for several years. Now the culinarian, who has been featured on international TV, teaches visitors how to make Thai dishes. The beginner class is popular as it will help you build a foundation for understanding how to approach Thai food in your kitchen back home. The six-hour experience involves making six dishes, maybe chicken-coconut milk soup, a fish cake, and fried chicken with ginger. The rate includes round-trip transportation, a welcome drink, and a coupon for ice cream. Book directly for a free apron or a discount. From $50 per person.

The Chiang Mai Thai Farm Cooking School โรงเรียนสอนทำ อาหารเชียงใหม่ไทยฟาร์ม

(thaifarmcooking.net; 081288-5989; 38 Mun Mueang Rd, Si Phum)

A couple named Sawat and Nathalie transformed a rice field into an organic farm, and now they offer cooking classes on the property. You'll see lemongrass, ginger, and galangal in the ground and will pick what you need for your recipes. Once in class, you'll each have a station with the equipment for a full day of cooking. You'll make a curry paste, prepare sticky and jasmine rice, create a curry and soup, stir-fry dishes, work with noodles, and concoct a dessert. There's a market visit, too. End your day dining with the group while you enjoy the fish pond, farm, and mountain views. Lemongrass tea, recipes, and transportation to and from your hotel are included. $50 per person.

ENTERTAINMENTS

Cabaret

Cabarets are such a relaxed yet invigorating way to spend an evening. **Chiang Mai Cabaret** (facebook.com/ChiangmaiCabaretShow) brings a splash of color to the already vibrant night bazaar. Ladyboys in elaborate feathered and sequined costumes put on quite the show, and they may get one or both of you up on stage as well. The drag performances at **Sixcret Show** (facebook.com/sixcretshow) are different every night of the week and may involve fire, clever lighting, and/or celebrity look-alikes. At **Miracle Cabaret Chiang Mai** (facebook.com/Miraclecabaretchiangmai), the nightly extravaganza brings in 200 performers whose on-stage sass may involve tiaras, glitter, and a whole lotta leg. A pre- or post-show restaurant meal is optional.

Old Chiang Mai Cultural Center ศูนย์วัฒนธรรมเชียงใหม่เก่า

(oldchiangmai.com; 053202-9935; 185/3 Wua Lai Rd, Haiya)
Enjoy a performance highlighting Lanna culture at the Khantoke dinner show, which has been entertaining visitors since 1970 ($25

per person). Costumed artists perform dances, among them the Flame Worshiping Yogis and the Swords Dance. As you watch, you'll have a regular, vegetarian, or Halal menu of Thai specialties. The cultural center has other performances that don't include a meal. One is the Hill Tribe Show, held outdoors, which features true tribe members, in traditional dress, sharing their ceremonial dances, whether Akha, Lisu, or Hmong. This is also often packaged with the Khantoke show.

Khantoke dinner show at Old Chiang Mai Cultural Center

NIGHTLIFE

Loi Kroh Road ถนนลอยเคราะห์

While you presumably already have overnight company if you're reading this book, Loi Kroh Road is still a fun place to visit. Girly bars abound: this means pretty, seductive women will try to lure you into drinking establishments. Otherwise, settle in for a casual beer at one of these places or a regular hangout. The area is near the Old City's moat heading toward the river, with the main bustle around Thapae Stadium. Retail and massage shops dot the area too.

Nimmanhemin Road นิมมานเหมินทร์ (นิมมานเหมินท์, นิมมาน)

You'll need to take a 15-minute taxi ride toward the airport to get to Nimman Road unless you're staying there, but don't let that dissuade you. This is the center of nightlife when you want the anti-backpacker experience, no matter your budget. Nimman Road and its side streets, mostly sois 7 and 9, are relatively posh compared to the rest of Chiang Mai. Dress up for craft cocktails at a rooftop bar, put on your sexy clothes for a wild night at a fab dance club, or just get your fix of a trendy experience, whether that's a gourmet burger, a cup of single-origin coffee, or a creative dinner made with flavors from around the globe. You'll find sports bars too where you can watch the game with others in an establishment with a fashion-forward kind of feel.

Old City เมืองเก่า

You might not notice nightspots when touring Chiang Mai's Old City during daylight hours, but they're there—although spread out. The hub, if there is one, is the loud and popular Zoe in Yellow, located near Ratvithi Road and Ratchapakhinai Road. Several additional hangouts are clustered around it, most catering to those with a backpacking budget and sensibility. Throughout the Old City, you'll find all kinds of places to let loose in whatever style you want after dark. Sip a brew in a beer garden, dance to electronic music, or party with women who rent themselves out.

LIVE MUSIC

Boy Blues Bar บอยบลูส์บาร์

(facebook.com/Boy-Blues-Bar-170272579657052; 089192-8527; Chang Moi Sub-district)

Thanks to a blues fan who goes by Boy, Chiang Mai has had a solid blues presence for more than a decade. This hard-to-find hangout on a side street near the night bazaar and Kalare food hall is the place for blues in Chiang Mai. Huddle over your drinks at a small table, or simply walk around and listen from the street. The stage is open-air and the sound travels into the market.

Hard Rock Café Chiang Mai ฮาร์ดร็อคคาเฟเชียงใหม่

(hardrockcafe.com/location/chiang-mai; 05327-7766; 115 Loi Kroh Rd, Chang Khlan)

Whether you're a Hard Rock virgin or have eaten the burgers and purchased the T-shirts at Hard Rock Cafés around the world, you'll get a kick out of the Chiang Mai version. First off, this restaurant has the Gold Burger, which is topped with a 24-karat gold embellishment. International flavors, milkshakes, and cocktails are part of the mix, as are live bands and, when they're not around, DJs. You can dance pretty much any time of the day or night.

North Gate Jazz Co-Op

(facebook.com/northgate.jazzcoop; 081765-5246; 91 1-2 Sri Poom Rd, Tambon Si Phum,

If you have a thing for some soulful saxophone, make time for a night at North Gate. It's not a fancy bar, by far. Instead, it's a chill spot for chilling to the sounds of live jazz bands, at least two a night (with jam sessions each Tuesday), inside or out. It's near the Old City's Chang Puak Gate.

Roots Rock Reggae @Maerim Roots Rock Reggae @ แม่ริม

(rootsrockreggae.business.site; 0819920-9079; 3009 Huai Sai, Mae Rim; daily 5pm-midnight)

Right in the heart of the Old City's club scene, Roots Rocks Reggae is a destination for a few brands of chill tunes. You'll hear singing in Thai and English, whether the bands' tunes are ragga, roots, rock, ska, or reggae. Nothing fancy, just drinks and music.

BARS

Myst

(facebook.com/MystMAYA; 061512-6768; 5 55 Moo 5, Huay Kaew Rd, Muang Chiang Mai; daily 5pm-1am)

Ready, set, TikTok: Order the Rainbow Bomb and start filming. It's a line-up of booze shots in a rainbow of colors, and each is smoking, literally, thanks to dry ice. The dramatic presentation is also a fine way to get smashed. This sassy sixth-floor bar and restaurant has city and mountain views. Time your visit for sunset. Settle in for a meal, a drink, or a shisha smoke. The highish prices are worth the splurge for the ambiance.

Oasis Rooftop Garden Bar โอเอซิสรูฟท็อปการ์เด้นบาร์

(facebook.com/oasisrooftopgardenbar; 081693-5019; 13/1 Soi Jang Sripoom 1, Sripoom Rd, Amphor Muang; Wed-Mon 5pm-midnight)

Since mojitos are Cuban, it seems topsy-turvy that there even is a run-off for which Chiang Mai bar has the best ones. Yet topsy-turvy is practically a theme at Oasis, where the mojito has been named the best in town. The bar is on a roof in the Old City, yet filled with plants as if it were at street level. Some decor pieces are modern, others timeless. Even the music mixes it up. So grab a seat, get a couple of drinks and snacks, and unwind at a place that has no solid rules.

THC Roof Top Bar

(thc-rooftop-bar.business.site; 080907-8802; 19 Mun Mueang Rd, Tambon Phra Sing; daily 5pm-midnight)

Take off your shoes, sit on pads at a low table, and let the chilling begin. They don't sell THC or the substance from which it's derived at THC, just drinks and food. Still, the mellow vibe pervades, in part from DJ-spun reggae, and some from the mountain and city views. THC draws a young crowd seeking low prices, yet the view and ambiance appeal to almost everyone with a small taste for adventure.

NIGHTCLUBS

Infinity อินฟินิตี้

(facebook.com/infinityclub.chiangmai; 05340-0085; 77/2 Chonprathan Rd, Tambon Su Thep; daily 6pm-midnight)

Nimman is Chiang Mai's trendy upscale neighborhood, and Infinity is a major nightspot there. It's designed in self-described luxury vintage London style, attending to details like comfortable seats and reasonable prices. The club fuses music, food, and art in its four zones, some indoors, others out. Depending on the day and the room you choose, you might dance your hearts out to soul music, electro, house, funk, jazz, or indie—live bands and DJs take the lead. Take a break with a tower of beer.

Warm Up Café วอร์มอัพคาเฟ

(facebook.com/warmupcafe1999; 05340-0677; 40 Nimmanhaemin Road, Suthep; daily 7pm-1am)

If Zoe in Yellow is the nightlife heartbeat of the Old City, the Warm Up Café plays that role in Nimman. Since 1999, this club has been rocking and rolling nightly—with several venues at once. One area may have a live band, another a DJ, the outdoor area a third kind of music. Expect hordes of enthusiastic young revelers, and sounds ranging from EDM to Breakbeats and rock 'n' roll. You can sometimes reserve a table in some of the spaces; check the Facebook page for details.

Zoe in Yellow โซอีสีเหลือง

(facebook.com/zoeinyellowchiangmai; 095695-6050; 40/12 Ratvithi Rd, Si Phum; daily 5pm-midnight)

If a night on the town for you two includes partying like a backpacker, head to Zoe in Yellow. This raucous enterprise is the nightlife hub of Chiang Mai's Old City. DJs spin hip-hop and electronic sounds while younger travelers down cheap drinks, dance off their jet lag, and get to know one another. Zoe in Yellow is surrounded by other bars, so head here and you'll be set for fun all night.

SHOPPING

Central Festival Chiang Mai เซ็นทรัลเฟสติวัลเชียงใหม่

(centralfestival.co.th; 05399-8999; 999/9 Moo 4, Super Highway Rd, Fa Ham; daily 11am-9pm)

Call it Fest to sound like a local, and shop like an American. Fest is the largest mall in Chiang Mai with 300 stores in its 70 acres (28 hectares) of space. Get your H&M fix, pick up any electronics you're missing, and otherwise bypass the chains for boutiques owned by locals: one specializes in tea. You can also go ice skating or watch a performance. The wavy exterior is noteworthy.

Kad Suan Kaew กาดสวนแก้ว

(facebook.com/kadsuankaew; 05322-4444; 21 Huay Kaew Rd, Su Thep; daily 11am-8:30pm)

Kad Suan Kaew was Chiang Mai's first shopping mall, and its prime location near the Old City and Nimman Road keep the crowds coming. It's built around a namesake department store and has a little bit of everything else: apparel, electronics, and restaurants. Bonus: bowling, a bar known for stocking choice beers, and a movie theater featuring Thai films.

CentralPlaza Chiang Mai Airport เซ็นทรัลพลาซาเชียงใหม่ แอร์พอร์ต

(centralplaza.co.th; 02021-9999; 2 Mahidol Rd, Pa Daet; daily

11am-9pm)

This five-story modern atrium-style mall has more than 250 stores, some kiosks featuring local handicrafts, others major chain stores. Robinson Department Store is the anchor. It also has an aquarium, restaurants, a multiplex with an IMAX theater, a supermarket, and a food court.

Maya Lifestyle Shopping Center

(mayashoppingcenter.com; 05208-1555; 55 Moo 5, Huay Kaew Rd, Chang Phuek; daily 10am-10pm)

A relatively new mall, this market embraces the "lifestyle" part of its name by appealing to upscale consumers with a striking freeform exterior, and trendy Thai and international stores and restaurants within. Shop for electronics on one floor and catch a movie at the multiplex on another. Croon to one another at a karaoke lounge and toast your retail rendezvous at a rooftop bar. Myst is a best bet at sunset for both views and cocktails.

MARKETS

Chiang Mai Night Bazaar เชียงใหม่ไนท์บาซาร์

(104/1 intersection of Tha Pae and Chang Klan Road Chang Klang; daily 5pm-midnight)

Shopping, shopping, and more shopping. Every single night, vendors set up stations to sell stuff—good stuff, cheap stuff, and fun stuff. Want a samurai sword? A watch? It's here, and you can probably bargain for an even better price than you think. Maybe this is the time to commission a painting of the two of you.

Khamthieng Flower Market ตลาดคำเทียง

(facebook.com/Kamthiengmarket; 053225-9589; 100 Talad Kham Thiang Rd, Paton subdistrict; daily 8am-6pm)

Flower, plants, ferns... you'll find variety aplenty at the Khamthieng

Flower Market, the largest such market in Northern Thailand. Even if you can't buy pieces here to plant in your own home, you might enjoy wandering around to get ideas. You'll see not only greenery, from starter plants to trees, but also gear for watering plants, decorating outdoor spaces, accessorizing fishponds, and more.

Sunday Market (Walking Street) ตลาดนัดวันอาทิตย์ (ถนนคนเดิน)

(Rachadamnoen Rd, Tambon Si Phum; Sun 4pm-midnight)
Every Sunday night, locals and visitors congregate at this outdoor market, which is closed to automobiles. Make the time for this one: You'll be able to shop for better-quality local crafts, often sold by the artist. Entertainers pop up regularly, so catch a puppet show or a dance routine. As always, plenty of vendors sell street food.

Warorot Market (Kad Luang) ตลาดวโรรส (กาดหลวง)

(warorosmarket.com; 01865-8958; Wichayanon Rd, Tambon Chang Moi; daily 5am-6pm)
Get a taste of true Thai life at Wararot Market, the biggest of its kind in this part of the country. Warorot is where locals shop for food to cook or heat up at home, for retail goods at fair prices, and for tasty bites to eat on the premises. The indoor space was transformed into a market in 1910 and today has three levels. The specialty is regional foods such as sausages and chili pepper pastes. The local sausages include sai ua, intestines stuffed with pork laced with herbs and curry paste that is often deep-fried, and sai krok Isan, a garlicky fermented pork-and-rice concoction often eaten grilled alongside sticky rice and raw chile pepper. One area has mostly Hmong and Chinese goods.

MASSAGES

Cheeva Spa Chiang Mai ชีวาสปาเชียงใหม่

(cheevaspa.com; 05321-1400; 4/2 Hussadhisawee Rd, Si Phum; daily 10am-9pm)

There's always something sexy about disrobing for a side-by-side spa experience. At Cheeva, a luxury spa with two local units, the Honeymoon Package plays up the playfulness. Over four-and-a-half hours, you will receive foot soaks and massages, revitalizing body scrubs, signature massages, a milky aromatherapy bath in a tub big enough for two, facials... and snacks.

Fah Lanna Spa ฟ้าล้านนาสปา

(fahlanna.com; 088804-9984; 57/1 Wiang Kaew Rd, Sripoom, Amphoe Muang; daily 11am-8pm)

Escape the Old City's hustle for a garden-like spa filled with luscious soothing treatments, from waxing's and facials to indulgent packages. Wooden planks connect various doorways, and shade trees including bamboo abound. The Fah Lanna Romantic may speak to you: You'll start with aromatic herbal steams held in a special cave, then on to body scrubs, a royal bath, aromatherapy oil massages, and facials. A smaller unit is open in the Nimman neighborhood.

Kiriya Spa Vana คีรียาสปาวนา

(facebook.com/Kiriya-Spa-Vana-in-Chiangmai-166271826765893; 05327-4923; 47 14 Samlarn Rd, Tambon Phra Sing; daily 10am-10pm)

When a walk-in parlor is less than you want and a big day spa is too much, think boutique: Kiriya meets that sweet spot in the middle. It has a garden setting, bold red and gold wall coverings, and other upscale touches. The chocolate almond body scrub is a mood enhancer, for sure, or you can go bigger with the Chocolate

Indulgence Ritual.

Kiyora Spa คิโยระสปา

(kiyoraspa.com; 05200-3268; 26 1 Chang Moi Rd Soi 2, Tambon Chang Moi; daily 10am-10pm)

Close to the Old City tourist sites, you can duck into Kiyora Spa for rejuvenation. Designed to resemble a teak wood manor, the spa has water features and an outdoor lounge for diffusing between treatments. Choose the same indulgence or package, Western or Asian, or go solo to each get exactly what you need most. Options include Lanna Traditions, healing you with foot reflexology, Thai massage, and a head/back/shoulder massage. Free transportation is available from certain hotels.

Lila Thai Massage ไลล่านวดแผนไทย

(chiangmaithaimassage.com; 05332-7043; 1 Intrawarorot Rd Soi 2, Tambon Si Phum; daily 10am-10pm)

Spa treatments usually seem self-indulgent, yet here you'll actually be doing good for other people while you enjoy yourself. Lila was founded by a former prison director for the purpose of training female ex-cons as certified massage therapists so they can support themselves. So, get yourselves a pair of Delight Candle foot massages, traditional Lanna massages, or maybe a couple of Coconut Ultimates. You'll feel terrific, and you'll help a worker remain independent.

Naruncha Beauty & Massage นรัญชาบิวตีแอนด์มาสสาจ

(facebook.com/narunchabeauty; 05327-3753; 130/1 Ratchaphakinai Rd, Phra Sing; daily 9am-10pm)

If a pampering spa experience isn't in your time or money budget, worry not. Naruncha will cover the basics with a Thai massage, only the ambiance will be simpler—a platform with mattresses lined up along one wall with a cheerful mural of trees on another.

The menu is simple, encompassing a variety of massages as well as manicures, pedicures, foot scrubs, body scrubs, and facials. A few packages add value.

The Giving Tree ต้นไม้ที่ให้

(thaigivingtree.com; 05332-6185; 5 13 Rachadamnoen Rd Soi 7, Tambon Si Phum; daily 10am-midnight)

One- and two-hour massages are available at The Giving Tree, a walk-in spot for foot soaks and Thai massages in the Old City. The offerings include packages of up to three hours. The most indulgent, Body Care Pack 3, will get you back in shape with a Thai massage, foot massage, stone therapy, and aroma oil back and leg massages.

The Oasis Spa โอเอซิสสปา

(oasisspa.net/destination/chiangmai/Nimman; 05392-0111; 102 Sirimanklajarn Rd, Suthep; daily noon to midnight)

One of five Oasis spas in Thailand, the Chiang Mai version may be the most fun. Its treatment rooms are located within a bright red mansion. Since you'll be in Lanna country, it's fitting to choose the Lanna Explorer package, a four-hour treat that you can book for two. A Thai herbal steam will chill you out so you're ready for purifying herbal body scrubs, facials, and King of Oasis signature massages. And that King massage? It involves aromatherapy, a hot herbal compress, and hot oil.

Zira Spa ไซร่าสปา

(ziraspa.com; 05322-2288; 8 Ratvithi Lane 1 Alley, Tambon Si Phum; daily 10am-10pm)

With 40 treatment rooms, you might call Zira a mega-spa. Here, in the Old City, you can unwind in a quiet courtyard and receive dual indulgences in en-suite treatment rooms. This award-winning facility was built to be a spa and designed in traditional Lanna style. Within its tasteful walls, submit yourselves to the Royal Honey Moon, a five-hour period of a whirlpool bath, reflexology foot massages, head/back/shoulder massages, Thai herbal hot compresses, body scrubs (choose a scent), body wraps (choose your fave), hot aromatherapy oil massages (choose your scent again), and six-step anti-aging facials.

TOURS

1 Day 4 Famous Temples in Chiang Rai 1 วัน 4 วัดดังในเชียงราย
(pagodaviewtoursthailand.com; 081386-1790; 60 Moo 1 Phahonyothin Rd, Pa O Don Chai)
Power through four Buddhist temples (refer below for more details)—each new and anything but humdrum—in one 13-hour day. On this private tour, you'll have your own driver and guide, who can adapt the itinerary to meet your whims. In addition to the four temples detailed below, you'll visit a few other notable buildings and have lunch at a Thai restaurant. $130 per person.

Wat Rong Khun The White Temple is an older structure that was purchased, renovated, and reopened by the artist Chalermchai Kositpipat in the late 1990s; construction is still going on. The art is kind of eery in a moving way, including sculptures of desperate hands reaching up from hell. Mythological creatures are also recreated here, all contributing to a frilly, ornate collection of gawk-worthy elements. The complex will eventually have nine buildings, among them a monks' residence, an art gallery, and a mediation hall. There is also a splashy gold building. It is frilly and ornate, and home to the restrooms.

Wat Sang Kaew Phothiyan Expect vivid, almost juvenile colors at this temple, where the name translates into some version of, "A lotus that sprouts and emerged from the water and emits light like a sparkling gem with brilliant light." something involving a lotus sprout emitting brilliant gem-like light. The main building, which debuted in 2006, is pointed and ornate. You'll see gold and red murals, a gold Buddha, and a bunch of brightly hued statues, many with an almost playful feel.

Wat Rong Seur Ten Known as the Blue Temple, this Buddhist site has you feel as if you're entering an undersea world. Royal blue walls, columns, and ceiling surround a giant white seated cross-legged Buddha. The exterior is deep blue too, with whimsical gold trim and a standing white Buddha. The Thai name refers to tigers, which once roamed this area. This is another new temple, built on the site of an ancient temple that hadn't been used in decades. It was completed in 2016.

Wat Huay Pla Kang This white frilly prayer hall is an unusual blend of Lanna and Chinese architecture. Its nine-story pagoda resembles a layered red-roofed cone, where dragons stand guard. Inside, you'll find Thai and Chinese style sandalwood statues. An enormous white seated Goddess of Mercy (Guan Yin) seated atop a hill on the same property is a third astounding structure. You can go inside this female statue and take an elevator up 25 stories to the top for a view of the mountains beyond. All of these buildings were added between 2001 and 2016.

1 Day Authentic Hill Tribe Tour ทัวร์ชาวเขาแท้ๆ 1 วัน

(thailandhilltribeholidays.com; 085548-0884; Nong Kwai, Mueang Chiang Mai)

Visit two or more hill tribes during this tour, where you'll see their villages and cultures close-up. A guide will drive you an hour outside Chiang Mai to Karen and Hmong communities. You'll see Karen bamboo stilt houses and cook lunch from local ingredients like jungle fern. Then you might visit a rice paddy or watch crafts being made. At the Hmong locale, you'll learn about their signature embroidery. Other activities vary seasonally and might include seeing a waterfall or local school. This is a customized tour, so you might opt to include a Baan Tong Luang village, home to members of Kayan, Lisu, Mien, and Palong tribes. From $115 per person.

Chiang Rai Day Trip Small-Group from Chiang Mai City with Golden Triangle เชียงรายวันเดียว – กลุ่มเล็กจากตัวเมือง เชียงใหม่กับสามเหลียมทองคำ

(tour-in-chiangmai.com; 053289-6445; 14 1st Floor, Ratchadamnoen Rd, Si Phum; daily 8am-8pm)

Take in Chiang Mai highlights in this full-day tour, which includes hotel pick-up. Just the two of you or with up to seven others, you'll see the hot spring at Mae Khachan, the Golden Triangle, and the House of Opium before a boat trip along the Mekong River. A highlight is Wat Rong Khun, a stunning, nearly filigreed white Buddhist temple with other-worldly elements like floating Buddhas, contemporary references such as a Matrix character, and hands jutting up as if by people in hell. It was built in 1998. Group tour cost $70 per person, private tour cost $160 per person.

Wat Rong Khun in Chiang Rai

Doi Inthanon +2 Hours Trekking at Inthanon National Park
ดอยอินทนนท์ +2 ชั่วโมงต้นไม้ทีอุทยานแห่งชาติอินทนนท์

(pagodaviewtoursthailand.com; 081386-1790; 319/99 Moo 2, T. Sanphaukwhan A. Hangdong)

Doi Inthanon National Park is home to the highest spot in Thailand, and that's only one of the highlights of this tour. From your hotel, you'll head to the park and its Wachiratharn Waterfall. Take a break at the Hmong Market before proceeding up to that peak. You'll also see where a king's ashes are contained and a pagoda with gardens. After lunch, spend the afternoon on a trek through farmland and by the Pha Dok Soew waterfall. End with a sample of locally grown coffee before heading back to Chiang Mai. From $100 per person. Private tours are available.

Full-Day Guided Tuk Tuk Chiang Mai Adventure and Rafting
ทัวร์เต็มวันพร้อมไกด์นำเทียวเชียงใหม่และล่องแพ

(viator.com; 0888651-9785)

Take three trips in one while you're in Chiang Mai. First off, you'll get to drive a tuk-tuk through the countryside during this full-day experience with up to 18 participants. Through the course of the trip, you'll visit elephants who live in a special home, see out-of-the-way temples, and learn about how monks live. Bonus: you'll get to ride on a river via bamboo raft. Lunch is included. From $175 per person.

Original Sunrise Tour on Mountains Top, Chiang Mai Landmark
ทัวร์ชมพระอาทิตย์ขึนบนยอดเขาเชียงใหม่แลนด์มาร์ค

(untouchedthailand.com; 084614-4078; 87/1 Moo 5 Don Kaew, Mae Rim)

When you meet up at 5am, just remember that sunrises are romantic. You'll be driven up a mountain to the temple Wat Phrathat Doi Suthep to see the sun come up over the city and the landscape around it. Bells ring, monks chant... and coffee is poured. You'll also be able to give food to monks, and to see temples in a jungle and in a cave. Breakfast is included. From $65 per person.

TEMPLES

Wat Chedi Luang วัดเจดีย์หลวง

(103 Prapokkloa Rd, Tambon Si Phum)

Unlike the colorful, newly built Buddhist temples on the outskirts of Chiang Mai, Wat Chedi Luang is an unadorned ancient complex smack in the middle of the Old City. Once considered the center of the Lanna Kingdom—marked by the Inthakin pillar—a pillar built in 1296 and moved to this temple, where it is held inside an ornate shrine in 1800—today the remains of this once-grand religious center are a spread-out array of buildings dating to the 1300s, partially renovated, partially decrepit. It's comprised primarily of three temples known as Wat Chedi Luang, which has Lanna-style architecture, plus Wat Ho Tham and Wat Sukmin. The famous Emerald Buddha lived here years ago and a replica is now on display. The Phra Chao Attarot statue of a standing Buddha remains on this site, as is an original sculpture of an elephant, joined by reproductions where the originals once stood by the naga(snake) stairways around the back and you'll find more treasures, among them a sitting Buddha with Chinese style elements. King Saen Muang Ma started the temple's construction in the late 14th century and his widow continued the project. Age has not been the temple's only enemy: a 1545 earthquake resulted in major damage, especially to the main pagoda, or chedi. You'll also see gum trees thought to have protective powers.

Wat Lok Molee วัดโลกโมฬี

(298/1 Manee Nopparat Rd, Si Phum; 05340-4039; daily sunrise-5pm)

A large brick chedi, or pagoda, has drawn worshippers to this temple on the northern end by the Old City's moat since 1527, when King Chettharat had it erected. There's an image of Buddha on each side, and thevadas (celestial) ones too. A wooden viharn went up a few years later, and it is made of wood with notable enhancements. The temple—probably royal at one time—itself is thought to date back to the mid-14th century. Until the Mengrai dynasty fizzled out in 1557, due to a Burmese invasion, they often buried the ashes of their people here. While you're visiting, stroll around the manicured garden, the mosaic art in the main hall, and several stupas too. When it's time to snap a photo, the stone elephants at the pedestrian entrance add an element of fun.

Wat Phra Singh วัดพระสิงห์

(2 Samlarn Rd, Phra Sing, Mueang Chiang; 05341-6027; daily 9am-6pm)

This Lanna-style temple is the opposite of decrepit, despite its origins nearly 700 years ago. Wat Phra Singh has elegance, and its sanctuary is adorned with intricate mosaic designs that tell stories. Named a royal temple by King Ananda Mahidol in 1935, this complex on the western edge of the Old City has another big draw: The Lion Buddha, or Prah Singh, allegedly brought to Chiang Mai from Sri Lanka and said to be based on an Indian statue of a Shakya lion. Serpent gables called naga stand guard. You'll also find a 1477 copper and gold Buddha here; it's known as Phra Chao Thong Tip. A 1477 library raised off the ground protects valuable documents. Other highlights include buildings with winged roofs, and ornate wooden carvings. Hundreds of monks live here.

Wat Phra That Doi Kham วัดพระธาตุดอยคำ

(05326-3001; Mae Hia, Mueang Chiang Mai District; daily 6am-6pm)

Take a quick taxi ride southwest of town to visit this quiet hilltop temple with great mountain views. It's known as Temple of the Golden Mountain, and the highlight is a 56ft-high (17m) seated white-and-gold Buddha built in the year 687. You can hit the grounds' gongs to create your own sounds between stops at other gems: an ornate Lanna-style ubosot ordination hall, and gold naga snakes held in the mouths of mythical marine monsters.

Wat Phra That Doi Suthep วัดพระธาตุดอยสุเทพ

(Mueang Chiang Mai District, Doi Suthep; daily 6am-8pm)
It seems an elephant selected this site in the 14th century. The story is that a monk went looking for a bone he'd dreamed about. He found the bone, which had special powers; half of it was sent into a jungle on an elephant. The elephant climbed through the jungle to the temple's current site, made some special sounds, then died. King Nu Naone then ordered his people to build a temple there. Whatever the origins, today Wat Phra That Doi Suthep is a Theravada Buddhist religious temple complex with viharns (dorms), bots (ordination halls), cloisters, and chedis (tower). Situated on Thailand's eighth-largest mountain, located just outside Chiang Mai, it sits within a national park. In addition to the 14th-century temple, there's also the International Buddhism Center and Bhubing Palace here. You'll see statues of that legendary elephant, for sure, as well as plenty of Buddhas and other religious symbols, plus murals. If you want a spell of good luck, go touch the bells: they have a rep for working.

Wat Sri Suphan วัดศรีสุพรรณ

(05327-4705; 100 Wua Lai Rd, Tambon Hai Ya; daily 6am-6pm)
Wat Sri Suphan is known as the Silver Temple, and indeed this five-century-old stunner near the Old City gate is an ornate structure that feels like a Thai version of your great-grandma's silver tea set—although parts are now made with aluminum and

other metals. The ordination hall, or ubosot, was first built in 1502 with elaborate repoussé panels. While those were destroyed over time, since 2003 modern-day silversmiths have recreated the silver exterior and even teach children how to work with metal. Only men are allowed inside since monks still use the interior; there they'll see a silver-and-gold Ganesha statue with Hindu elements, along with murals that incorporate Theravada, Zen, and Taoist Buddhist references. Take special note of writing on a stone it's in a pre-Lanna language known as Fhuk Kham. Silver panels in the main prayer hall share tales of Buddha's life, and Buddha statues here are silver-coated.

Wat Umong Suan Phutthatham วัดอุโมงค์สวนพุทธธรรม

(085033-3809; 135 Moo 10, Mueang Chiang Mai; daily 5am-8pm) It's not the tunnel of love, that's for sure, yet this tunnel-filled destination is surely worth your time. Wat Umong is a forest temple out near Chiang Mai University, a quick 10 minutes out of town. Its history is contested. King Mangrai in 1297? Or King Kuena, from 1380 to 1450? Whatever the origins, these 15 acres (six hectare) complex at the base of mountains has many riches: a replica of an Indian ashok pillar with lions; shrines within tunnels; a fasting Buddha statue nearly hidden in the woods; a museum/library; a meditation hall with an unpainted stupa (rounded roof); words of Buddha's wisdom tacked to "talking" trees; and a lake where you can buy food to feed catfish. It's said the tunnels were originally painted to look like the bush areas outdoors to keep a monk with psychiatric issues from wandering off the property to the actual bush areas.

Monk Chats

While in Thailand, you'll have the chance to feed alms to monks who pass by in a line, and to sneak peeks at them going about their business as you tour Buddhist temples. Want to meet them instead? You can sit down for a chat. Some Chiang Mai temples set up Monk Chat sessions for visitors, enabling you to learn about monk life and Thai culture in general. In return, the monks gain the opportunity to practice their English and to learn about you. Most of the monks who participate are young and are often accompanied by an instructor. The following are some of the options available:

Wat Chedi Luang Wander over to the monk chat tables outdoors anytime, any day, from 9am to 6pm.

Wat Doi Suthep Monks are on standby to chat from 1pm to 3pm every day.

Wat Sri Suphan Meet with monks daily from 5pm to 7pm before their meditation. You can stay until 9pm and try out the meditation yourselves.

Wat Suan Dok Chat with monks in a dedicated room on Mondays, Wednesdays, and Fridays from 5pm to 7pm.

Wat Umong and MCU Buddhist University Both offer the same monk chat hours: Monday, Wednesday, and Friday from 5:30pm to 7:30pm.

Wat Suan Dok Chat with monks in a dedicated room on Mondays, Wednesdays, and Fridays from 5pm to 7pm.

Wat Pha Khao If you prefer a less formal experience, stop by between 5pm and 9pm on weekends and see if you can find a monk willing to sit down with you.

Monk chat in Chiang Mai

ATTRACTIONS

Chiang Dao Cave ถ้ำเชียงดาว

(chiangdaocave.com; 094740-2294; 273 Moo 5 Chiang Dao)
North of Chiang Mai (70–90mins), more than seven miles (12km)
of caves draw visitors, and no wonder. This underground system
has 100 caves and five are available to see. Within is a Buddhist
temple (cover your shoulders, ladies), where you'll espy Buddha
and other statues along with carvings and other religious items,
not to mention the natural glory of the cave interiors. The guy
who lived in one of these caves for a millennium? That's just
legend. You'll need to hire a guide and rent a flashlight to explore
some of the caves. It's $1.50 per person to get in, $3.50 apiece for
a lantern (you'll need it), and another $3.50 for the guide.

Chiang Mai Centre Museums เชียงใหม่เซ็นเตอร์มิวเซียม

(cmocity.com; 05321-7793; Prapokkloa Rd, Si Phum; Wed-Sun
8:30am-4:30pm)
The Chiang Mai Centre Museums is a collection of cultural points

of interest. Within this museum there is the Chiang Mai Historical Centre and the Chiang Mai City Arts and Cultural Centre (see below).

Chiang Mai City Arts and Cultural Centre หอศิลปวัฒนธรรมเมืองเชียงใหม่

(cmocity.com/chiang-mai-art-cultural-centre)

Delve into Chiang Mai's history in this 1924 building with colonnades, a courtyard, and 15 rooms. Each of the rooms covers one time period of the city's past, starting with the prehistoric era and concluding with a video about Chiang Mai today. Rituals, crafts, architecture, and rulers are among the subjects covered.

Chiang Mai Historical Centre ศูนย์ประวัติศาสตร์เชียงใหม่

(cmocity.com/chiang-mai-history-centre)

Here Chiang Mai's history is presented using archaeological finds and photographs. Begin by taking in info about the ancient Lua community, which roots in Laos. The museum will then guide you through various dynasties, the years of Burmese rule, and archaeological finds.

Elephant Sanctuaries

Spend a full day with animals at the **Elephant Pride Sanctuary** (elephant-pride.com), where a local family lives on the property with elephants who once worked hard labor. Sign up for a visit and you will stroll through the jungle with your pachyderm friends, feed them bananas, and observe a river bath and a dip in mud. Lunch and air-conditioned transportation are included ($85 per person). At the **Maeklang Elephant Conservation Community** (maeklangelephantconservation.org), you'll be along the Maeklang River. Tours range from a half-day to two days ($57–$115 per person), staying overnight in a bamboo hut. With that option, you'll prepare elephant vitamins, wash the animals in the river, scrub their hides, clean the stables, and learn to cook Thai barbecue. **Elephant Nature Park** (elephantnaturepark. org) rescues and rehabilitates the gentle giants and other animals, including buffalo. Two can visit for a half or full day or stay overnight. You'll learn elephants' personal stories, and you'll see them bathe in pools and play in mud. Overnight adventures include hotel pick-up ($83–$192 per person). **Happy Elephant Home** (happyelephanthome.com) is a haven for elephants previously used in tourist activities. You can visit for the morning, the afternoon, or a full day, all with hotel pick-up. Change into classic tribal Karen clothing to learn about these creatures, lead them to the river, and watch them bathe and play. Longer visits include making a Thai lunch and frolicking in the mud alongside the animals ($30–$40 per person). **Elephant Rescue Park** (elephantrescuepark.com) offers four immersions, from the half-day Serene Boutique Elephant Care to the Overnight Elephant Care ($150–$205 per person). Everyone gets air-conditioned transportation, treats to feed the animals, an elephant bath, a visit to a park or waterfall, fresh coconut juice, and a meal. Bigger trips might involve making vitamin balls, planting elephant food, and cleaning the stable.

Highland People Discovery Museum (Tribal Museum of Chiang Mai) Highland People Discovery Museum (พิพิธภัณฑ์ ชนเผ่าเชียงใหม่)

(05321-0872; Lanna Rama 9 Park, Chotana Rd, Chang Phueak; Mon-Fri 8:30am-4pm)

This ethnographic museum highlights the lives of several Thai highland communities, among them the Mien, Karen, and Lua. You can visit typical huts, see their clothing and jewelry, and watch a movie about their lifestyles. Once a month you can shop for gifts and apparel made by tribe members.

Khun Chang Khian ขุนช่างเคียน

(Huai Kaeo Rd, Suthep)

Why go to Washington D.C. to see the cherry blossom trees when you can have a similar experience in Thailand? Every year around Christmas time, the pink-flowered trees blossom in the Khun Chang Kian Highland Agriculture Research Centre on Doi Suthep Mountain, about 40 minutes out of town. If you're visiting at just the right time, find your way to the highlands to see the Tiger King, or Nang Phaya Sua Kroang, trees, and the nature show they create.

Lanna Folklife Museum พิพิธภัณฑ์พื้นบ้านล้านนา

(cmocity.com/lanna-folklife-museum; 05321-7793; Prapokkloa Rd, Si Phum Sub-district; Wed-Sun 8:30am-4:30pm)

Learn about Lanna life at this museum, where 18 exhibits depict years past in the region including traditional dress. See what Lanna Buddhism temple courtyards were like and how they were used, take in sculptures, and understand Lanna music.

MAIIAM Contemporary Art Museum พิพิธภัณฑ์ศิลปะร่วมสมัยใหม่เอียม

(maiiam.com; 05208-1737; 122, 122, Moo 7 Tonpao San Kamphaeng; Wed-Mon 10am-6pm)

A private family with a long Thai history started this museum to share its personal collection of modern art, hoping that others would add their treasures to the mix. After renovating a 32,000ft^2 (2,973m^2) warehouse to a sleek design meant to showcase the art, rather than the building, the museum began filling the space. Natural and artificial light helps highlight the works, which are by Thai and Southeast Asian artists. The permanent collection has at its center the 1990s works of Chiang Mai artist Montien Booma and his peers. Visiting collections change regularly and span not only paintings and sculptures but also fashion, films, performing arts and design.

Museum of World Insects and Natural Wonders พิพิธภัณฑ์แมลงโลกและสิ่งมหัศจรรย์ทางธรรมชาติ

(facebook.com/MuseumOfWorldInsectsAndNaturalWonders; 05321-1891; 72 Siri Mangkalajarn Rd, Tambon Su Thep; Thu-Tue 10am-3pm)

A husband-and-wife team, he's a malaria guru, she's a mosquito maven, run this private museum. Mostly you'll see untold numbers of preserved bugs—we're talking butterflies, beetles, and spiders, plus way more. There are also paintings by the owners involving insects.

Queen Sirikit Botanical Garden ถ้ำเชียงดาว

(qsbg.org; 05384-1234; 100 Moo 9, Mae Rim; daily 8:30am-4:30pm)

These sprawling gardens, a half hour north of Chiang Mai, specialize in flora from Northern Thailand, and among those varieties focuses on flowers and plants whose populations are thinning. You'll find several breeds of orchids and palms. Stroll around to see them all, with the Doi Suthep Pui mountains rising above you and rainforest flanking the valley. A great deal of research takes place here too. Then see the sites from above by strolling the canopy walk over the jungle.

Royal Park Rajapruek อุทยานหลวงราชพฤกษ์

(royalparkrajapruek.org; 053114-1105; 334 Mae Hia, Mueang Chiang Mai; daily 8am-6pm)

Originally named the International Exposition for His Majesty the King, Royal Park Rajapruek is a botanical garden of sorts where agricultural research is performed. The plantings are clustered in zones spread over 200 acres (81 hectares). Among them are a 250-million-year-old pine tree, orchids, a Thai tropical garden including herbs, and an international zone with offerings from 24 countries. You can wander around, rent bicycles, or hop on a tram. Buildings of various architectural types are located around the property.

ADVENTURES

Balloon Adventure Thailand

(balloonadventurethailand.com; 096868-4176; 118 San Pa Pao, San Sai; daily 5.30am-10am)

Rooftop bars and mountain temples offer good views of Chiang Mai, but those vistas are nothing compared to what you'll see flying above the destination in a hot air balloon. Balloon Adventure will scoop you up from your hotel at 5:45am, serve you a welcome drink while you wait for the flight, then take you for a 50-minute tour at 6:30am. Celebrate with champagne and breakfast upon your return. $290 per person.

Bicycle Tours ทัวร์จักรยาน

(grasshopperadventures.com/location/day-bike-tours-in-chiang-mai; 061740-2233; 87 Bumrung Buri Rd, Muang Chiang Mai)

Explore Chiang Mai at a moderate pace with a bike tour led by Grasshopper Adventures. Each itinerary has plenty of stops where you can get up close with one element of the destination—and take a rest. You'll have four options: Bike Historic Old City Chiang Mai (half day) takes you down alleyways and inside the Old City walls; Chiang Mai Food Adventures by Bike (half day, at night), involves visiting a market and sample sweet and savory local specialties; Chiang Mai Countryside By Bike (full day) involves taking a train to ancient Lamphun before biking around temples and meandering through forest and countryside; and Chiang Mai Night Bike (half day) lets you pedal after dark when the temps cool—you'll see temples lit up, try hawker foods, and pass a night market. From $45 per person.

Chiang Mai Trekking with Piroon เชียงใหม่เดินปากับพิรุณ

(chiangmai-trekking.com/Trekking-Tours; 081961-1015; 12 Ratchapakhinai Rd, Chiang Mai)

Immerse yourselves in a less urban Chiang Mai by taking a multi-day trek with Piroon. Most of the trips are northwest of the city toward Mae Hon Son Province. The most popular tour takes three days. Highlights are swimming in a waterfall, hiking through jungle, visiting a Karen hill tribe, sleeping in a hut near the village, bathing an elephant, riding a bamboo river raft, and visiting a Shan village. Alternatively, you can book a one-day trip, which includes an elephant camp, a Shan village, a hike, a waterfall, and a bamboo raft trip. A "harder" version has more physical challenges. Join a group from $85 per person or book a private tour for $100 per person; prices increase for the longer tours.

Flight of the Gibbon เทียวบินของชะนี

(flightofthegibbon.com; 05301-0660; 106 Village, No.3, Huai Kaeo; daily 6am-11pm)

Ziplining over virgin rainforest is part but not all of the fun at Flight of the Gibbon, named for the apes that live in the area. Over the course of a seven-hour experience, you'll get to try several activities, including abseiling by rope down to the ground and climbing over the canopy on cargo nets. Lunch and transportation to and from the site (an hour from Chiang Mai) are included. From $150 per person.

WATERFALLS

Bua Tong Waterfall น้ำตกบัวตอง

The Bua Tong waterfall is beautiful, with white rocks that resemble cotton balls and striking white water streaming down. Yet the small waterfall is best known for being walkable—and we mean going up. The rocks are grippy, so you can take off your shoes and haul yourselves uphill at about a 45-degree tilt as the refreshing water cools your feet. This natural attraction is also known as the Sticky Waterfall; it is 90 minutes north of the Old City by car. You can buy snacks on-site and have a little picnic before or after your climb; many locals will be doing the same nearby.

Huay Kaew Waterfall น้ำตกห้วยแก้ว

Huay Kaew is absolutely beautiful, especially July through November when the waters flow heartily. It's a 32ft (10m) waterfall surrounded by lush greenery. And it's the closest waterfall to the Old City, located right near the Chiang Mai Zoo. Grasp hands and walk up the path to the right, dip into the shallow pools to cool off, and –if you have a towel or rent a bamboo mat—rest in comfort along the way. You can buy a meal and a memento by the entrance.

Mae Sa Waterfall น้ำตกแม่สา

Make a day of visiting the Mae Sa waterfall. This one is a series of waterfalls over 1½mi (2.4km), surrounded by wide rock, with jungle beyond that. Splash in some of the pools, picnic on the rocks... you can even rent a tent and stay overnight. Streets vendors set up in the parking lot, so you'll have food choices. Mae Sa is a half-hour drive from the Old City.

MUAY THAI

Boxing stadiums can be serious business, yet **Loi Kroh Boxing Stadium** is the arch opposite. You'll see fun matches for sure, and you can even step into the ring yourself. Your competitor, though, might be a ladyboy from one of the nearby bars or a hustler from the neighborhood pool hall. **Thapae Boxing Stadium** (facebook. com/Thaphae-Boxing-Stadium-593070844380006) is a laid-back Muay Thai boxing stadium, which makes it a great choice for casual observers. Most nights of the week you can watch locals who box for a living challenge each other. **Chiang Mai Boxing Stadium** (sites.google.com/xsorying.com/bookking/book-online) was built specifically for indoor Muay Thai matches and opened in 2016, so it's modern with striking circular colored lighting overhead. You can watch about half a dozen matches each night. Prices are higher here, but like the arena itself the fighters tend to be of a higher quality than elsewhere.

KOH SAMUI

Koh Samui

WHY GO

A beautiful retreat in the Gulf of Thailand, Koh Samui may well indeed be the romantic destination for your twosome. The tropical island is small enough to easily scoot around on a motorbike and large enough to have a good mix of culture, sports, dining, nightlife, shopping, and temples. With its own airport, Koh Samui is way easier to reach than its peers.

The island's landscape and businesses provide many special ways to up your amorous ante: Private dinners surrounded by tree canopy Gourmet picnics on secluded beaches. Lounge seating that floats above the water. Playing with pigs on a remote outer island. Clinking champagne flutes at a rooftop bar. Sharing a candlelit dinner for two on the beach. And being rubbed and scrubbed, then sharing a bubble bath, at a spa.

At 88 square miles (228km²), Koh Samui is half the size of another resort-island, Phuket. But that's still plenty of space to have your choice of beaches, some with powdery white sand, other sugary grains of gold. Snorkeling reaps coral reef surrounded by creatures of the glass-clear water. Nightspots range from relaxed to raucous.

You'll still find bits here of the fishing village culture that long defined Koh Samui. Alongside, contemporary hotels offer state-of-the-art services. The interior is jungle, offering ample hiking and viewpoint expeditions. Lodging facilities range from humble bungalows to five-star resorts.

Koh Samui's breadth of offerings comes with a downside: Some people find the destination more commercial than resort-y. Others adore the variety of offerings. If you decide Koh Samui is a good choice for you, visit knowing you have a range of activities to choose from whenever you step away from your sun loungers.

Maenam Beach

HOW TO GET TO KOH SAMUI

Koh Samui's selling points are countless, yet one jumps to the top: It has an airport, so you can fly here. The airport is owned by Bangkok Airways but a handful of other airlines use the facility too. (Talks are underway to build a bridge between Koh Samui and Nakhon Si Thammarat on the mainland.)

Please note: Between challenging websites, language barriers even online, and components that change with the season, it can be hard to pin down your best route. We advise hiring a travel agent to set up this leg of the trip for you. You can do that at home or in Thailand after you arrive. But googling for info on your smartphone an hour before leaving your current hotel? Not advisable.

Boat If you want to get as much time on the water as possible, skip the plane, or take it to Surat Thani and then switch to a ferry or speedboat. Ferries tend to be under $10 per person. You can also reach the island by ferry from Chumphon, Koh Phangan, Koh Tao, Krabi, and Ao Nang. Depending on the season, SeaTran, Songserm, and/or Lomprayah often have ferries to Koh Samui from these destinations, while ferrysamui.com has several speedboat routes. Before leaving, be sure to confirm if you are headed to the Nathon, Bangrak, or Maenam piers.

Bus Likewise, you can travel by bus from Bangkok. The trip will be inexpensive but long. You'll leave from South Bangkok's Sai Tai Mai Terminal. Private shuttles will drive you too, leaving from Khao San Road; they tend to be less comfortable. Bus/ferry packages are available. Again, if you book yourselves, look to 12go.asia for routes and packages.

Plane You'll find plenty of flights every day from Bangkok's Suvarnabhumi Airport, 90 or so minutes away, and also from Pattaya and Phuket, plus other countries. Look specifically at Bangkok Airways and Thai Airways. To save money, you can fly from Bangkok's Don Mueang on budget airlines as part of a package via Surat Thani with bus and ferry.

Train You can take a train from Bangkok to Surat Thani, then proceed to a ferry or speedboat. Again, train/bus/ferry packages are an option. The train portion alone ranges from $25 to $60 per person. Visit thailandtrains.com or 12go.asia for options. Take a bus to the ferry dock; five companies offer that service. It's $11 per person. Door to door, the bus-ferry leg of the trip should take three hours.

TRAVELING FROM THE AIRPORT

Once you arrive at Samui International Airport, what's next? Your choice.

Navigo and Grab The app Navigo (navigothailand.com) is Koh Samui's answer to Uber. You can order a ride from a smartphone app when you have internet service: It's about $17 between the airport and Fisherman's Village or Chaweng. The similar Grab app is here too, but doesn't yet have many on-island drivers.

Private car or minivan You can reserve (samuiairportonline. com) or pick up a regular burgundy and yellow taxi at the airport. Prices are set, and you will pay from $13 to $25 to your hotel, depending on how far you're traveling. For slightly more you can hire a private minivan, but a six-seater vehicle is probably unnecessary for just two of you.

Rental car Avis, Budget, Hertz, Europcar, and Sixt have airport counters if you're looking to rent a car for your stay. Rates begin at $19/day.

Shared minivan A cheaper option is a shared minivan, though be aware that it's likely to stop at other accommodations before your own. Again, reserve at samuiairportonline.com or find one at the airport; it will depart once at least five passengers are inside. Prices range from $3.50 to $21.

ARRIVING BY FERRY

If you're taking a ferry, you can end up at any of four piers on Koh Samui. Lipa Noi is closest to Surat Thani on the mainland. Koh Phangan and Koh Tai ferries go to Nathon Pier. If you're coming from Koh Phangan, you're likely to land at Bangrak Pier on the island's northwest. Maenam Pier, also called Lomprayah Ferry Pier and Pralarn Pier, greets ferries from Chumphon, Koh Phangan, and Surat Thani. Once you arrive, you'll find taxis and songthaew waiting at the dock for hotel-bound customers like you looking for a ride.

GETTING AROUND

If you have a rental car or the Navigo app and an internet package, you're set. Here are other options:

Motorbike/scooter rental This is how most people get around: Motorbikes and the smaller scooters are plentiful, affordable (around $9/day), and easy to use on Koh Samui's roads. Average-size couples can share one. Be sure to rent helmets too.

Motorbike taxi Motorbikes/scooters are mini motorcycles: If one of you is traveling alone, you can hail a taxi version and sit behind the driver. It's inexpensive and a little scary. Discuss the price before hopping on; it won't be high.

Songthaew are open-sided trucks that act as public busses. They're super-cheap; prices start at a couple of dollars a ride. Just confirm that the one you're about to board is headed in the right direction for your needs.

WHERE TO STAY

Koh Samui area map

Bophut บ่อผุด

Immersion into Thai life is what you'll find in Bophut. This beach area is home to Fisherman's Village, which until not long ago was, simply, a fisherman's village. These days, you'll find restaurants and bars here—most housed in the historic wooden buildings with Thai-Chinese character that served small-town life in the past. Bophut also has quite a few contemporary hotels, providing a welcome balance. A weekly market will give you ample souvenir-shopping time, while the beach is narrow yet lovely. Snuggled into digs here on the north shore, you'll have plenty of together time.

Chaweng เฉวง

If you're seeking anything other than peace and quiet, Chaweng is likely the Koh Samui destination for you. It's a quick ride from the airport, has a beautiful beach on the northeast coast (sunrise views!), loads of restaurants and retailers, and of course plenty of hotels at all price points. The Walking Street is great for browsing local goods, and you'll find designer goods in boutiques. If you lovebirds like your nights on the town, Chaweng has bars and clubs providing music and drinks. You're bound to meet new friends from around the world. Most nightspots front the sand, meaning you can extend your beach time into the wee hours.

Choeng Mon เชิงมน

Choeng Mon is impossibly romantic. Its string of beaches is white and small, each fronting its own placid and glass-clear bay. The sand is a bit sugary, but restaurants along the shore compensate, and water sports are easy to find. Many of the hotels are quite indulgent, and therefore of course on the pricier side. You can have delightfully subdued meals together and drinks in places where you needn't strain to hear one another. Chaweng is a quick 15 minutes away when you crave action; expect to choose to remain where you are.

Lamai ละไม

Beachtown-style mellow action, but not too much, makes Lamai the ideal alternative. This resort area further down the east coast also has a wonderful beach, and it's on the tranquil side for a popular island. Plus, you'll have easy access to restaurants, shopping, and enticing spas, plus the nightlife is rich here. Koh Samui's tourism growth essentially started on Lamai, meaning some lodging facilities are older. That generally makes them either more personable or less expensive.

Maenam แม่น้ำ

If you're seeking budget accommodations, Maenam is tops, and this north shore village is not the booby prize. The accommodations tend to be small and friendly, just not fancy, and maybe not air-conditioned. Water-sports vendors operate right from the gold-sand, crescent-shaped beach—which never feels crowded. Since wallet-watchers congregate here, meals and beers tend to be priced reasonably. And when you want a dose of special, treat yourselves to a meal or a beachfront massage (or a room) at one of the high-end resorts.

ACCOMMODATIONS

Amari Koh Samui อมารีเกาะสมุย $

(amari.com/koh-samui; 077300-3069; 4 14/3 Moo 2, Chaweng) Tucked into a quiet pocket of Chaweng Beach, this 139-room Amari resort has a contemporary Thai vibe with many home comforts. Floor-to-ceiling windows let the tropical sunlight pour into each guestroom, and all accommodations have free Wi-Fi and a terrace. Two freeform pools overlook the beach, Breezes Spa will quicken your unwinding time, and a fitness room will keep you trim. When you're hungry, choose from Prego Italian Restaurant, all-day Amaya Food Gallery, and Amaya Bar, which has wonderful water views. You can walk to town in 10 minutes and you'll be close to the weekly night market and airport.

OZO Chaweng Samui โอโซเฉวงสมุย $

(ozohotels.com/chaweng-samui; 07791-5200; 11/34 Moo 2, Chaweng Beach) Bright and modern with comfortable beds—chosen with much care—the OZO Chaweng Samui seems custom-made for Millennials and Gen-Zs, although couples of all ages will find much to like. Located on Chaweng Beach, the 208-room trend-forward resort has a swimming pool as well as a fitness center. There are two bars, one by the pool, the other on the beach. The cheerful dining spot Eat serves international foods by the pool for three meals a day while the Stacked Burger restaurant has American specialties.

SALA Samui Choengmon Beach Resort ศาลาสมุยเชิงมนบีชรีสอร์ท $$

(salahospitality.com/samui; 07724-5888; 10/9 Moo 5, Baan Plai Laem)

"Personal & Private" is the shtick at this hotel, which makes it ideal for couples. Of the 69 accommodations on-site, 53 villas and suites have their own swimming pools. Expect warm Thai style and modern amenities—and a spa makes the resort even better. You'll also have access to two restaurants, a beach bar, afternoon tea, and cooking classes. As for romantic meals, SALA Samui Choengmon takes the so-called cake. The chefs will put together one of four special just-for-you events. The first three are a chef-prepared barbecue dinner in your villa; a picnic packed to go; or a champagne breakfast that begins with Taittinger, which you'll pair with omelets, noodles... whatever Asian or Western foods you want. But it's the private tent dinner that is the ultimate gesture. Under a tent on the sand surrounded by hurricane candles, you'll be served a multicourse chef-made meal for just the two of you.

Sallamai Resort สัลลามัยรีสอร์ท $

(sallamai-resort.com; 084441-2149; 206/34 Moo 4, Lamai Beach)

This 10-room resort, set in the middle of this paradisiacal island, surrounded by jungle, will provide you with your own terrace, an Italian shower, and a stocked minibar. With a small upgrade, you'll also have an open-air, sea-view "bubble tub"—a whirlpool tub for two. When you can bear being with other people, there's also a shared swimming pool and garden, and Lamai Beach is nearby. An Eden for the amorous.

Thai House Beach Resort ไทยเฮ้าส์บีชรีสอร์ท $

(thaihousebeach-resort.com; 07741-8006; 131 Moo 3, T.Maret, Lamai Beach)

Bright polished guestrooms, a freeform pool with a whirlpool tub adjacent, a garden setting, and plenty of palm trees... what's not to like? Thai House is right on Lamai Beach, which is a fine place to enjoy seafood meals overlooking the gulf. Shaded lounge chairs await on the beach, as does a massage sala. (Sign up for massages daily. Why not?) Staffers wear traditional costumes, there's a shuttle to and from the airport, and you can request a private cooking class.

BREAKFASTS

Bar Baguette บาแกตต์บาร์ $

European

(barbaguette-samui.com; 094804-1221; The Wharf Samui, Bophut; daily 7am-7:30pm)

Pastries and coffee are taken seriously at Bar Baguette, a mall staple since 2015. Pastries, breads, and savory foods are made in-house daily, and Sasatorn coffee from the founder's hometown in Nan Province is brewed, dripped, and topped by a workforce who have the mantra, "Do it with passion or not at all." Breakfast is served all day. It ranges from fruit-topped pancakes and egg and sausage sandwiches to a smoked salmon breakfast bruschetta with eggs and guacamole. Curries, pasta, salads, and sandwiches are also available.

The Coffee Club เดอะคอฟฟีคลับ $

European, Thai

(thecoffeeclub.co.th; 092282-2115; Central Festival Samui, Chaweng; hours vary)

This Australian chain is a win for breakfast lovers, with a broad menu of day-starter (and other) meals, alongside frappés and coffees. These "all-day cafés" will bring you the avocado toast route, the eggs-and-bacon way, and Thai morning meals.

LUNCHES AND DINNERS

Baan Ya Jai Thai Restaurant ร้านอาหารไทยบ้านย่าใจ $$

Thai

(baanyajai.com; 099479-0707; 161/10 Moo 2 Choengmon Rd, Chaweng; daily 1pm-10pm)

Classic Thai cuisine by Chef Atitaya Paitoon draws locals and tourists to this Chaweng restaurant, a no-reservations favorite with an upscale decor. No mixy-matchy with other Asian cuisines. No western options. Just real Thai specialties made by an experienced chef. This is your place to get made-to-order pad Thai with pork, yellow chicken curry, grilled jumbo shrimp with tamarind sauce, and stir-fried morning glory. Glory be.

Dara Serene Restaurant ห้องอาหารดาราซีรีน $$

Seafood, International, Thai

(facebook.com/dara.serene; 0772-3323; 162/2 Moo 2, Dara Samui Beach Resort)

The food snobs among us always choose food over ambiance, preferring an exceptional bowl of curry in a dive than mediocre anything in a nice setting. Then there's Dara Serene. This hotel restaurant is located right on Chaweng Beach, and guests dine in shalas that are essentially sheer teepees lined up along the sand. Sunset? Stunning. Ask about adding on tasteful romantic ornaments to accessorize your personal dining area. Fresh seafood and southern Thai-fusion dishes provide a second reason to dine here.

Khaw Glong Thai Cuisine ข้าวก่องอาหารไทย $$

Thai

(khawglong.com; 089154-4560; 200/12 Moo 2, Chaweng; daily 1pm-9:30pm)

Seek out Khaw Glong on a side street near the Central Festival mall and you'll find a higher level of Thai cuisine than in many island spots. So popular is this Koh Samui restaurant that a second branch opened in Chiang Mai. The core concept is fresh everything: no prepped ingredients; no pre-cooked meals; no MSG. When you order, the kitchen staff chops up your vegetables and stir-fries to order. That's after you specify your preferred spice level. Begin with a duck salad or tuna in wild pepper leaves. Nine types of fried rice are on offer, including a variety with pineapple or crab. The menu lists several noodle options, plus soups, curries, stir-fries with basil, and even deep-fried tilapia, steamed perch, and sweet-and-sour chicken or pork. Many selections can be modified for vegetarians. The dining room is small and doesn't accept reservations, so time your visit for the shortest wait— namely between standard lunch and dinner hours.

Kob Thai กอบไทย $

Thai

(facebook.com/KobThaiRestaurant; 082534-9325; 101/18 Moo 3, Lamai Beach; daily noon-10:30pm)

Eat Thai classics under open-sided wood- or palapa-topped shalas at Kob Thai, near Lamai Beach. Each of the eight shalas is situated far from the others, giving you space to make goo-goo eyes in private. Lights in a variety of colors add to the otherwise casual ambiance once the sun sets. The garden setting has its own pool and, most notably, the restaurant serves traditionally prepared Thai foods. You'll get a taste of how locals eat—real curries, crab dishes, and stir-fries.

Lamai Veggie ละไมเวจจี $

Vegan, Thai

(facebook.com/LamaiVeggie; 089723-2061; 134/14 Moo 4, Lamai Beach; Mon-Sat 10:30am-4pm)

Lamai Veggie is the arch opposite of the bowls-and-smoothies vegan places. Here, in a frills-free streetfront—the exterior is covered with plants—you'll find meat-free versions of classic Thai foods. Thai curries, tofu, steamed veggies, stir-fries, and rice are plopped onto plates, nuthin' fancy. Kombucha and vegan desserts are available too.

Pizza Del Sol พิซซ่าเดลโซล $

Pizza, Italian

(facebook.com/Pizza-del-Sol-603566459703252; 093575-9330; 124/201 Moo 3, Lamai Beach)

There's grab-a-slice pizza, and there's let's-make-it-a-night pizza. The latter sums up Pizza Del Sol. This modern space has a grand tented entrance and contemporary backlit lighting inside. As for the menu, expect thin-crust pizzas and house-made pastas. Other Italian staples are here, too, like Caprese salad, bruschetta and a salmon steak.

Pure Vegan Heaven สวรรค์ของมังสวิรัติบริสุทธิ์ $

Vegan, International

(pureveganheaven.com; 07790-0464; 131/1 Moo 3, Lamai Beach; daily 10am-6pm)

Four of these "cruelty-free" vegan restaurants dot Thailand: Koh Samui's version has warm woods accented by deep greens, plus outdoor views and seats. Vegan guru Pure Raksapan, who also teaches kids about sustainable agriculture, is the brains behind the chain. Her so-called "guilt-free food" covers several categories. Offerings include a falafel bowl with quinoa and wild rice, a smoky barbecue bowl with jackfruit and sweet potatoes, Mexican-flavored faux poke, and juices.

Squires Loft $$

Steakhouse, Australian

(squiresloftthailand.com; 07742-3451; 24/36 Moo 1, Bophut; daily 5pm-11pm)

Squires Loft has a quarter-century history of serving steaks in Australia, and you can have the same experience in Koh Samui. The Premium grass-fed beef comes from Gippsland and Victoria. It's basted in a proprietary flavoring mix and topped with house sauces. Even the grills are Squires Loft-specific—they're built for the chain. Not big on beef? Chargrilled prawns with creamy garlic sauce, spare ribs, sausage, salmon, and a vegetarian platter are options. The dining room has an old-time feel with tiled floors and dark woods.

Stacked Burger เบอร์เกอร์ซ้อน $

Burger, American

(stacked-samui.com; 07791-5222; 14/3 Moo 2, South Chaweng Beach; daily 2pm-midnight)

If you need a dose of an Austin-esque eating scene, take yourselves to Stacked Burger. This is a super-serious burger joint in an upbeat polished setting with light woods, an open kitchen, and dangling Edison bulbs. Your burgers will be generous patties of U.S. grass-fed beef, and your buns will be baked daily on the premises. And the toppings? Pick from all kinds of combos, like The Cowboy, with barbecue sauce, bacon, cheddar, veggies, and the house sauce. We admire the Asian influence of the Samui Bad Boy: slow-cooked pork with cheddar, jalapenos, green salsa, pickled red onions, and barbecue sauce on a chili-lime bun. Stacked also caters to vegetarians with options like a grilled eggplant version called Save-a-Cow. The American menu continues with fries, onion rings, wings, chowder, apple crumble, and a Tomahawk steak for four. P.S. Check out the happy hour specials.

Supattra Thai Dining สุพัตราไทยไดนิง $$
Seafood, Asian
(facebook.com/SupattraThaiDining; 093282-8777; 32/6 Moo 4, Bangrak; Thu-Sun 6pm-10pm)
There's a description at Supattra of blue crab with wild betel leaf, and whole fish deep-fried, de-boned, and plated with a bundle of herbs. That's food porn talk right there. Request a deck seat at the sala-style restaurant; that way you can see the mangrove forest as you dig into your meal. Romantic! The base of all seafood dishes is fish or shellfish pulled from local waters. Supattra Schaden is the whiz behind the culinary accomplishments. And the wine list? That's the domain of her husband, Australia native Thomas Schaden.

The Hungry Wolf $
Vegan, European, Thai
(thehungrywolf.xyz; 094408-2243; 17/57 Moo 3, Chaweng Beach; daily 11am-9:45pm)
Hungry Wolf serves meat and great vegan options. Bypass the burgers with house-made buns and pizzas with scratch-made sauces for the sizeable vegan section of the menu. Here you'll find vegan OmniBeef and beetroot burgers, and also vegan pizza, green curry, burrito bowls, and linguini with garlic and olive oil.

Tree Tops Sky Dining & Bar $$
Romantic, International
(treetopsrestaurantsamui.com; 07796-0333; 92/1 Moo 2, Bophut; daily 6pm-11pm)

179

This is the place to woo your love. You'll be seated at one of only eight tables with water and mountain views, each table in its own mini shala, situated amid the canopy of a 120-year-old tree. The flavors are ambitious, delicately blending east and west. Croatian Chef de Cuisine Jakov Oršulić is the mastermind behind the menu. Your choices might include local prawns with lardo, mango bisque, fennel, and caviar, or a just-right egg yolk with foie gras and chorizo. For entrees, the day's choices could be Asian-glazed Kurobuta pork belly with popped barley, and white snapper with green curry and coconut chips. We suggest you start with a tropical cocktail, maybe the Lemongrass Wild Chill or Lychee Speer. Once the food comes, pair it with one of the cellar's 170 wines from 13 countries, Old World and New. Nine courses comprise the From the Sea to the Land tasting menu, available with and without wine pairings. Our advice: Go for the multicourse tasting menu so you can sup in the treetop a little bit longer.

Vikasa Life Café $

Vegan, International
(vikasalifecafe.com; 07742-2232; Vikasa Yoga, 211 Moo 4, Lamai Amphoe; daily 9am-10pm)
Located within a yoga center, the Vikasa Life Café promotes "whole food for life," prepared by a European chef—German-born Boris Lauder, a raw food specialist and author. The philosophy here involves "honest origins," and you can enjoy the artfully arranged, organic, and sustainably raised foodstuffs in a sleek restaurant that overlooks water and mountains. Locally made lemongrass-lime craft soda and Protein Reload smoothies are liquid contenders for your attention. After that, the menu ranges from chia jars and probiotic superfood bowls to raw pizza, beetroot sushi rolls, coconut ceviche, and pumpkin cashew gnocchi. Cocktails are available.

Zazen Restaurant ร้านอาหารซาเซ็น $$

Romantic, Fine Dining, Mediterranean, Thai

(samuizazen.com/bestrestaurantssamui; 07742-5081; 177 Moo 1, Samui Ring Rd, Bophut)

Specialties from the Mediterranean and Thailand are served on a terrace overlooking the beach at award-winning Zazen. It's a couple's kind of scene with more than 100 candles lit on and above tables each evening. Against this backdrop, the specialties of the two cuisines are prepared under the direction of a French chef who grows some of the herbs used. Focus on Mediterranean non-seafood main courses, listed under the title "Earth," like caramelized duck breast or a 150-day grain-feed beef tenderloin. Or go Thai with a prix-fixe menu: soup, spring rolls, prawn curry, sea bass, rice, and dessert. The wine cellar is well-stocked. On Thursdays and Sundays, performers in elaborate costumes dance for guests. And there's more! A Lobster Declination menu is filled with luxury foods like lobster and foie gras. You can also request a private candlelit dinner in a beachfront sala.

DESSERTS AND COFFEES

About Café Koh Samui เกียวกับ Cafe 'Koh Samui $

International

(07793-8167; 160/1 Moo 1, Mae Nam; daily 7:30am-5pm)

Nearly a dozen coffees are part of the quirky mix at About, a bright and colorful Mae Nam Walking Street pitstop where you might caffeinate with a German blend, Brazilian beans, or a Thai iced tea, among other options. The place is delightfully unpolished, with merchandise stuffed into jars, hanging from counters, and displayed in rotating racks. Order your beverage and settle into a weathered patio-style chair.

Boy's Organic Coffee $

Coffee, Thai, European

(facebook.com/Boys-Organic-Coffee-401322779879997; 089169-9396; 30/5, Ban Thongkrut Taling-Ngam; daily 7am-5pm)

Organic arabica beans grown in the highlands of Thailand are the foundation of the coffee menu at Boy's. The beans are morphed into hot and cold beverages, often with wistful hearts or cheery flowers created in foam at the top of your cup. With intentionally weathered woods, tasteful bouquets in small vases, and other thoughtful touches, this purveyor has an urban edge. Add on a butter lemon cake, brownie cheesecake, or carrot cake.

Cream Cafe Samui ครีมคาเฟสมุย $

Cake, French

(facebook.com/creamcafesamui; 065992-9096; 45 Moo 2, Chaweng Beach; daily 10am-10pm)

A cursive sign on a brick exterior beckons cake connoisseur to the Cream Café. This contemporary spot with loads of light shining through has seats inside and out. That gives you more places to indulge in the French pastries and simple Thai foods. Need a surprise? The custom birthday cakes are gorgeous, whether a frilly flower-topped affair or a superhero sensation. A full line of coffees, teas, and frappes are also available.

La Fabrique Samui La Fabrique สมุย $

Bakery, French

(facebook.com/lafabriquesamui; 07796-1507; 105/1 Moo 6, Lamai Beach)

La Fabrique is a small French bakery chain on Koh Samui, meaning you can seek out its sweets and such in more place than one. The shops have a kind of busy buzz, with single-serve desserts displayed on and above the counters. You can order breakfast and lunch meals too, and coffee drinks. Casual and colorful.

Leonardo Gelateria Italiana $

Ice Cream

(facebook.com/Leonardo-Ice-Cream-Factory-in-Lamai-Koh-Samui-258731444305250; 092847-7385; 137/2 Moo 4 Maret Maine Rd, Maret; Mon-Sat 9am-7pm)

French chef Philippe Leonardo prepares ice cream in Thailand using European techniques. The results are très magnifique because, as the logo says, the sweets are "homemade with fresh products." The menu has traditional ice cream in flavors like caramel with salt butter, and pistachio from Sicily. Sugar-free sorbets are also available. It's a simple dipping shop with bamboo and Thai touches.

Lolamui Café $

Cake, Coffee

(facebook.com/lolamuicafe; 07760-1607; 127/184 Moo 3, Island Ring Rd, Lamai; Wed-Mon 11am-5pm)

Homemade desserts and coffee made with beans from northern Thailand: no downside. Gather up your honey and head to this sweet spot for an interesting variety of sweets. Berry pie might be on the day's menu, or an unusual coffee cake. Maybe you'll hit the place on a taro coconut cake day, or find caramel cream banana cake on the menu. Plenty of cold coffee and tea drinks are available to go with your snacks. Take a seat inside, on the verandah, or out in the garden.

Pancake Island เกาะแพนเค้ก $

Pancake

(facebook.com/pancakeisland; 07724-7690; 26/48 Moo 4, Mae Nam; daily 9am-6pm)

Pancakes are not just for breakfast at Pancake Island, a plain restaurant with frilly entrees. Here pancakes are loaded with toppings, decorated with chocolate swirls and whipped cream flowers, and finished with scoops of ice cream. Bavarian Pineapple and Chocolate Forest are typical examples. You'll also find coffee drinks with latte art, whole cakes, sandwiches, fish cakes, and "breakkies."

Sweet Sisters Café $

Coffee, Asian, International

(sweetsisterscafe.com; 065953-8832; 57/3 Moo 3, Namueng Amphoe; Thu-Tue 11am-9pm)

Sweet Sisters bills itself as a fusion restaurant, and it opens late–though you'll want to make this a coffee priority stop. Opt for a cup of organic peaberry coffee, a flat white, or a "spicy" brew with cardamom, cinnamon, and ginger. Breakfast is served all day, from traditional Thai rice soup to pancakes, eggs, and green smoothies. Veggie bowls and Thai and Western snacks are also available. As for the rest: juices from local fruits, fish and shellfish caught wild, home-grown and local vegetables, free-range meat and chicken, and no MSG.

Swensen's สเวนเซ่นส์ $

Ice Cream, American

(facebook.com/We-Love-Swensens-294284244347936; Moo 2, Central Festival Samui, Chaweng,)

The American ice-cream chain Swensen's churns out cheerfully adorned desserts at this restaurant within a mall. Cookies, candies, ice creams, syrups, and toppings are stacked in a grand array of ways.

COOKING CLASSES

InFusion Cooking Classes ชั้นเรียนทำอาหาร InFusion

(infusioncookingclassessamui.com; 093784-8976; 149 Moo 1, Soi Khao Phra; Mon-Sat 7:30am-2:30pm, 5pm-7:30pm)

InFusion offers traditional and vegan Thai cooking classes in an air-conditioned facility. The school has an organic garden and often brings students on tours of a local market. There are more than 100 recipes in the repertoire, and you'll get to try some with a 2½ or 4½ hour experience. A favorite is the Authentic Thai Home Cooking Workshop, which starts with a market visit followed by a welcome drink, preparation of herbal beverages with ingredients from the garden, making and eating three dishes of your choice, and leaving with a small gift.

Island Organics Thai Cooking Class ชั้นเรียนทำอาหารไทย Island Organics

(islandorganicssamui.com; 089731-6814; 24/1 Moo 4, Chaweng; Mon, Tue, Thu, Fri 10:30am-2:30pm)

Thai Chef Lat will be your hostess and guide at this organic cooking school, where you'll use many house-raised ingredients (even farmed tilapia) at your personal cooking stations. You'll make curry pastes and coconut cream, plus possibly pad Thai, green curry, papaya salad, and/or mango with sticky rice.

Lamai Thai Cooking School ละไมไทยคุกกิ้งสคูล

(lamaithaicookingschool.com; 084096-4994; 126/80 Moo 3, Maret; daily 8:30am-12:30pm and 1:30pm-5:30pm)

Thai cook Khun Um will walk you through preparing a five-course meal at her school. You'll have some options: seafood salad or spring rolls? Green curry or Panang? You choose. The covered kitchen is open-air, and offers a view of the sea. No more than six of you will be learning at once, meaning that English-speaking Um will give you ample attention. Classes include hotel transportation, herbal and hot drinks, fruit, and recipes.

Smiley Cook แม่ครัวยิ้ม

(smileycooksamui.com; 082285-2919; 25/125 Moo 6, Chaweng; daily 9am-8pm)

Under cover within a garden near Fisherman's Village, chefs Monk and Bung are at the ready to teach you Thai cooking skills. A maximum of six people are in each class. Instruction is in English. Sessions start at 9am or 4pm, each lasting four hours. Every session begins with a half-hour at a market to buy ingredients, including introductions to exotic-to-Americans produce. Next, you'll prepare the four dishes you selected plus a banana and coconut milk dessert. You'll wind up your experience with a shared meal. Hotel transportation is usually provided.

ENTERTAINMENTS

Paris Follies Cabaret

(facebook.com/Paris-Follies-Cabaret-1718528401778733; 087030-8280; 166/92 Moo 2; Chaweng Beach)

Bikinis, boas, and feathered headdresses—the "ladyboy" cast members of Paris Follies go all out with the cabaret show, singing and dancing to upbeat tunes as the audience watches on. The music varies, from American pop to Bollywood to Latin American. Attend any of three different one-hour shows nightly. Sit up front and it might be you swaying your hips on stage with "Lady Gaga."

Starz Cabaret Koh Samui สตาร์ซคาบาเร่ต์เกาะสมุย

(facebook.com/StarzCabaretSamui; 084744-9074; 200/11 Moo 2, Chaweng Beach)

Invite a little not-quite Tina Turner into your night out. The Starz align for a whole lot of fun at this cabaret. Located in the Chaweng Beach area, this small theater turns out three 45-minute shows every night. See it for free if you purchase an (overpriced) drink. Divas and superstars, glitter and wigs are part of the performance, with talented cross-dressers "ladyboys" behind it all.

NIGHTLIFE

Soi Bar Solo ซอยบาร์โซโล

We won't say it's intimate, yet the neighborhood Soi Bar Solo is somewhat low-key compared to the others. Also near Chaweng Beach, this post-dinner hub is an LGBTQ magnet. Everyone is welcome in the bars, most of which are mellow. When you want a place to have fun, go see one of the two playful ladyboy cabaret shows in the area. Bar Solo itself, for which the strip is named, has closed for good, but that won't stop you from finding a good time. Chaweng Stadium (chawengstadium.com) hosts Muay Thai boxing matches twice a week—be sure to stop in to watch. For some classic rock, roll on over to the Jimi Hendrix Bar (facebook.com/pages/Jimi%20Hendrix%20Bar,%20Koh%20 Samui/134182390584162): Music your parents know is represented well here, along with indie sounds. It's a friendly place to unwind and maybe shoot some pool. K-Club (k-clubsamui.com) proudly flies its rainbow flag. Staffers pour cocktails and offer massages in its spa. There are even pop-up performances now and then.

Soi Green Mango ซอยมะม่วงเขียว

Soi Green Mango is Party Central on Koh Samui. The backpack contingent gathers on this stretch of the Chaweng Beach area to chug beers and watch go-go girls in action. Within this neighborhood, you have your choice of venue type. The eponymous Green Mango Club (thegreenmangoclub.com/green-mango-club-samui.html) is the Koh Samui outlet of a Thai party specialist. It looks like a treehouse. Explore assorted wooden stairways to find new places to dance: Hip-hop sounds boom from some areas, EDM from others. World-renowned DJs draw clubbers to Hush Bar & VIP Club Lounge (facebook.com/hushbarkohsamui). Once you get your drinks on—buckets flow here—duke it out with the boxing machine, dance to UK Garage or whatever sounds are throbbing, and leave little love marks on the chalkboard. Despite its name, Sweet Soul Café (facebook.com/SweetSoulCafeSamui) is no spot for a quiet little table in the corner. It's a club with no ceilings, where global hits and soul sounds spike the convivial imbibing-focused atmosphere. Buy shots from the Jägermeister machine—because, why not? The fun starts at 9pm. House music will draw your attention to CUBOS (instagram.com/cubosbar), owned by Australians. The party here—and it is quite a party—continues long after nearby bars shut down for the night.

Soi Reggae ซ. เร็กเก้

Also in the Chaweng Beach area, Soi Reggae is an after-dark gathering area, and it too is named for a club, in this case Reggae Pub. The mix here is not prudish—let's point to a bar with 69 in the name, another with the word sexy, and you may well find a willing third wheel to join you back at the hotel. Mostly though Soi Reggae is about the music, the booze, and the dancing. The businesses are huddled on a little peninsula. Reggae Pub itself (facebook.com/ReggaePubKohSamui) has been a gathering spot since 1988, then a beach bar. Today you'll find a two-story destination with a huge bar, a dance floor, TVs, and billiards. The music? Reggae for sure, and also rock and EDM, often shocking eardrums until the wee hours of the morning.

LIVE MUSIC

Bondi Aussie Bar & Grill, Chaweng

(bondiasia.com/bondi-chaweng; 080519-3931; 169/1-3 Moo 2, Chaweng; Mon-Fri 11am-midnight, Sat-Sun 9am-2am)
One of two Bondi bars on the island (the other is in Lamai), this is a spot for daily live music, generally from the bands Stone Age or Bandit. You'll also find other entertainment, plus food, and live

sports broadcasts of the AFL, NRL, and Premier League. Situated on Soi Green Mango, the entire place has an Australian theme.

Rasta Bar Samui ราสต้าบาร์สมุย

(facebook.com/RastaBar.KohSamui; 083181-5501; Chaweng Walk St, Bophut; daily 4pm-2am)

Get a Jamaican jam on at Rasta Bar, a reggae hangout. A red, green, and yellow color palette dominates, and the music memorializes Bob Marley. Pizza is made and sold on the premises. There's plenty of seating to watch the live performances.

The Palms Bar and Grill เดอะปาล์มบาร์แอนด์กริลล์สมุย

(thepalmssamui.com; 08463-0467; 162/6 Moo 2, Chaweng; Fri-Sat 5pm-midnight)

Three floors, restaurant foods, and live music every single night make The Palms a standout in Koh Samui. Come to this Soi Green Mango club for the sounds you like, then enjoy things like, maybe, a free shot and free Absolut Icebar admittance with your entry fee. As for that Icebar (icebarsamui.com), it's a sub-zero spot for an array of flavored vodkas. Grab a loaner coat and start drinking.

The Shamrock Club แชมร็อกคลับ

(facebook.com/shamrockirishpublamai; 084818-1266; 124/144 Moo 3 T., Maret; daily 5pm-2am)

You'll always find guitars and keyboards on stage at The Shamrock, courtesy of the OVADA Showband. Located along Lamai Beach, The Shamrock specializes in songs from the 1980s onwards, so you might get a little Michael Jackson, and a lot of whatever's hottest today. Sports games are often broadcast on TVs, a game is often in mid-play around the pool tables, and food is served.

BARS

Air Bar แอร์บาร์

(samui.intercontinental.com/air-bar; 07742-9100; 295 Moo 3, Taling Ngam; daily 5pm-midnight)

Located at the top of the InterContinental Hotel, the rooftop Air Bar is the ideal antidote to all those grunge bars and hopping clubs. Up here in the open air, you can see for miles in every direction—including Taling Ngam Bay and the Five Islands—while choosing from the likes of fine wine or top-shelf martinis. Actually, a Champagne Cocktail served with a fruity ice pop like the lime-flavored French72 might be just right. Want to make it even better? Book a Sunset package, which includes saved seats for the evening's sundown, two cocktails, and one tapa. Guitarists and saxophonists entertain regularly.

The International Bar บาร์นานาชาติ

(theinternationalsportsbar.wordpress.com; Soi Green Mango, Chaweng)

Sports, sports, and more sports. That's effectively the mantra at The International Bar. Shoot some pool, toss some darts, and have a chilled beer while watching soccer from around the world—"every game, every day," the website promises, with up to five live events being aired at once.

The Viper Room ห้องงูพิษ

(viperroomsamui.com; 081728-5495; 124/444, Moo 3, T., Maret; Mon-Fri 9:30am-3pm, 5pm-11pm; Sat-Sun 10:30am-3pm, 6pm-midnight)

"Rock pub and food" is The Viper Room's motto, and fittingly so, well, yea. To achieve a biker-bar vibe, Viper blasts loads of heavy metal, punk, and other edgy rock-ish music. You'll see posters of rock classic on the walls, along with guitars and T-shirts. If a few beers or Black Sabbath shots (black Sambuca) isn't enough to get you through the night, how about some chicken with cashews, a red curry, or hot dogs? Several whiskeys are in stock.

WOOBAR วูบาร์

(marriott.com/hotels/travel/usmwh-w-koh-samui; 07791-5999; 4/1 Moo 1, Tambol Maenam; daily noon-10pm)

Oh what a night. Or day. WOOBAR is decidedly Koh Samui's most interesting-looking watering hole, and it's really too classy for that description. Lounge seating on pods out in the water beg for SnapChat snapshots snuggling. This is an ultra-modern place to sit and sip, with the Gulf of Thailand around you, not to mention island views. Creative lighting after dark adds yet more oomph to the aura, the music is well-curated, and food is available.

BEACH CLUBS

ARKBar Beach Club อาร์กบาร์บีชคลับ

(ark-bar.com; 07796-1333; 159/89 Moo 2, Chaweng Beach; Fri-Sat 4pm-midnight)

Talk about sun and fun. ARKbar is all about both. Show up from 2pm on and you'll be immersed in an ongoing pool party, which transforms at some point into a beach party. DJs are behind the scene spinning tunes throughout, and there are nightly fire shows. The beach club sits at the heart of a resort, which itself was built for the kind of audience who wants to live at a beach club for a few days.

Elephant Beach Club เอเลเฟนท์บีชคลับ

(elephantbeachclub.com; 095420-8051; 159/75 Moo 2, Bophut)

Sit on lounge chairs and face the beach, with a bar featuring 50 signature drinks behind you and food at the ready. After dark, creative lighting adds hues of violet and pine to the setting, where you might lounge on a sun bed or even dine at a table for two just steps from the water. Elephant Beach Club feels made for couples, mixing a chill club vibe with a dreamy feel. Smooth jazz and R&B help, while dancers in cages add edge and the nightly fire shows provide excitement. Sometimes you'll happen upon a pool party or a hip-hop event.

SHOPPING

Central Festival Samui เซ็นทรัลเฟสติวัลสมุย

(store.central.co.th/; 02730-7777; 209/1-2 Moo 2, Chaweng; daily 11am-11pm)

When you need a dose of American-style shopping, Central Festival Samui has what it takes. The atrium-style mall has a couple of hundred stores, divided into themed areas: Bird Cage, Beach Town Market, Fisherman Village, and Chaweng Port. There's a Central Department Store, coffee specialists including Starbucks, the Japanese retailer Uniqlo, restaurants, and a food court with outdoor seating. (Hint: Break up your spree with a glass of wine.) High-tech rides, a movie theater, and a pirate-themed attraction can also be found here.

Chaweng Beach Road ถ. หาดเฉวง

When you want the opposite of American-style shopping, meander around the main sections of Chaweng Beach Road, which cover three miles (5km) long total. Official boutiques with walls, doors, and shelves are a source for handbags, higher-end apparel, and fashion by Thai designers. The section known as Chaweng Walking Street is fun for bargain hunting thanks to its stores, kiosks, and carts. Pick up movies and ankle bracelets, plus food from hawkers.

The Wharf Samui เดอะวาร์ฟสมุย

(07742-5500; 62 Moo 1, Bophut; Mon, Wed, Fri 2pm-11pm)
The Wharf Samui is a good bet for a blend of shopping styles: It's a polished, park-like outdoor area with open-front stores—most of them independents, rather than the chains you can find back home. The merchandise is an eclectic mix, from caftans to leather goods. Pick up a snack from the food court and eat at shaded tables. You'll also find a couple of proper restaurants and a spa.

MARKETS

Chaweng Walking Street ถนนคนเดินเฉวง

Much of Chaweng Road is fun to shop, and the Chaweng Walking Street section is a nearly mile-long (1.6km) market-like stretch. Here, vendors lay their goods out under tents—a lamp, say, flip-flops or knock-off Chanel cosmetic cases. Buy some merchandise you don't need but will surely enjoy, watch the free performances, and pick up a food you haven't tried yet in the hawker section.

Fisherman's Village Walking Street (Bophut Walking Street) ถนนคนเดินหมู่บ้านชาวประมง (ถนนคนเดินบ่อผุด)

(Bophut Beach Rd; Friday 5pm-11pm)
Bophut and its Fisherman's Village area are kind of quiet and quaint most of the time. On Fridays? Boom! Lively. Vendors pack the place with the kinds of cheap stuff that make tourists go ga-ga: earrings and dresses, bags and phone cases. Performers put on shows, food is dished out, portraits are sketched, and visitors turn out in droves to get a piece of the entire scene.

Lamai Walking Street ถนนคนเดินละไม

(Hat Lamai Road between the market and the bridge; Sun 5pm-midnight)
It's easy to spend your money at Lamai Walking Street. Simply stroll

around and you'll be tempted by various retailers' merchandise. On Sundays, the area expands into a destination—car-free for the evening, and filled with fun artisan goods, jewelry, and trinkets that make useful, or useless, souvenirs. Haggling is expected. And—surprise—street food is available in abundance, plus there are musicians and fire-show performers. This is also known as the Lamai Jai Dee Walking Street and the Lamai Sunday Night Market.

Maenam Walking Street ถนนคนเดินแม่

(Moo 1, Mae Nam; Thu 5pm-11pm)

The weekly Maenam Walking Street, located amid several restaurants owned by ex-pats, is the place to head If you want to contemplate dried crickets, taste less-unusual but still new-to-you foods, and browse untold numbers of retail stands. Small wooden Buddhas and decorate items carved from soap are among the items on offer. This small, U-shaped, open-air emporium near the beach is like the others, yet heavier on booze. You might even see a mobile cocktail cart hawking mixed concoctions. The food vendors tend to group together by type, so seek out the savories, then nibble your way around to the desserts.

Sharpen your Negotiating Skills

In traditional stores, the price is the price. But in Thailand's many markets you may be able to get that souvenir or item for less, often by as much as 25 percent. If you're savvy or they're eager for a sale (or overpriced), it's possible to get 50 percent off.

Here's how to haggle effectively: Hide your enthusiasm. Say something like, "What's the best you can do?" to urge the vendor to start the negotiations. If you're forced to go first and the vendor turns away like you don't exist, oops, you went too low. Move on; you'll probably find similar merchandise a couple of aisles down. If they immediately stuff the purchase in your bag when hearing your price, oops again, you offered too much. Pay, write off the experience as a lesson, and feel good about supporting an independent business person. Since you're traveling as a pair, you can do the retail version of good cop/bad cop. One can walk away while the other lingers, looking longingly at the coveted item. Otherwise, both of you should turn and leave. With luck the vendor will urge you back with a compromise price. If not, that's the end of it unless you return and pay the asking amount. If your currency is strong against the baht, the difference will be small for you anyway—assuming the asking price is fair, so heck, be kind and let the seller have a stronger profit margin.

MASSAGES

Conrad Spa Koh Samui คอนราดสปาเกาะสมุย

(conradhotels3.hilton.com/en/hotels/thailand/conrad-koh-samui-USMKSCI/amenities/spa-treatments.html; 07791-5888; 49/8-9 Hillcrest Rd, Tambon Taling Ngam; daily 9am-9pm)
Up on a hill with 270-degree Gulf of Thailand views and the recipient of several coveted awards, Conrad Spa is a luxury option. Case in point: Every treatment room has its own water-view balcony.

This hotel facility blends the old and new to provide treatments following new trends yet incorporating ages-old effectiveness. The three-hour Eden for Couples option provides gender-specific massages and facials plus a candlelit frangipani "Bathology" (a floral bath). Start saving up now. Before or after your sessions, spend time enjoying Tai Chi classes and other wellness offerings. You'll also find a relaxation lounge with rain showers and saunas. Simple massages are available at the main pool cabana.

Cyan Spa ไซอันสปา

(facebook.com/cyanspakohsamui; 094595-1017; 65/1 Moo 1 Fisherman's Village, Bophut; daily 1pm-8pm)

Classic Thai styling creates a fitting special, and place-appropriate, aura at Cyan Spa. Whether you're soaking in a bubble bath or receiving a massage, you'll be overlooking Bophut Bay and the expanse beyond. Facials, sauna soaks, and mani/pedis are among the services. Most of the lotions and potions used are made on the island.

Nan Maenam Massage น่านแม่น้ำมาสสาจ

(nan-maenam-massage-massage-spa.business.site; 061220-7317; 170/1, Moo 1 Walking St., Maenam; daily 10am-10pm)

You're supporting individual masseuses, especially women, at Nam Maenam, as each practitioner works for herself in this co-op parlor. The interior is cheerful and modern with reds and yellows. Massages, eyebrow tattoos, manicures, and pedicures are on offer.

Rey Wellness Massage

(facebook.com/ReyWellnessMassage; 086945-7949; 187 Moo 4, Lamai Beach; daily 10am-10pm)

A former Muay Thai boxer and current sports-massage therapist heads up Rey Wellness. Boy, does this staff know how to decrease your aches. They do more, of course, including relaxation massages, stomach massages, aromatherapy facials, and reflexology. Even coconut scrubs, inflammation therapy, and both Eastern and Indian "head therapy" are listed on the menu. Massage beds are lined up and separated by fabric curtains.

Swasana Spa สวาสนาสปา

(samuihotels.impiana.com.my/swasana-spa-in-koh-samui; 07744-8994; 91/2-3 Moo 3, Chaweng Noi Beach; daily 10am-8pm)

At Swasana Spa, treatments are designed for wrung-out travelers. Package names have words like "rejuvenating" and "stress reliever." Four Date Experience packages are meant for folks like you. It's hard to pass up Thai Spice for Two or In the Mood for Love, but Swasana Romance may be the one that woos you. For 3½ hours, you'll both enjoy a milky infusion, a body scrub or wrap, a Himalayan hot stone massage, and a detoxifying facial.

Tamarind Springs Forest Spa

(tamarindsprings.com/en; 085926-4626; 265/1 Thong Takian, Moo 4, Tambon Maret)

They'll have you at herbal steam caves, not to mention the natural rock plunge pools. Tamarind Springs is an award-winning spa located in a garden setting within a rainforest, which has been pampering visitors on its peaceful grounds since 1998. How can you resist? Designed to complement the natural environment, you can receive massages in a private pavilion meant for two, and those massages incorporate healing touches from several massage disciplines. Prakop herb treatments are available. Set aside a day and settle in for a four- or five-hour package. The Really Stoned incorporates a hot and cold stone massage, a facial or foot reflexology session, and the Steam & Dream, which allows you to—enjoy the natural rock cave and rock plunge pools as often and as long as you'd like.

The Anodas Spa Signature ซิกเนเจอร์อโนดาสสปา

(noraburiresort.com/spa-samui.html; 07791-3555; 111, Moo 5 Nora Buri Resort, Chaweng; daily 10am-8pm)

Gaze at the Gulf of Thailand from your comfortable perch within this hotel spa, whether on twin massage tables or in a bubbly tub. Healing techniques from the east and west are incorporated here into ways to make you feel great. Dive in together with the Honeymoon Package: Over 2½ hours, you'll both be scrubbed with a coffee-yogurt blend, massaged with aromatherapy scents, given natural facials, and invited to soak in a whirlpool tub milk bath. Sweet as honey.

TOURS

Angthong Marine Park Semi-Private Sunset Tour ทัวร์กึ่งส่วนตัวชมพระอาทิตย์ตกที่อุทยานทางทะเลอ่างทอง

(mobile.tourskohsamui.com/angthong.php)

Yay for yachts! On this full-day tour, you'll head to Ang Thong National Marine Park on a teak yacht with a whirlpool spa, exploring the 40-island area's shoreline, cliffs, and jungle. Over the course of the day, you'll stop to snorkel around coral reef in a sheltered bay, tour Emerald Lake with its sinkhole, and kayak to a secluded beach. A chef-prepared lunch is included. The tour ends after sunset. From $115 per person. Private options are available.

Just Jungle Eco Safari Tour เพียงแค่ Jungle Eco Safari Tour

(kohsamuitour.net; 061394-1444; 8/15 Moo 3, Chaweng Beach)

Play Tarzan and Jane (or Jane/Jane or Tarzan/Tarzan) on this six-hour jungle tour. After hopping into a 4x4 Jeep at your hotel, you'll go to waterfalls in Namuang, swim at their base, and traverse slippery stones on your backsides into a pool (additional fee). Those stones are known as "jungle water slides." Next up is zip lining in the mountains (additional fee) or simply enjoying more jungle time. Other stops include viewpoints, Hin Ta and Hin Yai Rocks (read more below), the Magic Buddha Garden (read more below), a large Buddha statue, and a rubber plantation. You'll be served a Thai lunch. From $61 per person.

Hin Ta and Hin Yai Rocks In case you had any doubt that Thailand is great for couples, Hin Ta and Hin Yai will set you straight. They are rocks, within a mess of other rocks, and they look like his-and-her genitalia—local lore calls them Grandpa and Grandma. You'll find them between Lamai Beach and Hua Thanon—head to the area and look for other tourists with cameras. A sign nearby spells out a whole backstory about a couple dying en route to marrying off their son. This area is a wonderful escape, with lovely sea views and a small beach near the non-touristy Hua Thanon Muslim fishing village.

Hin Ta and Hin Yai Rocks

Magic Buddha Garden The wonderful Magic Buddha Garden in this tour, also known as the Secret Buddha Garden, Magic Garden, Heaven's Garden, and Secret Garden, is a wonderland of small Buddha statues, along with others of people, gods, and animals, set amid lush gardens of indigenous flora, small waterfalls, rocky land, and a gentle stream—plus magnificent Koh Samui views. Durian farmer Nim Thongsuk started building it in the late 1970s, when he himself was in his late 70s. Your driver will take you through the two-hour tour and explain the stories told, which aren't self-explanatory.

Pig Island Koh Samui by Speedboat with Sunset (Exclusive Pig Feeding Experience) หมูเกาะเกาะสมุยโดยเรือสปิดโบ๊ท พร้อมชมพระอาทิตย์ตก (ประสบการณ์การให้อาหารหมูสุดพิเศษ) (gojotours.org; 02635-7374)
Pet pigs! Take a six-hour speedboat excursion to Pig Island, also known as Koh Madsum, where you'll feed and play with porkers on the sands of Pig Beach. You'll have a beach dinner of stir-fries and soup, then relax on sun beds, kayaking and swimming as you wish. Zip home as the sun sets. That's not all. You'll also snorkel off Koh Tan, likely to see coral and manta rays. A longtail boat option is available too. From $100 per person.

Private Island Gem Picnic and Snorkeling Tour ทัวร์ปิคนิค อัญมณีและดำน้ำดูปะการังบนเกาะส่วนตัว
(islandgemtours.com/tour/island-gem-picnic-tour; 07795-2686; 106/7 Moo 4, Maenam)
Picture this: a gourmet picnic on the beach of an island in the Gulf of Thailand. If you're looking to make a statement of love, this will do the trick. For this experience, you'll have a longtail boat or speedboat as the means to your destination. The standard itinerary—you can adapt it to your liking—is built around a Thai or Western meal set out on a lovely and quiet stretch of beach.

Minced larb, papaya salad, grilled chicken and pork are part of the Thai menu, while grilled Cajun chicken and pesto salad are among the American choices. Wine and beer are included, bubbly an add-on, and splurge out on some massages, too. Your six-hour outing will also include the chance to snorkel (gear included), plus plenty of opportunity to sunbathe. The honeymoon upgrade has a personalized gift too. From $320 per couple.

Top Sights of Samui City Tour สถานที่ท่องเที่ยวยอดนิยมของสมุยซิตี้ทัวร์

(viator.com/tours/Koh-Samui/6-Hours-Samui-City-Tour-with-Guide/d347-89944P5)

See Koh Samui's principal sites in one fun and easy six-hour tour. You'll be picked up at your hotel, driven to each attraction, and told interesting backstories. You'll begin big with What Phra Yia, the mountaintop Big Buddha Temple. At Wat Plai Laem, you'll see the Chinese Lady Monk, a tall statue with many hands. Take in another vista at the Lad Koh Viewpoint, then visit the anatomically shaped rocks at Hin Ta and Hin Yai (Grandfather and Grandmother). The Guan Yu Shrine, with its Chinese statue built in 2016, is up next. Other highlights include Namuang Waterfall and Nathon Town (the port area, with shopping). From $26 per person.

TEMPLES

Wat Khunaram วัดคุณาราม

(Route 4169, Na Mueang)

It won't be the sexiest moment of your trip, yet how can you pass up seeing the Mummy Monk? Creepy but fascinating, the temple has the seated remains of a modern-day monk named Luang Pho Daeng who wanted his corpse on display to teach people about the transience of human life, with regards to Buddha's insights.

His eyes are covered by sunglasses to hide disintegration. (Daeng died in 1973 at the age of 79.) Fun fact: Daeng was a monk as a young man, then got married and had six kids, then became a monk again. Monks and practitioners use the temple regularly; the rest of the grounds have the expected Buddhas and other religious attributes.

Mummified Monk Luang Pho Daeng at Wat Khunaram

Wat Phra Yai Ko Fan วัดพระใหญ่เกาะแฟน
(Route 4171, Bophut)
To see a gold Buddha, opt for Wat Phra Yai, where a 40-foot (12m) likeness propped onto a platform sits Mara-style in the center of a courtyard, with naga serpents adorning the stairway up. Big Buddha's hands are positioned in a way that represent the journey to enlightenment. While Big Buddha gets all the attention—heck, you might even see it from the air if you fly into the island—you'll find other Buddhas elsewhere, plus lots of religious icons for sale. Built in 1972, Wat Phra Yai is an active temple, and you might see religious rituals in action.

Wat Plai Laem วัดปลายแหลม

(Near Ban Plai Laem School, Plai Laem)

At the center of Wat Plai Laem sits a white, seated Guanyin goddess statue of mercy and compassion, with 18 arms, with each hand holding an object. Artist Jarit Phumdonming helped design this modern and vibrantly hued Buddhist temple with Thai and Chinese elements, incorporating old-time techniques. You'll find Buddhas aplenty too, notably a 100ft (30m) fat, Chinese-style laughing version. Expect to come across parishioners as well as tourists at this spot that hovers over the water on the northeast coast. You can food to feed the fish, the money from which will support the temple.

Wat Sila Ngu (Ou Wat Ratchathammaram) วัดศิลางู (Ou Wat Ratchathammaram)

The terra-cotta Sila Ngu, or "stone snake temple," is a small house of worship near Hua Thanon Beach with sculptures and has reliefs of warriors and sea monsters on its exterior. The roof has the bird-like garuda, though the inside is perhaps more striking: a golden seated Buddha sits on a high perch with gray elephants on either side. Other than that, it's almost all terra-cotta scenes, including monkey- and elephant-head gods. Sea creatures seem vicious: One is in the process of eating a human.

ADVENTURES

Canopy Adventures (Zipline) การผจญภัยบนหลังคา (Zipline)

(canopyadventuresthailand.com; 07730-0340)

Show up at the Secret Falls base camp and zip your way over the rainforest at up to 50 miles (80km) per hour. A driver will pick you up in a 4x4 and bring you to this hidden spot, where zip lines and rope courses await. There are 21 platforms altogether, with 15 cable rides that traverse 1¼ miles (2km) of jungle. Begin with fresh fruit before you're given training instruction and outfitted in safety gear. Your views will be treetops, waterfalls, and beaches. $50 per person.

Island Jet Ski Tours ทัวร์เกาะ Jet Ski

(kohsamuiwatersports.com/island-jetski-tours; 099369-7789; Lamai Beach, Ban Lamai)

Three- and four-hour jet-ski tours will take you to neighboring islands. The personal watercraft take minutes to learn, and then you'll be off into the water—on your own or sharing one vehicle. You'll start on Koh Samui and head to Koh Tan (Coral Island), Koh Matsum (Pig Island), and other Gulf of Thailand landmasses. You'll have time on land too, where you can have a meal, sip a cocktail, swim, and sunbathe. Morning and afternoon tours are available, and hotel transportation is included. From $265 per jet ski. Koh Samui Water Sports also offers jet boards, fly fishing, hoverboards, inflatables, wakeboards, banana boats, parasailing, sofa towables, water skiing, and flyboarding.

Samui Elephant Sanctuary ศูนย์อนุรักษ์ช้างสมุย

(samuielephantsanctuary.org; 095269-83434; 43/2 Taweerat Pakdee Rd, Bophut)

When they're done with logging and other grueling careers, some elephants are lucky enough to retire at one of two Samui Elephant Sanctuary locations. The outfit claims to be "the first ethical elephant sanctuary on Koh Samui," and the elephants live in a wooded area. During your visit you can feed the creatures, take them for a walk (or maybe they take you), and observe as they bathe and splash in the mud. Morning and afternoon programs are available. Both include hotel pick-up and return, a video intro, preparing elephant food, feedings, walks, watching elephants bathe, a vegetarian Thai buffet lunch, and water, coffee, and tea. $100 per person.

Samui Quad Motor สมุยควอดมอเตอร์

(samuiquad.com/en; 083645-9881; Soi 1, Maenam)

Take to the road—the rugged off-road. Quad Motor has a fleet of ATVs and its employees are ready to show the way. The outfit has trails and tracks amid the mountains and welcomes visitors for group tours and private ones. With others or just the two of you, you'll be brought to the Squad facility from your hotel and trained before taking the wheel. Then you'll follow a staffer into nature: streams, rock formations, mud, sand, viewpoints... stunning, and a helluva lot of fun to reach. With the two-hour tour, you'll stop for a drink at a bar set up near a remote waterfall. Cheers! One-hour tours are also available. From $95 per person for two hours.

YOGA'S

Absolute Sanctuary

(absolutesanctuary.com; 07724-7810; 88 Moo 5, Tambol Bophut)

If you want to return home from vacation feeling not only refreshed but actually inside-out better, consider staying at Absolute Sanctuary, which calls itself a wellness fitness resort. The programming? Weight management, de-stressing, detox, yoga, and Pilates, among other holistic disciplines. If you prefer only a bit of self-bettering, look at the yoga menu. Five-, seven-, and ten-day retreats are available, each starting with a personal wellness consultation and bio-impedance analysis. The lodging is in a boutique hotel with Moroccan touches. It is part of the Absolute You chain of boutique fitness studios.

The Yogarden โยการ์เด้น

(theyogardensamui.com; 085790-3409; 78 Moo 1, Laan Thong Rd, Fisherman's Village, Bophut)

An open-air yoga shala is the core around which this multipurpose studio is built. The YogaGarden is a nature-saturated complex surrounded by stone and palms. You'll find a lodging facility and a healthy foods café, too. Show up for one of the daily yoga or Pilates classes. You might enroll in a longer program, such as a yoga workshop or retreat, or perhaps a detox program. Here you'll also have access to naturopath's Chinese medicine experts and massages.

Vikasa วิคาสะ

(vikasayoga.com; 07742-2232; 211 Moo 4)

Vikasa has three main yoga shalas as well as private spaces. The facility has certified 1,000 yoga teachers over time, so you know a whole lot of learning is going on here. Created by yogi Konstantin Miachin, Vikasa was designed as a retreat, with lodging, for yoga practitioners seeking personal growth, although you can also take single classes and show up for the daily free meditation. The complex has an organic restaurant, juice cleanses, massages, Reiki instruction, and teacher training. The two of you might request a personal program—we think the private class where you learn to use Himalayan singing bowls will not only heal your spirits but also strengthen your bond.

Yoga House & Spa บ้านโยคะแอนด์สปา

(house-yoga.com/en; 082427-1284 145/1 Moo 4, Lamai Beach)

In the heart of Lamai, you can get a dose or 10 of any kind of yoga service that will make you feel better. This bright spot, under the direction of Master Valentin Voronin, offers a breadth of yoga and meditation classes, plus private training if you'd like sessions for just the two of you. In a private room, you can undergo Reiki, craniosacral therapy, acupuncture, biodynamic feedback, or sound training. Then there's the Chocolate Bliss spa package that includes a massage. (It's not yoga, but, hey, chocolate.) Vegan foods are for sale, as are yoga-related goods from singing bowls to bracelets.

BEACHES

Bang Po Beach หาดบางโพ

Bang Po, or Bang Por, is another beach few tourists know to visit. This nine-mile (14km) expanse of sand and sandy-bottomed shallow water is on the island's northwest coast. You'll find simple but plentiful food, and the crowd is scarce.

Bophut Beach หาดบ่อผุด

If you tend to like breaks during your beach visits, Bophut Beach might be for you. Just under two mile (3km) long and facing north, Bophut incorporates the personable Fisherman's Village and it also has minigolf, zip-lining, and a water park made of inflatables. Meals and snacks are easy to find, and drinking establishments tend to be of the flip-flops-and-Tees variety.

Chaweng Beach หาดเฉวง

Gulf of Thailand beaches on Koh Samui and other islands are renowned for being gorgeous—wide stretches of sand, attractive blue or green water, scenic backdrops. On Chaweng Beach, the swath of gorgeous extends for more than four miles (7km), and the sand is white and soft. Better yet, there's a coral reef offshore, which is excellent for snorkelers and divers. It's separated into sections: Chaweng Yai (big) and Chaweng Noi (small). Both face east, meaning they're good perches for sunrise excursions. Watch out for waves, which can make swimming a challenge and reduce the water's clarity. Chaweng is the bustle beach of Koh Samui: its people-watching superb, and nearby shopping and dining noteworthy. Vendors may even approach you with hot and cold foods. That said, it's still a mighty chill place, and nothing like the party beaches on some other Thai islands.

Lamai Beach หาดละไม

Further south on the east coast yet set off on its own between boulders, Lamai Beach is another popular choice. The water is calm, the sand is white and powdery, and you'll find restaurants and stores—there's just less of everything than at Chaweng, except serenity. The beach is especially wide, however, and the swimming is delightful—shallow enough for wading near shore, deeper further out.

Lipa Noi Beach หาดลิปะน้อย

Now we're on the west coast, which means sunsets. Yet Nipa Noi Beach has even more to offer. The sand is silky and white, the water is shallow near shore with a soft bottom, and the kayaking is easy. Plenty of trees provide shade from the sun. And not too many people will be in your way. This is just not a tourist hub. Of course, that may mean you'll likely find yourselves traveling elsewhere for dinner or groceries.

Maenam Beach หาดแม่น้ำ

Also facing north, Maenam Beach is a chill hangout shaded by palm trees. Many of the lodging facilities along the four miles (6½km) are right on the sugary golden sands, yet you won't feel crowded. Expect a lot of bungalow-style hotels that are unfussy shelters for unwinding. And the beach is pretty, lined with gardens and palms—plus tables set up for lunching right at the shoreline, facing the Gulf. The water isn't the best on the island; it's often not clear and may have jellyfish. You'll have extras though, like restaurants, massage parlors, and the kinds of stores that make running errands easy.

Thong Takhian Beach (Silver Beach) หาดท้องตะเคียน (ซิลเวอร์ บีช)

Get your cameras ready, friends—the good cameras, not the smartphones. Silver Beach is stunning. It's curved. It has boulders. Add in mountains and trees and see-through aqua water that often reveals fish swimming beneath you. Just a sliver of sand facing northeast from the center of the east coast, this strand doesn't even make it onto most maps. You may have to slip through one of the beachfront resorts to reach Thong Takhian, but don't be afraid to do so—the quiet beach itself is public. Oh, and this gem isn't too small: You can still get a Thai massage in a beachfront hut and a sea-view lunch at a hotel restaurant. Snorkeling and kayaking are good here.

KOH PHANGAN

Koh Phangan

WHY GO

Koh Phangan is two destinations in one: a lush tropical island, and a ravers' (hard-core partiers') paradise.

This 48 square mile (124km²) island has a lush jungle interior dotted with temples and waterfalls. A string of beaches rings the shoreline: white or gold sand; some with scenic stones, some without; often backed by shady mangrove or palm trees... these are blissful seascapes. Sand bars abound, hence the name's "ngan," which means sand bar in the Southern Thai dialect. Some stretches of shoreline are secluded while others have a few restaurants, bars, and massage huts, or even a bustling retail hub.

However, many of the island's visitors pay little attention to all that: They show up here to rave. Since 1985, Koh Phangan—then barely known to tourists—has grown into a destination for debauchery. Every month, the island's Full Moon Party on Haad Rin Beach draws up to 30,000 world-traveling 20-somethings, along with others drawn to late nights, loud music, and copious amounts of alcohol. There is no bigger event in Asia of this nature.

Half Moon and Black Moon parties are also regular events. That means the backpacking contingent and their fellow frolickers can find a way to let loose—with music, lasers, neon lighting, booze, and drugs—almost any time they visit.

If you're older, younger, and/or calmer, Koh Phangan still has a whole lot of appeal. The island has a bit of all you'll need, from resorts, spas, yoga classes, and retreats to water and land adventures, and interesting meals. The east coast is the mellowest, wherever you lodge, you can enjoy the beaches, bars, clubs, and restaurants overtaken by the various moon parties if you visit at any other time. Spend your days sunbathing on secluded beaches and diving pristine reefs. Simply check the dates before planning your arrival. And if you want to jump into the fray? Time your visit to coincide with the raves that most appeal to you. Drink and dance until the sun rises. We don't judge.

You can find starter information at tourismthailand.org/Destinations/Provinces/Ko-Pha-ngan/358.

HOW TO GET TO KOH PHANGAN

Simply put, the easiest way to get to the island is to take a ferry from Koh Samui to Thong Sala pier in the island's southwest: this is the route with the most options.

Koh Phangan is a half-hour or so ferry ride from Koh Samui. You can get a ferry at Samui's Maenam, Bangrak, or Nathon piers ($10 one way); book in advance at ferrysumai.com, 12go.asia/en, excursionsonsamui.com, and other websites, or ask for help at a storefront tourist office. It's also possible to reach the island via much longer ferry rides from Surat Thani town, Surat Thani airport, Phuket, Krabi, Ao Nang, Bangkok, and Nakhon Si Thammarat airport. See phuketferry.com for specifics.

Private speedboat is a faster and easier option, and you can be dropped off in Haad Rin in the southeast of the island instead of Thong Sala if that's more convenient. You'll find boats at Koh Samui's Fisherman's Village. Prices start at $30 but cost more if you book a reputable ride (recommended) through a tour office rather than jumping on an unregulated and possibly overcrowded boat.

If you're coming from Bangkok, the easiest route is to take an hour-long flight to Koh Samui and proceed as above, or to fly to Surat Thani, go to the Tapee Pier, and take a 2½-hour ferry ride from there ($32 per person). You can also ride the train to Surat

Thani then a bus to the ferry terminal from there; prices start at $13 and rise depending on air conditioning, sleeper cabins, and such. Expect the trip from Bangkok to take from nine to 22+ hours total. For an extra $17, you can buy a train/bus/ferry combo ticket. A comfy coach trip from Bangkok takes about 15 hours including the ferry and runs about $43 per person. There is also a more modest bus option, which will take you over on the car ferry. You'll find all these options listed on 12go.asia/en.

GETTING AROUND

Koh Phangan is relatively small. It has three town centers: Thong Sala, Baan Thai, and Haad Rin. Some other areas can be reached by car or motorbike, while you'll need a boat taxi to get to others.

Bicycle This won't get you from one coast to another; the island is filled with steep hills, plus some areas can only be reached by boat. But two-wheelers cost only a couple of dollars a day to rent and they're loads of fun when sightseeing. Some hotels lend them for free. If yours doesn't, stop into any of the rental shops along the island's west coast.

Longtail boat Longtail boats are a scenic and fun way to get from one waterfront locale to another. Each has a driver, who usually owns the boat; it's generally under $10 for a ride—these are private rides for the two of you, but that varies by season and distance. Agree on a price in advance.

Motorbike Motorbike rentals, also called scooters here, are quick and cheap, so rent a couple and zip from place to place with ease. Ask around to find a reputable place, because visitors sometimes get scammed. Expect to pay about $10 per day.

Motorbike taxi Keep it cheap without having to use a map or

GPS by taking a motorbike taxi. Negotiate the price in advance. Helmets are provided.

Rental car Cars and 4x4 jeeps will help you get around easily, especially handy if you want to seek out hidden mountain temples and such. From $25 per day, usually higher.

Songthaew Public busses are called songthaew; they're kind of pick-up trucks with benches and shade. They generally travel between Thong Sala and Haad Rin, on no particular timetable; feel free to ask the driver to drop you off elsewhere; she or he may say yes. Prices start at $1.60.

Taxi Regular taxis might fit up to ten people, dropping off and picking up passengers along the way. You might be able to flag one down, but usually you'll need a hotel or restaurant staffer to call one for you. Several at a time generally line up outside the raves. Rides start at $3.30 and depend on distance.

WHERE TO STAY

Koh Phangan area map

Baan Kai บ้านไก่

Baan Kai is relatively quiet and filled with lodging for budget-minded visitors, yet it's close and convenient to Koh Phangan's hot spots. The crux of Baan Kai is a village, a street that is ramshackle in appearance yet well-suited to provide all the essentials plus extras—cash machines, groceries, and travel services, for instance. In addition to a variety of restaurants, Baan Kai has bars aplenty and parties within those bars

Baan Tai บ้านใต้

Baan Tai has it all. This part of Koh Phangan, near Thong Sala and its ferry terminal, has a lovely long beach, and everything else you might want or need during your visit. You can hole up in a hostel or be pampered at a resort; there's easy access to food and drink in the village, as well as to tourist sights and attractions, plus assorted island activities. Music is seemingly everywhere, so you can always grab a pair of beers and settle in for a performance.

Haad Rin หาดรืน

Once a month, this is the wildest place on the island, and possibly in Thailand—home of the Full Moon Parties. The rest of the time, it's a lively destination popular with a young crowd fond of the partying life. You want restaurants? It has plenty. Bars? More than you'll have time to do shots in. Water sports? Oh yes. No one worries about the roar of motorboat engines in these waters. And the beach is beautiful, a long stretch of sand with palm trees for shade and a so-called Sea Walk lined with establishments offering food and drink.

Haad Salad สลัดผัก

Long ago, pirates hid at Haad Salad because it was hard to reach. Now it's a tourist area with a beautiful beach and a decent array of accommodations, restaurants, and bars—but no notable village to speak of. This northwest coast destination offers good swimming in winter and kayaking all year long. Dive operators will take you out to see hard and soft coral.

Haad Yao หาดยาว

Haad Yao is a fine place for beach bums. Stay in a sweet little bungalow and settle in with your sweetie: Your days will involve dinners at beachfront restaurants with twinkly lights, snorkeling the crystalline blue waters, and dodging the sun under palm trees that tower over the powdery sand. You can get to the busier beach called Chaloklum and the freshwater Lake Laemson from here.

Srithanu ศรีธนู

Choose Srithanu if you want a blissful beach stay that doesn't involve raucous all-night raves. In Srithanu, you'll find a rock-lined beach, resorts that are spread out from one another, and a nice little village filled with restaurants and other services. Enjoy the view from under a coconut tree and take a yoga class as the sun goes down. Srithanu has hotels at the higher end and an appreciation of the simple pleasures.

Thong Nai Pan ทองนายปาน

The sand is gold. The water is calm. There's a temple nearby, and a waterfall with a swimming area ready for a visit. Yes, there are giant lizards, but they're harmless and part of the tropical vibe. Thong Nai Pan has a little bit of the best of all Koh Phangan offers—assuming you want a party-free area. You can even practice yoga and try Muay Thai boxing here. Most of the lodgings are a bit nicer than elsewhere on the island, and a little pricier—all worth it for an idyllic environment, plus easy access to waterfalls in the jungle.

Thong Sala ห้องศาลา

You won't find a city anywhere on this remote island, but Thong Sala is the closest thing to it. Home of the ferry terminal at which you'll likely arrive and depart, this is where you'll find any island bustle. Its nightly food market is a must-see, especially on Saturday when it expands exponentially. If you need any service, this is the one place you're bound to find it. You can stay, eat exceptionally well, watch big games at a sports bar, food shop, and book day trips at the local travel agencies. You'll find hotels in every price category.

ACCOMMODATIONS

Buri Rasa Village Phangan บุรีรสาวิลเลจพะงัน $

(burirasa.com/phangan; 07795-6075; 55 Moo 5, Thong Nai Pan Noi Beach)

You'll find modern guest rooms with flat-screen TVs and DVD players at the Buri Rasa, a beachfront boutique hotel where various buildings face the pool, garden, or ocean. The restaurant, The Beach Club, spills onto the sand, where you can dine on barbecue as well as Thai and Western foods. The Nam Thai Herbal Spa is on the beach and uses herbs in its potions. Check the website for good promotional prices.

Cocohut Beach Resort & Spa โคโคฮัทบีซรีสอร์ทแอนด์สปา $

(cocohut.com; 098675-4345; 130/20 Had Rin Nai, Coco Beach)

Cocohut invites guests to "Live with nature, party with the moon" at its resort, up in the hills overlooking palm tree-dotted and quiet Leela Beach, and a short walk from the monthly party at Haad Rin. The 94 accommodations here range from deluxe guest rooms to two-bedroom beachfront villas. The property has a restaurant offering flavors from home and Thailand, and you can chill out with smoothies or cocktails by the meandering pool or on the beach. Cocohut Spa will set you up for massages and salon services, and you can make date night exceptional with a private dinner on the beach: you'll enjoy your meal under a decorated bamboo gazebo. A honeymoon package, also on the beach, includes a bridal bouquet and a bottle of sparkling wine.

Kupu Kupu Phangan Beach Villas and Spa by L'Occitane คุปุคุปุพะงันบีชวิลล่าแอนด์สปาบายล็อกซิทาน $$

(kupuphangan.com; 07737-7384; 69/13, Moo 4, Nai Wok beach) The Kupu Kupu offers romance, wedding, and honeymoon packages, so you know it's a special place for the two of you to be together. Its 41 accommodations are mostly villas and suites with private plunge pools. The resort's centerpiece is a vertical, infinity-edge sea-view swimming pool lined with cabanas. Breakfast is included. One of the two restaurants, the Rooftop Bar & Restaurant, offers sweeping vistas—and bingo nights. The Lilawadee Spa by L'Occitane has couples' treatments.

Le Divine Comedie เลอเทพคอเมดี $

(divinecomedyhotel.com; 091851-8402; 14/8 Moo 1, Tham Bum Baan Tai) Le Divine Comedie was designed for couples, so that's who stays at this budget-priced "truly handmade" boutique hotel on Baan Tai Beach. You'll get a local feel from the out-of-the-way location on a quiet stretch of sand yet have easy access to the destination's major sites and events. The rooms are ultra-comfortable with an urban edge—concrete elements, platform beds that appear to float, all set within a mélange of straight and curved clean lines common in the most contemporary spaces. The T-shaped pool provides sea views, plus it has submerged seats along the pool bar, where both fruit smoothies and trendy cocktails are available. Loungers are on the grass overlooking the beach and Koh Samui Island. The restaurant serves breakfast all day, among other meals.

Panviman Resort Koh Phangan ปานวิมานรีสอร์ทเกาะพะงัน $

(panvimanresortkohphangan.com; 07744-5101; 22/1 Moo 5, Thong Nai Pan Noi Beach)

At Panviman you'll be away from pretty much everything but each other, although the island's huge monthly party is only five minutes away. The creatively shaped infinity pool seemingly flows into the sea, while the breakfast restaurant has panoramic views of the Gulf of Siam and the golden sand adjacent to it. Your guest room, whether standard or a two-story pool villa, will feel luxe thanks to its abundant use of wood. This resort on crescent-shaped Thong Nai Pan Noi Beach is a scenic getaway that also has a spa and two lunch/dinner restaurants, one with seats jutting over the water.

Santhiya Koh Phangan สันธิญาเกาะพะงัน $

(santhiya.com/kohphangan; 07742-8999; 22/7 Moo 5 Ban Tai, Thong Nai Pan Beach)

The teak wood pool villas spread over 18 acres (7 hectare) of bay-view cliffs are enough to make this eco-resort special, yet that's just the start. This resort with a private beach has two pools, one with submerged chaises that resemble longtail boats, plus three restaurants, a spa, kayaking, paddle boarding, and a cute little make-shift shuttle van (essentially a songthaew) that zips guests around the property. Spend a day receiving twin indulgences at the Ayurvana Spa, where many treatments are performed in the open air with water views. Treat yourselves to the Phangan Moonlight Romantic Dinner: At a table for two, just steps from the water, you'll have the choice of two menus plus two glasses of wine each. Your meal might feature pan-fried sea bass and grilled beef tenderloin. End with sweet Thai banana in syrup with coconut mousse.

Sunmoon Star Resort Koh Phangan ซันมูนสตาร์รีสอร์ท เกาะพะงัน $

(sunmoonstarresortkohphangan.com; 086279-0166; 58/15 Moo 8, Haad Yao)

A spiffy modern guest room in a paradisiacal Thai island: That's a win. Sunmoon Star has garden-view, air-conditioned accommodations with balconies or terraces, TVs, fridges, sofas, and free Wi-Fi —all the fundamentals set into a lush setting and near beaches. There's also the Sun Moon Star Restaurant, so finding a meal is easy.

Zama Resort Koh Phangan ซามารีสอร์ทเกาะพะงัน $

(zamaresortkohphangan.com; 07734-9098; 81/5 Moo 8, Haad Chao Phao Beach)

Zama is a collection of air-conditioned bungalows with terraces set amid luscious landscaping. Its swimming pool is faces expanses of clear blue sea. Whether your bungalow looks at garden, pool, or sea, you'll have access to all the amenities: a private beach, a restaurant that greets you with bold artwork, a coffee shop, a snack bar, a bar, a yoga room, massages, and a shuttle.

BREAKFASTS

Beach Coconuts Bowls ชามมะพร้าวชายหาด $

Healthy, European

(beachcoconuts.negocio.site; 095279-4925; 108 Moo 1, Baan Tai; daily 9am-2pm)

The specialty here is Nice Cream Bowls: They're trendy food combos with a wellness bent, featuring superfoods like acai and spirulina. The Black Lava, for instance, lists "charcoal powder" along with the ingredient's mango, banana, and blackberries. In recent years, charcoal elements have been added to everything from foods to skin creams; the reason is that alternative medicine practitioners claim it removes toxins from the body. Others may include red dragon fruit, chocolate whey protein, or matcha. The dining room has a polished lightness with clever uses of rattan. The snappy space has a surfboard jive.

Pura Vida Café ปุระวิดาคาเฟ $

European

(facebook.com/Puravidacafe.pt; 065123-4598; 53/21 Moo 8, Haad Yao; daily 7:30am-5pm)

Pura Vida is a no-frills stop for breakfast and lunch in Haad Yao. It's owned by Portuguese ex-pats who have a way with eggs, acai, and foods from their homeland such as mushroom-stuffed chicken with a garlicky, creamy white sauce. Coffees are made from Thai and Columbian beans, breads are freshly baked, and all meals are cooked to order. Vegan dishes are available.

The Fat Cat Café คาเฟแมวอ้วน $

Mediterranean, European

(facebook.com/The-Fat-Cat-1076639089028396; 087622-0541; Walking Street Market, Taladkao Rd, Thong Sala; daily 9am-3pm)

The Fat Cat makes its menu seem straightforward: coffee, other drinks, breakfasts, and light meals. Take a closer look, and you'll see you can also get a Burmese salad, a pumpkin soup, house-made granola, and cashew butter, even coconut mini donuts. These foods and more are presented in a bright, simple space that opens to the street.

LUNCHES AND DINNERS

Ando Loco Mexican Restaurant and Bar Ando Loco ร้านอาหารเม็กซิกันและบาร์ $

Mexican

(andoloco.com; 085791-7600; 90/15 Taladkao Rd, Koh Phangan;

Thu-Tue 2pm-10:30pm)

Chef-owner Ando is a Chicago native who trained in simple and sophisticated Mexican restaurants before ultimately bringing south-of-the-border fare to this southeast Asian community in 2005. Playfully saying, "The nachos are calling and I must go," the website explains that many foods are sourced locally, except the signature guacamole's avocados, which hail from Australia. Margaritas come in ten fruity flavors. Dare you share the 20oz (600ml) Jumbo?

Auntie's Restaurant ร้านอาหารคุณป้า $

Thai

(Soi Krung Thai, Koh Phangan)

In-the-know foodies seek out this basic dining room that opens to a shopping street for warm service and tasty, inexpensive meals. The chalkboard menu is simple: seven Thai dishes such as red curry, tom kha gai (coconut-chicken soup), and chicken satay. Auntie's has free Wi-Fi but no atmosphere to speak of, but nobody cares.

Beachlounge $

Romantic, French, Thai

(facebook.com/restobeachlounge; 086870-4942; 89/1 Moo 1, Thong Sala Beach; daily noon-11pm)

Beachlounge serves French meals in a private beach setting. Indulge in stunningly sophisticated meals at a table set right on the sand or dine in the cozy interior with its wood-plank ceiling. You might fill up on fish with ginger sauce, banana blossom salad, or green curry chicken. As you dine, watch boaters and beachcombers go by, or take in the sunset. End with the mango and sticky rice: The rice is molded into a heart shape.

eat.co $
Vegan

(eat.co; 099305-6668; 72/1 Moo 8, Sri Thanu; daily 12am-9pm)

Vegan food that is made from scratch defines the two eat.co restaurants on Koh Phangan, a concept with a playful approach. Both locations serve breakfasts, wraps, and entrées. At the Sri Thanu outlet, fill up on the Cheesy Kebab Chip Bomb with hand-cut potato chips and mushrooms. A Thong Sala specialty is sweet: gluten-free waffles with coconut whipped cream, fruit, and caramel, and chocolate syrup.

Fisherman's Restaurant and Bar ร้านอาหารและบาร์ชาวประมง $$
Seafood, Thai

(fishermansphangan.com; 084454-7240; 62/1 Moo 1, Ban Tai; daily 1pm-10pm)

What a story, and what a meal. Chef-owner Khun "Lek" Thanaporn grew up in a local Baan Tai fishing family. He now buys fish for his popular restaurant from the Baan Tai community, and three of his 17 restaurant tables are old family fishing longtail boats that have been repurposed into dining areas with cushions as seats. Together with his Irish wife, Amanda, Lek has built Fisherman's into a beachfront choice for seafood meals, plus some classic and contemporary Thai dishes. Options include Lek's mother's yellow curry, grilled shrimp with dipping sauces, and steamed whole flat silverfish with lime, chili, and cilantro. Sip wine and cocktails—with house-made mix-ins and infusions—curled up on beanbag chairs and bamboo beach beds at the beach bar. Make reservations.

Jumpahom Thai Restaurant $
Thai

(jumpahom.wixsite.com/jumpahom; 081144-3934; 60/1 Moo 8, Haad Salad; daily noon-11pm)

With wooden beams and fences plus palms everywhere,

Jumaphom feels more like a treehouse than a restaurant. What a place to get a curry fix, especially if you're swinging in a hammock or seated on cushions. The food is awfully authentic—with the exception of the Western breakfasts and Italian pastas. Stick to Asian flavors like deep-fried fish with crispy garlic and pepper, glass noodle salads, stir-fries, fried noodles, or any of several curries, maybe massaman curry keng with coconut milk, potato, onion, and peanuts.

L'Alcove Beach Bistro $$

Romantic, Thai, French

(alcovephangan.com; 094579-3769; 15/1 Moo 6, Hinkong Beach; Tue-Sun 6pm-midnight)

L'Alcove is a rustic-chic seven-bungalow resort, and six nights a week it serves French and Thai dinners at its open-air bistro. Choose from 60 wines, and dine on a Gallic duck dish or a refreshing papaya salad as you watch the sun set and listen to musicians perform. If you prefer the beach to restaurant seating, just say so: you can choose your dining spot.

Mama Pooh's Kitchen $

Thai

(mama-poohs-kitchen.business.site; 086377-3569; 84/8 Moo 8, Haad Chao Pao; daily 10am-10pm)

Scratch-made Thai food is served in thatch-roof bamboo huts at Mama Pooh's, a rustic restaurant if ever there was one. The look is DYI, for sure, which adds to the charm. Try a Thai dish you don't know here, maybe kra praw moo kai daw, which is stir-fried pork with basil and a fried egg.

Nira's Home Bakery $

European

(facebook.com/Niras-home-bakery-120700347943551; 086595-

0636; Moo 1 Leabchaitalay Rd, Thongsala; daily 7am-5pm)
At 4am daily since 1985, Nira's has fired up the oven and started
making pastries and breads to be sold alone or used in sandwiches.
The coffee is freshly ground. Walk up to the counter to see the
day's goods and stay to eat at one of the inside tables or on the
covered patio. Muesli with tropical fruit and homemade yogurt,
BLT sandwiches, watermelon-feta salad, chicken and mushroom
pie, spaghetti Bolognese, burgers, pancakes, and Phangan-style
fried rice are among the diverse offerings in addition to the baked
goods.

No Name Thai Food Bistro $
Thai
(092541-4381; 127/16 Haad Rin, Koh Phangan)
In-the-know Thai food lovers show up at this tiny restaurant in big
numbers. The curries and pad Thai, plus steamy soups with glass
noodles, and mango with sticky rice, are all but legendary. Not a
place to come when you're in a hurry as long waits are common.

Peppercorn Steaks & Salads $$
Steakhouse, International
(facebook.com/Restaurantpeppercorn; 087896-4363; 58/28 Moo
8, Haad Salad; Sun-Fri 4pm-10pm)
While you can have salmon, lamb or even a vegetarian penne
with gorgonzola, wine, and cream sauce, mostly Peppercorn is all
about red meat. Settle into a wooden chair on a covered patio
overlooking the beach of Haad Salat Bay, and think steak: choose
your cut and size, then your sauce—such as forest mushroom
cream—and your side dish. The meat is from Australia and New
Zealand. Not your thing? Other options include duck a l'orange
and pork cordon bleu.

Pure Vegan Heaven สวรรค์ของมังสวิรัติบริสุทธิ์

Vegan, International

(pureveganheaven.com; 095858-3810; 64/46 Moo 8, Sri Thanu; Mon-Sat 10:30am-9pm)

Pure Vegan Heaven serves "clean and cruelty-free food" in four Thai locations, and the Koh Phangan unit is special: the restaurant serves vegan meals on a property with its own organic garden. Enjoy your food watching the sun set over the sea, and grab some veggies to take back to your room. The menu ranges from hot beverages like turmeric lattes with foam art to Greek salads and gluten-free nachos with vegan chili, chorizo, and cheddar.

Romanzo Tropicale $

Pizza, Italian

(facebook.com/RomanzoTropicale; 063630-6851; 15 Moo 6, Hin Kong Beach; Sun-Fri 6pm-10:30pm)

This restaurant's logo is a palm tree jutting out of the Roman Coliseum, and in true form the whole concept merges Italy and Thailand. Here you'll have your pizza overlooking Hin Kong Beach, where after dark dramatic backlighting adds to a ridiculously romantic vibe. Share focaccia or a pesto pizza, an octopus salad or a plate of house-made ricotta and spinach ravioli topped with a walnut and gorgonzola sauce. Grilled fish is also available. End the meal with a dessert pizza that involves Nutella.

Vintage Burgers, Friends & Booze วินเทจเบอร์เกอร์เพื่อนและ เหล้า $

Burger, American

(facebook.com/vintageburgerskohphangan; 095958-9011; Taladkao Rd, Thong Sala; daily 5pm-10pm)

When the craving strikes for an all-American meal, Vintage Burgers will fix you up. The hamburgers are big and cooked just right, and you can choose your toppings. The fries are noteworthy. Down them with a jumbo mojito and you'll be set for the evening. The super-casual space has simple bamboo tables and plants hanging from the ceiling.

DESSERTS AND COFFEES

Bubba's ของ Bubba $

Coffee, Healthy, European

(bubbascoffee.com/; 098807-6221; 59/4 Moo 1, Ban Tai; daily 7am-6pm)

Koh Phangan has two Bubba's outfits, each wonderful in its own way, and both based around coffee beans from Chiang Mai, Chiang Rai, and Tak Province. The air-conditioned Baan Tai branch specializes in vegan and traditional breakfasts, and also serves lunch and early dinner. Ingredients include grass-fed dairy products, eggs and poultry from free-roaming chickens, and baked goods and pasta from local vendors. Bubba's Roastery Haad Yao serves similar meals and also hosts roasting and coffee classes.

Crepes Corner $

Crepe

(facebook.com/pages/category/Restaurant/Crepes-Corner-Koh-Phangan-112352226835673; 065442-0643; 3 Soi Sukhumvit 63 Sukhumvit Rd, Khlong Tan Nuea; daily 11am-10pm)

Peanut butter, coconut custard, crab stick, ham, pizza—thin French pancakes are quite different here than in the little bistros back home or in Paris. Embrace it. Crepes Corner is a little kiosk in an area filled with kiosks: sit on a simple chair in the shade and enjoy your creation, whatever the flavor.

Dots Coffee กาแฟ Dots $

European

(facebook.com/dots.kohphangan; 092643-4320; 44/139 Moo 1;

daily 8am-8pm)

Dots is renowned locally for its super-serious java offerings, yet it also bills itself as a coworking space for digital nomads in search of speedy Wi-Fi. The specialty is hot and cold beverages, and pastries are available to eat with those drinks. Sometimes there is live entertainment. Workshops are held here regularly, maybe for storytelling or meditation.

Fresh สด $

Ice Cream

(facebook.com/fresh.sunsetwalk; 061852-8498; Sunset Walk, 103/4 Moo 1, Ban Tai; daily 5pm-10pm)

Look for the aqua-and-white-striped awning and you'll know you've found Fresh, known for "more than just ice cream," so the slogan goes. Maybe the day's chalkboard will tell you the flavor sour mango is available during your visit, perhaps "thick" chocolate with roasted nuts, or coconut with salted caramel syrup. The mojito ice creams have a following, surely since the treats, made with freshly squeezed juice, are a refreshing way to take the edge off.

Satimi $

Sorbet, Gelato

(facebook.com/satimifanpage; 099365-6963; 56 Moo 1, Tongsala; daily 10am-6pm)

Tropical and western ingredients, prepared with Italian craftmanship, add up to an intriguing line of gelato and sorbet at Satimi. Tucked away at the end of Walking Street, this purveyor of sweets in unusual flavors rotates interesting combos such as palm sugar caramel crisp, Thai tea, cinnamon cookie, and mocha macadamia.

The Sweet Café ร้าน Sweet Café $

Bakery, German

(facebook.com/The-Sweet-Cafe-116224741808140; 086775-8821; 45/3 Moo 1, Koh Phangan; daily 6am-8pm)

Small-batch baking of European specialties sets The Sweet Café apart from other bakeries. It bills itself as a "German Bakery and Restaurant." That would explain the fresh-from-the-oven Bavarian pretzels, rye breads, and apple crumble dessert. Coffee drinks, sandwiches, and fresh juices are also available. The shop has warm woods, shelves of books, and plenty of light.

Thong Sala Night Market ตลาดกลางคืนท้องศาลา $

Thai, International

(Tongsala Rd, Koh Phangan; daily 4pm-11pm)

This night market has many strong points, and dessert is one of them.

Food vendors abound, and you'll discover sweets here you won't find elsewhere, plenty of which—like pancakes—are made with coconut. The donuts come in bright cheery colors, Nutella is slathered on baked goods, and pastry makers display a variety of single-portion sweets.

COOKING CLASSES

Koh Phangan Vocational School โรงเรียนอาชีวศึกษาเกาะพะงัน

(thaiculture.education/workshops/traditional-thai-cooking-dessert; 07734-9233; 84/4 Moo 8, Koh Phangan)

Learn to cook papaya salad, pad Thai, fried cashews, coconut soup, or other dishes—two or three in total—at this hands-on school. Each session involves a recipe guide, an herb garden tour, drinks, a souvenir, and the chance to enjoy your creations while sitting by the lake. Private classes are available. You can also learn how to give Thai massages here. From $50 per person.

Proud Cooking การทำอาหารที่น่าภาคภูมิใจ

(proudcooking.com; 095376-8614; 34/1 Moo 4, Wok Tum)

No more than two other students will be in your group when you learn to prepare local favorites in the immersive lessons at this cooking school. You'll make coconut milk and curry paste yourselves and will cook other dishes too. What's more, you'll get to choose them—traditional, vegetarian, vegan, or gluten-free. The morning sessions last four hours and involve four dishes and hotel transfers. The afternoon session is a little shorter, includes three dishes, and does not include hotel transfers. From $40 per person.

Nongnooch Tropical Garden

(nongnoochtropicalgarden.com; 081919-2153; 34 Na Chom Thian, Sattahip District, Chon Buri; daily 8am-6pm)

A world-class botanical garden awaits—yet it's also kind of theme park-ish. A 40-minute drive south of Pattaya, Nongnooch, or Nong Nooch, spreads over 500 acres (202 hectares) and is filled with such beautiful flora that 5,000 people a day come to see it. Sections are dedicated to orchids and bromeliads, cacti and succulents, even plants native to Europe. Seek out the flower arrangements shaped like hearts—the perfect spot for a romantic photo. Many of the areas are sculpted and interspersed with large sculptures, 811 of the artwork dinosaurs. The T-Rex, for instance, is 45ft (14m) tall; it is one of six life-size replicas added in late 2020. While you're visiting, you're likely to see one of the regular cultural performances. You can also stop into a little zoo, where monkeys and elephants reside. Walk, rent bicycles, or even view the displays via a skywalk; then rent a paddleboat and head out to a floating garden.

Research is performed at Nongnooch too: The palm plants known as cycads are studied and preserved at a gene bank here. If you want more palms and petunias during your visit, stay in the on-site hotel or rental houses; there are two restaurants here, too. You can reach Nongnooch several ways from Bangkok. Choose the high-speed 997 "Sprinter" Rapid train to Ban Plu Tan Luang, which takes almost three hours and costs $6 one-way. (The 283 Rapid takes four hours.) From there, it's just a 15-minute walk to the gardens. A quicker option is to take a bus to Pattaya from Bangkok's Eastern Bus Terminal (departures every 30 minutes; $4 one-way). The trip takes from 90 minutes to 2½ hours, depending on traffic; from Pattaya, hop on a shuttle or taxi to the attraction. Alternatively, you can rent a car, arrange for a taxi or private driver, or take a Grab car for the two-hour drive. Too complicated? Book a ride with a tour company.

Nongnooch Tropical Garden

LIVE MUSIC

Jam Koh Phangan

(facebook.com/thejamkohphangan; 085923-0337; Moo 6, Hin Kong Beach; two nights weekly 7pm-1am)

Tap your feet to live music or play it yourself at Jam on Hin Kong Beach, where customers are invited to use the house instruments and equipment—even drum kits, synthesizers, and bass guitars—during open mic and jam sessions. Every so often magicians or fire performers take the stage, too. You'll be outside under string lights.

L'Alcove Beach Bistro $$

(alcovephangan.com; 094579-3769; 15/1 Moo 6 Beach, Inkong Beach; Fri and Sun 6pm-11pm)

This romantic French and Thai restaurant are also a wonderful open-air venue for low-key performances in a magical environment. Every Friday and Sunday starting at 6pm, dancers, singers, musicians, or fire show performers take to the stage. Split a bottle of one of the 70 wines, take a seat amid the twinkly lights in the venue and watch all you want. No cover charges.

Loccos PizzaBar

(loccos-pizzabar.business.site; 064723-4197; 53/21 Haad Yao Rd, Koh Phangan; daily 7:30pm-10pm)

Light, bright, and open-sided, this pizza and pasta restaurant has live music every night. Show up anytime from 7:30pm to 10pm and you can enjoy the sets while sipping wine or a tropical cocktail, or maybe eating dinner or a snack. Cello and guitar, and Sunday Saxophone, are typical offerings.

Rasta Home Koh Phangan ราสต้าโฮมเกาะพะงัน

(facebook.com/rastahome.kohphangan; 084910-0673; 58/24 Moo 8, Surat Thani; daily 10pm-2am)

Head to Rasta Home any Friday evening at 10pm and you're bound to hear reggae, rock, or roots blasting at its outside concert venue. The restaurant, between Haad Yao and Haad Salad, has an open-mic set-up once a week. If you two are crooners, step onto the stage when it's your turn. Otherwise, grab a beer from the bamboo bar, get comfy on a floor cushion, and enjoy the ride. You can also order some Thai food from the kitchen.

BARS

2CBar Sunset 2CBar พระอาทิตย์ตก

(facebook.com/2CBphangan; 093292-6545; 55/8 Thongnaipan Yai Rd, Thong Nai Pan Yai Beach; daily 11am-9pm)

When it's time to reset, join hands and head to this hilltop bar. You'll have an inspiring view of Thong Nai Pan Bay and the greenery and hills beyond it. Your seats may be floor cushions or backless benches. Order a watermelon daiquiri or Singapore sling just before sunset and turn your eyes toward the best show ever. DJs spin tunes some nights, starting at 5pm.

Amsterdam Bar อัมสเตอร์ดัมบาร์

(095018-4891; Wok Tum, Koh Phangan; daily noon-1am)

Arrive nice and early at Amsterdam Bar. This place is popular, so you'll want to secure one of the better spots for your sunset view on a cliff with broad ocean views—as reggae music plays. It takes a short uphill stair hike to get to this two-level venue, but it's worth the trouble. A couple of cold beers, a couple of chaises around the pool, or seat cushions on the ground, and you'll be ready to join the good-vibe group participating in this Koh Phangan tradition.

SOHO Koh Phangan Bar and Food Delivery

(sohophangan.com; 080537-2554; 44/56 Moo 1, Thong Sala; daily 9:30am-1am)

Brick walls and wood furnishings are the backdrop for this airy bar serving craft beers and American food. Across the street from a night market, it's a go-to for sports fans, as international games play on large TV screens—SOHO airs all live Premier League games and will play back others upon request. Fourteen beers and ciders are on tap.

Three Sixty Bar ทรีซิกตีบาร์

(facebook.com/Threesixtybar360; 082561-9874; 85/2 Moo 7, Koh Phangan; Tue-Sun 11am-10pm, Mon 4pm-8pm)

Three Sixty, as it is known, claims to be the only bar in town with 360-degree views. True? We're not sure. What we do know is that the sunsets are phenomenal—hills, sea, the whole shebang. Three Sixty Bar has three levels and DJs often spin electronic tunes. The open-sided establishment has a ceiling that's carved and painted with funky designs. The beams are graffiti-filled, and the floor looks similar. A strip of boardwalk-like wood offers plenty of places to take in the vista in the open air. So, grab a pair of adult beverages and let the evening begin.

BEACH CLUBS

Ban Sabaii Beach Club วนสบายบีชคลับ

(facebook.com/bansabaiibeachbar/; 087883-7277; Ban Tai Beach)

Lighting in deep jewel tones illuminates the beach day and night at Ban Sabaii, a Ban Tai Beach party haven. Rather than compete with the island's biggest events, it latches on to them. Ban Sabaii offers up its libations and sunset views after each moon-themed event. You'll also find Blue Moon and Acid Moon parties here, the latter "a night of deep psychedelic trance." That goes with the music, which is described as trance including "slow funky," progressive, and psychedelic. That's day and night, revelers, so you may be jamming while splashing in the sea.

Beach Bars

A ragtag wooden structure with a palapa roof, the beachfront **Freeway Bar** (facebook.com/Freeway-Bar-Bamboo-Tattoo-125999384125387) in Hin Kong serves up not only food, drinks, and smoothies, but also tattoos, paintings, leather goods, and necklaces. Live music plays regularly. Yao Beach is home to **Vagga Bar** (vagga-bar-see-through-boutique-resort.business.site), a more polished establishment where "B.B.Q. FOOD & DRINK" are on offer on and by the sand. Curl up with cocktails on beanbag chairs or sit side by side while dining to a sunset view. **Sunset Walk** (sunsetphangan.com) on Baan Tai Beach is home to the Bliss Espresso Bar for a beachfront breakfast, and Bar Yamyen for all kinds of cocktails including the Tomyum Martini with lemongrass, kaffir lime leaves, chili, and vodka. The expansive drink menu also lists a couple dozen types of gin. You can have a meal at a table or on beach cushions or beanbags. Dinner might be a cheeseburger, chicken schnitzel, stir-fried garlic tofu, or deep-fried pork, Thai-style.

Blackmoon Culture วัฒนธรรม Blackmoon

(blackmoon-culture.com; Bac's Bay Beach, Ban Tai)

Peace out at Blackmoon Culture, often called the Black Moon Party. With a hippie-dippie New Millennium-style groove, this small-by-comparison beachfront party is no quiet escape. Still, it's by default a relatively mellow way to party with a crowd on Koh Phangan. The event's mantras are peace, trance, and dance, and they're applied to this gathering on Ban Tai Beach on the night of each month's new—or black—moon. The music is psytrance and progressive, definitely not mainstream, spun by resident and guest DJs. Lighting and other decorations tend towards neon's and artistic shapes. $20 per person.

Full Moon Party ฟูลมูนปาร์ตี้

(fullmoonparty-thailand.com; 087884-0910; Haad Rin Beach, Koh Phangan)

Some couples book a stay in Koh Phangan for the beaches, food, and activities. Many plan their entire visit around the Full Moon Party. This internationally renowned monthly mega-bash held on, or right before or after, the full moon brings up to 30,000 young adults together for a night of wild fun at crescent-shaped Haad Rin Beach, where a string of bars and such help the fun along. Jugglers juggle, fire artists wow, and music blasts from several stages—reggae here, trance there, techno too, and more. Participants get their bodies painted with glow-in-the-dark colors. A few words of caution: Booze buckets prevail, but be safe and only buy from permanent bars that have good reputations to maintain. Don't go barefoot as sharp objects often find their way to the sand. Say no to the fire games, as injuries occur regularly. Know that having drugs in your possession can land you in jail: Skip the mushrooms, the yaba, the ecstasy, all of it. Put all valuables in your hotel safe, as myriad lodging robberies happen during Full Moon hours. And keep out of the water; not only is it used as a free bathroom, you can drown if drunk or drugged in the sea in the dark; the undertow increases the risk.

Full Moon Party at Haad Rin Beach

Half Moon Festival เทศกาลไหว้พระจันทร์

(halfmoonfestival.com; 091445-1444; Ban Tai)

You'll rave about this rave, a bold and bawdy dance party held one week before and one week after Koh Phangan's Full Moon Party. Half Moon is a horde of revelers gathering around three music stages, and you can enjoy them all, whether you opt for blacklight body painting or not. The main stage emits thundering's of progressive trance or underground music throughout the night, while the Cave tends toward R&B and hip-hop sounds, plus smoke effects and indoor UV paintings on concrete walls. At the G Floor, funky house music creates yet another vibe. Each of those three areas has some sort of outrageous lighting. Fire shows? Of course. Held in a jungle clearing a bit north of Ban Tai Village, Half Moon costs about $50 per person, extra for VIP privileges, available online and through hotels in advance. Well-kept restrooms and other amenities, including light meals, are available.

Jungle Experience ประสบการณ์ในป่า

(facebook.com/JungleExperiencePartyKohPhangan; 084837-2370; Ban Tai Jungle; semi-monthly)

Pack your glitter eyeshadow and skimpiest clothes to groove at the Jungle Experience, a raucous all-night party with top DJs spinning techno, house, and progressive sounds nonstop. Dance like your lives depend on it twice each month: ten days before and the day before Koh Phangan's Full Moon Party. Be sure to seek out the performance artists at this unleashed event in a tree-free section of the Baan Tai jungle. Extraordinary lighting adds to an otherworldly feel. Fire shows, graffiti art, sculptures, and lasers are also part of the excitement. When you need a break, you can buy a meal and rest in a Chillout Zone, and close your eyes in the Disco Nap area. Taxis are always available for a safe ride back to your hotel. Tickets are available at ticketmelon.com. About $15 per person, plus more for extra experiences.

Ku Club กู่คลับ

(facebook.com/kuclubkohphangan; 07723-8855; 100/5 Moo 1, Ban Tai)

"Celebrating not imitating," it says on the exterior of Ku Club, an open-air nightclub located on the property of The Beach Village resort. Several resident DJs entertain regularly, and they take care to play music you won't hear elsewhere in Koh Phangan. Some nights you can show up just for the sunset and a drink in the chic space resembling the original version in Ibiza, Spain. Skittle vodka and ice cream cocktails are popular among the beverage choices.

MARKETS

Chaloklum Sunday Food Market ตลาดโฉลกหล่ำวันอาทิตย์

(Chaloklum Pier; Sun from 5pm)

The quiet fishing village of Chaloklum comes alive each Sunday as its pier fills up with food stalls and, not surprisingly, souvenir vendors as well. Grab a few dishes to share: try authentic local foods like spicy fish wrapped in banana leaf or a grilled coconut sweet. If you eat before sunset you can enjoy the water views. Mellow live music often plays up on a stage.

Thong Sala Night Market (Phantip Food Market) ห้องศาลา ไนท์มาร์เก็ต (ตลาดอาหารพันทิพย์)

(098957-1857; 44/160 Moo 1, Thong Sala; 5pm-10pm)

The Phantip Food Market, or Thong Sala Night Market, is a bustling market located within Thong Sala. You can pick up inexpensive Thai foods in the outdoor section, or head to the indoor businesses in two buildings surrounding that area for more food vendors. Come Saturday night, the market gets bigger and better. It also takes on additional names such as the Saturday Walking Street Market and Talad Kao Market, as it takes up space along the Chinese Walking Street/Thong Sala Walking Street.

MASSAGES

Ayurvana Spa

(santhiya.com/kohphangan/spa; 07742-8999; 22/7 Moo 5, Ban Tai)

Poolside, or overlooking the pool or Thong Noi Pan Beach and the sea beyond, Ayurvana Spa has settings as magnificent as its treatments. The five-hour Santhiya Honeymoon Package starts with a Thai herbal steam and soak in a milky mineral bath. Then you'll be off for body scrubs or wraps, aromatic massages, foot massages in the open-air, and facial treatments.

Eyo Thai Massage เอโยนวดแผนไทย

(facebook.com/Pariphat9999; 082885-6253)

If you're after the massage, not the ambiance, Eyo Thai Massage, also referred to as Eyo Health Massage, will get what you need. This barebones facility off Hin Kong Road between the post office and Flash Express offers Thai massages, with oil and without.

Kanda Massage กานดามาสสาจ

(facebook.com/KandaMassage; 086423-2629; 79/28 Moo 1, Soi Krungthai Bank Thongsala; daily 9am-10pm)
Kanda Massage is a cheerful little house filled with massage therapists and aestheticians who work hard to please each guest. Body scrubs, aromatherapy, reflexology, waxing, manicures, and pedicures are all available, along with the expected Thai massages.

Panviman Spa ปานวิมานสปา

(panvimanresortkohphangan.com/spa.html; 082276-1895; 22/1 Moo 5, Thong Nai Pan Noi Beach)
Have your Thai massage lasts 60, 90 or even 120 minutes at this hotel spa, located up on a hill with sweeping bay views. You'll find lots of massage variety here: A Thai yoga massage builds in stretching so you'll be more flexible and your blood will flow better. Swedish, stress release, aroma well-being, Phangan herbal healer, Tibetan stone... we could go on. You might choose the Love Forever Ceremony: this pampers you both with an herbal steam infusion and Jacuzzi soak, plus the body scrub, massage type, and facial of your choice.

Papaya Massage นวดมะละกอ

(facebook.com/papaya.massage; 093743-2945; 76/10, Seetanu Rd Moo 8D; daily 10am-10pm)
Every massage bed is adorned with different fabrics at Papaya Massage, adding a lush feel to a simple space. All lotions and potions are natural, and all massage therapists have experience before joining the staff. The staff will gift you a banana and a cup of herbal tea before you depart.

Pure Relax Massage Phangan เพียวรีแล็กซ์มาสสาจพะงัน

(purerelaxspa.com; 081621-1170; 145/7 Moo 1, Thong Sala; daily 10am-11pm)

Pure Relax is a modern-day spa offering individual treatments and packages. Buy a package and you'll be driven to and from your hotel. You can get a bikini or Brazilian before beach time. You needn't be newlyweds to enjoy the Honeymoon package: this starts with an herbal Thai steam, then continues with body scrubs, body wraps, a fruit and juice break, and full aromatherapy body massages. The finale is an Indian head massage plus a facial. Did we mention you'll share a bottle of prosecco before heading back?

Revive Massage นวดฟื้นฟู

(facebook.com/WatPhoCertified; 082130-3117; 76/8 Moo 8 Ao, Sri Thanu; daily 10am-10pm)

Thai massages and therapeutic massages are on offer at Revive, and a staffer will help you figure out which is best for you at any given time. The setting is a sunny street front with platform beds lined up and separated by curtains. Coconut oil, aloe vera, and foot massages are also available.

Sanya Massage Spa ซันย่ามาสสาจสปา

(sanyamassagespa.com; 082278-6957; 126/17 Moo 1 Taladmai Rd, Koh Phangan; daily 10am-10pm)

Sanya Massage is a one-stop-shop for beauty and wellness treatments. Not only can you receive a Thai, oil, herbal compress, or other massage here. You can also have just about any part of you waxed—make that any part, indeed—and get your finger- and toenails spiffed up.

Tanaporn Massage House บ้านนวดธนพร

(facebook.com/Tanaporn-Massage-House-Thong-Nai-Pan-Noi-Koh-Phangan-247290788641353; 081078-7814; 8/29 Moo 5, Ban Tai; daily 9am-9:30pm)

A lovely setting with woods, outside views, and rich décor touches including bamboo ceilings, flowing drapes, and decorative fabrics makes this massage house a step above most competitors. The menu includes a wide variety of massages plus facials.

TEMPLES

Chinese Temple of Mercy (Kuan Yin Temple) วัดจีนแห่งความ เมตตา (วัดเจ้าแม่กวนอิม)

High on a hill near Chaloklum, this ornate three-building Buddhist temple draws visitors and locals looking for luck. The design has Chinese elements such as dragons, as well as a large Buddha. The temple was constructed in 1992, allegedly inspired by a woman's dream about fishermen needing a lighthouse. The lighthouse never happened, but the temple did, and within is a statue honoring the Buddhist goddess of mercy, named Kuan Yin, also spelled Guan Yin.

Wat Chaloklum วัดโฉลกหล้า

(Moo 7, Chaloklum)

An ornate white temple with a fanciful roof and gold accents makes Wat Chaloklum especially attractive. This temple is easy to visit, as it is situated in the center of the fishing village for which it is named. A variety of Buddha and other statues are on the ground.

Wat Khao Tham (Mountain Cave Monastery) วัดเขาถ้ำ (สำนักสงฆ์ถ้ำภูเขา)

(watkhaotham.org; 087974-9465; Soi Hua Hin 101, Khao Tao)

Seek out this little monastery on a hill above Baan Tai, overlooking the Gulf of Thailand. The building, which has ornate elements around the doors, has much to see, starting with a Buddha and elephant statues out front. It has a reclining Buddha, a temple with what looks like a footprint from Buddha, and paths through the woods. Inside, you'll see assembly and ordination halls. The facility belongs to the Thai Forest Temple family, a strict sect. While it's good manners to avoid the monks and their homes, you'll be free to seek out the abbot. You might also come across a meditation retreat (in Russian or English); in that case, shhh.

Wat Maduea Wan วัดมะเดื่อหวาน

(Near Phaeng Falls, Koh Phangan)

Five-headed dragons flank a dramatic outdoor stairway at this Buddhist temple. At the top, on a hill, you'll find a historic temple where locals come to worship. It's a white building with a red roof. A highlight is a copy of the Buddha's footprint; the original is at Wat Phra Phutthabat in Saraburi. Durian trees thrive near another building at the foot of a hill.

Wat Paa Sang Tham วัดป่าแสงธรรม

Located near the Chinese Temple, this 2014 Buddhist temple was built to honor the Taoist goddess of mercy. Also called Ph Saeng Dhamma, it is colorful and loaded with statues, plus you'll find a giant gold rock situated up a stairway outside. The forested setting is the serene backdrop for Buddha statues, including a laughing Buddha, and elephants. Dragons and Taoist gods adorn a shrine.

Wat Samai Kongka วัดสมัยคงคา

(094603-3651; Thong Salad North, Koh Phangan)

Maybe you'll show up for a meditation experience, maybe to be horrified. Either way, once you get a look at this temple's depiction of hell—the Buddhist version—you'll be glad to have added it to your itinerary. A colorful, embellished gate will greet you; once inside, you'll essentially tour Buddha's life via paintings, plus those sculptural depictions of sinners getting their due. Additional sculptures around the grounds enhance the experience. Consider hiring a guide so you can understand the Buddhist, Hindu, and Tao references.

ADVENTURES

Bottle Beach Viewpoint จุดชมวิวหาดขวด

Bottle Beach, or Haad Khuad, is a taxi boat-ride away ($5) from Chaloklum Beach or Haad Kkom Beach. Once you're on this divine strip of sand on the northern end of Koh Phangan, head behind the food vendors toward the mountain and look for a simple hand-painted sign to the viewpoint. Hoof it into the trees and keep following the path for around an hour. At the top, very carefully head onto the huge rocks to see water and hills stretching on seemingly forever. If you're a more avid hiker, you can first walk an hour or two to Bottom Beach from Haad Khom Beach, before heading up.

Viewpoint at Bottle Beach

Jungle Flight Adventure Park

(081086-8479; Baan Tai; daily 8am-6pm)

A local resident with rainforest expertise and ecological awareness runs this small park for adrenaline junkies. It has zip-line rides, jungle walks, and ATV adventures. No reservation is necessary: just find the sign at Baan Tai mountain and choose your pleasure.

Kitesurfing เล่นว่าว

(Breeze Surf Club; 082277-3374; 145/10 Moo 1 T., Ban Tai)

Feel the wind beneath your wings by kitesurfing with this local outfitter. Breeze has programs for kitesurfing (aka kiteboarding) beginners, intermediates, and skilled enthusiasts. Equipment is provided with all lessons, or you can just rent the gear if you know what you're doing. A private starter lesson for the two of you will cost about $100. Breeze also offers windsurfing and stand-up paddle boarding.

Paradise Waterfall น้ำตกสวรรค์

The beaches are so pretty it'll hard to pull yourselves away for other attractive sites. With their gushing (or trickling) waters and scenic backdrops, waterfalls are inherently romantic. On Koh Phangan, one of the best is Paradise Waterfall, located inland near the Chinese Temple. We suggest you drive over on a rental scooter by following Chaloklum Road. (Otherwise find a taxi to take you.) The water runs down a wide expanse of rock, which itself is flanked by lush green jungle; you might approach it on rental scooters—just follow Chaloklum Road. Once you're there, after taking look-at-us-in-Paradise photos, you may want to dip into the Paradise pool for a swim or swing over it on rope swings. While you're here, zip over to Phaeng Waterfall too; it's only a few minutes away. That one, within Than Sadet National Park, is steep and also jungle-encased. It's majestic during the wet season, but entirely dry—and far less exciting to look at—from December through March.

Phaeng Waterfall and Khao Ra Viewpoint น้ำตกแพงและจุด ชมวิวเขาระ

As we said above, Phaeng Waterfall is in the same general area as Paradise Waterfall and also easy to get to. Phaeng Waterfall is within Namtok Than Sadet National Park; when there's enough water, you can take a dip in waterfall pools. When it's dry, even the waterfall may be MIA. While you're in the area, seek out the Khao Ra Viewpoint, the highest point on the island. You'll start and end at Khao Ra Terrace and traverse jungle and dirt path on your way up. Your reward for the steep three-mile (4.8km) energy expenditure will be views of green mountains and blue water.

Phangan Bicycle Tours พะงันไบค์ทัวร์

(phanganbicycletours.com; 065059-2283; 99/121 Moo 1, Thongsala) See the Koh Phangan that residents know from a cycling tour. Book a morning or afternoon adventure, and you'll pedal 10½ miles (17 km), at a moderate pace, past coconut plantations, a temple, a market, and villages as a guide shares fun information. From $40 per person.

Scuba Diving ดำน้ำลึก

(sailrockdiversresort.com; 080885-7268; 15 Moo 7, Koh Phangan) Koh Phangan's only PADI Career Development Center, Sail Rock works with everyone from new divers to advanced ones, and even runs snorkeling trips. The destination is usually Sail Rock, a dive site with whale sharks, batfish, and barracuda living in the water around a giant rock. Sail Rock Divers is part of a resort in serene Chaloklum, and has air-conditioned classrooms for the schoolbook parts of instruction.

Secret Mountain ภูเขาลับ

(facebook.com/secretmountain.kohphangan; 097949-4159; 42/3 Baan Nai Suan, Moo 2, Khao Mai Ngam)

Opened to the public for the first time in 2015, Secret Mountain, or Baan Nai Suan, is a scenic spot visited by few tourists. At this elevated establishment, there's a bar, a pool (you'll need to pay to use it), and wonderful views. That's it, but it's more than enough for couples seeking a peaceful and polished home base for taking in Koh Phangan's phenomenal vistas. Thai and western meals and music are sometimes available.

The Challenge Phangan เดอะชาเลนจ์พะงัน
(challengephangan.com; daily 10am-6pm)
It's hot in Thailand, and The Challenge is a fun way to cool off. It's a water obstacle course, kind of like Survivor without having to sleep under a tree. You'll climb, swing, and paddle from beginning to end. Balancing on beams and rolling barrels are also part of the test. If you make it, you'll be rewarded with a cocktail. $18 per person.

MUAY THAI CLASSES

Exercise in proper Thai fashion by taking a class at a Muay Thai gym. **Diamond Muay Thai** (diamondmuaythai.com) gives a discount for first-time visitors, enabling you to get a taste of Thai boxing from a one-time pro. Classes are held every morning and again in late afternoon Monday through Saturday, while training programs offer a more intensive option. Train and Stay packages involve two two-hour classes a day and way more plus basic or plusher on-site accommodations **Phangan Muay Thai & Fitness Gym** (phanganmuaythai.com) has a low student-teacher ratio so even beginners get ample attention. Muay Thai, strength, and cardiovascular training are all a focus. Sign up for a private trainer for just the two of you. Dietary supplements are sold retail here. **Muay Thai Chinnarach** (muaythaichinnarach.com) welcomes everyone from first timers to elite fighters to train at the facility, which has been around since 2005. It is run by a two-time world champion, Master Chin. First-timer classes can involve a Muay Thai focus, or a blend including fitness or shedding pounds. You can train for one day or three weeks.

YOGA

Jaran's Yoga-Wellness-Eatery Yoga-Wellness-Eatery ของจรัล
(jaransphangan.com; 095962-8124; 82 Moo 5, Koh Phangan)
Yoga, wellness, and healthful food blend beautifully at Jaran's. You can join a yoga class here any day of the week (mountain views!), maybe Hatha/flow, perhaps restorative and therapeutic. You can sign up for a special event such as Ecstatic Dance, or you can indulge in holistic therapies designed for healing and relaxation. Whatever you choose, be sure to stick around for house-made, plant-based, locally sourced meals and snacks at Jaran's Kitchen.

Orion Healing Centre ศูนย์การรักษา Orion
(orionhealing.com; 07744-5966; 15/2 Moo 8, Sri Thanu)
Since 2006, founders Daliah and Ari have blended yoga with reiki, breathwork, and meditation at Orion, which also functions as a detox retreat. In drop-in classes, you can practice Hatha yoga, Vinyasa, and other disciplines. You can also book a yoga retreat together. The Orion facility includes three yoga shalas and a café, wellness lounge. and waterfront "healing oasis" with beanbag chairs and hammocks.

Samma Karuna สัมมากะรุณา
(facebook.com/sammakaruna; 08396-93794; 84/13 Moo 8, Haad Chao Phao)
Samma Karuna describes itself as an International Awakening & Healing School, plus a yoga teacher retreat. During your Koh Phangan stay, you can participate in a yoga class, or Mindfulness

in Intimacy Training.

The Yoga Retreat โยคะรีทรีท

(yogaretreat-kohphangan.com; 07737-4310; 65/4 Moo 8, Haad Salad)

Join yogis in the jungle at The Yoga Retreat, where you'll face palm-covered hills while doing your downward dogs. Drop-in classes are held every day, with Ashtanga, Yin, and Kundalini among them. If the two of you want yet more yoga, sign up for a yoga retreat lasting six to 30 days. Yoga-detox retreats are also on the schedule. On-site rooms are available if you'd like to lodge on the property during a yoga or detox retreat.

Wonderland Healing Center ศูนย์การรักษาวันเดอร์แลนด์

(wonderlandhc.com; 07737-7377; 77/7 Moo 3, Koh Phangan)

Wonderland is a healing and detox center located in a tropical environment surrounded by palm trees and mountains. It's a resort with 37 guestrooms, vegan foods, a pool, and an herbal steam sauna. It has a full calendar of daily classes like Vinyasa yoga, held in a two-story shala, as well as sound healing and nature treks. We suggest you get a Healthy Day pass (from $50 per person). That entitles you to exercise classes, two meals, and participation in whatever other activities are on the calendar during your visit. Wonderland is also big on yoga retreats and other multi-day educational experiences.

BEACHES

Bottle Beach หาดขวด

If you want the ultimate Koh Phangan beach getaway, Bottle Beach is the bomb. Located far from anything on the island's north coast, Bottle Beach is reachable only by boat taxi or a two- to three-hour hike. (You can also ride a scooter but it can be dangerous when the steep roads are slippery.) Your reward is space, solitude, clear water, and clean sand with a backdrop of palm trees and a smattering of beachfront restaurants. Hop in kayaks for a spin around, and then settle back onto the sand for more downtime.

Haad Rin หาดริน

If you prefer a scene with your sand, Haad Rin is the place for you. Once a month, the island's renowned Full Moon party takes over this beach on the peninsula jutting off south Koh Phangan. The rest of the time, the bars still line the Sea Walk, water-sports operators are at the ready to get you a Jet Ski or banana boat, volleyball nets are always available for a volley on the sand, and enough restaurants are around to keep you satisfied. The beach has two sections, Haad Rin East, or Haad Rin Nok, with more hotels and the better beach but water that's not quite as great, and Haad Rin West, or Haad Rin Nai, a more laid-back area and less of a party hub.

Haad Salad หาดสลัด

Haad Salad, or Salad Beach, may be on the same island as Haad Rin yet it is the opposite in every way. This northwestern hideaway is tranquil, with only a few hotels and restaurants. Its splendid blue-green water is so shallow that the two of you can sit right in it and relax the day away. Cliffs covered in foliage surround the beach, adding to the secluded, serene feel. The lack of motorsports helps too. Coral is right offshore so you may want to rent snorkel gear from a beachfront hotel or local dive shop.

Haad Yao หาดยาว

If you like your beautiful beach filled with amenities, then Haad Yao might be your choice. You can stay in accommodations right here on the island's northwest coast, or just visit for the day. When you need a break from the white sandy stretch that slopes down toward calm, swimmable waters, there's plenty to do. Restaurants give you choices for lunch, bars options for drinks. You can even get a massage here. The snorkeling and diving are excellent at a coral reef close to shore and, of course, you can find a dive operator without walking far.

Mae Haad and Koh Ma แม่หาดและเกาะม้า

It's hard to fathom how a simple island beach offers much, yet Mae Haad has so much going on. The shoreline itself, on Koh Phangan's north end, is gorgeous with sandy white sands. You can spend your days swinging in hammocks and receiving massages without heading to town. Great, right? Better yet, during low tide you can walk along a sandbank to Koh Ma, which is a quiet island traversable by foot. The waters surrounding Koh Ma are so rich with marine life that snorkel and dive tours favor it. You'll find red snapper, multicolor coral, and turtles.

Thong Nai Pan ทองนายปาน

You like a lively beach but not a party scene? Choose the Thong Nai Pan duo, Noi and Yai, each a cove with wonderful sunrises, plenty of restaurants, and just a moderate number of sunbathers. Swimming is good here, and sometimes there are waves to play in. Located along the northeast coast, each cove has its own personality—but, in both cases, views of jungle-topped mountains. Noi's village offers laid-back restaurants and bars. Yai has a longer stretch of sand, hiking trails, and even yoga classes on the beach. Hop on a scooter and you can bop back and forth between the two. It takes about half an hour to walk it.

PHI PHI ISLAND

Phi Phi
Island

WHY GO

Mix beauty, adventure, and the exotica of being out in the middle of the Southeast Asian Andaman Sea, and you have a getaway the two of you will warmly recall for decades to come. That's what you'll find in the Phi Phi Islands. Pronounced "pee-pee," this is a cluster of six islands within the Mu Koh Phi Phi National Park marine sanctuary. The crux, nature-wise, is stunning clear water that's exceptional for diving amid coral, set against dramatic limestone peaks that tower up overhead. If scuba isn't your scene, enjoy the water another way: Travel by boat to explore island caves and monkeys living in the wild.

All of the development is on just one island: Koh Phi Phi Don, which has two rocky sides separated by a slim mile-long (2km) landmass. That isthmus is simple: beaches on along both edges—making it look sort of like a lopsided butterfly—with tourist hotels and services in the center. That's it, just beautiful Thai beach and all you'll need to enjoy it.

In 2004 the island was massively destroyed by the Indian Ocean tsunami, which caused thousands of deaths. Koh Phi Phi Don has since been rebuilt and today is as busy as ever. You can walk essentially anywhere in the central area—to French croissants, longtail boat water taxis, hippie jewelry, and margarita-soaked Mexican dinners. For a dose of immersion with nature away from the beach, the Ao Lo Dalam viewpoint is a half-hour hike away. What you won't see: automobiles, i.e. cars or trucks. Motorbikes are the only way to get around other than a boat or your own two feet. If the island's petite central area is too populous for you as a pair, look into the east coast, Long Beach, or Laem Thong.

The other main island is Phi Phi Leh, a rocky outpost with exceptionally pretty beaches. Here, Maya Bay—featured as the eponymous sands in the 2000 film *The Beach*, starring Leonardo DiCaprio—is safe for camping, although it was closed for renovations at the time of writing. Sometime by 2022, Maya Bay is expected to re-debut with features aimed at sustainability. Ten thousand newly planted corals will inhabit its waters. Only 1,200 tourists a day will be allowed to visit; that will be controlled via electronic tickets. Viking Cave is worth a detour; not only is it pretty, it's a source for the birds' nests used in Chinese specialty dishes. The other islands are Koh Vida Nok, Koh Phai (Bamboo Island), Koh Young (Mosquito Island), and Koh Bida Nai; none is inhabited. To learn more about any and all of the Phi Phi Islands, check the official tourism website, visit phiphi.com. It has useful information.

As for romance, the Phi Phi islands have a smattering of sensational options. You can go with classic moves like candlelit dinners on the sand, or adventurous ones like snorkeling with sharks. For more pedestrian chill-pill time, play pool at a hangout. Want to light up the night? Watch one of Koh Phi Phi's many fire shows at night. You can also join the audience of a Muay Thai boxing match, then put on padded gloves and play-punch it out in front of an audience.

Day trips are a big appeal here, either by joining a tour group, or, if you have the cash, chartering a private tour. You can spend a day at another island beach, hop around to a variety of scenic spots via boat, or get active with activities such as hiking or diving. Some require a long water taxi ride or hike to reach: Your reward is an entirely new experience.

Maya Bay

HOW TO GET TO PHI PHI

The journey is half the fun. Most visitors reach Phi Phi via Phuket's Rassada Pier ($10 to $25 per person, depending on the season) or Krabi's Klong Jirad Pier ($12 to $15 per person). Both have ferries that take 90 to 120 minutes, although floatplanes and speedboats decrease time on the water for a higher fee. Ao Nang and Koh Lanta also have transportation here. If you're staying in accommodations far from the center of Koh Phi Phi Don, email your hotel in advance to pre-arrange the final leg of your trip. Get more info at phuketferry.com.

GETTING AROUND

It's not just cars and trucks that are absent on Phi Phi Don. Besides motorbikes, you won't see transportation other than feet and boats. To get around you'll walk and hike, hop in a water taxi or hire a private boat.

WHERE TO STAY

You'd think with only one inhabited island, choosing a locale would be easy—especially since that island is less than 4 square miles (10 km²). Think again. Koh Phi Phi Don has distinct vibes in its four main neighborhoods.

Phi Phi Don area map

Laem Tong

If the thought of dodging crowds makes Phi Phi Don sound appalling, book a stay in Laem Tong. You can only get to this tranquil spot on the island's northeastern reaches by water taxi from Tonsai Village, which takes up to an hour, or, sometimes, by ferry from Krabi or Phuket. (*Definitely* get specific instructions from your hotel before heading here.) The area, which means "golden bay," has a few accommodations, leaning towards high-end, plus a palm-shaded 0.6-mile (1km) beach. If you're into water sports, choose a resort that has equipment. Overall, this is the place to spend time just for the two of you, soaking in the sun, snorkeling the nearby reefs, and lunching alfresco on seafood cooked by members of the local community, known as sea gypsies. You can also participate in a hotel cooking class or sand volleyball match, while fine-dining options make for special dinners, especially private dinners for two on the sand. End-of-day views from the Phi Phi Sunset Pier are particularly special.

Long Beach

If you want a laid-back beach vibe but with access to the island's tourist facilities, Long Beach is your best bet. This part of Phi Phi Don is a short but rugged stroll away from Tonsai Village most people take a five-minute water-taxi ride instead. The beach itself is a soft white sand strand that faces southwest—the view includes the limestone cliffs of Phi Phi Leh, and the Shark Point snorkeling site is nearby. Rent a deck chair, head out in a kayak, enjoy side-by-side massages... the pleasures here are few, simple and divine.

Phi Phi Central Area

If you want easy access to everything, this is the place for you. Restaurants, bars, dive shops, tour boats, souvenir shops, and, of course, lodging facilities are all here. You can roll out of bed from your cottage, B&B, or hotel and walk to essentially any activity, whether that's getting a tattoo (henna or permanent) or buying a sundress. You'll see longtail boats lined up by the dock, along with motorboats ready for the day's excursions. Need breakfast first? Bakeries and cafés with trendy coffee drinks await.

Tonsai Village is the heart of the hub, located between Loh Dalam Bay and Tonsai Bay. Loh Dalum is mighty vibrant too—in tropical-island terms at least, followed by Tonsai East, a strand of white sand that's home to affordably priced accommodations plus some stores and restaurants. Choose Tonsai West if you want to flip between serene and social.

Phi Phi East Coast

If nature is what kick-starts your amorous intentions, Phi Phi's East Coast is for you. If not, skip to the next section, since it takes two hours by foot (a half-hour by boat) to get here from Tonsai Bay. This blissful, rugged area has mountains, a small town with places to eat and drink, and access to narrow beaches along the 2½ miles (4km) of coastline, with few people on them. Within this eastern part of Phi Phi Don, Rantee Bay has the island's most placid water, and Loh Bagoa (aka Loh Ba Koa) is noteworthy for its mangrove forest.

ACCOMMODATIONS

Panmanee Hotel โรงแรมปานมณี $

(panmaneehotel.com; 07581-9379; 55 Moo 7, Ao Nang)
The spiffy Panmanee Hotel is located in the center of it all, near Ao Tonsai Pier and the Koh Phi Phi Viewpoint. You'll have all you need at a budget price, including air conditioning, Wi-Fi, a fridge and a TV.

Phi Phi Island Village Beach Resort พีพีไอส์แลนด์วิลเลจบีชรี สอร์ท $$$

(phiphiislandvillage.com; 07562-8900; 49 Moo 8, Ao Nang)
Seventy acres (28 hectares) of tropical foliage with a half-mile-long (800m) beach will be your playground during a stay at Phi Phi Island Village. With four restaurants, three bars, a dive center,

swimming, and a spa, any time here will rev up the romance factor. Upgrade to one of 12 hillside pool villas and, in addition to soaking up the Loh-Ba-Gao Bay views, you can start the day with a private Jacuzzi soak. Plus, a staff member will deliver breakfast and high tea daily. With thatched roofs and plenty of space to roam, this luxury escape has a rustic feel. You may even happen upon a hammock here and there. Ask about private dinners for two on the beach, and get pampered with a Lover's Care Package at the Wana Spa—a milky Jacuzzi soak, coconut scrub, and aromatherapy massage. Check the website's Promotion's page for deals.

Phi Phi The Beach Resort พีพีเดอะบีชรีสอร์ท $

(phiphithebeach.com; 062191-4945; 177 Moo 7, T., Ao Nang) Choose the type of villa best for your time together—some have a partial or full sea view, and settle into serenity at this quiet resort along Long Beach. Your days will blend as you meander from oasis-style swimming pool to Thai massage, from dining room to beach bar—where a fire show entertains guests after dark. Your villa will have its own balcony with a sunbed. Blacktip Scuba is a PADI dive facility located on the property. Thai wedding packages include a Long Drum procession; Western-style packages a floral arch. Honeymoon deals feature a candlelit beach dinner and a three-hour boat tour.

P.P. Erawan Palms Resort ป. เอราวัณปาล์มรีสอร์ท $

(pperawanpalms.com; 07581-8713; 45/9 Moo 8, Leamtong Beach) What makes P.P. Erawan Palms most special? Maybe it's the beachfront massage hut with side-by-side beds. Or perhaps the Goodview Restaurant, one of three dining areas, with sunset views of a pier and cliff. Then again, the swim-up bar alone may make your stay. Or just the fact that you can only reach this Laem Tong Beach haven by boat. Bottom line: dreamy. Book yourself a room or bungalow with a balcony along the half-mile (800m) white-sand beach, in the verdant garden, or up in the hills, and prepare to escape every care. Check the website for promotions.

Zeavola Resort ซีโวล่ารีสอร์ท $$$

(zeavola.com; 07562-7000; 11 Moo 8 Laem Tong, Ao Nang)
Zeavola Resort is so romantic that you'll swoon from the beachfront setting and the teakwood suites, for starters. The eco-friendly hotel is set along white and sandy Laem Tong Beach, with accommodations in villas, many nestled into a lush hill. Your villa might have an outdoor rain shower or even its own plunge pool. You can dine in either of the restaurants, or have the staff bring your dinner to your villa or the beach for a private candlelit repast. It gets better: You can book a sunset cruise for just the two of you, which will transport via longtail boat to a neighboring island, where staff will set up a wine tasting with small bites for you to enjoy together as you watch the sun go down. Back at the resort, all spa treatments are offered in tandem, adding to the romance. Try the Local Wave: Over three hours, you'll be massaged or scrubbed with sensual oils selected for loyalty, fidelity, fascination, or undying love. Zeavola also has beach seating, a pool, diving, a boutique, and a fitness center. Reserve in advance for special pricing.

BREAKFASTS

Aroy Kaffeine อรอยคาเฟอีน $

International
(095257-5452; 125/48 Moo 7; daily 9am-5pm and 6pm-10pm)
In its new location a ten-minute walk from Tonsai Pier, Aroy is an easy choice pre- or post-dive. The coffee choices are well-respected by connoisseurs. Lovingly prepared breakfasts and other foods have helped this place grow a strong reputation. The

granola is made with both maple syrup and peanut butter, and is served with fresh fruit. Pancakes with Nutella are a treat too. You'll dine near a lagoon in a sweet little building with a V-shaped roof. Aroy has its own granola, nut butters, and other packaged items under the JaJa Coffee & Spice label. Pick up the Golden Milk powder as an immunity booster.

Mon Cafe Ma Boulangerie มนต์คาเฟมาบูแลงเกอร์ $
Bakery
(facebook.com/Mon-caf%C3%A9-1198176336927247; 089706-2702; 125/25 Moo 7; daily 7am-8pm)
Breakfast, brunch, and baked goods are the canvas upon which Mon Café builds its business. Enter through the cheerfully colored street-front entrance and sit in the artsy feeling dining room with an open kitchen—or take over an outdoor table—and dig in. Take a break over a coffee, croissant, sandwich, or big ol' plate of ham 'n' eggs. Mon Café serves smoothies, too.

Phi Phi Bakery พีพีเบเกอรี $
Bakery
(facebook.com/phiphibakery; 07560-1017; 97 Moo 7, Ao Nang; daily 7am-5pm)
Start your day here with pancakes topped with bacon, a donut fresh out of the oven, or a plateful of eggs Benedict. Run by the same family since 1989, they also serve up croissants, Danishes, desserts, and old-fashioned birthday cakes, along with coffee. Later in the day, try the salads, pizzas, and sandwiches.

Unni's Bar & Restaurant $
Thai, International
(unnisrestaurant.com; 091837-5931; 125/36 Moo 7, Ko Phi Phi; open daily)
With the tagline, "Tequilas, limes and good times!", you know

Unni's will be a fun stop for dinner. (And breakfast is a sure bet here, too.) The local unit of a three-restaurant chain, this one is attractive with dark-wood floors and furnishings, and crisp, light walls. Start with a bagel and a bloody Mary. Or get The Dream with your eggs: it's a Frappuccino-like refreshment with espresso, chocolate, Bailey's, and whipped cream. An acai bowl is served with muesli, sliced banana, and exotic fruit. Avocado toast is one of many vegetarian options.

LUNCHES AND DINNERS

ACQUA Restaurant Phi Phi ACQUA Restaurant พีพี $

European, Thai

(acquarestaurantphiphi.business.site; 083181-6915; 125/18, Ao Nang; daily 11:30am-10:30pm)

Whatever you're in the mood to munch on, you'll find it at ACQUA. A rustic-chic stop for casual bites, you can take a break from your beach bliss for muesli, waffles, chorizo, or pasta—or massaman curry and tom yum soup. Grab a drink or three to go with it—hey, no one's driving—and stay for the live music.

Anna's Restaurant ร้านอาหารแอนนา $

Thai, European

(facebook.com/pages/category/Thai-Restaurant/Annas-Restaurant-512900225414475; 085923-2596; 111 Moo 7, Ao Nang; daily 10:am-6:30pm)

Expats, diners and tourists flow in and out of Anna's all day long, whether to fuel up with a British breakfast or get a taste of Thai cooking, all at fair prices. The dining room is reasonably attractive with dark woods contrasting with light floors and walls. Fans are located throughout. There are a few tables outside the front door.

Dow Restaurant ร้านอาหารดาว $

Vegetarian, Thai

(dow-restaurant.business.site; 082201-1220; 125/34 Moo 7, Koh Phi Phi; daily noon-10:30pm)

Located near Phi Phi Island's Ao Tonsai Pier, Dow is casual and friendly. Within its unfussy brick-walled dining room you can eat essentially any kind of food you want, and for a low price. Vegans can be assured that the plant-based meals here have no surprises such as fish sauce. Sit back and enjoy.

Efe Mediterranean Cuisine Restaurant ร้านอาหาร Efe Mediterranean Cuisine $

Mediterranean, Turkish

(facebook.com/eferestaurant; 095150-4434; 125/22 Moo 7, Soi Babai; daily noon-10pm)

Turkish foods are the specialty at Efe, so expect specialties such as kebabs (try the fire-seared lamb kofte kebab), falafel, and hummus here. Pizzas, wraps, and burgers are available, too. The small dining room has warmly hued walls and Middle Eastern fabrics; outdoor seating is available.

Grand PP Arcade

Vegetarian, Healthy, International

(facebook.com/GrandPPArcade; 080538-2608; 104/16 Moo 7, Ao Nang; daily 8am-3pm, 6pm-1pm)

Airy and filled with plants indoors and out around its wooden tables and chairs, Grand PP Arcade is essentially an attractive diner with vegan and non-vegan foods. Have a hearty American-style breakfast, or a meat-free curry, and be sure to take a couple of cupcakes back to your hotel. The cooks have a great attitude about adapting any dish to meet your dietary restrictions.

Italiano Bar & Restaurant $

Pizza, Italian

(italianorestaurantphiphi.com; 07560-1065; 92 Moo 7, Mueang; daily 11am-11pm)

House-made pasta, thin-crust wood-fired pizzas, grilled seafood with Mediterranean flavors, and plenty of wines to go with them, bring regulars to this Italian restaurant. Burgers, Thai dishes, and paninis are also on offer in this restaurant set in the hub of Ton Sai Village. The dining room has a festive lightness.

Mama Ping มาม่าปิง $

Seafood, Asian

(facebook.com/pages/category/Local-Business/MAMA-PING-1446774478980483; 092701-2933; Ao Nang, Mueang; daily 9am-9:45pm)

You're on an island: so eat at the beach. Mama Ping, self-described as a Sea Gypsy Restaurant, serves up bountiful platefuls of food right off the sand. The dining area is draped with festive beads, while the seafood is right from the water. And the staff will hack the top off a coconut any time you want a refreshing drink.

P Monster Burger เบอร์เกอร์มอนสเตอร์ $

Burger

(facebook.com/MonsterBurgerPhiPhi; 088008-8299; 125/29 Moo 7; daily 12am-10.30pm)

You don't have to travel halfway around the world to get a big juicy burger with interesting toppings. But you can. Monster Burger lets you choose the patty and your own toppings. That patty could be beef, but soft-shell crab, fish, shrimp, chicken, and meat-free falafel or mushroom options are also available. Select a type of bun, the cheese, the veggies, the sauce, the side dish, and then the extras, such as caramelized onions, smoked salmon, or avocado. The space itself is contemporary-casual with basic tables and benches, plus a mix of light and medium woods. It's not a place to linger, fingers intertwined.

October Resto ตุลาคม Resto $

Seafood, Thai

(october-resto.business.site; 081797-7177; 90 Moo 7; daily 8:30am-11:45pm)

Sample seafood fresh from the sea at this extremely informal restaurant with a wide menu. Take a seat in the light, bright dining room, choose your meals from the photos of dishes that cover the walls, and dig in. Choices include barbecued lobster with butter and garlic, steamed fish with lemon sauce, sweet Thai pancakes, tuna sandwiches, and vegetarian items such as coconut soup with mushrooms.

Only Noodles ก๋วยเตี๋ยวเท่านั้น $

Thai

(Ao Nang, Mueang; daily 10:30am-10:30pm)

A bright little spot that's decorated more like a kindergarten classroom than a restaurant, Only Noodles has a strong rep for serving up just noodles, and great noodles at that. Every dish is prepared to order, so if you want squid, vegetables, chicken, or beef, just ask, and the cooks will jump into action. Your choices are pad Thai, or yellow, glass, or "big" noodles prepared as you request. Big portions, low prices.

Pad-Thai Restaurant ร้านผัดไทย $

Thai

(facebook.com/pages/category/Local-Business/Pad-Thai-restaurant-Phi-Phi-Island-121940251209308; 084846-3921; Loh Ba Kao Beach)

Quietly set behind the Phi Phi Island Village Beach Resort, this restaurant with its plain name dishes out a legendary version of the iconic Thai pasta dish. The rustic restaurant is open-sided and the cooks fire up the food in the open air. Despite the name, Pad-Thai serves up a broad menu including non-noodle dishes, much of its fresh seafood. Cocktails and coffee are also served.

P.P. Wang Ta Fu ป. หวังต้าฝู $

Japanese

(facebook.com/PPWangTaFu; 07581-6588; 88, 88/1 Moo 7, Ao Nang; daily 11am-9:30pm)

When you need a sushi fix, P.P. Wang Ta Fu has the chopsticks ready. Sashimi, nigiri, maki, temaki... each has its own section on the menu. And if one of you is craving spaghetti instead? Worry not: Start with garlic bread, then go for pasta carbonara. You'll find Thai, American, and Chinese flavors here too, all in a friendly little storefront space.

DESSERTS

Qoori Qoori Café $

Cake, Ice Cream

(facebook.com/qooriqooricafe; 081951-6767; 125/131 Moo 7, Ban Tai)

Simple but scrumptious, the Qoori Qoori Café serves house-made ice cream, desserts like chocolate fudge cake, and tropical fruit drinks. Maybe get a scoop of vanilla with chunks of mango on top, or an orange-mango soda to drink. Playful signage outside leads to a simple counter-service atmosphere with few tables. Pay mind to the sign, "Vacation Calories Don't Count." You can take a board game from the shelf and play while you snack.

The Mango Garden สวนมะม่วง $

Mango, Thai

(themangogarden.com; 091989-2965; 73 Moo 7 T., Ao Nang)

Walk past the bold and clever bulb-illuminated signage outside The Mango Garden and you'll find fresh and trendy sweets inside. The original unit of a dessert concept now based in Bangkok, The Mango Garden offers authentic and multi ethnic twists on mango desserts. You can get an exceptionally satisfying mango with sticky rice, knowing the mangos are of the Nam Dok Mai variety and the rice is from "the best rice fields in the Mae Chan District, Chiang Rai Province." Have the dish with white rice, or go for blue, colored with butterfly pea flowers. Or you can go in another direction— maybe mango-coconut pudding or mango waffles. Smoothies and coffee drinks are also available. Wooden crates are used for décor, representing the way mangos are transported.

Mango with sticky rice

COOKING CLASS

Pum's Cooking School โรงเรียนสอนทำอาหารของปุ้ม
(th.pumthaifoodchain.com/cookingschool.html;   07560-1425; 125/40 Moo 7, Ao Nang)

Chef Pum has been cooking Thai food since she was a child, and through traveling she has expanded her repertoire tremendously. Today she runs a namesake restaurant plus an educational arm that teaches important info about herbs and sauces, how they relate to chicken and vegetables, and "how to be lazy in the kitchen," as the website says. Most days, the school has three classes, and you can choose from the 40 curries, stir-fries, and other dishes that appeal most to the two of you. Options range from Pum's Mini-Me, for mastering one or two recipes, to Pum's Grand Chef, a full-day experience featuring Pum herself and her signature dishes.

Land of Smiles

The term "Land of Smiles" is often used to describe Thailand. Maybe we're just buying into the marketing hype, but the people do come across as friendly.

The saying has substance behind it, too. Just as Alaskans allegedly have names for various kinds of snow, Thais describe specific types of smiles. *Yim yaw* is a playful "I told you so" version while *yim cheun chom* displays pride or admiration for someone. The smiles are sometimes phony. As for people, Thais tend to hide negative emotions behind up curled lips. If you'll be in Thailand for an extended period, you'd do well to learn how to look behind the smile to discern what someone is truly feeling. Or, go with the flow and move on conflict-free. The goal of some insincere smiles is to avoid confrontation.

Plus, being friendly gets the job done. Tourism is a tremendous part of the Thai economy. Giving visitors a big ol' smile before taking them on a taxi ride, serving a meal, or heading up a tour to a deserted island is good for business.

BARS

Banana Bar บานาน่าบาร์

(bananabarphiphi.blogspot.com; 087330-6540; 117/13 Moo 7 Soi, Koh Phi Phi; 11am-1am)

In case the views aren't stunning enough around the island, head higher to Banana Bar, located on the roof of the Banana Sombrero Mexican restaurant in Tonsai Village near Pagarang Residence. Climb up the steep spiral staircase and find a grungy looking space. You'll be seated on floor cushions which themselves are atop worn-out wood, along with bamboo shalas (open-sided structures with pointy roofs). Arrive in time to see the stunning sunset views. Maybe you'll catch a hula hoop contest (enter and that'll keep you laughing for years), a movie, or a fire show. Get daily updates on Twitter at @BananaBarPhiPhi.

Reggae Bar Phi Phi เร้กเก้บาร์พีพี

(reggaebar-bar.business.site; 091034-6598; Opposite the Main 7-Eleven, Main Town Centre 125/55, Ton Sai Bay; daily 6pm-1am)

Usually drinking is the main point of a bar, and Reggae does have five bars, yet here it's the sideshow. Reggae Bar Phi Phi hosts Muay Thai (Thai boxing) matches every night. First the professionals play but then—Oh yes!—you can get in the ring yourselves. You'll receive a bucket of something spiked if you do, and might receive a medal too. This Central Tonsai establishment also has TV screens and pool tables.

SPORTS BAR

The Dubliner Irish Pub ผับไอริช Dubliner

(the-dubliner-irish-pub-bar.business.site; 091034-6598; 25/81 Moo 7; daily 8am-1am)

The Dubliner is the opposite of tropical—it's like an Irish-American sports bar in any U.S. city. You'll get whiskey and Guinness and plenty of TV screens, for sure, not to mention a hearty English breakfast, or a plate of pad Thai. Live sports events play for all to watch, a DJ spins tunes, and drinking games make the crowd friendly. Are you two competitive? If so, you can both take the Burger Challenge. Finish the 1.7-pound (800g) whopper in 30 minutes and it's free.

BEACH BARS

Moonlight Beach Bar มูนไลท์บีชบาร์

(facebook.com/pages/category/Bar/Moon-Light-Bar-Phi-Phi-Island-370026623416933/; 089725-4341; Ao Nang, Mueang; daily 8am-1am)

It's kind of odd to pair a palapa roof with sleek lounge seating and pulsating techno music, but hey, anything goes at the beach. Moonlight has a club feel to it, and beach mats with backs, so you can sit up facing the sea, drink in hand, and let you meld beach-world and club-world into one.

Slinky Beach Bar สลินกีบีชบาร์

(facebook.com/slinkybeachbarofficial; Central Loh Dalum Beach; daily 7pm-2am)

Remote Asian islands aren't generally about the night scene, but Slinky Beach Bar is the exception. This is a place to let loose. Staffers give out free shots early on to get guests grooving, and from there your on-the-sand experience might involve dancing to EDM DJs and live musicians; it may also mean body painting or involve buckets of liquid courage. So get your dancing shoes on—actually, flip-flops are better in case you're on the sand—and stick around for the fire show that has the crowd going wild.

Sunflower Beach Bar & Restaurant

(facebook.com/Sunflower-Beach-Bar-Restaurant-Phi-Phi-83729338647; 080038-3374; 102 Moo 7, Ao Nang; daily 11am-11pm)

You'll hear talk of fire shows at Sunflower, and of course they're worth a detour. But, to get the most out of your visit, come early and plan to hang around. Sunflower is right on Loh Dalum Beach and it's what we'd call and extended-stay kind of bar. Lay side by side in a hammock or sala; order drinks, nab a book, shoot some pool, borrow a board game, or have a bowl of curry. The playlist is ever-changing, and at night live acoustic music takes over. This is what downtime is all about. (If you must use your smartphones, you'll find the Wi-Fi relatively speedy here.)

The Beach Bar เดอะบีชบาร์

(facebook.com/The-Beach-Bar-Phi-Phi-Island-104126027665073; 061212-5892; Moo 8, Baan Lo Ba Kao; daily 1pm-1am)

Don't dress up. The Beach Bar is an ultra-ultra-ultra-unfussy place to unwind—with the help of alcohol. "Chill out hippie style". Unfinished-wood furnishings, colorful pendants, plants, and some Jenga and Connect Four... that's it. Peace, man.

BEACH CLUB

Ibiza Beach Club อิบิซาบีชคลับ

(facebook.com/IbizaBeachClubPhiPhi; 081968-3640; In the middle of Loh Dalum Bay; hours vary)

You'll feel like you're on Phuket, not remote Phi Phi, at Ibiza Beach Club. This scene involves DJs, dancing, drinking, and fire shows on the sand.

NIGHTCLUB

Carlito's Beach Bar & Nightclub บาร์ริมหาดและไนท์คลับของ Carlito $

(facebook.com/carlitosphiphi; Tonsai Village, Ao Nang; daily 11am-2am)

This nightspot, located in a Tonsai Bay hotel hub, is best known for its "fire poi dancing," which involves a chain and flames. Guests can learn the technique during daylight, then try it out after dark as a DJ spins upbeat music. The stage is set on the sands of Chaokoh Beach and patrons watch from plastic chairs. The rustic two-building establishment is a chill hangout all day long, a seller of buckets mixing booze and energy drinks. It also serves food and offers beach yoga sessions.

MASSAGES

Baan Sabai Thai Massage บ้านสบายนวดแผนไทย

(baansabaithaimassage.wixsite.com/home; 07581-2256; 125/10 & 125/13 Moo 7; daily 9am-11pm)

Rejuvenation treatments are the name of the game at Baan Sabai, and after all that sunbathing, diving, and dining, you may want to go the pampering route. While this spa isn't fancy, it offers a range of services including gel manicures, eyelash tinting, and Brazilians. Hot-stone, milk cream, aloe vera, and of course traditional Thai massages are among the body services on offer.

The Pier Massage นวดท่าเรือ

(094709-3545; Ao Nang; daily 10am-11pm)

When you want a massage but not a splurge, The Pier Massage will take care of your aches and pains. This strip-mall business has a team of practitioners who work their magic, with mattresses lined up neatly along a wall. Request spots side by side and ooh and aah in unison as your body's kinks and aches are released.

TOURS

Blanco Boat Party ปาร์ตีเรือบลังโก

(facebook.com/BlancoBoatPartyThailand; Blanco Beach Bar & Hostel, 276 Moo 7, Loh Dalum)

If you have a yen for time out on the town, bring that party onto the water. A local bar hosts the Blanco Boat Party, where the 18+ crowd can tour the islands while drinking and listening to a DJ's tunes. Snorkel, paddleboard, and kayak gear are included. During the six-hour excursion on an unfancy boat, you'll encounter Monkey Beach, Viking Cave, Maya Bay, Loh Samah Bay, and Pelah Bay. The expedition ends with a buffet dinner. About $40 per person.

Full-day Tour by Speedboat ทัวร์เต็มวันโดยเรือเร็ว

(Phi Phi Travel and Tours, phiphitravelandtours.com, 11am-7:30pm)

Join a group and tour all five of the Phi Phi Islands by speedboat. You'll start the day with a (safe-for-people) snorkel with blacktip reef sharks around Phi Phi Island, then relax on a Bamboo Island beach. After a lunch of fried rice and fruit, swim and snorkel around more islands, stop by the Viking Cave, snorkel more, see magnificent Maya Bay, and watch a sunset over the Andaman Sea. Not quite romantic enough? Choose an after-dark bioluminescent swim in Tonsai Bay; the water appears to glow in the dark, thanks to microorganisms that live in it. Snorkel gear, life jackets, water, soft drinks, lunch, fruit, the national park fee, and the services of an English-speaking guide are included. About $130 for both of you.

Long Tail Boat Phi Phi เรือหางยาวพีพี

(longtailboatphiphi.com; 091213-4005; 125/2 Moo 7, Ao Nang)

Take a half- or full-day private longtail boat tour from a company that will customize the itinerary to your liking. Snorkel equipment, life vests, fresh fruit, and bottled water are included. The half-day Bamboo Island Route (about $110 total for both of you) for example, will take you to Long Beach with views of Phi Phi Ley, then Loh Moo Dee Bay, Rantee Bay, and Bamboo Island, for snorkeling by a coral reef. A full-day three-island package (around $225 for two people) will cover Wild Monkey Beach, Viking Cave, two emerald lagoons in Phileh Bay, Los Samah Bay, Maya Bay (from a distance), and Rantee Bay, ending the day with snorkeling at Shark Point and a stop at another Monkey Beach.

Longtail boats at Phi Phi Don

Shark Watch Tour ทัวร์ชมฉลาม

(The Adventure Club; diving-in-thailand.net; 081895-1334; Moo 7, Muang)

Add a once-in-a-lifetime experience to your once-in-a-lifetime trip to Thailand. On the Shark Watch Tour, you'll swim amid blacktip reef sharks with no more than snorkel equipment and a wetsuit. Experienced guides from The Adventure Club, a five-star PADI dive operator, will guide you—although you must have prior snorkeling experience. Up to seven of you plus crew will depart Phi Phi Island in the morning to see the sharks. You'll receive a briefing beforehand, a 90-minute swim with the non-dangerous creatures, and learn more about sharks on the way back.

HIKING AND VIEWPOINTS

All those tree-colored limestone peaks that flank Phi Phi Don's resort area and contribute generously to the island's beauty? They are ripe for climbing. The most popular viewpoint is actually a trio of three consecutive areas. You even have two choices: a longer, less steep route, or a quicker, more challenging one. If you're not big on hiking, you can also drive to the viewpoints atop those mountains on a motorbike, or hire a motorbike taxi for round-trip transportation. Either way, the views along the way to the top trail are lovely. You'll need to pay a small entrance fee at the first viewpoint. There, you'll have access to restrooms, and you can pick up a snack to power up for the rest of the trip.

To hike to the viewpoints, begin at the eastern end of Tonsai Village, and follow signs for Viewpoint 1. A second sign to follow says Tsunami Evacuation Route. Climb the stairs and continue walking to the first viewpoint, where you'll have a terrific view that encompasses both Loh Dalum and Tonsai bay, which are divided only by a thin isthmus yet have water of completely different colors. Continue to Viewpoint 2 for another few minutes to get an even better take on that scenery, and ditto to Viewpoint 3, about 10 minutes further along, which will also have the thinnest crowds. You can buy a drink at a little shop here before heading back. If you're on wheels, find the paved road near the Phi Phi Arboreal Resort and follow the signs.

BEACHES

Packed, secluded, or in-between, every Phi Phi Island beach has distinct attributes.

Loh Dalum Beach

On the northern edge of Phi Phi's thin center strip, Loh Dalum Beach is the other place to join a crowd and get a tan. That said, the daytime hours here are relatively sedate, actually, with sunbathers and kayakers populating the half-mile (800m) beach, lapped by placid emerald water. It's fun to sun yourselves, grab a local lunch from a hawker, and maybe rent yourselves a banana boat and head into the bay. Once the day ends, Loh Dalum Beach is yet another center for nightlife, as the beach bars fill up with young adults ready to get the party started.

Loh Moo Dee Beach

Early and late in the day, Loh Moo Dee Beach is a true getaway. The fifth-of-a-mile (300m) of white sand and transparent water on the southern part of the island's east coast are pristine, and few people will be around. Signs say the property is private, but stay put; it's owned by the government. Soak up the sun (or stay in the shade), buy lunch at a shack, and find fish in the water. The snorkeling is superb. Midday is an exception to Loh Moo Dee being a dreamy beach. At that time, tourists arrive in off-putting numbers and the boats that bring them are noisy. If you're staying in the central part of the island, to get here you can take an interesting walk, ride a motorbike, or hail a longtail boat taxi.

Tonsai Beach

Tonsai Beach is two destinations in one. It's pretty, for sure, and conveniently located in the center of the strip that's the heart of the island. Although the sand, sea, and views are stunning, this beach gets crowded with revelers. It's fun, but not necessarily tidy or tranquil. Plus, the water is occasionally not swimmable when the tide recedes. If you want quiet, head to the silkier, calmer western edge. At night, the fire shows might be worth a detour. Tonsai Beach is also near rock-climbing sites. You'll see backpackers in hiking shoes alongside bikini-clad party girls.

Viking Beach

Viking Beach, on Tonsai Bay, is a tiny tenth-of-a-mile (160m) shaded beach in a great location. It's to the east of busy Tonsai Beach yet way quieter, as it's home to a single resort, which has a restaurant. If you're fit, you can walk to Tonsai and Long Beach, to the west. A little jungle will be part of your adventure.

HUA HIN

Hua Hin

WHY GO

When you want a break from Bangkok's bustle, head to Hua Hin. It's a lovely beach community on the Malay Peninsula loaded with open-air attractions, not to mention the leisurely pace so alluring in waterfront resort towns. Today, this long-time fishing port is also a hub for sumptuous spas, beachside seafood dinners, and more night markets than you'll have time to explore. Much of your stay will be outdoors, whether gobbling up street foods, walking uphill to visit a giant Buddha, or swaying to the sounds of an open-air concert.

In recent years, Hua Hin has become, say, The Hamptons for city folks, or—if you believe the marketing message—the "Thai Riviera." It is certainly an easy and accessible way to mix up your Thai vacation.

That's in part because it's close. You can get to Hua Hin in as little as three hours. Bangkok residents with extra cash have long taken the trip to this stretch of beaches along the Gulf of Thailand. Recent years have seen visitor and residents' numbers increase thanks to the construction of new housing. This has brought with it a surge in services: More trains travel here now, new shopping malls have popped up, the number of golf courses continues to rise, and ancillary businesses of all types have expanded in numbers.

Romantic activities take many forms here. You can hole up in a spa suite that has its own pool. Gaze at the ocean over cocktails at a rooftop bar. Learn to prepare green-mango salad in a private class. Hang out at the beach on oversized daybeds. Or meander market stalls for small gifts by local artisans. If golf is your game, Hua Hin has plenty of options, so plan tee time for two.

Hua Hin doesn't seem to have an official tourist office, but you can find useful information at tourismthailand.org/Destinations/Provinces/Hua-Hin/240 and tourismhuahin.com.

HOW TO GET TO HUA HIN

There's an excellent range of transportation options for getting to Hua Hin from Bangkok since the destination is not on an island that can be accessed only by boat. You can fly, take the train or bus, or even drive or hire a taxi from the city. You'll find more details on all options at kiwitaxi.com/blog/how-to-get/bangkok-hua-hin.

Bus If you're traveling by bus from Bangkok, the Southern Bus Terminal has the most public busses to Hua Hin and the Mo Chit terminal has fewer. It's about $1.60 each way. If you're leaving directly from Bangkok's Suvarnabhumi Airport, you can take a VIP coach to Hua Hin via airporthuahinbus.com for $10 per person.

Car It takes 2½ to three hours to drive from Bangkok to Hua Hin, via routes 35 and 4. You can rent a car in the capital.

Flying Hua Hin Airport (minisite.airports.go.th/huahin; huahin@airports.go.th) is small and flying to it from Bangkok is rarely your best bet. AirAsia and Thai AirAsia are its only airlines; at the time of writing, commercial flights run only on weekends, and only to and from Chiang Mai, Bangkok, and Udon Thani. Takeaway: Flight flexibility is limited. Expect more options within the next couple of years because an airport expansion is currently underway.

Train Several trains a day run from Bangkok to Hua Hin's train station, which is in the town center. Most take 4¼ to 5½ hours. Comfort, speed, seat reservation options, and price levels vary. Choices are Ordinary, Rapid, Express, and Special Express.

Prices range from $4 to $30. You can book tickets at railway. co.th, thailandtrains.com, and 12go.asia. More tracks are under construction so you should have more options by the end of 2022.

Taxi One option worth considering is to hire a taxi from Bangkok. A private taxi service, in a regular car or a fancy one, costs $60 and up. Start with thaihappytaxi.com and tommytaxibangkok. com/huahin. You might be able to haggle a street cab for less— assuming you find a driver willing to go that far.

GETTING AROUND

With a decent pair of flats, it's possible to traverse Hua Han by foot. There are plenty of other options available, which are especially handy if you want to explore the nearby communities of Pranburi and Cha-am.

Bicycle and Motorcycle Hua Hin is small enough that a pair of bicycles might be your best wheels, and rental places abound. Motorbike rental is also available. Ask your hotel concierge or desk clerk for nearby recommendations.

Motorbike taxi Motorbike taxis are easy to find, quick and cheap.

Rental Car Budget, Avis, and local companies have autos to rent, ideal if you want to explore beyond Hua Hin.

Samlor A bit like giant bicycle rickshaws, in a samlor you'll snuggle into the back seat and a driver will peddle up front. You won't spend more than a few dollars, even with luggage.

Samlor driver waiting for passenger

Songthaews Songthaews are like pick-up trucks where the backs are turned into open-sided shuttle busses. For less than a dollar total, the two of you can hop a ride from one beach area to another.

Tuk-tuks Open-sided transports similar to golf carts with a driver, tuk-tuks are a big deal in Thailand. A short trip will cost a couple of dollars.

WHERE TO STAY

Hua Hin area map

Bo Fai

Head toward the airport, about 15 minutes outside of Hua Hin, and you'll find Bo Fai. This is where locals live, alongside ex-pats who've settled in the area. In exchange for dreamy sprawling resorts, you'll have interesting restaurants, bars with local color, community-oriented businesses, and decent prices—not to mention the opportunity to explore the condos and houses both posh and plain where people reside full-time. Golfers often choose this area because it's close to the greens. While the beach is nearby, life in Bo Fai centers around town—paved streets, tile-roofed buildings with trees interspersed, and mountains beyond.

Central Hua Hin

If you like to step out the door and be near people, food, markets, and malls, choose your accommodations here. You'll be close enough to Hua Hin's namesake beach that you can hit the sand whenever the mood strikes, yet you'll pay less for your room and have sightseeing and nightlife options practically outside your front door.

Cha-am

Cha-am is less of a scene, so it's your best bet if you're seeking quiet time alone. Most hotels have good restaurants, bars, and activities, so you won't need to go elsewhere to fill your time. You can stay in fancy digs here, or moderately priced ones. However, you'll be disappointed if you're looking for a wilder night scene. Cha-am is about 16 miles (26 km) to Hua Hin, so you're unlikely to make the trip daily.

Khao Takiab

Khao Takiab is elusive, in a wonderful way. It's tiny, and it's filled with personable boutique hotels and bungalows. It's also peaceful, giving off a real lazy-beach-days vibe, yet it has the charm of its fishing village origins. You'll be tempted to hike up Chopstick Hill, aka Monkey Mountain, as a golden Buddha statue with palms facing out lives at the park accompanied by plenty of macaques. A couple of temples are around there too. If you like to dine out often, you'll need to hop on a cab or tuk-tuk now and then because Khao Takiab is so small that it is short on dining options. Khao Takiab is two and a half miles (4 km) from central Hua Hin.

Pranburi

About 15 miles (24 km) south of Hua Hin, Pranburi is the beach resort town you want if you're enamored by beach basics: sand, sun, sea. If you care more about malls, markets, and bars, choose another neighborhood. If you're looking for a luxury resort for your romantic vacation, there's a good chance it'll be located here—and filled with amenities that'll make you feel like royalty. The beach is uncrowded, and you'll see mountains across the water. Pranburi is also a convenient launching spot for a day trip to Khao Sam Roi Yot National Park, which is a 45-minute drive away.

ACCOMMODATIONS

Cape Nidhra Hotel Hua Hin โรงแรมเคปนิทราหัวหิน $$

(capenidhra.com; 03251-6600; 97/2 Petchkasem Rd, Hua Hin)
The Cape Nidhra offers so much that you may never leave the property during your visit. Your room will be a spacious suite with its own pool and wooden deck, perfect for when it seems like too much trouble to venture down to the ocean front swimming pool. The activities here are all adults-oriented: Sign up to learn Muay Thai boxing, fruit carving, or Thai massage. For meals, choose from the Euro-Asian menu and enjoy the pool views. You can also opt for room service—maybe you can eat au naturel in your private pool?—or a beach dinner for just the two of you under the stars: The setting is dramatically romantic, with an illuminated open-sided tent. Be sure to make time for a whiskey-and-cigar date at the rooftop bar; you'll have Gulf of Thailand vistas.

G Hua Hin Resort & Mall จีหัวหินรีสอร์ทแอนด์มอลล์ $

(ghuahin.com; 03251-5199; 250/201, Soi 94 Phetchkasem Rd, Hua Hin)
The G is all about convenience, with oodles of extras. The boutique hotel's 79 guestrooms and suites are bright, large, and modern, with a balcony that has a private whirlpool tub or a daybed overlooking the saltwater pool. What's more, you'll be adjacent to an upscale shopping mall and near the major tourist sites. A free shuttle service will get you around town. Also at The G: a fitness center, a formal restaurant, a hair salon, and a nightclub. That nightclub, EAST, is a sexy spot on the roof with a backlit bar and lounge seating.

Let's Sea Hua Hin Al Fresco Resort $$$

(letussea.com; 03253-6888; 83, 188 Soi Hua Thanon 23 Nong Kae, Hua Hin)

This entire resort is designed for adults and staffed with Holiday Hosts who are trained to dote unobtrusively. During your stay, you'll be in one of 40 suites, each with its own rooftop garden or poolside balcony. Adjustable ambient lighting and Bose Bluetooth speakers make it easy to get the vibe going. Dine on Thai specialties like roasted duck curry with lychee and pineapple at the namesake restaurant, and unwind at the three bars and lounges—at the Sand Lounge, you can sip and snack in the pool or on the sand. Indulge in a Sea Blue couples' treatment at the Gaia Spa, which is open-air yet air-conditioned. For under $40 daily a piece, you can upgrade to the Z-Luxe Club package, which offers a host of VIP services. For instance, you'll be entitled to have happy hour cocktails and canapés at the beachfront bar each evening, and complimentary access to Thai massage and culinary lessons. Bonus: Gaia Spa therapists will apply sunblock for you during a 15-minute procedure.

Long Beach Inn ลองบีชอินน์ $

(longbeach-thailand.com; 086064-5841; 223/4 Moo 4 Sam Roi Yot National Park, Hua Hin)

You'll get bang for your baht at the Long Beach Inn, a value-priced hotel with a lot to offer near Sam Roi Yot National Park and Dolphin Bay. This inn has only 11 rooms, divided among three villas, and each has a terrace. The Honeymoon Suite includes a whirlpool tub. Lots enhances the deal: TV and minibar in the room; a swimming pool; bicycles to borrow; and a lounge with pool table and darts. You can even rent golf clubs or order a Thai massage.

My Way Hua Hin Music Hotel มายเวย์หัวหินมิวสิคโฮเทล $

(mywayhuahin.com; 032516-5567; 20/35 Soi Hua Hin 108, Hua Hin)

The My Way hotel is like a Hard Rock at a Motel 6 prices. The entire resort is infused with music references: you might have Rolling Stones artwork on your bedroom wall, or a Frank Sinatra likeness; a lamp will resemble a saxophone; and an acoustic guitar may hang in the room. Feel like serenading your S.O. with a ukulele, or even a piano? It'll be delivered to your doorstep. Rock, jazz, or classical, this hotel will help get your groove on. The My Way has a pool, free shuttle service, a fitness center, and a breakfast restaurant. Each lodging unit is air conditioned with a fridge, TV, and DVD player. It's located near the beach and the Vana Nava water park.

Putahracsa Hua Hin พุทธรักษาหัวหิน $$

(putahracsa.com; 03253-1470; 22/65 Naeb Kaehat Rd, Hua Hin)

Sleek, white, and modern with a pool that appears to drift into the sea, Putahracsa brings urban flair to the shores of a quiet beach. All guestrooms abut the pool, while the villas—which have open-air tubs or pools—are near the sand. You can have a barbecue prepared by a private chef and served on your terrace or pool deck. If you prefer to get out, enjoy a similar feast-for-two at the Oceanside Beach Club & Restaurant. Learn to cook at on-site classes; practice yoga, chanting, and meditation with a pro; and, when you're ready to scoot around town, use the free bicycles or tuk-tuk service to see the sites.

Ruenkanok Thai House Resort เรือนกนกไทยเฮาส์รีสอร์ท $

(ruen-kanok-thai-house-th.book.direct/en-us; 03253-7112; 21/14 Nong Kae-Takiap, Hua Hin)

The Ruenkanok is a modest hotel. That said, this hideaway has quite a bit to recommend it. Thai-style villas are spread around the lushly landscaped property, and guests are greeted with a welcome drink. Once settled in, you can use the pool, which is adjacent to an ornamental pool filled with Thai sculptures and lily pads. Your accommodations will be air conditioned with a TV and CD player as well as slippers. You'll be a third of a mile (536m) to the beach. When hunger strikes, walk over to the Khingkanok Café for familiar Thai flavors. If you'd rather do your own cooking, use the grills by the pool. Grab a pair of bicycles when you feel like taking a ride.

BREAKFASTS

Amber Kitchen ครัวอำพัน $$

Buffet, Thai, International
(marriott.com/hotels/hotel-information/restaurant/details/ hhqmr-hua-hin-marriott-resort-and-spa/5749498; 03290-4666; H 107/1 Phetchakem Rd, Hua Hin; daily 6:30am-11pm)
Bright and tailored with upholstered seats and a wall of floor-to-ceiling windows, Amber Kitchen is an all-day restaurant at the Hua Hin Marriott. For breakfast, there's an a la carte option, but the buffet has too many tempting foods to pass up. You'll find the bacon and eggs you love back home alongside Thai and other Asian specialties. Fruit juices, cold cuts, live cooking stations, a raw bar, and desserts are all part of the experience.

Bliss cafe & restaurant บลิสคาเฟแอนด์เรสเตอรองท์ $

European
(facebook.com/blisshuahin82; 097991-0177; 178/221 Soi Hua Hin 82 Phetkasem Rd, Hua Hin; Fri-Wed 9am-8pm)
Light, bright, sweet, and flowery, bliss looks like a café in an American coastal resort town. The feminine setting is the place to unwind over a cup of coffee or tea, home-baked goods, and meals such as peach-cinnamon pancakes, or a European breakfast with

eggs, bacon, sausage, and hash browns. There's also pizza and pad Thai, not to mention beer, pasta, steaks, and salad. Uplifting tunes play in the background.

Hangtime Lounge $

European

(facebook.com/hangtimelounge; 080341-8706; Lemon house 51, Tambon Hua Hin; Tue-Sun 7am-8am)

From a Sundowner smoothie with ginger, honey, orange, pineapple, and coconut oil, to a lamb filet dinner with thyme, pomegranate, and potato... it feels like you can get almost everything at Hangtime. Wraps, bagels, muffins, and full breakfasts are served in a contemporary-casual dining room with wood tables and chairs. The German chef-owner is a kiteboarder (and martial artist), hence the assorted water-sports items hanging from the walls and ceiling.

SEA Harmony Eco House & Café $

Asian

(seaharmony.business.site; 085109-2680; 8/10 Takiab 6 Nong Kae, Hua Hin; Thu-Tue 9am-8pm)

House-grown organic fruits, vegetables, and herbs are woven into meals at this restaurant within the SEA Harmony Eco Lodge. Sea Harmony is also a destination for coffee drinks, as the beans are from Thailand's Chiang Rai district and roasted locally. Breakfast choices include a gado gado salad made with Indonesian vegetables, poached eggs, and a peanut dressing; and the Issan Breaky, featuring Thai sausage, a Spanish omelet, vegetables, and sticky rice; a Thai breakfast soup; and a full English breakfast. The chefs are happy to help guests with gluten, celiac, and other dietary requests.

LUNCHES AND DINNERS

31 Burger 31 เบอร์เกอร์ $

Burger, American

(facebook.com/31burgerhuahinbranch; 083290-0159; 62 4/62 Naebkehardt Rd, Hua Hin; daily 10am-10pm)

Whether you want a big beefy burger, a fish fillet on a burger bun, or a vegan patty made from chickpeas, 31 Burger will set you up. Buns of white, red or black, a variety of viscous toppings including "hot mayo" or truffle sauce, beers... it's a good choice for an inexpensive American-style meal.

DAR Restaurant ร้านอาหาร DAR $

Barbeque, Thai

(darrestaurant.restaurantwebexperts.com; 095767-8827; 222, 61 Petchkasem Rd, Hua Hin; 10am-9pm)

Real Thai people cook real Thai food at DAR, two restaurants a minute apart: One is a freestanding building with table service, and the other is a counter-service operation in a row of counter-service operations. Both are near the Grand Night Market. DAR specializes in the local take on barbecue but the wide menu has many other options. Delivery is available.

Hua Hin Vegan Cafe & Wine หัวหินวีแกนคาเฟแอนด์ไวน์ $

Vegan, Asian, International

(facebook.com/huahinvegancafe; 092536-6241; 100 Soi Hua Hin 74/2, Hua Hin; daily 10:30am-10pm)

Vegan foods with Asian and Western flavors bring plant-based diners to this café with indoor and outdoor seating. The bright interior has wooden spoons and strings of garlic festively hanging from above, with light woods creating an inviting space. Coffee, smoothies, pizzas, and full entrées are on the menu. Vegan desserts are also available.

Jek Be-Ak เจ๊กเบ – อค

Seafood, Thai

(03251-3672; Dechanuchit Alley, Hua Hin; daily 6:30am-1pm, 5:30pm-8:30pm)

This plain yet bustling restaurant with seats inside and out, Jek Be-Ak gets rave reviews for its Thai dishes, especially the seafood ones. Expect to wait in line for your steaming dishes of soft-shell crab, shrimp with noodles, and pork with basil. You'll feel like a local. Prices are low.

La Terrasse Seafood La Terrasse ซีฟู้ด $$

Romantic, Seafood

(facebook.com/La.terrasse.hua.hin/; 03251-1393; 11 / 1 Naresdamri Rd, Hua Hin; daily 10am-10pm)

Bountiful plates of fresh seafood are the specialty at La Terrasse, which is also beloved for its expansive dining terrace set out over the water. Some nights are Dine & Dance affairs with live music. Lunch deals with an appetizer, entrée, and wine, beer, or coffee are a good deal.

Luna Lanai Beach Bar $$$

Romantic, Thai

(facebook.com/LunaLanaibytheSea; 03270-8000; 1573, Petchkasem Rd Sheraton, Cha-am; daily 10am-10:30pm)

Why have your meal in a ho-hum dining room when you can have it overlooking the sea? Luna Lanai has seats perched above the water; even better, you can arrange for a romantic culinary rendezvous right on the sand for just the two of you. Seated under a draped frame and surrounded by hurricane lanterns, you'll indulge in a four-course meal. Expect dishes like spicy red seafood curry with pineapple, or stir-fried chicken with cashews and dried chilis.

Mamma Mia — Cucina Italiana & Pizza $$

Pizza, Italian

(mamma-mia-italian-restaurant.business.site; 03251-2250; 8/4 Naresdamri Rd, Hua Hin; daily 11:30am-10:30pm)

Share a wood-fired pizza, or go all-in with pasta, steak, lamb chops, and desserts, at this award-winning Italian restaurant with outdoor seats overlooking the Gulf of Thailand. Meats and many other ingredients are imported, while the breads, pastas, and sweets are created in-house. The menu is extensive.

Moom Muum Noodle & Rice Café ร้านก๋วยเตี๋ยวหมูต้มยำ $

Thai

(facebook.com/moommuumhuahin; 04556-5692; Soi 94, Hua Hin; daily 10am-9pm)

If you're the types to moon over noodles and rice, Moom Muum will give you a fix. The setting is simple: just a few seats at tables that look hand-painted, all open to the street in nice weather. The food is the typical pad Thai, soups, stir-fried noodles, and curries, here prepared with a special warmth and sold at modest prices.

Ogen Hua Hin Restaurant ร้านอาหารโอเจนหัวหิน $

Vegan, Middle Eastern

(ogen-hua-hin-restaurant.business.site; 092260-0376; 250/131 Petchkasem Rd, Soi 94 opside hotel Narawan, Hua Hin; daily 11am-10pm)

Specializing in Middle Eastern foods, this simple space in the center of Hua Hin—which opens to the street—includes many vegan selections on its menu, in addition to fish and meat dishes. Falafel, hummus, and baba ghanoush are among the plant-based options.

Oraya's Restaurant ร้านอาหารอรยา $

Thai

(02543-6835; 23/2 Selakam Alley, Hua Hin; Mon-Sat 11am-10pm)

A thin no-nonsense family-run staple with knick-knacks to warm the space up, Oraya's is a beloved local go-to for low-priced green chicken, garlic prawns, yellow curry, and other Thai flavors. Each dish is prepared to order.

Royal Indian Restaurant $
Vegan, Indian
(huahinindianrestaurant.com; 02221-6565; 392 1 Chakkraphet Rd, Wang Burapha Phirom, Hua Hin; daily 10am-11pm)
Delve into Indian curries and vegan specialties like *channa masala* and *jeera aloo* at the Royal, where the vegan section of the menu lists a dozen options. You can have your meat-free meal inside the bustling dining room with floor-to-ceiling windows, at a sidewalk table, for take-out, or even delivered to your hotel room.

The Beach at Anantasila Restaurant & Bar เดอะบีชทีอนันตศิลา เรสเตอรองท์แอนด์บาร์ $$
Romantic, International, Thai
(thebeachatanantasila.com; 03251-1879; Nong Kae, Hua Hin; daily 7am-10pm)
Order the multicourse Thai menu, a la carte Western items, or the four-course Romantic Dining Experience with an amuse-bouche (free tiny appetizer) and a palette cleanser (about $125/couple). No matter your choice, you'll be thrilled with your table, shaded if necessary, overlooking the beach and water. This hotel restaurant also has a selection of wines and an assortment of signature cocktails.

The Corner Steakhouse & Churrascaria $$
Steakhouse, Vegetarian, Brazil
(facebook.com/the.corner.steakhouse.churrascaria; 097221-7890; Soi 112, Hua Na, Hua Hin; daily 11am-9pm)
Brazilian steakhouses are renowned for their variety of grilled

meats served from skewers at the table. The Corner takes the concept further, urged on by the owner, the son of Brazilian gauchos. Here you can indeed get your red meat fix, with grain-fed Australian ribeye and grass-fed strip loin, but that's just the start. You can also help yourselves to a vegetarian buffet, Thai classics, pizza slices, and even the makings of a coffee bar. Greek salad, snow fish fillet, spaghetti Bolognese... the menu is extensive and some items are all-you-can-eat. The dining room is woodsy and attractive. Entertainers often perform.

The Social Salad สลัดสังคม $

Healthy, Thai, European

(thesocialsalad.org; 081809-5083; 1/8 Chomsin Rd, Hua Hin; daily 8:30am-9:30pm)

It's easy eating green at The Social Salad, where healthy Western and Thai foods make up the menu. Locally sourced and organic foodstuffs are used when possible. You can go fitness-club light here with smoothies and design-your-own salads. Plenty of heartier choices are available too, including Italian pastas, Thai curries, and British-inspired fish and chips. The dining room is homey with shelves full of knick-knacks.

Tsunami Sushi Buffet Huahin สึนามิซูชิบุฟเฟต์หัวหิน $

Buffet, Japan

(tsunamisushibuffet.com; 03272-1122; 143/34 Soi 75/1, Phetkasem Rd, Hua Hin; daily noon-8:30pm)

Like its peers, the Hua Hin branch of this buffet chain specializes in Japanese food. For one set price, help yourselves to all the sushi rolls you want, as well as sashimi, cooked skewered proteins, and more—200 items in all.

DESSERTS AND COFFEES

Baan Gliwang บ้านกลีวัง $
Cake
(baan-gliwang.business.site; 03253-1260; 11 Naebkehardt Rd, Hua
Hin; daily 9am-6pm)
Baan Gilwang takes the cake when it comes to dessert in Hua
Hin. Sit under a patio umbrella and relax to ocean views in a lush
garden setting with a cool beverage and a slice of cake. Fresh
coconut gateau is a signature item, and blueberry cheese pie is
also popular. Chocolate comes in many forms, such as a double
fudge brownie, layer cake, and a square with caramel and nuts.
Savory items including crab dishes are also available.

Bello Dolce $
Gelato, Italian
(bellodolceicecream.com; 03251-0114; 36/139 Nongplub Rd, Hua
Hin; hours vary)
A chain with both stationary ice cream counters and mobile tuk-
tuk units, Bello Dolce sells gelato made with Italian ingredients as
well as sorbet blended with locally raised fruits such as banana,
passionfruit, and mango. It sells other desserts as well, so you
might pick up an American-style chocolate chip cookie or a
tiramisu. Can't choose? Just ask, and you can have your ice cream
scoop sandwiched between two cookies. You'll also find Bello
Dolce products on local restaurant menus, and at markets and
festivals around town.

Chatchai Market ตลาดฉัตรไชย
Thai
(Dechanuchit Rd, Hua Hin; 03251-3885; daily 5am-4pm)
Forget fancy restaurants. You can bond in bliss tasting local flavors
at Chatchai Market, opened in 1953. Stroll through at your leisure,

eyeing the whole fish, skewered meats, dried shellfish, and items you'll never be able to name. (If you're squeamish, ask questions to avoid dishes like pig's blood soup.) Some of Thailand's luscious fruits can be found dried here, the perfect carry-along snack for your daily travels. You can also sample local desserts, likely handmade by the purveyor. Prices are reasonable. Our choice: *roti gluay*, a fried banana pastry with condensed milk on top. Cooking utensils make for practical souvenirs. And, heck, pick up some fresh flowers for the hotel room on your way out.

Eighteen Below สิบแปดด้านล่าง $

Ice Cream

(facebook.com/18belowicecream; 081751-7057; 4 62 Naebkehardt Rd, Hua Hin; weekdays 11am-5pm, weekends 11am-8:30pm)

This ice cream purveyor sells its wares in a spiffy, bright shop with minimalist white seating, a little garden area, and a neon sign reading, "So Scooping Good." Another sign promises the ice cream is "home-crafted" from premium ingredients with neither preservatives nor additives. Whether you want a simple scoop or an ice-cream float, you can choose from flavors such as black sesame, mint leaves and chip, lemon cheesecake, "meaty coconut" or Thai tea. Slices of cake and pie are also available.

Il Gelato Italiano $

Gelato, Italian

(IL-Gelato-Italiano-Icecream-Hua-Hin-386905678102422; 03264-6526; 19/4 Hua Hin 61 Alley, Hua Hin; daily 10:30am-9pm)

A colorful sign greets you at Il Gelato Italiano, setting the tone for a cheerful storefront with cartoon graphics on the wall and seating inside and out. In Hua Hin since 1993, Il Gelato dishes out Italian-style ice cream. You can get a straightforward cup or cone, or even a banana split. If you're feeling adventurous, try a Blue Lagoon (it's swirled in a cup and topped with a paper umbrella);

a waffle with ice cream and whipped cream; or, inexplicably, an ice cream creation described as, and resembling, spaghetti Bolognese. Another oddity is "ice cream fried eggs." Caramel, orange, "blue sky," and cappuccino are sample flavors.

Mae Nong Nooch แม่นงนุช $

Thai

(facebook.com/MaeNongNuchHuaHin; 03251-1035; Dechanuchit Alley, Hua Hin Province; daily 7am-6pm)

You'll find mango with sticky rice throughout Thailand, but this is where you *need* to try it. Mae Nong Nooch has been making and serving this iconic dessert since 1941. This family-run shop has a devoted following, in large part because the signature dish is devotedly created using classic cooking techniques: The rice is steamed with pandan leaves and mixed with sugar, salt, and cream of coconut immediately upon being cooked to the right texture. Arrive hungry, because you'll also want to try the coconut tart, and the peanut-filled sticky rice dumpling. Or the fried crab when that's available. As the window sign says, "First we eat, then we do everything else."

Swensen's สเวนเซ่นส์ $

Ice Cream, American

(swensens1112.com/en/#!; 02103-5999; Swensen's Hua Hin Clock Tower, Hua Hin; daily 10am-8pm)

Swensen's has long served up all-American ice cream sundaes in North American malls. In Hua Hin, you can get a taste of it near the Clock Tower. Take a seat and order a classic Tower, which is a tall stemmed parfait glass loaded with sweets, banana slices, and other toppings, or opt for a Unicorn or Mermaid indulgence. Every day is sundae here. Be sure to check out the flavor of the month.

The Chocolate Factory โรงงานช็อกโกแลต $

Chocolate, Cake

(facebook.com/chocolatefactoryhuahin; 061172-8887; 95/4 65 Petchkasem Road, Hua Hin; daily 11am-10pm)

Bright and modern with a pitched ceiling, the Hua Hin outlet of The Chocolate Factory is a terrific place for the two of you to gorge on sweets together. Sauce painting—designs artfully created out of sauces on the plate— is part of each dessert's presentation. You might start with a proper meal, maybe a pizza, steak, or grilled sausages, but then get serious with sugar. White or dark chocolate lava cake will make your day, or try the sweetcorn crème brûlée. The Bingsu Chocolate is a mound of sweetened shaved ice encased by a tepee of chocolate candy sticks; it also has chocolate chips on top and a shot glass of chocolate milk alongside. Order a box of chocolate candies to go at the retail shop, or maybe a truffle or 10. There is live acoustic music on Saturday nights.

Together Bakery & Café $

Cake

(03253-1059; 72/3 De Chanuchit Rd, Hua Hin; daily 10:30am-11pm)

While at the night market in which it's housed, stop at the Together Bakery—together of course—for cake and coffee. Pick up a packaged cake to go, or sit under shade to enjoy a slice on the spot. The specialty is a soft coconut cake layered with coconut cream and infused with the gentle flavor of pandan. Strawberry milk cake and Thai tea cake are other options. Coffee drinks, milkshakes, wine, and cocktails like whiskey sours are also on the menu.

Coffees

If just a standard pot or pod cup of coffee won't do, despair not. Hua Hin has plenty more ways to chase the perfect bean. **Osot**

Place (facebook.com/osotplace) is a cute, chilled street front spot near Hua Hin Temple where a young crew brews, cools, and adds artful foam designs to a variety of java drinks. You'll know the origin of your beans, and can get specialty beverages with, say, Glenlivet and whipped cream. **Yummy Corner Noodle & Café** (facebook.com/Yummyhuahin) is a homey, woodsy, purposely cluttered retreat with a chalkboard explaining the specifics of its coffee drinks. It serves food too, and even has a noodle menu and a list of ice creams. But in-the-know caffeine fiends stop in for the lattes, americanos, and macchiatos. Prices are low. Both a roaster and a purveyor of coffee drinks, **Velo Café Rock 'n Roast** (facebook.com/velocafehuahin) is a delightful choice for an espresso, cold brew, or iced latte with honey, maybe accompanied by a toasted sandwich, lemon Madeleine, or almond éclair. Narrow and snazzy with a multicolor wood floor, mustard walls, and white accents, this counter-service establishment often has jazz coming through the speakers. **Black Monster Café** (facebook.com/ blackmonstercafe) comes across as higher-budget than its peers, with a striking marquee outside punctuated by the playful likeness of a black monster. Inside, "where all the mischievously good things happen," you can order at the counter for a piccolo, latte, or affogato, made with a bean type you select. Cakes, smoothies, and a few savories are also available.

FOOD TOUR

Feast Thailand ฉลองประเทศไทย

(feastthailand.com; 095461-0557; 11, 186 Soi 43 Hua Hin, Hua Hin) Let locals lead you Hua Hin's best food. This food tour company is owned by Thai residents and is run by knowledgeable guides. Join a group tasting or arrange for your own private tour for two. Six itineraries are available, including the three-hour Sunset

Local Eats ($50 per person): You'll head first to a market where you can watch chefs stock up for their restaurants, then visit two restaurants and a street vendor, sampling 15 different foods. Fermented pork sausages, steamed pork and rice dumplings, Chiang Mai noodles, salted crusted grilled fish in lettuce leaves, and assorted sweets are some of what you'll try. Another option, the Foodies Food Tour ($50 per person), is a morning excursion. It starts with a Thai breakfast of pork and rice porridge, and Thai iced coffee, which will wake you up for the day. Next up are a couple of yellow curries, a braised duck specialty, green papaya salad, and 12 other samples from various parts of the country.

COOKING CLASSES

Bamboo Thai Cooking Class Hua Hin แบมบูไทยคุกกิ้งคลาสหัวหิน
(bamboothaicooking.com; 092517-8422; 1337/29 Phetkasem Rd, Huay Sai Tai, Cha-am)
The teacher of this school, Anya, has spent her life in both Thailand and Australia, so she can teach the best way to prepare the Thai foods she grew up with while speaking English. She grows herbs and produce too, and uses some of what she reaps in her cooking lessons; you'll get to tour her garden. Her friendly classes, $42 a person, include transportation to and from your hotel, an e-recipe book, a lesson in making curry paste, and the cooking of four dishes, three savory and one sweet. Your menu might feature pandan chicken, papaya salad, Thai custard, coconut soup, or prawn tom yum soup. Express classes are similar but involve making only a curry paste and one dish.

Hua Hin Thai Cooking Academy สถาบันสอนทำอาหารไทย หัวหิน
(huahinthaicookingacademy.com; 086004-0839; 210/4 Phetkasem Rd, Soi 82, Hua Hin)

Whether you select the beginner or vegetarian four-hour curriculum ($45 per person), you'll receive not only instruction but also hotel pick-up and either a market tour or a fruit-carving lesson. A full-day alternative involves 10 dishes and costs $85 per person. The academy has English-speaking instructors and invites you to select one each of curry, stir-fry, soup/fried rice/noodles, and salad or dessert before arriving.

Spice Spoons ช้อนเครื่องเทศ

(anantara.com/en/hua-hin/restaurants/spice-spoons; 07742-8300; 43/1 Petchkasem Beach Rd, Hua Hin)
Within the Anantara resort, Spice Spoons' A Culinary Journey is a one-day program (9am to 2pm; $80 per couple). Book two days in advance, and upon arriving you'll have a sort of immersion experience. Start with a welcome drink, then tour a hydroponic garden, mushroom house, and market, learning about local ingredients, tasting snacks, and drinking Thai coffee. You'll make something with gold leaf at the Huay Sai Tai Temple, then return to the hotel to prepare and eat the dishes you selected—maybe steamed sea bass, massaman beef curry, or spicy prawn salad. You'll depart with a certificate, an apron, a cutting board, and recipe cards. The cooking portion is held in a kitchen with lagoon views. Add-on options: napkin folding, table setting, and fruit and vegetable carving.

Thai Cooking Course Hua Hin หลักสูตรการทำอาหารไทย หัวหิน

(thai-cookingcourse.com; 081572-3805; 19/95 Petchkasem Rd Soi 19, Hua Hin)
This school has been teaching visitors to prepare classic Thai dishes since 1999. The classes are hands-on and begin with a market tour. The owner and primary instructor is a woman named Beau who grew up in her parents' restaurant kitchen. Today she

shares her skills within a professional kitchen. Each lesson involves learning how to choose ingredients, prep, and cook them. In the one-day course ($50 per person), you'll spend time in the Chatchai Market before making coconut cream and curry paste plus a few dishes, and tasting them at the end. The Express Class ($32 per person) is a shorter version. Book a session for just the two of you ($215): You'll prepare four dishes in addition to curry, plus get a market tour, e-book, and more.

NIGHTLIFE

Soi Bintabaht

You can split a bottle of bubbly in your room or clink cocktails at a rooftop bar or beachfront lounge. But when you want a night out in Hua Hin, Soi Bintabaht is the place to go. Also known as Walking Street, presumably for the monks who walk through daily at dawn, this is a hub for hedonism after dark—relatively speaking. Strut through the main drag and weave amid the various narrow roads and you'll happen upon big bars and small ones, flashy nightclubs, and the occasional restaurant. Outdoor seats beckon guests to each venue. So, if you want to watch the big game, dance, sip a Guinness, or get a tattoo or massage, just wander until you find the best crowd for you.

LIVE MUSIC

A couple of drinks, a good music act... always a great way to spend a night out together. Here are some Hua Hin highlights. **Hua Hin Beer Garden** (huahin-beergarden.com) is an outdoor bar with alfresco seating. Musicians perform every Tuesday, Friday, and Saturday, and pageants and dance parties are held here. Thai and international foods are served. Grab seats at a long table and make new friends at **Father Ted's Irish Pub &**

Steakhouse (facebook.com/fathertedsthailand). The Irish-owned restaurant serves food all day long, and has live music some evenings, televised sports games on others. Quiz Night is fun too. Someone's making music on stage every night at the dark and cozy **London Bar & Guesthouse** (facebook.com/London-Bar-Guesthouse-1657985231155153), so grab a spiked cider, wine, or beer and chillax. Or dance. The tunes are mostly classic rock 'n' roll. With an indie night, and bands called names like Greasy Café, you're always apt to hear new sounds at **Ra Ruen Chuen** (facebook.com/RARUANCHUNBAR). Head outside, where rows of tables with plastic chairs set up big crowds for an evening of drinking and humming along to whoever's on stage. Go for a Caribbean beach bar vibe at **Reggae Bar Hua Hin**, where you can shoot pool and play foosball while listening to musicians. There are two good nightspots inside the Hilton Hua Hin Resort & Spa. **Hua Hin Brewing Company** (hilton.com/en/hotels/hhqhihi-hilton-hua-hin-resort-and-spa/dining) has burgers, steaks, and live sport screenings, while its **Beer House** offshoot (hilton.com/en/hotels/hhqhihi-hilton-hua-hin-resort-and-spa/dining) has guests dancing daily to R&B, rock, and 90s tunes from the live band in a dark-wood venue.

BARS

EAST Rooftop
(facebook.com/easthuahin; 094937-0586; G Hua Hin Resort & Mall, 250/201 Petchkasem Rd, Hua Hin; daily 5pm-midnight)
Located on top of a hotel, EAST Rooftop is the perfect start or end to an evening. Dim lighting with sensual backlit accents set an in-the-mood cadence. Cuddle together on a sofa under the stars and take in the views of buildings and mountains where you might hear techno music, or arrive for Candy Pink Night (dress

accordingly)... either way, you're bound to wind up on your feet dancing.

Elephant Bar ช้างบาร์

(centarahotelsresorts.com/centaragrand/chbr/restaurant/ elephant-bar; 03251-2021; Centara Grand Beach Resort & Villas Hua Hin, 1 Damnernkasem Rd, Hua Hin)
Whether you're 18 or 80, you'll feel all grown up at Elephant Bar. It's an open lobby lounge within a hotel, with upholstered living room-like seating. It's known for the Heritage Fizz cocktail, and you can choose from many whiskeys. A musical trio entertains with relaxing music, often jazz.

Le Bar Francais Hua Hin Wine Bar

(facebook.com/LebarfrancaisVineHuahin; 03251-6318; 12/3 Damnoen Kasem Rd, Hua Hin; daily 11am-12:30am)
This sophisticated little storefront is a quiet spot to split a bottle of wine. It is said to have one of Hua Hin's best selections of wines from around the globe. You can also pick up a bottle or case to bring back to your hotel.

Vana Nava Sky วานานาวาสกาย

(vananavasky.com; 03280-9949; 129 Petchkasem Rd, Nong Kae; weekdays 5pm-midnight, weekends additional hours)
Located more than half a mile (800m) off the ground—with a through-the-glass view down—this sky-high 27th-floor bar was designed by Ashley Sutton and the cocktail recipes are courtesy of "mixsultant" Joseph Boroski. Take in the views—up and down, ocean and buildings. Toast your luck at being at the top of the world, and snack on Thai, Japanese, and Mediterranean small bites.

SPORTS BARS

El Murphy's Irish Bar & Grill Bar & Grill ของ El Murphy

(facebook.com/El-Murphys-Irish-Bar-Grill-120311454646796; 03251-1525; 25 Selakam Alley, Tambon Hua Hin; daily 7am-1:30am)

When you need a night of jeans, Ts, and no pressure at all, this is the place to slow your pace. El Murphy's has plenty of brews on tap plus a wellspring of whiskeys. Grab some suds, maybe a bite (the breakfasts are huge), and see what's happening on the 16 high-definition TV screens. Live music often plays. There are a few seats outside.

Take 5 Sports Bar & Live Music ใช้เวลา 5 สปอร์ตบาร์และดนตรีสด

(facebook.com/take5huahin; 02438-8392; 1/83 Nong Kae-Takiap, Nong Kae; daily 11am-11:15pm)

Talk about having it all. At Take 5 you'll be able to catch the big game from back home on any of seven big screens, or dance to live music or whatever tunes the DJ spins. Or you might have a meal of Indian or Chinese food, local Thai dishes, or the kinds of pub staples you love. Grab a beer, take it indoors or out, and shoot some pool. Special events are sometimes held on the roof.

BEACH CLUBS

Oceanside Beach Club โอเชียนไซด์บีชคลับ

(oceansidebeachclub.com; 03253-1470; 22/65 Naeb Kaehat Rd, Thap Tai)

Oceanside is a stylish way to spend your beach days and nights, come sun- or candle-light. Oversized white daybeds on a wooden pavilion face the ocean under shade, and open-air table seating in similar hues, under a roof, is great for dining. Order drinks and dinner, or time your visit for a themed night, maybe an opera supper or tapas, or an event where everyone wears all-white attire. The daytime music is soothing, while after dark musicians tend toward acid jazz and Latin sounds.

Shoreline Beach Club ชอร์ไลน์บีชคลับ

(facebook.com/ShorelineBeachClub; 03261-6600; 17/74 Takiab Rd, Hua Hin)

Located on Takieb Beach, the beach-club element of the Amari hotel has a pool, a variety of seating options, a beachside grill, and a lounge with energizing music. Buy tickets so you can play for the day. Separately, return for events such as a New Year's Eve party or a Loy Krathong (banana trunk) celebration; in other words, the facility conjures up event themes regularly. The after-dark pool parties are kind of sizzling, so check the schedule.

So Beach Party ปาร์ตีชายหาด

(so-sofitel-huahin.com/things-to-do/happening/so-beach-party; 03270-9555; So Hua Hin, 115 Moo 7 Tambol Bangkao, Phetchaburi)

Sofitel went all party-chic with its boutique Hui Hin hotel, and the So Beach Party best represents that. Young, beautiful people gather here bi-monthly—locals, celebs, couples like you—for partying in the most jet-set style on Cha-am Beach. Dress on your wilder side, and don't be surprised to find yourself competing in a limbo competition while strangers applaud, or in sand volleyball after a grilled seafood dinner. Pop the prosecco and expect a whole lot of barefoot dancing.

NIGHTCLUBS

Panama Bar

(facebook.com/Panama-Hua-Hin-369420590136893/) is a disco with a range of music including hip-hop, reggae, and EDM, plus events like Glow in the Dark night. **Sugarland** (sugarland-club.

com) bills itself as a hybrid. It has a lounge with premium spirits and a pool table, plus the largest club in Hua Hin, featuring DJ sounds, light shows, and a high-tech sound system. Live bands play nightly at 8pm. Note: Sugarland is the bar at Paradise Village restaurant. Urban music—electro, hip-hop, and house—draw people to **Sam Sam Bar** (facebook.com/SamSamBar). Snuggle side by side on a banquette, shoot some pool, and enjoy the laid-back aura. The two-story **Blue Monkey** (facebook.com/ bluemonkeyhuahin), with blue lighting throughout, has an American bent with beer pong along with hard-to-find-here booze like shooters and absinthe. Hear the house and hip-hop sounds. You'll also find a dance floor and a pool table.

SHOPPING

Blúport Hua Hin Resort Mall บลูพอร์ตหัวหินรีสอร์ทมอลล์

(bluporthuahin.com; 02136-1250; 8/89, Soi Moo Baan Nongkae, Nongkae; daily 10am-9pm)

Whatever you're looking for, Blúport is bound to have it. For starters, this massive mall has 100 restaurants in its Dining Port, from a Sizzler steakhouse to the Korean-cuisine Sukishi, not to mention sushi, coffee bars, and pizza. It has many styles of clothing, jewelry, shoes, and beauty salons, plus a high-end grocery store on the ground floor and a six-screen multiplex on the second. If you want to giggle like schoolchildren, join the little ones at Whaley Port, a theme park designed to feel like the underwater world inside a whale's stomach—you might get into a video-game competition at the Game Port section.

Market Village Hua Hin มาร์เก็ตวิลเลจหัวหิน

(marketvillagehuahin.co.th/en; 03261-8865; 234/1 Petchkasem Rd, Hua Hin)

Shopping a block from the beach? That's kind of dreamy if you're a beach- and retail-loving duo. This light and airy atrium-style mall has a range of stores—many that you will know—as well as a multiplex and bits of Hua Hin culture and history, some indoors, some out. For example, the mall periodically hosts art exhibits and small concerts. The basement level has low-cost wares, including a reasonably priced foot massage, while you can pick up groceries at the ground-floor supermarket or lunch at the food court. Home goods are on the second floor and services like hair salons on the third. A bowling alley and cinema are other entertainment options at Market Village. Regular events such as soccer matches and concerts are held; check the website for details.

Seenspace

(seenspace.com/huahin; 092350-0035; 13/14 Hua Hin 35, Hua Hin; weekdays 11am-9pm, weekends 10am-10pm)

Let's not get too literal about Seenspace's slogan, "Eat Play Stay Relax" (or as the Facebook page says, "Eat Lay Play Relax"). Just enjoy the beachfront location and the slick industrial-chic vibe—the exterior is unpainted concrete—that makes the mall feel like a scene. The mall is built around a park with trees, beanbag chairs, and string lights. Dip into the pool bar for a cocktail, lounge on the beachfront daybeds, or dance to live music when you're not, say, looking for new earbuds or jeans. There are 200 stores in all, plus a boutique hotel and several restaurants.

The Venezia Hua Hin & Cha-am เดอะเวเนเซียหัวหินและชะอำ

(facebook.com/Venezia.huahin; 03244-2823; 1899 Petchkasem Rd, Cha-am)

Few activities are more romantic than a gondola ride along the canals of Venice. Surprisingly, you can cross that off your wish list in Hua Hin. The Venezia mall has a Venetian theme, down to the replica St. Mark's Square and clocktower, while the stores and restaurants are housed in replicas of Venetian homes. Sounds a little Vegas, doesn't it? Besides food and apparel, you'll find a small train, a garden, a dancing fountain, an illuminated heart, a horse-drawn carriage, and other photo ops and activities.

MARKETS

Cha-am Wednesday Night Market/Railway Station Market ตลาดนัดกลางคืนวันพุธชะอำ / ตลาดสถานีรถไฟ

(Cha-am, Phetchaburi; Wed 5:30pm-10pm)

Get lost in a sea of locals and tourists at the weekly Cha-am Night Market. This is the ideal choice if one of you loves shopping and the other loathes it: One area is the designated Falang Husband Minding Centre. It's like a meet-up for men ditched by women who are eager for a retail spree. The guys sit together at long tables, beers in hand, and pass the time. You'll find a large array of merchandise and food here, in typical night market fashion. Be on the lookout for some unusual items, such as fine knives.

Chatchai Local Market ตลาดสดชาติชาย

(tourismthailand.org/Attraction/chatchai-market;   03247-1005; Dechanuchit Rd, Hua Hin; daily 5am-4pm)

The chic new markets are tons of fun, but for a taste of older Hua Hin choose Chatchai, or Chat Chi, which has been in the same building since 1926. Look for the seven eaves on the roof before entering; they were added to honor King Rama VII. During the day, locals head here for groceries: One vendor might sell only chili pastes, another fish or Chinese donuts. As the day winds down, the foodservice focus amps up. You'll be with other tourists as you try vendors' specialties. Possibilities are a bowl of pig's blood soup, and a snack of sticky rice served in bamboo.

Cicada Market ตลาดจักจั่น

(cicadamarket.com; 099669-7161; 83, 159 Soi Hua Tanon 21, Nong Kae; Fri-Sun 4pm-11pm)

Cicada Market is several destinations in one: It's a night market that starts before sundown, yet also a destination for performing and visual arts, street food, and a beer garden. It's located in a leafy area so shade abounds, and water elements add character. In addition to vendors selling merchandise, much of it handmade and a large percentage legitimate "art," you can spend time watching comedy, magic, and other shows at the Cicada Amphitheater, and tapping your feet to musical performances in the garden. A section called Cicada Cuisine section has street foods, Thai, Western, and others.

Hua Hin Night Market ตลาดโต้รุ่งหัวหิน

(facebook.com/Huahin.nightmarket.walkingstreet;   03251-3885; daily 5pm-1am)

Located near the train station, Hua Hin Night Market is a bustling after-dark enterprise, and it's loads of fun, though it doesn't have a distinguishing characteristic like some of its peers. You can shop, not surprisingly, for shirts and jewelry, designer knock-offs, and hand-crafted souvenirs. And you can eat: The typical and tempting array of flavors are on offer her. Try a grilled-to-order lobster, a kebab, papaya salad, or stir-fried noodles.

Seafood at Hua Hin Night Market

Tamarind Market ตลาดมะขาม

(facebook.com/tamarindmarkethuahin; 088611-1644; 17/75 Soi Huana Village, Nong Kae)

While Tamarind Market doesn't have the upscale sheen of Cicada, it's an appealing hub for an inexpensive meal to the sounds of live music. This enterprise bills itself as a "Chic and Chill Festival Evening Market." It's in a small park with tamarind trees near the beach and is made up of two sections. One has food stalls with both Thai foods (one booth is labeled "Variety Spicy Salad") and international items, and loads of seating in open areas. Then, in the back, bolder eaters will find more authentic Asian foods that are as high on flavor as their setting is low on atmosphere.

The Grand Night Market เปิดท้ายหัวหินแกรนด์

(facebook.com/JEABRADANT; 081692-4580; 39/11 Chomsin Rd, Hua Hin; Wed-Mon 3:30pm-midnight)

Get a snack, have your feet rubbed, pick up a new pair of sandals... and eat. At this night market, some of the restaurants are permanent stalls while others are tented. Overall, it's the regular story in another nice space: food, drink, and all kinds of retail opportunities. You know—narrow aisles, portable kitchens side by side, loads of color, plenty of enticing aromas, and, of course, shoppers and diners bopping from vendor to vendor.

MASSAGES

Chillax Health Massage

(chillaxmassagehuahin.business.site; 083236-5914; 1/42 Nong Kae-Takiap Rd, Nong Kae; Thu-Tue 10am-6pm)

This classic storefront Thai massage parlor offers several treatments in addition to the standard "Thai massage." Options include deep-tissue, sports, Thai oil, office syndrome relief, Relax & Refresh, feet and legs, and head massages.

Niwaschon Traditional Thai Massage นิวาสชนนวดแผนไทย

(facebook.com/Niwaschon-Traditional-Thai-Massage-1776124672464533; 080987-9019; 104/3 Naeb Kehardt Rd, Hua Hin; daily 10am-11pm)

Niwaschon looks like a standard walk-in parlor, yet it adds extra touches so your visit will feel more special. You'll be greeted with cookies and tea, and massage chairs are adorned with attractive linens, pillows, and flowers. Aroma foot massages, Thai herbal compress massages, mani/pedis, and classic Thai massages are all on offer.

Nurul Nashita Massage นุรุลนชิตามาสสาจ

(facebook.com/nurulnashitathaimassage; 098829-4492; 23/2 Soi Hua Hin 57, Dechanuchit Rd, Hua Hin; daily 10am-11pm)

When a quick fix will make all the difference, walk into Nurual Nashita for a foot massage, or maybe an herbal hot-compress massage. Either will get you back into sightseeing mode in no time.

Thai Thai Massage นวดแผนไทย

(thaithaimassagehuahin.com; 084318-2451; Soi 57, 20/1 Dechanuchit Road, Hua Hin; daily 11am-10:30pm)

Graduates of the Bangkok Wat Po Massage School comprise the staff of Thai Thai, a street-front stop with several offerings. Facials, sports massages, hot herbal massages, and even physiotherapy complement the standard assortment of traditional Thai, head, foot, and head/back/shoulders treatments.

The Barai บาราย

(thebarai.com/barai-spa; 03251-1234; 91 Hua Hin, Khao Takiap Rd, Hua Hin)

Now you're talkin'. This hotel spa has racked up luxury awards for the work done within its 18 treatment rooms and eight residential spa suites. You could make a vacation of this type of indulgence. The spa suites are spacious accommodations that, besides other perks like walk-in closets and/or private pools, have designated private spa treatment areas. There or at the spa itself, you can get any of dozens of treatments or day packages—even holistic therapy like lifestyle consultations and personal training sessions. Why not both receive crystal energy balance massages? We're talking hot stones, warm oil, and specially placed crystals for a restorative 90 minutes. The Couples Harmony package, for spa-suite guests, involves a jasmine body scrub, the crystal energy massage, and a mini facial.

The Spa at InterContinental Resort Hua Hin สปาที่อินเตอร์คอนติเนนต์ลรีสอร์ทหัวหิน

(huahin.intercontinental.com/spa-and-wellness; 03261-6999; 33 33 Petchkasem Rd, Hua Hin)

Wellness treatments of all types are available at this upscale hotel spa, a serene sanctuary offering massages, facials, and beauty treatments as well as morning yoga, detox services, and even private Tai Chi instructions. Lovebirds can exhale together with the Duo Retreat: You'll start with a jasmine body scrub and an apple-green tea, detoxifying wrap, then surrender to any of their hour-long massages. And then? Mini facials. You might opt for the 14K Golden Facial. The mask used to remove toxins is, indeed, made with real gold.

TOURS

2-Day Wildlife Tour in Kaeng Krachan National Park ทัวร์ 2 วันในอุทยานแห่งชาติแก่งกระจาน

(thainationalparks.com/kaeng-krachan-national-park/guided-tours/2-days-wildlife-tour-in-kaeng-krachan; November-July)

About 90 minutes from Hua Hin, Kaeng Krachan National Park

is a 1,125 square miles (2,914km2) expanse with 420 species of birds, macaques, and other wild animals like leopards, crab-eating mongooses, and barking deer. This two-day immersion is different every time, but it's always fascinating. You'll pay upwards of $500 for your private tour for two. A typical experience might involve animal-spotting drives, jungle hikes, a night walk, meals, and a tented campsite.

Khao Sam Roi Yot National Park อุทยานแห่งชาติเขาสามร้อยยอด

(thainationalparks.com/khao-sam-roi-yot-national-park; 03282-1568; Moo 2, Ban Khao Daeng Khao Daeng, Kui Buri; daily 8am-3:30pm)

This national park ($7 per person) is best known for its Phraya Nakhon Cave, yet it has so much more to enjoy in its 38 square miles (98km2). The park's name means "Mountain with 300 Peaks," so of course the views of its limestone hills are stunning, and the Gulf of Thailand backdrop makes it more so. What's more, you might see other caves, canals, and wetlands. Wading birds are easy to spot, and in the fall all kinds of birds stop in on their annual trek south for the winter. Consider visiting the park as part of a guided tour that includes the Kui Buri Wildlife Watching Area (thainationalparks.com/kui-buri-national-park), home to wild elephants, gaurs, and other animals. The parks are an hour south of Hua Hin and there are no public transportation options to get there. If you don't take a tour, rent a car or arrange for a taxi. A car might be best because sites within the park are spread out. A bicycle would be handy for this too, but that would be tricky for most tourists to arrange. The Khao Sam Roi Yot website provides a link to a day-long expedition that includes taxis both ways from $75 and up; this amount covers entrance to most park attractions, and offers add-on options such as Kui Buri.

Monsoon Valley Vineyard ไร่องุ่น Monsoon Valley

(monsoonvalley.com/en; 081701-0222; 1 Moo 9 Nong Phlap, Hua Hin; daily 9am-6:30pm, to 8pm Nov-Mar)

If you enjoy drinking wine together, why not see where it comes from? Monsoon Valley Vineyards has several options. Take a tour of the vineyard in an oversized tuk-tuk ($3.50 per person): The guide will explain how wine grapes are raised in a tropical climate. Upgrade to the Day Out, which might involve a meal at The Sala bistro and wine bar, time at an elephant sanctuary, mountain biking around the vines, bottle painting, and/or a "Wine Safari" that involves seeing wildlife at Kuiburi National Park. Attend a harvest party in February or March. Or sign up for a Wine & Tapas, Wine & Dine or Vineyard to Wine Bar experience ($55–$65 per person).

Private Floating Market and Petchaburi Excursion ตลาดน้ำ ส่วนตัวและเที่ยวเพชรบุรี

(thailandtours.travel/thailand/hua-hin/huahin-excursions/ private-floating-market-and-petchaburi-excursion; 085094-3444)

See area highlights in one day on a private tour: A guide will take you to a floating market, where you'll be taken on a longtail boat to an area where vendors in their own boats and in stalls sell street food, apparel, and mementos. You'll then proceed to the city of Petchaburi for lunch, followed by the historic Khao Wang (Phra Nakhon Khiri) mountaintop summer palace or the Khao Luang cave, where Buddhas statues and other pieces sit within. The tour also includes Wat Mahathtat Buddhist temple. $125 per couple.

Sam Roi Yot & The Secret Cave สามร้อยยอด & ถ้ำลับ

(thailandtours.travel/thailand/hua-hin/huahin-excursions/sam-roi-yod-the-secret-cave; 085094-3444; Rama IV Road 4033 Sam Roi Yot, Sam Roi)

Take a day trip to Khao Sam Roi Yot National Park—"the Mountain with 300 Peaks"—to see the highlights, stress-free. An English-speaking guide will pick you up at your hotel and drop you back off at journey's end. After an hour's drive through pineapple groves and a fishing village, you'll hike from a beach to Phraya Nakhon Cave, home to a historic king's throne and majestic natural illumination. You'll have lunch before heading back. $100 per person.

ANIMAL SANCTUARIES

Hutsadin Elephant Foundation มูลนิธิช้างหัสดินทร์

(hutsadin.org; 03282-7098; 176 Moo 7 Nongplub Rd, Hua Hin; daily 9am-4pm, English-speaking 9am-1pm)

Help the *mahouts*, or elephant keepers, tend to their giant charges at this nonprofit sanctuary for animals past their prime. Just show up on a weekday and ask to volunteer. You can hear a lesson about Asian elephants ($10 per person), take a half-hour walk beside an elephant ($25 per person), or do a combo of both those activities ($33 per person), or, weather-permitting, shower the elephant and have your photo taken ($13 per person).

Rescue P.A.W.S. Day Visit กู้ภัย P.A.W.S. วันเยียม

(rescuepawsthailand.org/day-visits; 090232-8709; 65 Khao Tao Temple, Nong Kae)

If the pair of you are pup lovers, spend a day doing good in Thailand. This dog-rescue organization, whose name stands for Providing Animal Welfare Through Sterilizations, invites you to join in rounding up homeless dogs and cats so they can ultimately be placed in loving homes. You'll be driven through Hua Hin neighborhood's, seeing local sights as you do so, before heading to the Gulf for a swim with these would-be pets. $43 per person.

> ### Treatment of Elephants
>
> In Thailand, as in much of Asia, elephants have had it bad. They are used for tourism purposes. These huge creatures may be strong, but they're not machines. They suffer through overworking and abuse, and are sometimes malnourished.
>
> In recent years, animal sanctuaries have opened up all around the country, many specializing in elephants. In these facilities the pachyderms are safe from mishandling—at least the ones we recommend throughout this guide.
>
> The sanctuaries are expensive to run, so many raise funds by inviting people to visit. Your experience can be as simple as a couple of hours touring around for a modest fee. Or, for a higher price, you might spend two nights at a sanctuary. During that time, you might help the animals walk around, and take a mud and regular bath. You might also assist in preparing their vitamin-rich feed.

CAVES

Phraya Nakhon Cave

(thainationalparks.com/khao-sam-roi-yot-national-park; Rama IV Road 4033, Sam Roi Yot; daily 8am-3:30pm)

The biggest tourist site within Khao Sam Roi Yot National Park, 45 minutes south of Hua Hin, the Phraya Nakhon Cave has several elements. There's the mammoth cave part, complete with stalagmites and stalactites and all, but it also has two sinkholes, plus a green and gold royal pavilion called Phra Thinang Khuha, built in 1890 so King Rama V had a place to rest under its four-gable roof during his visits. Sometimes the sun beams through a sinkhole and lights up the structure in a mystical, magnificent way. You'll climb up a challenging stone trail for about three-quarters of a mile (1200m) to get into the cave, then descend on what may be a wet path to explore the interior. Drive or take a taxi to this cave, about an hour south of Hua Hin, and wear lightweight shoes with a good grip because caves can be slippery.

Sunbeam through a sinkhole at Phraya Nakhon Cave

Tham Khao Luang Cave

(tourismthailand.org/Attraction/tham-khao-luang;   03247-1005; Khao Wang Rd, Thong Chai, Phetchaburi; open 24 hours/day) History buffs will want to visit for the multiple Buddha statues within this cave temple, and possibly even to see the Chakri Dynasty's coats of arms carved into one of the statues. You might just want to get close to the monkeys that hang out here. Either way, Tham Khao Luang is relatively easy to visit. It's on a small hill, an hour outside of Hua Hin, reachable by foot or car. The temple itself was only used as such for about a century; it was started by King Mongkut and enhanced by King Chulalongkorn. The cave's seated and reclining Buddha statues aside, the interior is best to see early in the day: At the time, the sun often shines through a hole in the top. The effect is magnificent.

TEMPLES

Wat Huay Mongkol วัดห้วยมงคล

(081858-6661; Thap Tai, Hua Hin; daily 5am-10pm)

Monk Luang Phor Thuad is said to have performed miracles—one involved transforming ocean water into a life-saving drinkable version, and you can see a 39-foot-tall (12m) statue of him sitting in meditation pose within this park. Pilgrims may be at your side. It's common to walk in circles under the belly of an elephant statue here, and/or burn incense near a fallen teak tree imbued with special meaning, if you want to ring in some luck. Besides luck, you can bring home some knick-knacks; souvenir versions of the monk, and of King Taksin the Great, are for sale.

Wat Khao Krailat วัดเขาไกรลาส

Wat Khao Krailat, or Krailas, four miles (6.4km) outside of town, sits boldly atop a mountain. Climb some stairs to reach this temple that is home to monks even today, and meander hand in hand among the many distinct Buddha statues—including a reclining white Buddha, as well as the fishponds, before heading back. The sea views are wonderful.

Wat Khao Sanam Chai วัดเขาสนามชัย

(03253-6604; 69/7 Petchkasem Rd, Hua Hin; daily 8am-5pm)

A white structure with a graceful white multi-layered roof, adorned with gold, this religious center includes a Buddhist shrine with a gold Buddha statue and an ordination hall. Sunset views of the harbor and town make this hilltop temple a popular evening destination. It's a 10-minute car or taxi ride from the center of Hua Hin.

ATTRACTION

Mrigadayavan Palace พระราชนิเวศน์มฤคทายวัน

(mrigadayavan.or.th; 03250-8444; 1281 Petchkasem Thanon Phet Kasem, Cha-am; Thu-Tue 8:30am-4pm)

Maybe you two talk about getting a little vacation home by the sea? His Majesty King Rama VI did, though he wanted to keep it simple—for royalty. And so, early in the 1900s, he had Mrigadayavan Palace built as a place to heal from his rheumatoid arthritis. The location was chockful of hog deer, so the name is a tribute to a place in India where Buddha first preached, and where deer lived; the name means "hog deer stream." He also declared the land a wildlife sanctuary. The king died after his first two visits; its 16 teak buildings and 23 staircases were eventually abandoned, but these days the palace is open for exploring. Group tours point out both Thai and Western design details. Reserve your spot at least a week in advance, whether for a traditional tour—you'll be appointed a session based on what interests you, or an "upper-level tour," which delves into architectural detail.

ADVENTURES

Cha-am ATV Park ชะอำเอทีวีปาร์ค

(cha-amatvpark.net/en/; 095828-9454; 760/7 Soi Borkam, Cha-am; Thu-Tue 9am-5:30pm)

Rough it, while smiling, at Cha-am, where you can ride all-terrain vehicles on three rugged tracks. Curves, hills, potholes, *water hazards?* —you've got this. While here, you can also shoot with bows and arrows in the eight-target archery area, or join a paintball battle in a shaded stadium.

Hin Lek Fai Hill Viewpoint เขาหินเหล็กไฟ

(tourismthailand.org/Attraction/khao-hin-lek-fai)

Hua Hin, together with its coastline, makes for a nice view from above. To see that, take a trip less than two miles (3km) west to Hin Lek Fai Hill, also called Flintstone Hill, which has half a dozen viewpoints. Best at dawn and, second-best, dusk, the top of the mountain offers vistas of the town, its beach, the Gulf, the fishing pier, and a golf course. Peacocks and other birds reside on the hill. Locals will be jogging and cycling up the hill alongside you. Kiosks offer snacks and drinks.

Hua Hin Bike Tours หัวหินไบค์ทัวร์

(huahinbiketours.com/tours; 081173-4469; 8/12 Takiab 6, Nong Kae)

You can tool around town on any rental bike, but join a half, full-, or multi-day tour to see Hua Hin in another way. Nine options are available, and most start about 7:30am and conclude at 2:30pm or 5:30pm. The Hua Hin Hell Ride ($65 per person), for seasoned cyclists, goes through back streets, off-road along train tracks, through non-tourist neighborhoods, and up some steep mountain. Gears, Grapes & Vineyards ($115 per person) is longer but milder. Stops include a monument, a country road, a temple, a Dole packing plant, and a vineyard, where you will get to sample the wares. You can ride the 11 miles (18km) back or hop on the truck.

North Kiteboarding Club

(northkiteboardingclub.com; 083438-3833; 113/5 Petchakasem Rd, Hua Hin)

Hua Hin's wind and water—sandy beach, riff-free—make it a good place for kiteboarding from October through May, and North Kiteboarding Club will set you up. Serious kiteboarding couples can choose from three packages, for seven, 10 or 14 nights. You'll receive intensive instruction, supervised kiting, a place to stay, and daily breakfast. For a briefer experience, choose the introductory course ($130 per person) that'll give you all the basics.

Vana Nava Water Jungle วานานาวาวอเตอร์จังเกิล

(vananavahuahin.com; 095828-9454; KM.#198, 760/7 Soi Borkam, Tambon Cha-am; Mon-Thu 11am-4pm, Fri-Sun 11am-6pm)

Vana Nava is an eco-sensitive 8-acre (3.2-hectare) water park with 20 slides and other rides, set amid 200,000 trees and plants. Scream in glee together as you whiz down the Boomrango, an anti-gravity tube slide, and The Abyss, one of the world's largest waterslides. And consider having pictures taken at Vanadio, a professional underwater studio offering costumes and props, from Muay Thai outfits to glam gowns.

GOLF

Banyan Golf Club บันยันกอล์ฟคลับ

(banyanthailand.com/hua-hin-golf; 03261-6200; 68/35 Mooban Hua Na, Tambol Nong Gae)

A relative newcomer, Banyan opened in 2009. The award-winning, championship Pirapon Namatra-designed 18-hole course is par-72, has views of sea and mountains, and offers up six types of tee boxes, so you're set no matter your level of play. The golf carts are high-tech with GPS systems in English and other languages, and the pro shop is well-stocked with apparel. Stop by the Terrace restaurant for a post-game bite and a selection of wines, or the clubhouse's Mulligan's Pub, with several whiskey varieties and cigars.

Black Mountain Golf Club แบล็คเมาน์เทนกอล์ฟคลับ

(blackmountainhuahin.com; 03261-8666; 565 Moo 7, Nong Hieng Rd, Hua Hin)

You'll think you're in Palm Beach, not Hua Hin, when you see Black Mountain, a golf-club community just west of Hua Hin. It opened in 2007 and quickly garnered many awards—even before expanding its golf offerings in 2016. It has villas, a water park, a wakeboard park, and other amenities. At its heart are two manicured golf courses, one with 18 holes, the other nine. Asian PG tours are often held here.

Royal Hua Hin Golf Club รอยัลหัวหินกอล์ฟคลับ

(santiburi.com/huahin; 03251-2475; Amphur Hua Hin, Prachuabkirikhan)

Royal Hua Hin is Thailand's oldest golf course, and that alone makes the fairway worth a detour. It is surrounded by 240 acres (97 hectares) of lush greenery. Serving golfers since 1924, this 18-hole, par-72, Gulf-view facility has roots back to 1919, and its original clubhouse still stands. Don't be surprised if a monkey nabs your ball.

Springfield Royal Country Club สปริงฟิลด์รอยัลคันทรีคลับ

(springfieldresort.com/golf; 03270-9256; 208 Moo 2, Sampraya, Cha-Am)

Golf legend Jack Nicklaus himself designed the 27 holes at Springfield Royal, where golfers are surrounded by woods and mountains. This is a great place to take lessons, as groups are small, and the coaches use analysis to assist with helpful feedback. Five sets of tees are available. You'll also find a pro shop, putting and chipping greens, and a clubhouse with a restaurant.

BEACHES

Cha-am Beach หาดชะอำ

If you're bored to tears on a serene strand, consider Cha-am Beach instead. It has loads to do yet never feels crowded. Join a soccer match, treat yourselves to massages under parasols, or head into the water on a parasail. Plan for a seafood meal here, and at a reasonable price. The place fills up on weekends.

Hua Hin Beach ชายหาดหัวหิน

The golden sands extend for 4½ miles (7km) on Hua Hin Beach. This is a lovely but busy strand, right along the Gulf of Thailand. That works if you like to break up your sunbathing with a horseback ride or personal watercraft adventure, and sunbeds here and there are an enticing way to recover from the sports. As for wading in the water, it's doable and nice, but can be rocky. When it's time for a bite, restaurants and vendors are easy to find.

Khao Kalok Beach หาดเขากะโหลก

The sand is white and soft, trees add shade, and the water is shallow. Khao Kalok, which also goes by Pak Nam Pran, is a mighty relaxing breed of beach. Rent a couple of deck chairs from a vendor and settle in for a de-stressing session. The beach is backed by Skull Mountain. Turn around any time you want to trade a sea view for a mountain view. When you're ready for a bite, restaurants are nearby.

Khao Tao Beach หาดเขาเต่า

Frankly you won't hear much about Khao Tao, so choose it if you're into crowd-free beach experiences. The small strands—it's two beaches in one—are located between twin rocky areas. Both Small Sand Beach and Big Sand Beach are quiet, but there's the chance to receive a massage in a hut. Swimming is easy here. Plan to eat just-caught fish at a restaurant while you're in the area.

Suan Son Pradipat Beach หาดสวนสนประดิพัทธ์

One of Hua Hin's four other beaches, 3.7-mile (6km) Suan Son is where the locals go. It's owned by the military and has only welcomed civilians and visits since 2001. The sand is smooth, the swimming fine, plus there's a whole lot of shade. The name means "sea pine tree garden" due to the trees behind the sand. You're apt to find an impromptu soccer match. Plenty of restaurants offer meals with a scenic backdrop.

MUAY THAI CLASSES

Work off some of that fried street food with a class or five in Muay Thai, a form of boxing. **Por Promin Muay Thai Camp** (porpromin.com), under the direction of the renowned Kru Kin and his wife Miriam, offers camps for newcomers and others. If you can't spare 10 days to attend a camp, book a private lesson for the two of you. The studio is only 10 minutes from central Hua Hin. Pro boxers will be your instructors at the **King of Muay Thai Gym** (kingofmuaythaigym.com). You can drop in pay-as-you-go for about $15 or commit to a Stay & Train program with an apartment or hotel room. Near the Blúport mall, **Amazing Muay Thai Gym & Fitness** (facebook.com/AmazingMuayThaiGym) has a walk-in gym and Muay Thai training. Mix some Muay Thai into your regular exercise routine at **Elite Fight Club** (facebook. com/elitefightclubhuahin). Here you can pick up the boxing basics while also doing yoga and CrossFit elements. Daily classes are straight Muay Thai, Abs & Booty, Western Boxing, and Elite Fight Fit. If you're *really* into getting fight-fit, stay in the on-property bungalows.

YOGA

Chiva-Som ชีวา – สม

(chivasom.com/hua-hin/yoga-for-life;   03253-6536;   73/4 Petchkasem Rd, Tambon Nong Kae)
Chiva-Som is a wellness retreat. It has classes all day long, including hatha yoga, HIIT, and Aqua Aerobics with hand buoys. Most guests stay here, enrolled in educational and exercise programs or retreats. The facility includes a gymnasium, a spa, studios, shalas, and pavilions dedicated to Pilates, yoga, dance, Tai Chi, relaxation, and "refunction." On a yoga retreat, you'll build up knowledge about not only poses but also meditation, ayurvedic

cleaning, and mind-body-spirit connectivity.

Shakti Yoga Hua Hin

(huahinyoga.com; 095307-8767; Soi 67 Petchkasem Rd, Hua Hin)
Focused around empowerment, the Shakti Yoga Studio is above
all convenient. It's in the center of Hua Hin and has mats, blocks,
and straps for all to use. You'll practice on the second floor with
garden views out of big windows. While you'll probably choose
this place for their beginner, flow, and power classes, you'll
probably end up sticking around for the rooftop pool and deck,
and the Japanese café.

KRABI

Krabi

WHY GO

You'll have tough decisions to make when planning a trip to Krabi. Which scenic beach should we choose? White sand or gold? Clear blue or clear aqua water? Stunning limestone cliffs—on the beach or seen from it?

If you're looking for a romantic beach getaway, Krabi is likely to be a good destination for you. Here, you can lodge in luxury and spend full days at a spa. You can hike or camp in national parks with fascinating landscapes. Then there's scuba diving, elephant visits, rock climbing, hot springs, yoga retreats—you'll find it all.

Krabi is actually a province that stretches 1,818 square miles (4,709 km²). The namesake capital and nearby resort areas are on southern Thailand's west coast, where Krabi hugs the Andaman Sea. More than 150 offshore islands are part of the province.

Ao Nang is the hub, Krabi Town the capital, and you'll find hotels ranging from intimate inns to luxury resorts in some other areas as well. Longtail boat captains will zip you over the pristine waters for a moderate fee, so it's possible to visit a new island every day. In the busier areas, you can take a break from the beach to shop alongside locals at a market, visit temples in unusual places, and spend your evenings drinking fine wines, or tropical cocktails, as the sun sets.

Poda Island in Krabi Province

HOW TO GET TO KRABI

Most international flights to Krabi involve a change at Bangkok, which at most is 90 minutes away by air, although Singapore, Darwin, and Kuala Lumpur all have flights to Krabi Airport (KBV; krabiairportonline.com). Flights from any of these destinations can be under $100 per person. The airport is a 15-minute taxi ride from Krabi Town, 25 to 45 minutes from Ao Nang. You can also get to Krabi overland from elsewhere in Thailand and Southeast Asia. For up-to-date information, consult a travel agent, walk into a storefront tour office, ask at your front desk, or visit websites such as krabi-tourism.com, phuketferry.com, thailandtrains.com, 12go.asia, busonlineticket.co.th and rassadapier.com.

Bus It's a 12-hour bus ride from Bangkok's Southern bus terminal, also called Sai Tai Mai (economy $20 per person, VIP $35 per person), and a three-hour bus ride from Phuket ($4 per person). The bus will drop you off at the Krabi Bus Terminal (Bor Khor Sor) in Talat Kao, just north of Krabi Town. From there, regular taxis, and group taxis called songthaew, will be outside and ready to take you to Krabi Town or Ao Nang.

Car It takes two to three hours to drive from Phuket to Krabi, and the roads are reasonably well marked. From Bangkok, it'll take at least ten hours driving along the Gulf of Thailand.

Ferry There are ferries to and from Krabi's Klong Jilad Pier, to and from Phuket and Phi Phi Island (from $15 per person for both destinations), as well as ferries between Krabi province's islands. You can also choose a group speedboat (80 minutes; $40 per person) or charter a private one from Phuket (prices start at $350 per person).

Taxi A taxi ride from Phuket costs about $85.

Train Krabi doesn't have a train station. You can take a train part of the way, from Bangkok's Hua Lamphong station to Surat Thani (at least nine hours; $17 to $60 per person). Then, take a 20-minute taxi ride to the bus terminal. From there, you'll have a two-hour bus ride to Krabi after a shuttle.

TRAVELING FROM THE AIRPORT

Airport transportation You can book a taxi or executive car in advance to take you from the airport to your hotel at krabiairportonline.com/transportation. Alternatively, you can go to the taxi stall in the airport and hire a taxi from there. It's about $20 for a cab to Krabi Town, $27 to Ao Nang. You can also pre-book a taxi or limo at krabiairportonline.com/transportation and airmundo.taxitender.com.

Bus A shuttle bus runs from the airport to Krabi Town and Ao Nang several times a day and costs under $5 per person. The route is fluid; the driver will drop you off at your destination. The shuttle service can also get you to the Klong Jilad Pier, Klong Muang, and Khao Kwang Beach. The shuttles are run by Pichet Transport (facebook.com/Pichet-Transport-Company-Limited-1456627334631676; it's best to inquire at the airport rather than hunt down the schedule, written in Thai, available online.

Rental vehicles Renting a car or motorcycle at the airport or in town means you can easily venture out to see the parks, temple, and other out-of-town sights. Avis, Budget, Europcar, Hertz, and Sixt all have counters at the airport. Pure (cars.purekrabi.com) and Drive (drivecarrental.com) are options elsewhere in the area.

GETTING AROUND

Most tours, cooking classes, and other group activities will drive you door to door if you're staying in the main resort areas, except for Railay. Otherwise, you can take one of the following options to get around:

Local bus These are open-sided vehicles called a songthaew; prices are extremely low.

Motorbike taxi Hop on the back of a two-wheeler, into a motorbike sidecar, or into a tuk-tuk; you'll find them parked wherever tourists gather. Drivers wear brightly colored vests. Prices tend to be under $2 for any trip.

Regular taxi Use these for short trips or negotiate a full-day rate for a bigger trip. It's about $85 for a whole day of transport, and that's whether you go to one destination, such as Phuket, a series of smaller, closer ones, like local temples and scenic hikes.

Longtail boat Eager locals are always happy to zip you across the water to another beach for a modest fee.

WHERE TO STAY

Krabi area map

Ao Nang อ่าวนาง

Ao Nang is the heart of it all, and the tourist center of Krabi Province. Its streets are chockful of shops and restaurants, and its sand has water sports and longtail boats to nearby beaches. When you want a special dinner for two, Thai-island style, book yourselves a table at a waterfront seafood restaurant. This is also the place to head for nightlife in Krabi.

Klong Muang คลองม่วง

Want one-on-one time surrounded by beauty with few distractions? Klong Muang, north of Ao Nang, is the place for you... The hotels are boutique or leaning toward high-end; this is a place where infinity pools and Jacuzzi villas are ubiquitous. Most hotels are directly on the beach. Those strands themselves are long, white, and empty, with glass-clear water. They're not excellent for swimming, yet splendid hotel swimming pools compensate well. Bonus: The waters are all but free of commercial boats, so the beach is truly serene. The town itself is little to speak of beyond a few bars and restaurants. On Klong Muang, you'll probably travel only from your room to beach to resort restaurant etc. When it's time for an adventure, visit the national park near Tubkaek Beach. The area has an old-time feel yet thoroughly modern accommodations.

Koh Lanta เกาะลันตา

Koh Lanta is one of Thailand's largest islands, yet many of its hotels are only open in high season. That leaves plenty of room for couples visiting from May through October to roam its soft-sand beaches such as Phra Ae, Bakantiang, and Klong Bao, plus the tiny strands within Klong Chak National Park. Some Koh Lanta beaches are ideal for getting massages side by side, splashing around in empty waters, or for a special dinner for two on the sand after dark. Koh Lanta is a couple of hours' drive from Krabi airport, three hours if you choose a public bus. There are three ways to get here: Take a minivan taxi from the airport (it's about $100 for up to six people, so seek out fellow riders). Choose the Express Transfer minivan/speedboat/hotel-transfer combo (also $100). Visit kolanta.net/get-to-koh-lanta to book in advance. Or, find your way via taxi or bus to a ferry. Alternatively, you can take a minibus or ferry from Ao Nang, as well as from the Phi Phi islands, Phuket, and Ko Jum. Visit 12go.asia/en/travel/krabi-airport/koh-lanta for options.

Krabi Town ตัวเมืองกระบี่

Krabi Town is the capital of the whole Krabi area, and it has a bustle you won't find elsewhere. That said, this is Thai-island bustle, meaning it's laid-back compared to Bangkok and even Phuket. Krabi Town highlights are the graceful white modern temple Wat Kaew Korawaram, sitting atop a hill, and two adjacent undistinguished-looking riverside parks (seek out the waterfront Monument of Black Crabs statue, which resembles sparring crustaceans). Four of the traffic lights on busy Maharaj Road at Manus Borarn Square are presented playfully: Identical statues of a prehistoric man hover over the autos, each holding the canister containing the red, yellow, and green lights. Elsewhere, statues of sacred animals, including twin elephants holding streetlights, are on pillars above the traffic. You can get your retail fun done on Walking Street and at markets. When you want to see what else Krabi Province has to offer, you'll find it easy to get to other destinations from here.

Nopparat Thara นพรัตน์ธารา

If you want the convenience of Ao Nang Beach without the commercialization, try nearby Nopparat Thara. The 3 mile (5km) beach is halved by a river. Families swim in the calm waters, locals might be beside you, and only a few businesses cater to the sunbathers. Pavilions and benches provide a reprieve from the sun and sand. At low tide, you might be able to walk to outlying islands.

Railay ไร่เลย์

If you're after beauty over convenience, Railay may be your best bet. To get to this mini peninsula, which is technically Nang Cape, you have to take a boat from Krabi Town, Ao Nang, or Ao

Nammao. The beach here is broken into East and West Railay, Phra Nang, and Tonsai, divided by cliffs. Stunning beaches, soft white sand, limestone cliffs, and fascinating caves will greet you—all of which are walkable. Some people come for the rock-climbing, and, surprisingly, nightspots are part of the scene. But this is more a place for sarongs than snappy cocktail dresses.

ACCOMMODATIONS

Avani Ao Nang Cliff Krabi Resort อวานีอ่าวนางคลิฟกระบี รีสอร์ท $

(avanihotels.com/en/ao-nang-krabi; 07562-6888; 328 Moo 2, Ao Nang)
You'll be near all the action of Ao Nang at the Avani, featuring 178 accommodations in the heart of the destination. This modern cliffside hotel has views of the Andaman Sea; choose the Ocean Wing so you can watch the sun set from your balcony. The resort has five restaurants, one of them by the swimming pool, while another is on the roof with lovely vistas and a menu of flavors from around the world. To work off all the meals, join Muay Thai and other exercise classes in the wellness center.

Ban Sainai Resort บ้านใสในรีสอร์ท $

(bansainairesort.com; 550, Soi Ao Nang)
Massages by the saltwater pool. Hammocks at every turn. Private thatched-roof cottages. Bansain may be a five-minute shuttle ride from the center of Ao Nang, yet when you're at the resort you'll feel every bit of the tropical-island life. Lushly landscaped and timeless in feel, Bansain is a place to sloooow doooown. It's also a place to stay healthy; you can even get superfood smoothie bowls by the pool. The Sai Nai restaurant serves Thai food, but you'll have to hop on a shuttle to town if you want spirited beverages— Bansain is alcohol-free.

Beyond Resort Krabi บียอนรีสอร์ทกระบี่ $

(beyondresortkrabi.com; 07562-8300; 98 Moo 3, Klong Muang Beach)

Why compete with Krabi's limestone cliffs? Instead, the 211-room Beyond was designed to blend into the scenery, its low-rise design with freeform curves flowing seamlessly into the stone, sand, and sea around it. Located on Klong Muang Beach, beyond has an oasis-style pool lined with palm trees and lounge chairs. You can stay in a cottage or villa—maybe even one with a private pool—and request the adults-only area of the resort. Grab a bite to eat at the air-conditioned indoor restaurant or, especially for dinner, book a table at the beachfront restaurant so you can dine under the stars by candlelight. Beyond also has a spa with two treatment rooms, and a fitness center.

Centra by Centara Phu Pano Resort Krabi เซ็นทราบายเซ็นทาราภูพาโนรีสอร์ทกระบี่ $

(centarahotelsresorts.com/centra/cpp; 075607-8889; 879 Moo 2, Soi Ao Nang 11)

Centra, a bright hotel built in 2016, has everything you'll need during your visit. The guest rooms have bright neutral colors with whimsical Asian design elements, plus balconies with views of either the pool or the cliffs. Dramatic cliff views, in fact, can be seen from almost everywhere at Centra—even the swimming pool. The pool itself has shaded seats; chairs submerged in it. The restaurant Mix Bistro is right by the pool, serving Thai and western foods all day long. The beach is a quick, free-shuttle ride away.

Layana Resort & Spa ลยานะรีสอร์ทแอนด์สปา $$

(layanaresort.com; 07560-7100; 272 Moo 3, Phra-Ae Beach Saladan)

Layana is an adults-only beachfront resort on the quiet western end of Krabi, boasting a gold-sand beach with spectacular sunsets, a large saltwater infinity pool, and a fitness center for guests of its 59 balconied rooms, suites, and villas. It also has a restaurant, two bars, and a library. Join thrice-weekly yoga classes on a specially designed platform in the garden, be indulged in any of six indoor spa treatment rooms, or receive foot massages in an outdoor massage sala. The Layana Romancing package, spread over four hours, will pamper you with a sauna stay, a sea-salt scrub, a Dead Sea caramel mud wrap, a floral bath, a Swedish massage, and an aromatic facial. Now that's the way to bond.

Sunrise Tropical Resort ซันไรส์ทรอปิคอลรีสอร์ท $

(sunrisetropical; 07581-9418; 39 Moo 2, Ao Nang)
Take a longtail boat from the mainland to Sunrise Tropical Resort, where the motto is "Let Sunrise lighten your life." It's a lushly landscaped 28-room hotel on Railay East Beach. Spend quiet days wading into the sea, dipping into the shaded freeform pool, and dining at the all-day restaurant. One evening, request a candlelit dinner for two by the pool; you'll be under a special tent. Sunrise is also a five-minute walk from Railay West, and 15 minutes from Phra Nang Beach. It's a 12-minute walk to Princess Cave.

BREAKFASTS

89 Café 89 คาเฟ่ $

Thai, International
(facebook.com/89cafe; 082654-4992; 10/1 Chofa Rd; daily 6:30am-11pm)
Sit by the window or on the front porch and watch Krabi Town pass by while you have the day's first coffee at 89 Café; enjoy foam art on your lattes and cappuccinos. Go all out with a big breakfast: vegetarian or carnivorous, this place will fill you up. The granola is made in-house, the omelets are prepared to order, and the waffles are just the thing to get you going. Thai and Western meals are served through dinnertime.

Cafe 8.98 คาเฟ 8.98 $

Healthy

(cafe898.com; 07565-6980; 143/7-8 Moo 2, Ao Nang; daily 7am-11pm)

In both Ao Nang and Klong Hang, Café 898 is set up to kick-start your day. This mod Starbucks-esque place draws ex-pats and Western tourists for morning coffee drinks made from Arabica beans from Thailand and the South Pacific, as well as smoothies, breakfast bowls, and all the expected breakfast foods, from waffles to eggs.

Easy Café อีซีคาเฟ $

European, Thai

(facebook.com/pages/Easy%20Cafe/826227060902618/; 081457-2366; 30 Kongka Rd, Muang District; Tue-Sun 7:30am-6pm)

Get your daily get-up-and-go at the Easy Café, where the barista-prepared coffee drinks are destination-worthy. The food options are good too, and bountiful. Go big with a full English breakfast, baked beans included, or opt for breakfast sandwiches, croissant sandwiches, omelets, French toast, porridge, and even pancakes.

LUNCHES AND DINNERS

Ao Nang Buffet อ่าวนางบุฟเฟต์ $$

Buffet, BBQ, Thai

(avanihotels.com/en/ao-nang-krabi/restaurants/ao-nang-buffet; 07562-6888; 328 Moo 2, Ao Nang; daily 6pm-10pm)

"Dine without limits" the website of the hotel buffet says invitingly. Within the Avani hotel, with dining tables spilling onto the sidewalk, you will be free to fill up on grilled marlin and squid, as well as lamb, sausages, and beef. Elegantly presented salads are set out, and chefs will top your papaya or fruit salad as you request. Grab a curry, a pasta dish, or sushi roll slices. Desserts are bite-size, making it easy to taste several.

Baitoey Seafood ใบเตยซีฟู้ด $

Seafood, Thai

(baitoey.com; 07561-1509; 79 Kongka Rd, Paknam Muang; daily 10am-10pm)

While you're bound to find food you'll enjoy on Baitoey's 18-page menu, the setting alone will win you over. The restaurant, opened in 1988, is a cheerful blue and white building set along the Krabi River next to Thara Park. The feel is relaxed yet special, whether you choose a table inside or in the fresh air overlooking the river. From that perch, you might try spicy salad soup feather seaweed salad, or clams with hot and sour curry with sea bass and coconut shoots. Much of the seafood comes from the river itself.

BUZZ Café $

Vegetarian, Healthy, Mediterranean

(facebook.com/buzzcafeaonang; 080718-1331; 873 Moo 2, Ao Nang; daily 9am-5pm)

BUZZ is all about organic food and drinks. The name may refer to the honey used to sweeten desserts naturally, or could refer to the serious cups of coffee served here. Breakfast bowls are a specialty, and although BUZZ isn't meat-free it has many vegetarian and vegan options. Stop in for a refreshing smoothie, or maybe a slice of cake that's not made with refined sugar.

Carnivore Steak & Grill $$

Steakhouse

(carnivore-thailand.com; 007566-1061; 127 Moo 3, Ao Nang; daily 12:30pm-10pm)

When you have a hankering for a big meal, Carnivore will satisfy. The restaurant has a huge menu, much of it built around Australian and New Zealand steak, as well as lamb and other meats. Choose from more than a dozen side dishes and five sauces. For starters, lobster bisque and grilled mushrooms are among the options.

Expect several beer and whiskey choices too.

Crazy Gringo's Restaurant ร้านอาหาร Crazy Gringo $

Mexican

(facebook.com/crazygringosrestaurant; 085339-8272; 93/2 Moo 3, Muang Krabi; daily 10am-midnight)

You'll need margaritas or cervezas to get past the noise at Crazy Gringo's. It's a high-volume Tex-Mex joint dishing out chimichangas and nachos, just like you'd get back home. Live music, hot chili peppers, and rows of tables are a fun setting for a night when you just want to slum it, in a good way.

D&E's Jungle Kitchen $

Thai

(facebook.com/DEs-Jungle-Kitchen-524490487660745; 091158-4949; 33 Moo 2, Ban Ao Nang; Mon-Sat 11am-10pm)

Get into the Thailand groove at D&E's. This family-run restaurant, right near the Ao Nang Mosque, is made up of a bunch of thatched bamboo huts at which guests are served home-style local meals. The stir-fries, noodle salads, and curries might sound the same as dishes served in other Thai restaurants, but here they're more like what local residents eat at home.

Govinda's Restaurant ร้านอาหาร Govinda $

Buffet, Vegetarian, International

(govindasaonang.business.site; 099363-2158; 32/24 Moo 2, Ao Nang; daily noon-10pm)

Plant-based eaters will find whatever they crave at Belinda's. This spacious second-floor dining room is cheerful with twinkly lights, and a mishmash of colors. It has a buffet as well as a regular menu. Indian breads, American hamburgers, Mexican fajitas, Spanish empanadas, Italian lasagna—all meat-free or using substitute proteins. Fruit drinks are also available.

Hong Ming Vegetarian Food หงหมิงอาหารเจ $

Vegetarian, Asian

(07562-1273; 4/1 Pruksa Uthit Rd, Muang Krabi; Mon-Sat 6am-6pm)

Hong Ming is small and simple, a counter-servery dishing out a few curries, soups, and noodle dishes, all of which are meat-free. You'll need to use hand motions as your server may not speak English, but that's part of the charm. Sit at one of the few tables and enjoy the flavors.

Jenna's Bistro & Wine $$

Fine Dining, International

(jennasbistro.com; 07569-5152; 328/3 Moo 2, Ban Ao Nang; daily 11am-11pm)

If you like to rendezvous over rosé, Jenna's is the place for you. This polished restaurant would be at home on the main street of any United States tourist town, with its upholstered seating and tasteful wall coverings, not to mention sidewalk tables. You'll find labels from North and South America, Europe, New Zealand, and Australia. The food spans the globe too: Expect Thai specialties like massaman curry, but also Australian Black Angus steaks, French cheeses, and Italian specialty hams. The seafood platter alone crosses continents, with Norwegian salmon, New Zealand mussels, North Atlantic lobster. And heck, who can say no to a New York-style cheesecake made with Tahitian vanilla bean?

KoDam Kitchen ครัวโก๋ดำ $

Thai

(kodamkitchenaonang.com; 062723-1234; 155/17, Soi Khlong Hang 4, Moo 3, Khlong Hang Rd, Ao Nang; daily noon-9pm)

You might feel like you're at a party at KoDam Kitchen, as the thatch-roof restaurant's seating is an outdoor assortment involving long tables and a colorful array of plastic chairs. KoDam has a huge menu, and photos will help you choose. The signature Seafood Jarn Ron, which is shellfish in broth, is appealing, and a variety of items are wok-fried with chili paste and herbs. The chicken drumsticks in creamy massaman curry are another must-have. Then again, how do you pass up on pineapple-fried rice? Take-out is available.

Longtail Boat Bar & Restaurant $$
Romantic, Italian, Seafood, Thai
(facebook.com/longtailboatrestaurant; 07563-8093; Seafood St, 32/17 Moo 2, Ao Nang; daily 1:30pm-10pm)
Follow a narrow road near Ao Nang Beach to Longtail Boat, and you'll have quite the seafood experience. This casual restaurant serves fresh-from-the-sea lobster, blue crab, and more, prepared with Thai flavors. The chefs also specialize in Italian food, including house-made ravioli, gnocchi, and fettucine. Watch the sun go down from your perch on the terrace, or dine indoors in air conditioning. Be sure to end with fried banana; it's served with ice cream.

Ruen Mai Restaurant ร้านอาหารเรือนไม้ $$
Thai
(facebook.com/ruenmaikrabirestuarant; 089288-3232; 61/17 Moo 3, Kukkak; daily 10:30am-4pm, 5pm-10pm)
If you are going to have one all-out special meal during your time in Krabi, make it Ruen Mai. It will be an experience. The restaurant is in Klong Chilat, between Krabi Town and Ao Nang. Enter past the weathered wooden sign to discover conical huts, bamboo, water, and jungle-like foliage. Organic herbs and vegetables are grown within this space, and you'll eat in the fresh air here too. The food is authentically southern Thai—so true to the area that you'll be glad the friendly staff is willing to answer questions. Options include turmeric-fried fish, crab with coconut milk and

chaplu leaves, and stir-fried shrimp with tamarind. Take-out and delivery are available.

Taj Palace ทัชพาเลซ $

Indian

(tajpalace.net; 086951-1369; 111 Moo 2, Highway No. 4203 440 Moo 2, Ao Nang; daily 11am-11:30pm)

The flavors of India, plus some pizza and pasta, have helped build Taj Palace into a long-standing restaurant in Ao Nang. Owned by Diwakar Rai, the restaurant, with a staff of 25, has won awards. The menu features Indian specialties such as garlic naan, mushroom biryani, and chicken vindaloo, alongside Thai curries and stir-fries. Then there's the American breakfast, spaghetti alla puttanesca, and margherita pizza. Go with it: you're on vacation.

Tong Talay Seafood Buffet ทองทะเลบุฟเฟต์ $$

Seafood, Buffet

(facebook.com/Tongtalay.seafood; 083526-7398; 889/5 Moo 2, Ao Nang; daily 4pm-11pm)

If you can't get enough of all the luscious, exotic fish and shellfish pulled from Krabi's crystal-clear waters, head to Tong Talay so you can try out a wide variety in one sitting. Look for mounds of giant river prawns, local clams, and the oysters so often credited as aphrodisiacs. Much of the variety at this cavernous restaurant is raw and laid out on ice; you select your faves and cook them yourselves on a small tabletop grill. Cooks will grill fish to order for you. Take some spoonful's of sauces like green curry, or red curry with crab meat, along with toppings. Tong Talay will drive you to and from your hotel for free.'

Umberto's Italian Cuisine อาหารอิตาเลียนของ Umberto $$

Pizza, Italian

(umbertorestaurant.com; 098548-3332; 125 Moo 3, Ao Nang; daily 1:30pm-9:30pm)

For lunch it's hard to resist a hand-tossed pizza at Umberto's, a restaurant that's been serving up authentic Italian food since 1988. Yet chef-owner Umberto Barbieri will tempt you with so many other fine foods—plus dozens of wines—that you're sure to be back for a special dinner. Begin with any of the eight varieties of bruschetta before trying a house-made pasta. You might choose gnocchi with truffles, or spinach-stuffed green ravioli. Australian meats and Andaman seafood are the basis of the main entrées. That might mean a garlic-marinated lamb chop or beef osso bucco with risotto.

DESSERTS AND COFFEES

Cafe 8.98 คาเฟ 8.98 $

Cake, Coffee

(cafe898.com; 07565-6980; 143/7-8 Moo 2, Ao Nang; also in Klong Hang; daily 7am-11pm)

These two sister cafes may be known for coffee, but their desserts are just as destination-worthy. Going for a Tribeca NYC aura, the cafes not only have freshly roasted coffee beans but also signature desserts, including chocolate cake and banana splits. Cheesecakes and puddings are other options.

Häagen-Dazs $

Ice Cream

(haagendazs.co.th; 07563-7701; 162/86 Moo 2, Chaweng Beach; daily 11am-11pm)

Krabi's unit of this international ice-cream brand will scoop out cones and cups to your liking, with toppings or without. Local flavors include Royal Milk Tea, and yuzu citrus and cream. The Red Dream drink is especially refreshing on a hot day, made with raspberry sorbet and syrup plus soda.

Lion & Shark สิงโตและฉลาม $

European

(facebook.com/LionandShark; 086904-6613; 247/3 Moo 2, Ao Nang; daily 7am-10pm)

Superfood freaks, here's your breakfast place. Lion & Shark specializes in fruit bowls, juices, and smoothies, plus a wide array of hot coffee beverages and bigger meals like egg dishes. But mostly you'll see bowls of superfruits with granola at every table. The side-street setting is Seattle-stylish with sofas, plants, and lots of light.

May & Mark เมย์ & มาร์ค $

Coffee, International

(facebook.com/MayAndMarkHouse; 081396-6114; 34 Maharaj Rd, Soi 10, Pak Nam; daily 7am-9pm)

Known around town as May and Mark's House, this spiffy "restaurant and coffee gallery" with glass walls facing the sidewalk and front patio roasts its own coffee and bakes its own bread. The restaurant serves a varied multinational menu all day long, drawing a lot of customers for its American breakfast. Iced lattes go gloriously with a big plate of eggs. Smoothies, burritos, and pancakes are other options. Indian and Mexican specialties are among the other menu items.

Krabi Sinocha Bakery กระบี่สินโอชาเบเกอรี $

Bakery

(facebook.com/KrabiSinochabakery; 07561-2246; 86 Maharaj Rd, Pak Nam; daily 7:30am-7:30pm)

From festive birthday cakes with floral touches to a slice of something sweet packaged to go, this counter-service bakery near the night market will give your sweet tooth a smile. Cold beverages are also sold here, and there are some seats.

Sprucy Café & Bakery $

Cake, Crepe, Coffee

(sprucy-cafe.business.site; 081080-8008; 289/25 Uttarakit Rd, Pak Nam; daily 7:30am-6pm)

Since 2005, Sprucy has been brewing coffee, pouring tea, and treating Krabi locals and visitors to house-made honey toast, waffles, crepes, and cakes. The café is oh-so-urban, with brick walls, sofas, and a slow drip seemingly always in progress. The sweets tend to lean French, and there's a mango crepe that may call your names in at breakfast time.

The Coffee Club เดอะคอฟฟีคลับ $

Australian

(thecoffeeclub.co.th; 061403-6254; 273, Moo 2, Ao Nang; daily 7am-9:30pm)

With over 400 units worldwide, the Australian-based Coffee Club chain serves three meals a day, and breakfast is a specialty. In its Krabi version, you'll find a contemporary glass and wood storefront, indoor and outdoor seating, and a wide menu. Pair your morning coffee with cereals, eggs, pancakes, or other hearty fare. The coffee itself is Australian-style, made from signature Brazilian, Colombian, and Indian beans roasted in Melbourne and ground in the restaurant to order. There are beach views out the back windows.

Two Scoops สองสกูป $

Gelato

(facebook.com/Twoscoopsgelatoanddesserts; 089724-2791; 73/1 Moo 3, Saladan Ban; daily 11am-6pm; open seasonally)

Two Scoops makes its own gelato and it dishes out plenty of other sweet treats too. Check their Facebook page for specials such as lemon meringue pie and a weekly kombucha. It's all served out of a cheerful pink building.

COOKING CLASSES

Smart Cook Thai Cookery School (smart-cook-thai-cookery-school.business.site) is a classroom in an open-sided hut that is outfitted with portable burners, giving everyone the chance for a hands-on experience. A maximum of nine students attends each class, and you'll get to choose the dishes you want to master. At **Ya's Cookery School** (yacookeryschool.com), Chef Chonlaya Laothong (Ya) offers several one- and three-day culinary classes, starting with info on local produce and ending with a meal and a recipe book. Three-day guests can stay in the two-bedroom villa on-site. **Thai Charm Cooking School** (thaicharmcookingkrabiaonang.com), also in an open-sided hut, focuses on "Healthy Thai dishes you can make at home." You'll choose seven savory dishes to learn, plus you'll practice cooking two classic desserts.

ENTERTAINMENTS

Ao Nang Krabi Stadium สนามกีฬาอ่าวนางกระบี่
(aonangkrabistadium.com; 07562-1042; 100 Soi Nopparatthara, 13 Moo 3 Tumbun, Ao Nang)
Get a taste of Thai boxing, called Muay Thai, and get in shape as well. This stadium welcomes guests for one- and two-hour training sessions for $10 to $15 per person. You can also watch boxing matches three times a week; they're held Monday, Wednesday, and Friday at 9pm. Also called Raja II, this stadium is said to be the third-largest in the country after two in Bangkok.

Temple of a Million Beers วัดล้านเบียร์

Wat Pa Maha Chedi Kaew is a must-see for the beer enthusiasts among you. Also known as Temple of a Million Bottles, Wilderness Temple of the Great Glass Pagoda, and Temple of a Million Beers, this house of worship is literally made of beer bottles. (Concrete, too.) It started as a do-good project in 1984: Tired of litter, monks in Sisaket asked locals to contribute empties so they could build a temple on village burial ground. Long story short, 1.5 million Leo, Chang, and Heineken discards make up the foundations of the temple, dormitory, prayer rooms, and crematorium, plus the water towers. The caps? Mosaics. Construction continues as beer bottles come in. The temple is in the Khun Han District, in Thailand's northeast near Cambodia. It's a seven-hour drive from Bangkok, 13½ hours from Chiang Mai. This is a world of rice paddies, fruit farms, and waterfalls.

NIGHTLIFE

Ao Nang Center Point อ่าวนางเซ็นเตอร์พอยท์

(49/2 4203, Ao Nang)

Built in 1999 and renovated in 2010, Center Point is literally the center point for downtown action in Ao Nang. It's a three-story mall on the beach with a mélange of nightspots, in addition to stores and restaurants. A night out here might involve dinner first—Mediterranean, Mexican, whatever you want. Then you can bop between bars: the spots on the bottom scream to get your attention with bold signage; heading upstairs, female pole dancers and ladyboys—the general term here for transvestites and transgender women—will gear you to clubs and a cabaret. Tattoos? Yes, that too. In all, Center Point is like a miniature of Phuket's Bangla Road and Bangkok's Soi Cowboy. It's near the Burger King on Central Beach Road.

Soi RCA ซ. อาร์ซีเอ

(Ao Nang; diagonally opposite McDonald's; daily 6pm-3am)
The sign officially says RCI Entertainment, and if the polish of Center Point isn't your jam, try this nightspot, which has a more organic feel—plus plenty of outdoor seating. You'll find about a dozen bars, most geared toward single men—yet couples can enjoy the drinks, accouterments, and people-watching. Some of the bars are straightforward, maybe with sports on TVs, others friendly for those shopping for, ahem, a third wheel. Put it this way: One is called the Climax Bar. Don't be surprised to find yourselves involved in some drunken game of Connect Four or a round of pool or whatnot. Let loose and let the evening carry you.

LIVE MUSIC

Bar

Bamboo Bar แบมบูบาร์

(facebook.com/Abowtenboom; 095030-6418; 8 Maharaj Rd, Railay Beach; daily 6pm-2am)
You're in Thailand, so let your drinking hole *feel* like Thailand. Bamboo Bar is the relocated incarnation of a Krabi mainstay. It's the Thai version of a tiki hut—an ultra-casual open bar. Yet good cocktails are served, musicians entertain, patrons get friendly, and no fashion statement is required.

Boogie Bar บูกีบาร์

(facebook.com/Boogie-Bar-305427986243811; 088594-6915; 459 4203, Ao Nang; daily 3pm-1:30am)
This Ao Nang favorite has retro decor elements and loud live music seven nights a week—most of it Western. Grab a drink, tune in, or shoot a game of pool.

Chang Bar ช้างบาร์

(Moo 2, National Hwy 4203, Ao Nang)

Bouncy, boldly colored letters flag Chang Bar, as if shouting, "Let's party!" Inside, you'll find plenty to drink, roaring music, and a dance floor, plus plenty of ladyboys adding color to the scene. Drag shows create a whole other playful vibe on the second floor.

Full Moon Cocktail Bar ฟูลมูนค็อกเทลบาร์

(fullmoonbar.in.th; 088768-9932; Moo 2, Ao Nang Beach; daily 2pm-2am)

Part bar, part tattoo shop, Full Moon is a mellow place to spend time together over a few drinks. On Wednesday, musicians entertain with some sort of mellow music—folk, reggae, rock. A small draft Chang beer is less than $2. Spend $80 total and you'll depart with a free T-shirt.

Krabi Weekend Night Market ตลาดนัดกลางคืนกระบี่

(Soi 10, Maharat Rd, Opposite City Hotel, Krabi, Fri-Sun 6pm-9:30am)

Crowds gather here on weekend nights to fill up on the inexpensive foods dished out by vendors at this night market. While you down kebabs and fruit and crickets—or whatever floats your street-food boat—you can watch the live entertainment: it could be a band playing, a fire show, or an impromptu dance party.

Reggae Town Bar & Restaurant

(facebook.com/Reggae-Town-2116757938353579; 082806-1776; 4 48/3 Moo 2, Ao Nang; daily 11am-1am)

Chill to reggae sounds or watch a soccer match in this lively spot filled with mini flags and banners, plus Bob Marley reminders. Check for happy hour, the "beer buffet," and other specials. And yes, you're apt to wind up dancing.

Tew Lay Bar ติวเลย์บาร์

(062959-9395; Ao Nang, Mueang)

Tew Lay Bar is just a square, with a bamboo bottom and a simple roof, a few stools on each side. It's directly on Railay Beach and serves drinks in the ultimate chill-out setting. There's a treehouse kind of platform too, and a hanging basket seat, plus reggae tunes as a backdrop. At sunset, you'll fall in love with each other all over again.

The Last Bar & Restaurant

(093683-7229; Railay Beach East 633 Moo 2, Ao Nang)

The last bar on the Railay strip, this aptly named beach bar has a whole lot to offer. There's booze, of course, but also several pool tables, and nightly DJs, often live entertainment, too. You might catch a Muay Thai boxing match on the premises. Dancing? That happens organically in every free space on the floor. There's a restaurant too, which keeps different hours. When you need sustenance with your liquid refreshments, you might be able to order from a restaurant that's on the premises, if it happens to be open; the hours don't always coincide.

Tipsy Bar ทิปซีบาร์

(facebook.com/tipsybaraonang; 096030-9340; 4203 Highway, Ao Nang; Mon-Sat 5:30pm-midnight)

Unfinished woods, open sides, low seats, string lights, and pineapple wedges on the rims of cocktail glasses: you'll have no worries hanging out here. Your biggest concerns will be whether to shoot some pool or have another green mojito, make new friends or seclude yourselves in a corner.

Koh Lanta Bars

Half-moon parties, Black moon parties, just-because beers instead of breakfast—the rough-and-tumble **Freedom Bar** (facebook.

com/suppasert) structure at Klong Khong Beach's Lanta Emerald Bungalow is open for quixotic couples' rum-and-Cokes all day, every day, from 8am to 2pm. A DJ gets folks dancing after dark. **Ozone Beach Bar** (facebook.com/ozonebar), a relative old-timer in Koh Lanta, has two parts: a beach bar, and a beachy beachfront dance club with tunes spun by DJs. If you're up for a lively night, choose Thursday, for free entry and a scene on the sand. Even the name **Moonlight Sunset Lounge Bar** (moonlight-resort. com/Facilities) is for sweethearts. You'll find this one within the Moonlight Exotic Bay Resort in Koh Lanta, and we recommend you find it before the sun goes down. Cuddle into a cabana with fruity cocktails and watch the show in the sky. Think peace signs and bamboo when it comes to **Rock Beach Bar** (facebook.com/ rockbeachbar), where sunset views from tables and floor cushions are especially fun accompanied by cocktails served in pineapples. On the edge of Koh Lanta Yai and within the Cococape Resort, this beach bar also has fire shows and entertainment. Thatch-topped **Pangea Beach Bar & Kitchen** (facebook.com/pangeabeachbar) offers meals, sunsets, and beverages on Long Beach. Those sunsets? They come with sounds from a live DJ.

SPORTS BAR

The Irish Embassy สถานทูตไอริช

(irishpubskrabi.com; 72/4 Moo 3, Nong Thale; daily noon-1am) When you want to watch a major sports game on TV, or even just be with others who enjoy spending time that way, grab a beer at one of the Irish Embassy bars. Every setting is different, yet each is a warm and friendly spot for a Western bite to eat and an ale on tap. The original Koh Lanta location has a pool table and darts; the Ao Nang unit is the newest and most contemporary; while live music often plays at the Klong Muang unit.

PUB CRAWL

Ao Nang Krabi Pub Crawl อ่าวนางกระบีผับ Crawl

(bodegahostels.com/tickets/ao-nang-krabi-pub-crawl)

"Bring your liver," the website says, to join this pub crawl. If overdrinking is your kind of fun, buy tickets ($15 each) to meet up with your new beer buddies on a Monday, Wednesday or Friday night. Drinking games begin at 7pm, and the actual crawl starts at 11pm, ending after you hit four bars minimum for 45 minutes to an hour each. Your booze-soaked adventure will include a bucket at Bodega Ao Nang, several shots, and a T-shirt.

SHOPPING

The three-story tall **Vogue** (facebook.com/VOGUEKRABI) mall near the Krabi night market is also the name of the sole department store here. Inside, it looks like any hometown Macy's, with racks of Levi's branded apparel, shoes, make-up, and other expected merchandise. You'll find a supermarket, a food court, and other businesses within. **Outlet Village** (outletmallthailand.com/our_ branch/11) will get you well-priced name-brand goods, many that you know like Wacoal, Speedo, and Adidas. It's on Krabi Town's Petchkasem Road near across from Num Furniture. **Catalunya Walking Street** in Ao Nang is for vacation-style shopping: stores, kiosks, galleries, lodging, bars, and restaurants along an L-shaped pathway, starting at the south end of Ao Nang Beach Road.

MARKETS

Ao Nang Night Market อ่าวนางแลนด์มาร์คไนท์มาร์เก็ต

(109 Moo 3, Ao Nang; daily from 4pm)

Do you buy a belt, or drink coconut water from the fruit? Pick up an ankle bracelet, or treat yourselves to mango with sticky rice? The choice is yours at this night market, a lively spot for eating and indulging your retail weaknesses. Some nights, the market hosts entertainment like a fire show or a Muay Thai boxing demonstration.

Chao Fah Pier Food Market
(Chao Fah Pier on Kong Ka Rd near the boxing stadium, daily 5pm-12:30am)
Every evening at 5pm, a parking lot near the pier empties of vehicles and fills with food vendors. A few dozen specialists in grilling, frying, and more hand over desserts, snacks, and meals for mere baht, including specialties unique to southern Thailand such as grilled seafood. Plastic seats are clustered around tables.

Krabi Town Walking Street ถนนคนเดินเมืองกระบี่
(Pak Nam, Muang; Fri-Sun 5:30pm-10pm)
Cocktails served in bamboo, bags of snacks, skewered meats, tie-dyed dresses, colorful toys... Krabi's Walking Street is essentially a night market three evenings a week, and the two of you can have fun perusing sarongs and feasting on street food. Pick up a locally made craft for your mantle back home, watch people sing, karaoke, and get snockered on Long Island Iced Teas.

Maharaj Market ตลาดมหาราช
(69 Maharaj 7 Alley, Pak Nam; daily 3am-10am)
Live like a local for a few hours and wander the aisles of the Maharaj Market, also called the Morning Market, an indoor affair where residents, not to mention chefs, do their grocery shopping. This market is divided into sections, such as "FOOD – FLOWER" and "GROCERY ITEMS." The regional pickled vegetables sold here are a specialty. Fresh flowers, local curries, barbecued poultry, fruits, and vegetables... you'll find plenty to keep you snapping photos and eating.

MASSAGES

All Day Massage and Sea บริการนวดตลอดวันและทะเล

(facebook.com/Alldaymassage.spa; 095708-5746; 247 Moo 2, Tumbon Ao Nang)

All Day is a well-dressed version of the classic walk-in spa. It has a contemporary entrance, and its massage beds are firm, tidy spaces with curtains for privacy. A row of upholstered chairs is set for foot treatments.

Anchan Massage อัญชัญมาสสาจ

(anchanmassage.com; 080865-0342; 347 Saladan, Ko Lanta; daily 10am-10pm)

When you need to heal from hikes and cave explorations, get a side-by-side treatment at Anchan Massage. You can receive the typical side-by-side food treatments and also, in a nicely decorated private room, get facials, massages, and waxes. Consider lying on parallel beds while receiving relaxing oil massages.

Ao Nang Haven Massage

(aonanghaven.com; 094079-5262; 304 Moo 5, Ao Nang; daily 9am-11pm)

Body scrubs, Thai massages, aroma oil therapy... your wish is bound to be available at Ao Nang Haven Massage. Book a room for two and sign up for the 90-minute Signature P.L.U.S.H. Therapy. It involves massages from the head to the lower legs using the spa's own massage oil and wax oil balm.

Body Kneads Thai Massage มุนวดตัวนวดแผนไทย

(bodykneadsthaimassage.business.site; 098315-1623; 12/14 Chao Fa Alley, Tambon Pak Nam)

Walk in off the street and have your body reset with a Thai massage in Krabi Town. Foot, oil and back massages are also available at this simple space, which has dim lighting and curtains between each massage bed.

Boossabakorn Spa & Beauty บุษบากรสปาแอนด์บิวตี้

(boossabakornspa.com; 07569-5615; 132/35 Moo 2, Ao Nang; daily 9am-10pm)

From simple foot massages to unusual full-body treatments, this moderately priced day spa has many options. The Golden Sexy Skin Sneha Hot Massage Candle, for example, involves hot liquid being dripped onto the body from an Ayurvedic candle. The usual benefits are to get rid of toxins and relieve pain, though the spa's website claims the "golden shimmer" left behind is "a trigger for romance and passion."

Massage Corner มนวด

(massagecorner.shop; 081271-5399; 155/17 Moo 3, Ao Nang)

What a stylish little spot to get your Thai massage or other wellness encounter. House-made coconut oil is often used in treatments, along with other natural ingredients. Whether you have therapists skillfully and simultaneously manipulate your bodies in the outdoor pavilion with mountain views, or opt for inside, you'll have time to unwind. Hot coconut oil massages, sesame oil massages, French manicures, yogurt body scrubs—there are a few dozen options to choose from.

Radarom Spa

(radaromspa.com; 07569-5524; 43/2 Moo 2, Ao Nang Beach)

Free transportation from your hotel is an extra reason to choose Radarom, an upscale day spa with an array of treatment options. The Honeymoon Escape package will treat the two of you to body scrubs, hour-long massages, and facials. You'll receive a snack of cookies and tea before departing.

Sa-bai Thai Massage สบายสบายนวดแผนไทย

(sa-bai-thai-massage-massage-spa.business.site; 087334-2112; 12/15 Chaofa Rd, Pakmun; daily 9am-10pm)

When simple is best, grab a spot at this Krabi Town massage parlor, where the mattresses are on the floor and a few people can receive foot treatments at one time. Facials, body scrubs, waxes, and mani-pedis are available in addition to massages.

So Spa with L'Occitane So Spa กับ L'Occitane

(sofitelkrabiphokeethra.com/wellness-hotel-krabi/so-spa; 075662-7800; 200 Moo 3, Khlong Muang Beach A.Muang Krabi; daily 10am-8pm)

A luxurious hotel spa with L'Occitane products is enough to draw massage lovers to this retreat. Using French and Thai influences, the award-winning tranquil space has 12 treatment rooms and a dramatic pool. Enjoy the Aromatic Dinner package, which includes a Jacuzzi bath for two, aromatherapy massages, and then a candlelit dinner. Ooh-la-la.

TOURS

5 Island Sunset Cocktail Cruise ล่องเรือค็อกเทลยามพระอาทิตย์ตก 5 เกาะ

(krabisunsetcruises.com/en/sunset-cruise; 089719-7344)

Every day at Ao Nang (1:15pm) and Railay (1:30pm), guests are swooped up onto a century-old wooden Siamese Junk boat to head out for an active tour until 8pm. You will be brought to the limestone island Poda; Chicken Island, with a chicken-shaped rock formation; and Si and Ta Ming islands, both great for snorkeling, with time to swim, snorkel, kayak, and/or paddleboard. Not your thing? Watch from the deck, taking in the views. You'll head back just in time to see the sun set from the boat. At the end, you'll swim in bioluminescent waters near Pranang Beach. A Thai buffet dinner, fruit, and soft drinks are included; spirits are for sale. About $90 per person.

Deep Mangrove and Canyon Kayak Tour in Krabi ทัวร์พายเรือ คายัคปาชายเลนและแคนยอนในกระบี่

(firstlevelkayakingtrip.com; 063395-4868)

Immerse yourselves in the different breeds of landscape in this morning tour. You'll start by kayaking in the Andaman Sea amid towering limestone cliffs. Next up is a jungle-canyon landscape, then a mangrove forest filled with monkeys, all by kayak. Includes hotel pick-up, kayak, and life vest. About $40 per person.

Emerald Pool, Hot Springs and Tiger Cave สระมรกตน้ำพุร้อน ถ้ำเสือ

(krabitrek.com/tour-krabi-jungle-springs-emerald.shtml; 087274-4011)

Krabi's Tiger Cave Temple is a significant site, and KrabiTrek has built a full tour around seeing it. In addition to the renowned cave temple, the full-day experience will bring you to Namtok Ron Hot Spring for a steamy soak in healing mineral waters as well as the Emerald Pool for a swim.

Full-Day Jungle Tour Including Tiger Cave Temple, Crystal Pool and Krabi Hot Springs ทัวร์ป่าเต็มวันรวมถึงวัดถ้ำเสือสระ คริสตัลและบ่อน้ำพุร้อนกระบี่

Krabi's most special sites are spread out. This group tour run by Trip Store Krabi makes it easy for you to see three of them in one easy seven-hour trip. An English-speaking guide will bring you to each. One is the mountaintop Tiger Cave Temple (Wat Tham Suea) and its Mountain Temple; the area includes caves, archaeological finds, and jungle. The cave began its transformation into a sacred site in 1975, when a Vipassana monk spotted tigers while he was meditating there. Today you'll want to seek out tiger paw prints, a cave protrusion that resembles a big cat's paw, and the statues of Buddha. If you're fit, take the challenging 1,200+ step stairway to the summit to get close to a large golden Buddha, additional religious structures, and a view in all directions, including Krabi Town, sea, jungle, and cliffs. On this tour, you'll also visit Namtok Ron Hot Spring and waterfall, and the Emerald Pool (Sa Morakot) for a freshwater swim in stunning green water. In the middle, you'll have a Thai restaurant lunch. From $42 per person.

Krabi 4-Islands Tour by Sea Eagle from Krabi ทัวร์ 4 เกาะกระบี่
(tripstorekrabi.com; 084067-9979; daily 8am-10pm)

Hop onto a speedboat with English-peaking guides and explore the area via these four- to six-hour tours. The tours are often offered in the morning and again in the afternoon. You'll likely stop at Pranang Beach to swim and enjoy the beach, Tub Island for snorkeling and exploring, Chicken Island to see a magnificent limestone rock and to snorkel, and Poda Island to visit a bamboo plantation and have a beach lunch or barbecue dinner. $40 per person includes transportation to and from your hotel.

ANIMAL SANCTUARIES

Ao Nang Elephant Sanctuary ศูนย์อนุรักษ์ช้างอ่าวนาง
(aonangelephantsanctuary.com; 065390-9925; 272 Moo 6, Ao Nang)

Spend time with retired elephants at this sanctuary, which keeps them fed and healthy in their golden years. During your visit, a tour guide and elephant keeper will help you cook for the animals, entertain them, cool them off with mud, and give them a bath. The three-hour program includes hotel transfers, a shower, and an English guide. About $10 to $16 per person.

Krabi Elephant House Sanctuary ศูนย์อนุรักษ์ช้างกระบี่
(krabielephanthousesanctuary.com; 05383-8380; 567/3 Moo 4, Tumbon Saithai)

Mahouts are people who live with elephants—we're talking

day and night. You'll see some and visit with the animals at this sanctuary via one of four programs. During your time here, you will at the very least feed elephants, walk in the forest with them, and participate in a bath and mud spa. Bigger programs may include preparing meals and herbal medicines for the creatures, making paper from elephant poop, and visiting the Emerald Pool and hot springs. Book your spot at least a day in advance. From $55 per person.

Bathing elephants at Krabi Elephant House Sanctuary

Krabi Elephant Sanctuary ศูนย์อนุรักษ์ช้างจังหวัดกระบี่

(krabielephantsanctuary.com; 095126-5261; 83/13 Moo 4, Tambon Ao Luel, Ao Luek)

When elephants are past their prime for tourist or logging jobs, they are welcome at this sanctuary, where no rides by visitors are allowed and the setting is a natural one for the animals. Half-day visits involve hotel transfers, feeding elephants sugar cane and bananas, take photos, hearing about their behaviors, taking a mud bath with them, applying skin treatments, and bathing alongside the elephants in a river pond. About $80 per person.

Lanta Animal Welfare ลันตาสวัสดิภาพสัตว์

(lantaanimalwelfare.com; 084304-4331; 629 Moo 2, Ko Lanta; daily 9am-4pm)

If a homeless animal in Krabi has had a hard time, there's a good chance Lanta will come to the rescue. You can take a behind-the-scenes tour: just ask, and a host will set you up to see how animals are doctored, sterilized, and cared for. Free.

CAVES

Diamond Cave (Tham Phra Nang Nai) ถ้ำเพชร (ถ้ำพระนาง)

(Ao Nang, Muang)

One of Krabi's niftiest caves is also among the easiest to see. It's just a ten-minute walk from any of Railay beaches. It's illuminated, and you'll go through on a walkway that is quite manageable. It's about $7 per person to get in, but you'll be rewarded with stunning limestone formations, sloped walls, and vertical natural carvings.

Khao Khanap Nam Mountains and Cave เทือกเขาและถ้ำเขาขนาบน้ำ

(tourismthailand.org/Attraction/khao-khanap-nam; Muang, Krabi)

Even before you see its signature sites, you'll know you've reached Krabi when you spot Khao Khanap Nam. They're a pair of oddly shaped limestone mountains, separated by a river, and they're a 15-minute boat jaunt from Krabi's pier. You'll see stalagmites and stalactites, but will be lucky not to see the many (long-gone) skeletons once discovered here; many are thought to be the remains of Japanese soldiers from World War II, who may have died of thirst or by flood. A 25,000-year-old skeleton was also found here. Also in the cave: prehistoric paintings, and carvings of ancient men making tools.

Khao Mai Kaew Cave ถ้ำเขาไม้แก้ว

(Moo 6, Koh Lanta Yai; 089288-8954)

Call each other Wilma and Fred as you head into the Khao Mai Kaew Cave. It's dark and it's slippery, but if you're willing to deal with slimy ladders and bamboo bridges, you'll get to swim in a cave pool with views of stalagmites and stalactites. Don't let the bats drive you batty; you'll be in their home, after all. To reach this inland cave from Koh Lanta's Old Town, rent a motorbike and follow Route 4245 northeast, then turn left on the only major road you'll hit and ride for another few minutes.

Phra Nang Cave (Princess Cave) ถ้ำพระนาง (ถ้ำเจ้าหญิง)

(Phra Nang Beach, Phela)

This cave, which is right on Phra Nang Beach (a quick and inexpensive boat ride away from Railay Beach, then a ten-minute walk), is fun to explore. The reason to go, though, is a collection of, um, male genitalia standing jutting from the ground. They're made of wood, and many are wrapped in brightly colored cloth. They are said to have something to do with long-ago offerings to the Hindu god Shiva, fishermen's safety, fertility or the princess goddess Phra Nang.

TEMPLES

Chinese Temple วัดจีน

(Ao Nang, Muang)

You'll need to ask locals in Ao Nang where to find this modern complex known as the Chinese Temple, which has a playful design. Climbing up the entry stairs, you'll pass sculptures of dragons and lions in various colors. Then you'll walk under giant face-to-face pink elephants. At the top, green dragons with gold scales flank a multi-armed god, which has the likeness of a small person on its lap. At the end is a three-tier white Chinese-style building with a green roof. You'll see gold people in a boat, gray people praying, a realistic-looking giant bird, and myriad takes on Buddha.

Wat Bang Thong วัดบางทอง

(07565-6014; 46 Swine 3 Na Nuea, Ao Luek; daily 8am-6pm)

Wat Bang Thong is a new relatively new Buddhist temple built in Ao Leuk, an hour north of Krabi Town and Ao Nang. The temple has Thai and Hindu elements. It has a giant Buddha within its colorful interior, and many gold ones ringing the building. Its newly built chedi, a bell-shaped tower called Wat Mahathat Wachiramongkhol, is 230 feet (70m) high and looks almost Central American in it style yet as many distinctly Indian details. Its pagoda is gold. Walk up close and you'll see small statues in many parts of the exterior a swell as paintings of otherworldly characters. The grounds also have life-size elephant statues wearing ornamental accents, along with colorful intricate designs on building exteriors.

Wat Kaew Korawaram วัดแก้วโกรวาราม

(07561-1252; Issara Rd, Pak Nam; Tue-Sun 10am-5pm)

Looking down on downtown Krabi, Wat Kaew Korawaram is a stately white Buddhist temple with a blue-tiled roof, approached via a staircase along which gold Naga sculptures stand guard. Go inside to see a large Buddha and other artworks. It was built in 1887.

ADVENTURES

Half Day Koh Klang Culture Cycling ปั่นจักรยานเทียวเกาะกลาง ครึ่งวัน

(kskrabi.rezdy.com/308669/half-day-koh-klang-culture-cycling; 088445-8256)

Talk about stimulation. With this four-hour tour, you'll take a longtail boat across the Krabi River, hop on your bicycles in Koh

Klang, and cycle to a village. Led by a guide, you'll pass duck, chicken, and vegetable farms, rice production, and coastal birds. Reset with Thai snacks before heading back. The terrain is flat throughout. About $85 per person.

Krabi Rock Climbing ปีนผากระบี

(krabirockclimbing.com; 095028-3143; 625/17, Railay Beach, Ao Nang; daily 9am-6pm)

Krabi's limestone peaks rival its stunning waters as the reason people visit. Learn to climb those rocky surfaces or, if you're experienced, plan a more advanced rock-climbing challenge. Railay-based business invites the two of you to book a private lesson or to learn with other beginners. Full- and half-day beginner experiences are available, as are two- and three-day more advanced adventures, and multi-pitch and deep-water options. $40 to $210 per person.

Saithai Mountain ATV Adventure สายไทยเมาเท่นเอทีวีแอด เวนเจอร์

(facebook.com/SaithaimountainATVadvantureKrabi; 083092-4225)

Take a ride on the wild side and scoot around Saithai Mountain on ATVs. The local outfitter will take you on beginner or advanced tree-lined trails, and will also plan tours of the area's tourist sites.

Thai'd Up Adventures

(thaidupadventures.com; 098909-2885; 95 Moo 2, Sai Thai; daily 8:30am-4pm)

Hey Jane and Tarzan! Swing above the trees with Thai'd Up, located 15 minutes from town. This facility has two-hour, half-day, and full-day opportunities for zip-lining over two courses, plus top-rope climbing and rock climbing. The wires go up to 820 foot (250m) long and 200 foot (60m) high. ATV rides are an add-on. From $40 per person.

HIKING AND VIEWPOINTS

Khao Ngon Nak Viewpoint (aka Dragon Crest) จุดชมวิวเขา งอนนัก (หรือที่เรียกว่า Dragon Crest)

(Khao Ngon Nak National Park, Nong Thale)

Hike up Dragon Crest Mountain to Khao Ngon Nak to see Krabi from above on this hike, which will take four or more hours round-trip. The steep portions have ropes and such to hold on to, and you'll see a waterfall and streams along the way. At the top, you'll have vistas of rolling hills, pointy peaks, and lots of green, seemingly going on forever. On a clear day, you'll even spot the Hong Islands and Koh Yao Yai. The hike starts about half an hour outside of town. Take a cab, wear sturdy shoes, and pack water and snacks.

Khao Ngon Nak viewpoint

Railay Viewpoint จุดชมวิวไร่เลย์

(319 Moo 5, Baan Ao Nam Mao, Ao Nang)

Railay Beach has east and west portions, and each has an entrance for a hike up to its namesake viewpoint. From the east beach, walk uphill for 20 minutes. Most of the work will be on rocks, but there are vines and trees to grab onto. The view at the top is of pine trees, peaks, sand, and water. From Railay West, your route to a stunning, similar view starts on the sand and diverts into several trails. Go as far as you're comfortable, then stop, as the final stretch involves a wall of rock, so it's not for everyone. You'll still get wonderful scenery if you decline the final stretch.

Tab Kak Hang Nak Hill Nature Trail เส้นทางศึกษาธรรมชาติ เขาทับก๊กหางนาค

(6024, Tambon Nong Thale, Amphoe Muang)

Serious hikers will enjoy this trail, a 4½ mile (7.2km) hike to see greater Krabi. Starting about half an hour outside of town, the trail involves challenging roots and trees with little in the way of stairs or pavement. Wildflowers will compensate, not to mention sweeping views of the unusual landscape of rolling hills and craggy peaks, much of its emerald green. Expect the adventure to take three to four hours round-trip.

NATIONAL PARKS

Khao Phanom Bencha National Park

(thainationalparks.com/khao-phanom-bencha-national-park; 061232-4901)

This park is smaller than Mu Ko Lanta, at 19 square miles (50km2), and located just north of Krabi. It'll take you up to 40 minutes to reach from your hotel by automobile. Head to the visitor center, as it's easy to access the waterfall and circular hiking trails from there. The landscape is lush montane forest and about 200 types of birds reside within. Wild animals like tapirs and clouded leopards might also lurk quietly, but you're not likely to see them. The waterfall is Huai To Falls, and it tumbles a half-mile in seven tiers (800m) into smaller falls; swim in the ponds between levels. All but the final tier is easy to walk to. Khao Pheung Cave is another highlight. Bats and geckos live among its stalagmites and stalactites. You can rent tents or bungalows within the park. To reach this park, drive a rental car or scooter, or take a taxi; the road trip, mostly on Route 4, will take about 40 minutes.

Mu Ko Lanta National Park อุทยานแห่งชาติหมู่เกาะลันตา

(thainationalparks.com/mu-ko-lanta-national-park; 081090-1466) Thailand designated Mu Ko Lanta as marine park in 1990, and the 52-square-mile (135km2) expanse in southern Krabi includes several islands. You're most likely to visit Ko Lanta Yai, where the local people, known as sea gypsies (Chao Ley), live and practice ancient rituals. Ko Lanta Noi is popular too. The smaller islands, which are closed from mid-May through October, are excellent for diving and snorkeling. In all, the landscapes involve rain, mangrove and beach forest, lots of splendid white-sand beachfront, hiking trails among the challenging hills, and a number of caves. If you want more than a single-day look-see, book a stay. Your choices will be a two-room bungalow near the headquarters on Laem Ta Nod ($50) or a campsite in the same area or on Ko Rok Nok, a beach with ultra-clear water; permission is required. There is a restaurant, although the menu is limited. It also costs $7 per person to get into the park. To reach Mu Ko Lanta from Krabi, take a ferry ($30-$40 per person) from Krabi's Khlong Jilad Pier to Koh Lanta, then drive a motorbike or take a 40-minute taxi ($25 per person) or minivan ($17 per person) ride from Koh Lanta.

BEACHES

Ao Nang Beach หาดอ่าวนาง

Unless you're on Ao Nang Beach for a drink or meal, you'll probably be there to leave: As the shoreline at the center of Krabi's main tourist town, Ao Nang Beach is the main place to hop on a longboat to go to a different beach. That's not to say it's not lovely: the sand is lined by palm trees on one side, calm water on the other. But this is more a place for shopping, dining, and beer-sipping, not to mention renting water-sports equipment and hopping on tours. The sunsets are wonderful.

Kantiang Bay อ่าวกันเตียง

For a whole other beach experience, check out Kantiang Bay. In high season, take a two-hour ferry ride from Krabi Town; otherwise, get here on a minibus plus a speedboat, available at select times. Your reward will be an arched white-sand beach backed by shade trees and lined with a small variety of hotels, from basic to luxury. You'll look at mountains and boats, not hordes of tourists. The diving from here is worth a detour.

Phra Nang Beach หาดพระนาง

It doesn't take much to make a beach romantic, yet Phra Nang may set the bar for others worldwide. This quarter-mile (400m) stretch of sand is white and soft, and lapped by pristine calm Railay Bay water. Park yourself for the day, grab lunch from a longtail boat, and scuttle under a limestone cliff for shade. The Princess Cave is here, filled with giant wooden penises, and a second cave offers nice little hikes. It takes 20 minutes by boat to reach this beach from Ao Nang.

Railay Beach หาดไร่เลย์

Reachable only by boat, and offering smooth sand and views of extraordinary cliffs, Railay Beach—really four beaches in one—is a wonderful getaway. You'd think development would spoil the perfection. But how can you complain about the chance to have a massage in a setting this spectacular? Or to do some Muay Thai boxing? You can even have lunch at a beach café. Once you reach this peninsula via quick boat ride, you'll find it easy to explore by walking around. In fact, the beach has no vehicles at all. Rock climbing is available here.

Tub Kaek Beach หาดทับแขก

When you want the ultimate escape—quiet sand, pristine water, a tête-à-tête over a private candlelit dinner—take the 30-minute taxi ride to this destination, also known as Tubkaak. Or, stay here. Tub Kaek has a handful of resorts, each hugging a bit of the 1.2-mile (2km) gold-sand beach. Day-trippers should expect most, if not all, meals to be at the resorts, as few vendors sell food here. Hike through the landscape on a trail, and watch an exceptional sunset. Oh, and make time for *The Hangover Part II* before you arrive; parts were filmed here and at the Ritz-Carlton.

MUAY THAI CLASSES

The **Lanta Muay Thai Complex** (lantamuaythaicomplex.com)—owned by a woman, Pensri "Penn" Keeratimetakul—has beginner and other classes, sparring opportunities, and the chance to use the gym near Khlong Dao Beach. **Lanta Muay Thai Academy** (facebook.com/lantagym) invites you to take group or private classes in Koh Lanta, or stop by for fitness sessions. **Bull Muay Thai** (bullmuaythaikrabi.com) calls itself a training camp, and the Ao Nang facility welcomes walk-ins for any group training class; they're held at 8am and 4pm daily. Shuttle service is available. Bull Muay Thai has not only a gym but also a pool, restaurant, bar, and store. At **Honour Muay Thai Gym Ao Nang Krabi** (honourmuaythai.com), you can spar near Ao Nang amid limestone peaks. Owners Howard and Ajarn Yodchai Noi have set up a place mostly for week and longer intensive-training stays, but welcomes walk-ins for group training sessions. VIP private training is another option. **Emerald Muay Thai Gym** (emerald-gym.com) says invites newbies and pros, on Monday and Saturday. The Ao Nang gym staffs current and former pro fighters. Brazilian Jiu-Jitsu lessons are also available.

YOGA

Lanta Yoga ลันตาโยคะ

(lanta-yoga.com; 089019-5911; 557 Moo 2 Saladan, Koh Lanta)
Tucked away from the hubbub of Koh Lanta, Lanta Yoga teaches yoga classes in an open-sided shala surrounded by nature. Classes are Vinyasa flow, adapted for all levels. The same owners run the nearby Fruit Tree Lodge; a modest hotel comprised of traditional Thai-style bungalows.

Oasis Yoga Bungalows โอเอซิสโยคะบังกะโล

(oasisyogabungalows.com; 085115-4067; 15 Moo 3, Saladan, Koh Lanta)
If all yoga, all the time, triggers romance for your duo, book a stay at Oasis Yoga Bungalows. This is a serene place to take yoga classes, steps from the Koh Lanta beach, then retreat to one of 13 poolside bungalows, each with a hammock—and also air-con and Wi-Fi. The on-site restaurant serves fresh-focused daytime meals, and the bar offers cold-pressed juices, signature cocktails, and craft beers. You can take a few classes or participate in a retreat.

Samadee Yoga สมะดีโยคะ

(samadeeyoga.com; 081538-2343; A 539 Moo 2, Aonang Soi 2/1, Ao Nang)
Several types of yoga are offered at Samadee, so you'll find calming practices and physically challenging ones—all with a view of the jungle, English and Thai instruction, breathing exercises, a mantra, and a bit of meditation. Options include Vedic Hatha yoga, Kundalini yoga, yoga Nidra, and gentle or dynamic flow, among others. You can also book a private class or take harmonizing workshops together. Teacher training is another option.

Shambala Marina Yoga & Reiki ชัมบาลามารีน่าโยคะและเรกิ
(marinayoga.com; 094320-5335; 524 Moo 2, Ao Nang Soi 1)
Yoga is on the calendar seven days a week at this studio, catering
to all levels. You can also take a reiki class, learn chakra breathing
techniques together, plan for a yoga retreat, or try out healing
practices such as sound bowls and ear candles. Teacher training
is also available.

KOH TAO

Koh Tao

WHY GO

Koh Tao is small, yet this pretty island packs in a wallop of wonders. For starters, this palm-fringed destination in the Koh Samui Archipelago, at just a bit more than eight square miles (21km²), is a global diving hot spot: here, the robust scuba community offers a tremendous amount of instruction and pro training—not to mention good dive sites and surprisingly low prices. Koh Tao means "turtle island," and you may well see the namesake creatures during your dives. Harmless sharks are also in some waters.

If scuba isn't your jam, you'll still find lots to love in this wee spot in the Gulf of Thailand. The beaches that string the island are white or golden, lively or tranquil, bare or boulder-dotted. The water: pristine and gorgeous bays, one after another.

Lovely romantic restaurants and bars provide special meals, and spas encourage couples' treatments. If you like a crowd with your courting, head to Sairee Beach or the Mae Haad area. There you'll find bars filled with fun-loving vacationers.

Koh Tao has a handful of viewpoints too, offering panoramic vistas as a reward for a hike or a drive. In sum, this little locale has a whole lot to love. You could easily spend a week here and not get bored.

Mountain view of Sairee Beach

HOW TO GET TO KOH TAO

If Bangkok is the center of the Thai universe, Koh Tao is a distant star. Which means: No bus. No train. No plane. No car. Boat is the only way to reach this destination. But that's easy. First off, you'll need to travel to Chumphon, Surat Thani, Koh Samui, or Koh Phangan by plane, train, bus, or automobile. Some combo tickets are available: Consider using a travel agent to help—any storefront will do, or email your hotel in advance for guidance. Other options are the websites 12go.asia, busonlineticket.co.th, directferries.com, lomprayah.com, seatrandiscovery.com, and songserm.com. In the end, you'll arrive by water at Mae Haad Pier on the island's west coast.

Catamaran and speedboat If you're in Chumphon, you can take a 90-minute catamaran ride to Koh Tao with Songserm. The Lomprayah Catamaran runs from Koh Samui and Koh Phangan. Again, check online for up-to-date info.

Combo tickets Bus-and-boat tickets are sold by Songserm Express and Lomprayah Catamaran, for journeys starting in Bangkok. The bus portion takes eight hours, the boat portion up to three hours but the prices are low, with the whole trip coming in at $55 per person one-way total. Train-ferry combos are the same price and take 18.5 hours by train, plus the ferry ride.

Ferry The Seatran Discovery (seatrandiscovery.com) ferry runs from Koh Samui and Koh Phangan. The journey lasts 75 minutes to 2½ hours and prices start at $20 each way per person one way. From Chumphon, a Songserm ferry runs daily and takes under three hours for about the same price each way.

GETTING AROUND

Koh Tao is small and all the tourist areas are along the shoreline, so it's easy to get around. Essentially, one road circles much of the island: No matter your mode of transportation, turn out the front door of your lodging facility and you'll find your destination easily.

Bicycle Bicycles won't get you as far, but you'll burn off some of that panang curry and beer, and it'll be easier to stop at a whim along the way. Some hotels have their own fleet. From $5 a day.

Longtail boat If you want to visit outlying islands without abiding by a tour's schedule, you can rent kayaks from a vendor along the beach or hire a longtail boat. Simply agree to a round-trip price with the person guy running your motorized vessel. You can also hop from pier to beach this way. From $5 or $50 for a whole day.

Motorbike/scooter Rent a motorized two-wheeler for your stay, or a pair of them if you don't fancy squeezing onto one seat. Then you'll be able to get anywhere on the island—except the mountaintop viewpoints. You can rent in any number of specialty shops along the west coast or, in some cases, request pick-up/drop-off from your hotel. From $10 a day.

Motorbike taxi If you want to keep it cheap but not do the driving, sit on the back of a motorbike taxi, although that might be challenging for two of you at once.

Songthaew Thailand's answer to buses and taxis, on Koh Tao the songthaews—four-wheel-drive trucks that can handle the rugged road—can be found at all the major tourist areas. You pay based on distance, which is rarely more than $7 for the two of you. These are also referred to as taxis on the island.

WHERE TO STAY

Koh Tao area map

Chalok Baan Kao Bay อ่าวโฉลกบ้านเก่า

If you're more a sun, sand, and sea duo than a beer-for-breakfast pair, Chalok may be perfect for you. This crescent-shaped area near the southern tip and overlooking its namesake bay has divine white sand and calm water for swimming. In fact, the sea is so clear you might swoon. You can see Ang Thong Marine National Park, plus the islands of Koh Phangan and Koh Samui, in the distance. Activities, restaurants, and bars are never far, and you can easily reach the other tourist areas when you want a change of scenery, nightlife, or a water-sports adventure.

Mae Haad แม่หาด

If all that prettiness without some rowdiness seems boring, Mae Haad might be your best bet. You'll probably arrive at the ferry dock here, on the western coast, and this is the place to get cash, buy sundries, find that funky sarong, and rent motorbikes. Most of the lodging here is budget-friendly, though boutique properties offer more chic, personable options. You'll have plenty of dining choices and convivial nightlife, but the beach is small and not as special as its peers elsewhere on the island. The snorkeling, though—there's a shipwreck right offshore.

Sairee Beach หาดทรายรี

If you two are a social pair, this is your spot. Sairee Beach has exceptional sunset views and plenty of wonderful meal options. Beach lovers will enjoy calm swimmable water, boulders, shady palm trees, and wooden beach huts, all lined along arch-shaped white sand. It's also party central: Beach clubs, bars and more attract fun lovers after dark. That includes the backpackers living on pennies a day and those who have spa days and luxury tours before hitting the cocktail menu. There's a coral reef offshore.

Tanote Bay อ่าวโตนด

Sunrise views are reason enough to stay in or visit Tanote Bay, and that's not the only selling point. This east coast area has a big, sensational, and blissfully quiet, gold-sand beach, and it's surrounded by tropical beauty. Rent a kayak here and take time to walk within the lush tropical landscape beyond the sand. You can easily reach three viewpoints by foot. Your choice of hotels will be limited (but varied price-wise)—a boon if you like your beaches bare.

Thian Og (Shark Bay) เทียนอ๊อก (อ่าวฉลาม)

Black-tip reef sharks—don't worry, they're not aggressive—

abound in Shark Bay's waters, a fun reason to spend time here on the south coast. A whole bunch of turtles hang here too. The beach is white and never chaotic—all the better for one-on-one time in paradise. You can snorkel, have a nice meal... and sun yourselves some more.

ACCOMMODATIONS

Ban's Diving Resort บ้านดำน้ำรีสอร์ท $

(bansdivingresort.com; 07745-6466; 3/1 Moo 1, Sairee Beach) Bright, comfortable, and modern air-conditioned rooms greet you at Ban's, a great hotel on Sairee Beach for couples who dive. You'll be free to use the swimming pools, fitness center, and in-house conservation center that highlights the resort's eco-friendly initiatives. A restaurant, bar, convenience store, and ATMs are also on-site, alongside the PADI dive offerings. These range from beginner to pro courses, as well as fun diving and more serious outings for advanced scuba enthusiasts. More than 250,000 divers have been certified here. Ban's has four large dive boats equipped with refreshments, and rental equipment certified by Aqualung.

Cape Shark Pool Villas เคปชาร์คพูลวิลล่า $$

(capesharkvillas.com; 07745-7121; 21/9 Moo 3, Shark Bay) Maybe you'll have natural stone walls in your room, like in The Hideaway Villa, perhaps "only" a private infinity pool. From studios to five-bedroom villas, Cape Shark offers a romantic setting perched over the Gulf of Thailand. Thatched roofs abound, as does the natural, tropical charm and plenty of amenities—an outdoor pool and sun terrace among them. Ao Luek beach is a quick walk away and free shuttles will bring you there as well as to town. You can rent snorkel gear and have massage treatments here.

Chaantalay ชานทะเล $

(chaantalaykohtao.com; 084545-0919; 35/8 Moo 1, Koh Tao)
Less than half a mile (800m) from Sairee Beach, Chaantalay is a sharp-looking budget-friendly hotel with many extras. In addition to comfortable air-conditioned rooms with TV and free Wi-Fi, there's a mountain-view pool with pool beds as well as a pool bar, billiards table, restaurant, sun deck, garden, and fitness center. You can even rent bicycles here and get help planning outings at the tour desk.

Jamahkiri Resort & Spa จามาคีรีรีสอร์ทแอนด์สปา $

(jamahkiri.com; 07745-6400; 21/2 Moo 3, Koh Tao)
Jamahkiri offers three honeymoon packages, which tells you how ideal this hotel is for couples. Even the smallest of those includes spa pampering, a private boat tour, and breakfast in bed. Yet Jamahkiri is just as sweetalicious without the package. The seaside accommodations, from traditional guestrooms to three-bedroom villas, are air conditioned with plenty of natural light and decorated with traditional Thai touches. You'll eat in an open-sided restaurant, and can take the edge off at the pool bar or seated in the wine cellar. Happy hour runs every day from 5 to 9pm. A spa offers a variety of therapeutic treatments, and the full-service dive center has instruction, high-end equipment, and two boats for excursions, and they never take more than four divers per divemaster. A marina is on the premises, as is a fitness room. The resort makes eco-efforts, from using low-energy light bulbs to sorting recycling and initiating road clean-up efforts.

Monkey Flower Villas มังกีฟลาวเวอร์วิลล่า $$

(kotaovilla.com; 092423-1639; 19/6 Moo 1, Koh Tao)
If you're looking for a whole lot of privacy in a whole lot of space, Monkey Flower villas is for you. This privately owned getaway with tropical landscaping has four villas, each spacious

and comfortable, some with private decks and pools. You'll be a three-minute walk from Sairee Beach, though a private car and driver will bring you to and from there or anywhere else on the island. A concierge is on call around the clock. A waterfall and a pond stocked with catfish and carp are on the premises. At check-in, you'll receive a phone to use during your stay. The drivers' contact info, activities, and restaurants will be pre-loaded into the contacts list.

The Tarna Align Resort เดอะ ธ นาอะไลน์รีสอร์ท $
(tarnaalignkohtao.com; 07760-1843; 33 Moo 1, Koh Tao)
The Tarna Align is romantic on its own, and it offers add-ons that make it ridiculously so. Stay at this boutique resort, a five-minute uphill drive from Sairee Beach, and you can request a special dinner in your villa or even a sunset dinner cruise with chef-prepared courses and a butler to serve them. On property, all three restaurants—Thai, Japanese, and Western—are located on the highest floor to provide water views. The bar? It's on the roof and the vistas are sublime. Even the simplest guestrooms are individually decorated soothing sanctuaries of neutral tones with contemporary accents. You'll also have access to swimming and an on-premises cooking class. The Align has a dive school with a saltwater pool for practice and a two-story dive boat with food, drinks, a lavatory, and a shower. Stay-and-dive packages are available, and the Align will meet lower rates if you book directly.

View Point Resort วิวพอยท์รีสอร์ท $
(viewpointresortkohtao.com; 091823-3444; 27 Moo 3, Koh Tao)
Nestled beside boulders right on the water, View Point Resort is a secluded spot ideal for two people in love. Each villa and cottage bring the outdoors in, as local woods and stones are integrated into the design. Your thatch-hut accommodation might have a private pool with an air-conditioned interior and be just a short walk to

the quiet beach. Others are farther from shore yet offer balconies facing Chalok Baan Koa Bay or the natural jungle landscape. A freeform pool stands above the bay, The Cape restaurant and bar uses herbs grown on the property, and the Chillax Hut is a prime place to receive massages. Book yourselves the Sunset Toast & Candle Light Dinner on the Beach. You'll begin by reclining on Thai pillows as the sun sets, nibbling on canapés and sipping bubbly. You'll follow with a three-course meal. Other packages can include couples' massages and speedboat excursions.

BREAKFASTS

Breeze Koh Tao บรีสเกาะเต่า $$
International, Mediterranean
(breezekohtao.com; 093553-4799; 9/94, Moo 2, Koh Tao; daily 7:30am-10:30pm)
When you want to be seated for a proper table-service breakfast, head over to Breeze, a Mae Haad beachfront restaurant featuring international flavors, fresh seafood, and plenty of vegan options. If tables aren't your thing, settle into beanbags or chaises. The breakfast menu is ample. Choose an American-style meal of pancakes served with banana, tamarind, chocolate, candied walnuts, and salted caramel. Or go yogi-style: smashed avocado on toasted ciabatta with roasted tomato, poached egg, and feta cheese. The Full English is also available, with baked beans and all. Later in the day, return for pasta, burgers, and a dessert board designed for sharing, loaded with panna cotta, dark chocolate fondant, and sorbets. Sunset views are a plus at dinnertime.

Living Juices น้ำผลไม้ที่มีชีวิต $
Vegan, Heathy
(facebook.com/LivingJuices; 090916-8967; 14/12 Moo 1, Laville View Kohtao Guest House; daily 8am-4pm)

When "SUPER FOODS" jumps off the menu in bright orange type, you know this Sairee restaurant is a good bet for a healthy day-starter meal. Living Juices is all about that, from house-made protein bars and coffee drinks to "Living Bowls": fruit mixes topped with house-made granola, coconut milk, SuperBoost trail mix, bananas, and shredded coconut. Hang around a bit and you may receive advice on eating well, or even official coaching. The juices on offer are varied: the Royal Flush is red from beets, while the Healthy Starburst is carrot-orange.

The Factory Café $
Vegan, Healthy, International
(facebook.com/thefactorykohtao; 098718-6712; 9/284 Sairee Beach; daily 8am-5pm)
Brunch is available all day at the bright and rustic beachside Factory Café. This Sairee Beach whole-foods enterprise offers up a bunch of superfood smoothies and cold-pressed juices, as well as bowls, wraps, and baked goods. It's all vegetarian—much of it vegan—with organic and locally raised ingredients used whenever possible. Banned: refined sugars, MSG, and hydrogenated oils. Grain or quinoa Yogi Bowls are hearty ways to start the day. The eggs Benedict, cinnamon porridge, and shakshuka are also tempting. Other options better suited to later in the day include a meat-free Philly Cheesesteak sandwich and pesto pumpkin tofu scramble. And be sure to add on a dragon fruit- and passion infused water.

LUNCHES AND DINNERS

995 Duck 995 เปิด $$
Duck, Asian
(facebook.com/pages/995%20Duck/2244351832241973 Tay, Koh Tao; daily 9am-3:30pm, 5:30pm-9pm)

Sometimes called 995 Roasted Duck, this is a Sairee Beach Chinese restaurant that's all—surprise, surprise—about duck. The highlight is assorted roasted duck entrées served in soup with noodles or on a plate with rice, though the restaurant does a whole lot more than that—and, of course, all with duck. Prices at this street front restaurant are cheap, and there's usually a line, so head out before you're too hungry.

Babaloo $
Vegan, Thai
(facebook.com/babaloo.tao; 098861-2503; Chalok Baan Kao Beach, Koh Tao; daily 8am-10pm)
With a conical palapa roof, Babaloo provides an authentic Thai setting. The food is meat-free vegan and vegetarian. From curries to vegan "duck" spring rolls and sweet-and-sour entrées, every dish is cooked to order. Choose vegan fish, chicken or duck substitutes. Ginger tofu with mushrooms and a Thai spinach omelet are typical selections.

Cantina de Koh Tao แคนติน่าเดอเกาะเต่า $
Mexican
(facebook.com/cantinadekohtao; 093364-9277; 9/62 Moo 1, Sairee Beach; daily 10am-10pm)
Thousands of miles from Tijuana, or even Texas, you can have a fiesta of flavors by dining at this "Mexican grill & cantina". Get your fill of breakfast burritos, veggie taco plates, Baja fish tacos, and fajita wraps. Time your visit for a Tuesday when chips and salsa cost are free and margaritas and tacos are discounted. The salsas, masterminded by the Californian owner, are made in-house. The no-fuss dining room opens to the street.

Coconut Monkey ลิงมะพร้าว $
Vegan, European
(facebook.com/CoconutMonkeyKohTao; 093640-4522; 25/92

Moo 2, Mae Haad Beach; dally 8am-5pm)

It's all about fresh, right on the beach, at Coconut Monkey. All day long, take in beach views while enjoying espresso or fresh juices, or fueling up on overnight oats with fruits and caramel, a granola-yogurt combo, or a vegan banoffee pie, all made in house. Omelets and vegan chili, breakfasts, and bowls are also available.

Flaming Hog BBQ บาร์บีคิวหมูไฟ $

BBQ, American

(facebook.com/flaminghog99; 085781-3275; 9/62 Moo 1, Sairee Beach; daily noon-10pm)

Hickory-smoked in Koh Tao? Why not! "BIG Jim Anderson, the BBQ KING!!!!" turns out grilled chicken and ribs, along with corn on the cob, potato salad, and coleslaw at this casual American-style barbecue joint with bamboo seating. The chicken smokes for up to seven hours. Miss chili? You can get it here—Texas- or Colorado-style.

Hippo Burger Bistro ฮิปโปเบอร์เกอร์บิสโทร $

Burger, American

(facebook.com/Hippoburgerkohtao; 085226-2648; 9/38 Moo 1, Sairee Village Ban Ko Tao; daily 11:45am-11pm)

Miss your hipster burger hangout back home? Hippo will fill the gap. Its premium beef burgers have all kinds of toppings, and so do other varieties—Hawaiian pork, teriyaki chicken, and lamb with feta, for example. A bean and lentil patty will satisfy vegans. The Hippo makes sauces and buns in-house, and the drinks menu extends to all-things-trendy: fruit or blended ice-cream shakes, fruit juices, pale ale, and hard cider.

Infinity Thai Food อาหารไทยอินพินิตี้ $

Thai

(infinitykohtao.com/restaurant and facebook.com/InfinityKohTao; 07733-2809; 5/44-45 Moo 2, Mae Haad; daily 10am-9:30pm)

Located in an inn, Infinity serves its Thai specialties—and American options like a chicken club sandwich with fries—in a bright, natural dining room that opens to the outside. Thai-fried chicken with cashews is a staple, along with panang and massaman curries. The full menu is large; it's divided into sections like "Fried," "Small on rice" and "The plates not spicy": It'll be easy to match a section to your likes. Fresh fruit shakes are a refreshing addition.

Koh Tao BBQ Buffet เกาะเต่าบาร์บีคิวบุฟเฟต์ $
Buffet, Thai
(koh-tao-buffet-bbq.business.site; 088449-8191; Chalok Moo 3, Koh Tao; daily 5pm-10pm)
For about $6 apiece, you can get your fill of Thai flavors. A nondescript spot with indoor and outdoor seating, this all-you-can-eat restaurant puts out stainless steel chafing dishes of many foods. Choose what you want, then, back at the table, warm some fish, shellfish, meat, and/or vegetables over a tabletop cooking device. Once cooked, you can start dipping the foods in a variety of sauces.

La Carotte Qui Rit $
Vegan, Thai
(facebook.com/pages/La%20Carotte%20Qui%20 Rit/782117988547593; 096730-9188; Ban Ko Tao, Mae Haad; daily 10am-9:30pm)
Meat-free Thai meals cater to vegetarians and vegans at La Carotte Qui Rit, a colorful open storefront. The menu is broad, encompassing curries, noodles, stir-fries, and even sweets. The portions are generous and the prices are low. The specialty is lui suan noodle, which looks like little sushi roll slices but is entirely plant-based, filled with veggies, and is topped with cashews and sesame seeds.

La Pizzeria $

Pizza, Italian

(facebook.com/lapizzeriakohtao; 090279-1300; Nay Pon Rd Walking St, Sairee Beach; daily 11am-11pm)

A white likeness of Italy on a deep red wall marks La Pizzeria, an Italian specialist that opens to the street. Stop in for a pie—there are a few dozen varieties—or pasta, calzones, risotto, lasagna or eggplant parmigiana. The restaurant makes the ricotta stuffed into its ravioli, the spinach is grown on an organic farm, the pesto is prepared in-house... you get the idea. Daily specials are posted regularly. Takeout and delivery are available.

P.Oy's Place ป. อ้อยเพลส $

Thai

(facebook.com/Poysplace; 062069-1030; 5/68 Moo 3, Chalok Bann Kao; Tue-Sat 11am-9pm)

Pornsri "P.Oy" Piper, a chef with decades of experience in London and Thailand, and her family run this Thai restaurant on the lower road toward Chalok. Stop in for a slow-cooked massaman chicken curry with khao soi, or maybe for one of their Indian Nights to try the pork vindaloo and South Asian chicken curry. The sticky chicken wings nearly have a cult status. Essentially, just show up, take a seat in the open-sided dining area and expect fresh, chef-made Asian food.

Pranee's Kitchen ปราณีคิทเช่น $

Thai

(pranees-kitchen.business.site; 07745-6924; 9/1 Moo 2, Mae Haad; daily 8am-9:30pm)

Koh Tao may be newly popular for tourists, yet the family behind Pranee's Kitchen has been dishing out garlic pepper chicken, shrimp pad Thai, and spicy-and-sour kaeng som curry for three decades. Located in the Ananda Villa hotel the open-sided restaurant in the Mae Haad area kind of has it all: coffees, fruit shakes, breakfast including pancakes, cocktails, burgers, pasta, steak, and panang, green, massaman and red curries, as well as other Thai dishes.

Seafood by Pawn ซีฟู้ดบายจำนำ $

Seafood, Thai

(facebook.com/seafoodkohtao; 093530-9324; 2/77 Moo 2, Mae Haad Village; daily 11am-10pm)

The hand-painted sign marketing Seafood by Pawn has a homemade feel, and that matches the food at this stand in the Green Mango Food Court in Mae Haad Village. Grilled fresh fish and Thai classics are made with love. (You can get some Western dishes too, from Greek salad to a Western omelet.) Dine in a traditional Thai-style open-sided, pointy-roofed shala surrounded by greenery: your meal might include a whole fish, maybe stuffed or pan-fried, or tempura prawns and calamari.

The Gallery Restaurant ห้องอาหารเดอะแกลลอรี $$

Thai

(thegallerykohtao.com; 07745-6547; 20/27 Moo 1, Sairee; Thu-Tue noon-10:30pm)

When you want a dose of urban panache in your tropical island getaway, here's your top pick. The Gallery is a fine-dining hotel restaurant that also has an upstairs lounge called The Gold Bar and a fine-art photo gallery. Exceptional ingredients are used to create Thai meals here, and each plate is artfully arranged. The chefs are so determined for guests to enjoy each dish that they provide separate spoons for each so the flavors don't mix. Order a la carte, or opt for "Trust the Chef": After learning your preferences, the head chef will design a multicourse meal just for the two of you ($30 per person). Dining indoors or out, you'll enjoy views of Sairee and Mae Haad bays from the hillside position.

Tukta Thai Food ตุ๊กตาอาหารไทย $

Thai

(10/1 Moo 3, Koh Tao; daily 11am-10pm)

A Thai shala hut with open sides is the setting for local flavors at Tukta, where colorful soups and chilled beers make almost any day better. Located in Mae Haad, the restaurant serves a broad menu of meats and seafood but also accommodates vegetarians and gluten-free diners with ease. It fills up nightly, so arrive on the early side.

VegetaBowl $

Vegan

(facebook.com/vegetabowl; 084692-7749; 9/281 Moo 1, Sairee Beach; daily 11:30am-8pm)

Eating healthy "bowl" meals helps keep those hearts healthy, and VegetaBowl went all-in on the concept. Its vegetarian and vegan menu items involve fresh ingredients with sauces, nut butters, and dressings made on the premises by the Canadian chef. As for the no category: frying, MSG or preservatives. Gluten-free options abound. Sugar-free smoothies are available, along with choices like the Wellness Bowl, filled with roasted sweet potato and pumpkin, hummus, veggies, and sprouts with a garlic-tahini sauce. Quesadillas, cookies, and falafel burgers are sometimes available.

Whitening Bar & Restaurant ไวท์เทนนิงบาร์แอนด์เรสเตอรองท์ $$

Romantic, Seafood, European, Asian

(facebook.com/Whiteningkohtao; 083941-4199; 9/246, Moo 1, Sairee Beach; daily 11:15am-11:45pm)

Lest you think Sairee Beach is all backpackers and dive suits, Whitening will set you straight. In Hamptons style, this waterfront restaurant is all white. The menu is creative and upscale—pan-seared duck breast, pad cha seafood (shellfish cooked at a very high temperature)—and at night candles illuminate each table. Some of those tables are directly on the sand. A little wine, a dose of sunset... this is why you traveled to Thailand. Dinner isn't mandatory—you'll enjoy Whitening just as much sipping happy hour concoctions to soothing music. The beach view never gets old.

DESSERTS AND COFFEES

Cafe Culture วัฒนธรรมคาเฟ $

Coffee, European

(089616-1556; 10 Moo 1 Walking St, South Sairee; daily 8:15am-8pm)

Hey, it takes energy to sunbathe on the beach all day. Step into Café Culture on your way to or from Sairee Beach to rev up with coffee. The baristas here create adorable animal art—just ask: cutie-pie bears, puppy dogs, a wistful heart, or a rainstorm, perhaps a bunny rabbit or swan... sip as you look at each other with puppy dog eyes. Basic lattes and Americanos comprise the coffee menu, and there's a matcha green tea latte—also customizable with designs on top —too. Breakfasts, sandwiches, salads, and juices are also available.

Koh Tao Thai-Riffic เกาะเต่าไทย – ริฟฟิค $

Cake, International

(facebook.com/KohTaoThaiRiffic; 088442-9877; 9/251 Moo 1, Sairee; daily 10am-9pm)

Chances are you'll spend a lot of your Koh Tao stay in Sairee. That gives you more chances to indulge in sweets at the Thai-Riffic bakery on Nay Pon Road. Order a birthday or other special-occasion cake in advance, or just show up for the house-made ice cream, cookies, or slices of whatever is in stock. As for cakes, that might involve familiar flavors or Thai tea, orange, or "choco mocca caramel." With luck, you'll arrive at a time when brownie cheesecake slices are ready to serve, or black forest cake or strawberry choux. Plenty of coffee and tea beverages are available to pair with your treats.

Monsters มอนสเตอร์ $
Ice Cream
(monsters-ice-cream-shop.business.site; 098398-7224; No. 11/1 Moo 2, Koh Tao; daily 11am-9pm)
Rolled ice cream—ice cream that is flattened, then rolled into thin layers with toppings such as candies and cookies... that's the gist of Monsters, a simple, cheerful waterfront sweets shop on Tanote Bay Road near the Mae Haad Pier. Half the fun is watching a staffer manipulate your ice cream to order. The other half? Eating the colorful concoctions.

Permpoon Ice-Cream เพิ่มพูนไอศครีม $
Ice Cream
(facebook.com/pages/PermPoon%20Coffee%20Bar%20By%20 The%20Pool/556926461425483; 07745-6126)
Homemade gelato is the calling card at Permpoon, a dessert specialist in Sairee. Look for flavors such as biscuit brownie, tiramisu, strawberry cheesecake, and rum raisin. The shop uses cookies, some with faces, to create cheerful characters with scoops of ice cream. The café itself is shabby chic with plants and pastels.

The Beer Masons เบียร์เมสัน $
Coffee, International
(thebeermasons.com; 086024-6024; 17/59 Moo 1, Sairee Beach; daily 9am-midnight)
Why does a sign touting "Organic Coffee 9am–7pm" hang outside

a craft beer bar? Well, it's good for business, plus java jives with "superb protein pancakes" and Indian-influenced morning foods. And hey, the coffee is special. We're looking specifically at the nitro-infused cold brew, which for under $2 will keep you alert through the day and probably half the night. Should you choose to have yours stirred into Irish coffee, we won't judge.

The Factory Café $
Coffee, Vegan, Healthy, International
(facebook.com/thefactorykohtao; 098718-6712; 9/284, Sairee Beach; daily 8am-5pm)
Rev up with coffee at this health-food restaurant on Sairee Beach. The coffee menu has the expected espressos, lattes and mochas, and also a Dirty Turmeric latte; it has turmeric paste stirred in, presumably to help with inflammation. Choose your milk, while teas and "herbal tonics" are also available, along with fresh juices and smoothies.

Zest Bakery & Coffee House $
Coffee, International
(facebook.com/Zest-255762929862; 077456-1778; Mae Haad, Sairee; daily 7am-5pm)
Have a heart of foam top your latte at Zest, a three-unit chain caffeinating the beach crowd on Koh Tao. The hot coffee drinks are a mainstay, made from beans grown in Thailand, though they're not the only reason to visit. American breakfasts include hash browns, while there are also vegan options (think: lentils), porridge, muesli, juices, lassis, pastries, Niçoise salad, and sandwiches... stop in any time before sunset.

COOKING CLASSES

Idjang's Kitchen

(idjangskitchen.com; 062218-2864; Jitsin Village, Sairee)

The restaurant Idjang's Kitchen specializes in "Seasoning with Love," and its culinary team will teach you how to do the same. Have a private class for two or join up with four others for a session, held in an open-air kitchen. The syllabus focuses on making the most of fresh ingredients. You'll select the recipes you want to tackle, maybe glass noodle salad or prawn cakes, then you'll go through the steps of making a few, getting tips and lessons along the way from Idjang herself. From $50 per person.

Parawan's Thai Home Cooking Classes ชันเรียนทำอาหารไทยทีบ้านของปารวรรณ

(parawanthaicookingclass.com; 087511-4654; 13/82 Moo 1, Sairee Beach)

Step into Parawan's home and make three dishes that you choose, with her guidance. Whether your menu features papaya salad, fried rice, banana with coconut milk, or other Thai favorites, you'll be ushered through the prep steps in this open-air rooftop studio that accommodates eight, each with a personal prep area and cooking station. From $50 per person.

Thai Cooking with Joy ทำอาหารไทยกับจอย

(thaicookingkohtao.com; 090867-9048; 33/18 Moo 1, Sairee Beach)

Learn to prepare Southern Thai dishes on an outdoor rooftop with Joy, whether you're new to cooking or kitchen masters. The class will have a maximum of six of you (private options are available) practicing the making of three dishes in three hours. Your choices might be spring rolls, massaman curry, or tom kha soup. From $50 per person.

ENTERTAINMENTS

The Queen's Cabaret คาบาเร่ต์ของราชินี

(facebook.com/The-Queens-cabaret-Kohtao-241332126391727;
087677-6168; Sairee Beach, Koh Tao; nightly 10:20pm)
Live it up watching a ladyboy show on Sairee Beach. Every night,
a cast of well-attired drag dressers perform seductive, and Abba,
acts to an enthusiastic crowd. And guys, don't sit too close if
you're averse to becoming part of the entertainment; the singers
are likely to pull a couple of guys onto the stage.

MUAY THAI CLASSES

At **Island Muay Thai** (muaythaikohtao.com) you can see pros
fight it out Thai-boxing-style once every week or so. You can
also take private lessons using the full-size ring for sparring.
Monsoon Gym & Fight Club (monsoongym.com) welcomes
visitors to group training classes and also teaches Jiu jitsu, HIIT,
and 10th Planet techniques. You can participate in a full-service
fight camp, too.

NIGHTLIFE

Sairee Beach หาดทรายรี

Sairee Beach isn't just a party scene during the day. After dark, the
energy level really ramps up. Club-like crowds gather and dance
at clubs right on the sand, where swimming pools, bands, and
DJs are the hubs for dancing around. Even regular beach bars are
destinations here: Some put on fire shows or have big TV screens
for watching sports matches. On Sairee Beach, SangSom Rum
(made in Thailand) has become the go-to spirit for buckets of a
get-smashed drink that combines this otherwise fine liquor with a
caffeinated energy drink, whiskey, and cola.

LIVE MUSIC

Fishbowl Beach Bar

(facebook.com/fishbowlbeachbar; 062046-8996; 3/1 Moo 1, Sairee Beach; daily noon-2am)

If you dance on the bar, you receive a free shooter. That should give you an idea about Fishbowl, a thatched-roof long-timer that's home to nightly live music, fire shows, and late-night DJ scene. Fishbowl is almost like an American bar mitzvah for grown-ups: You'll be invited to play games, maybe burning limbo or beer pong. Less rowdy partiers will enjoy the bean-bag-for-two seating.

Good Vibe Bar

(facebook.com/goodvibebar; 086053-0300; 2/34 Moo 3, Mae Haad; select nights 6pm-2am)

Welcome. Really, you'll feel welcome. The Good Vibe Bar is aptly named. Sometimes musicians entertain, often guests do. Whether you're talented or merely brave, you can step onto the stage and join the jam: the mic is often open. That means you could end up dancing the Macarena with strangers in the open air.

BARS

The Beer Masons เบียร์เมสัน $

(thebeermasons.com; 086024-6024; 17/59 Moo 1, Sairee Beach; daily 9am-midnight)

You could spend your time at The Beer Masons trying to draw the line of how founder Marek Novak went from Czechoslovakia to Thai dive instructor to cave-diving filmmaker to craft beer bar founder. Or you can drink. More than 500 craft beers are for sale here on Sairee's Walking Street, plus hard ciders, all in a convivial Irish pub kind of environment—no shocker since the current owner is Belfast native Jimmie O'Murray. There's a "snacks chef" on staff, meaning the food menu is worthy of the brews.

SPORTS BAR

Reef Sports Bar & Restaurant

(reefbarkohtao.com; 089988-4902; 5/15 Mae Haad; daily 8am-11pm)

When you want to see a soccer match or other sports game, head to central Mae Haad. This sports bar is just what you need, with its six screens tuned to live sports and free Wi-Fi in case you want a personal look-see too. You'll also find a pool table and board games within the friendly, woodsy space. About those hours: If a big game runs to 3am, you will not be kicked out, and you sure won't be alone. Or hungry. You can always pick-up nachos with chili or a chicken zinger burger with fries and coleslaw.

BEACH BARS AND CLUBS

BND Beach Club บีเอ็นดีบีชคลับ

(facebook.com/bndbeachclub; 099494-4625; 3/2 Moo 1, Sairee Beach; daily 4pm-2am)

If beachfront clubbing is your ultimate experience, BND may be your dream destination. This is a beachfront club with three levels. We're talking live Latin music, international DJs, and dancing; Wine Down Wednesday sunset gatherings on the roof; fire shows for a wow factor, and then there are a couple of pool tables, a lounge, and TVs with sports games. This all happens right on Sairee Beach with water views from just about everywhere.

FIZZ beachlounge

(facebook.com/fizz.beachlounge; 086278-7319; 14 Moo 1, Ban Koh Tao; daily noon-1am)

Up on the northern stretch of Sairee Beach, FIZZ is both beach bar and restaurant. The soundtrack is soul funk disco; it'll mellow you out in a sensual sort of way. Sit in side-by-side beanbags with a small table in front and watch the longtail boats, sunset, or moon and enjoy the evening. A frosty martini or beer here is a welcome break from the party bars. And hey, you can have Thai curry or a beef or vegan burger.

LEO Beach Bar by the Rock ลีโอบีชบาร์บายเดอะร็อค

(facebook.com/leobeachbar.bytherock.kohtao; 081356-2223; 2/4 Moo, Ban Hat Sairee; daily noon-2am)

At the southern end of Sairee Beach, LEO is yet another beach bar packed with foreigners wanting a wild night out. The fire shows are phenomenal here, DJs get the crowd on their feet, and the drink list is long. You can even get a decent bite to eat. Grab a Leo Strong Brew beer and prepare for Latin music, or techno, or whatever's on the menu when you show up. Don't be surprised if you wake up covered in body paint.

Lotus Bar โลตัสบาร์

(lotusresortkohtao.com/facilities/lotus-bar or facebook.com/lotusbar.kohtao; 07745-6272; 9/9 Moo 1, Sairee Beach; daily 5pm-2am)

Backlit in blue and right on the beach, with one of the best fire shows on the island, Lotus Bar is far more than a washed-up-looking drinking establishment at a resort—although it is that, too. Located near Sairee Beach's strikingly horizontal palm tree (you'll know it when you see it), this easy-going establishment has reasons to visit all evening long: sunset happy hour is from 4pm to 7pm; 2-4-1 buckets are sold from 8:30pm to 11pm; and musicians entertain nightly from 7pm to 9pm, after which DJs take over. Settle into Thai loungers on the sand, get yourselves some oversized drinks—maybe the ones in plastic kiddie pails served with two straws—and let the rest of the day unroll at its own pace.

Maya Beach Club มายาบีชคลับ

(mayabeachclubkohtao.com; 080578-2225; South Sairee Beach; daily noon-2am)

Maya aims to stand out from the other place's by making tourists get drunk on the beach in several ways. It courts a daytime crowd as well as a night one. It pours top-shelf cocktails and fine wines. It has DJs every day of the week, with live music from 6pm to 8pm. And—bear with us here—it has a "no cheese" music policy. Its tunes, instead, are "from a variety of genres that aren't crappy remixes." So maybe it's not quite as different as the marketing copy says. Still, it's a wonderful place to do the drinking-together-in-paradise bit, take in a fire show, and maybe go out into the water on paddleboards as the DJ spins. Tapas and sushi are available.

Pirate Bar บาร์โจรสลัด $

(facebook.com/piratebarkohtao; 07745-6457; 25 Moo 3, Chalok Ban; daily noon-2am)

If you dare to pass the skull-and-crossbones sign posted boldly for all to see, you'll get to play the buccaneer way at Pirate Bar. The extremely chill beach bar in a hard-to-find Chalok Bay location encompasses two private beaches, plenty of shade, more than plenty of drinks, and water play plus fire shows. Swashbuckling? Let's hope not. On Mondays, settle in for Movie Night. All the fun without the frenzy.

Victor Bar วิคเตอร์บาร์

(facebook.com/VictorsBar10.10; 07745-6602; Sairee Beach, Koh Tao; daily 2pm-midnight)

Call it Victor Bar or Pool Bar, this Sairee Beach drinking hole has an interior that practically glows with jewel tone lighting, as well as a deck with wooden bench tables, a beach area with beanbag chairs... and a swimming pool. Did we mention the pool table? The food? You can hang out here for hours, in other words, morphing from sunbathers to swimmers to diners to drinkers to dancers. And yes, since it's nearly mandatory on Sairee Beach, Victor has DJs and fire shows.

PUB CRAWL

Koh Tao Pub Crawl ทัวร์เกาะเต่าผับ

(facebook.com/kohtaopubcrawl; 061458-8221; Sairee Beach; Mon, Wed, Fri, Sun from 6pm)

Pub crawls are generally relatively intimate bar-hops among a small group of strangers, yet on tiny Koh Tao up to 150 people join in with the Koh Tao Pub Crawl. Four nights a week, you can show up at 6pm and for about $16 apiece be part of a near-legendary drinkathon. The event starts at Choppers Sports Bar on Saidee Beach and continues to four other bars. Over the course of the evening, you'll receive free buckets, shots, and shirts, happy hour prices, discount cards, professional photography at a pool party, entrance to a cabaret show, live music, a beach party, and, if you're lucky, prizes.

MASSAGES

Let Impress Massage (facebook.com/Impress-Massage-933371633428562) help you heal after diving. It's a short walk from Sairee Beach and is great for a foot or Thai massage. **Majestic Spa** (facebook.com/Majestic-SPA-Koh-tao-493431280717387) has its own building in Sairee and includes more upscale offerings like stone massages. Sauna spells with Thai herbs, pedicures, and massages are yours overlooking Sairee Beach at **Paradise Massage** (facebook.com/Paradise-

Massage-292534544192926). In the Chalok Bay area, **Family Thai Massage** (tripadvisor.com/Attraction_Review-g303910-d14796327-Reviews-Family_Thai_Massage-Koh_Tao_Surat_Thani_Province.html) will do the trick for foot, oil, and Thai massage treatments.

TOURS

PADI Discover Scuba Diving in Koh Tao—Half Day and Two Dives

(scubabirds.com; 082818-1030; Blue Diamond Resort, 24/21, Moo 2, Mae Haad)

See the underside of Koh Tao's waters with this half-day beginners' dive in the Gulf of Thailand. All the scuba equipment is included, along with the guidance of PADI-certified instructors, viewing of a diving video, credit toward certification, and refreshments. You'll see the Japanese Garden in Koh Nang Yuan, or instead Mango Bay, as you get accustomed to using your equipment. Later, dive twice for at least 40 minutes each time before turning back. Ask about photo add-ons. No experience necessary. From $125 per person.

Full-Day Snorkeling Adventure Around Koh Tao

(facebook.com/wetravelkohtao; 092791-4966; 3/99 Koh Tao, Surat)

Make it an extra-fun day of snorkeling with We Travel, which has music playing aboard its air-conditioned boat, which itself is equipped with a water slide, a diving board, floating sun beds, and a climbing wall. You'll depart from Mae Haad Pier and head to top snorkel spots including Shark Bay, Aow Leuk, Hin Wong Bay, Mango Bay, and Koh Nang Yuan. You'll also get a little land time, hiking to the Nang Yuan viewpoint. Includes hotel transfers, lunch, and refreshments. From $31 per person.

TEMPLE

Temple Koh Tao วัดเกาะเต่า

Temples needn't be ancient to be beautiful, spiritual, and worth a visit, and this new hilltop structure, opened in 2018, is proof of that. A white main building with red and gold accents is the center, with pointed, elegant hook shapes along the top. You'll find art inside. Weddings, funerals, and such are held here often, and monks' study and teach here, with the instruction open to the public. The temple came to be after the death of monk Ajhan Suang, who built a pavilion on the island. His follower Ajhan Wanna began the process of having the temple constructed in his mentor's honor. Located between Mae Haad and Sairee Beach near the Koh Tao School.

Buddhism

Wat means "temple" in Thai, and you'll find these religious structures throughout Thailand—at least 30,000 of them. Most are Buddhist, since 95 percent of residents practice this religion, and many of the temples have architectural influences from China and India, as well as other cultures. They tend to differ vastly from one to another. Explore enough and you'll see not only ornate traditional temples but also cheery modern ones. As for Buddha? He takes many forms in sculptures and other media, as do other gods depicted.

Buddhism has been in Thailand for centuries, probably 250 years before Christ made his appearance on earth. In fact, the Thailand we know today evolved from the merging's of various Buddhist kingdoms over time. Today, young Thai men often spend at least three months living as a monk during their teenage years. The tradition is meant to conjure up good karma, among other benefits.

It's important to behave respectfully when visiting a temple. For starters, cover your shoulders and knees, even if it's just wearing ratty pants and tossing a scarf over your shoulders. You'll need to take off your shoes and place them in a designated area, and should also pocket your hats and sunglasses. If you come across monks, don't assume it's OK to snap a photo. If seems appropriate to do so at that time, ask if you can take their picture. Smoking and eating inside are not allowed.

There are a few more rules to bear in mind. Don't pose next to a Buddha, although it's fine to take a pic of the Buddha alone. Don't point at a Buddha either; it's inappropriate. Always make sure your feet are lower than the statue's.

ADVENTURES

Diving

Koh Tao is petite yet it has a huge reputation for diving. Scuba enthusiasts from around the world make it to this little dot in the Gulf of Thailand to explore underwater. The reasons are numerous: The area still has living coral reef worth seeking out, along with shipwrecks, limestone formations, and an array of fish as well as blue-spotted ribbon-tailed stingrays and turtles. While summer months are best, divers can have good experiences year-round with warm water at 84°F (29°C) and few currents. Many operators offer instruction and excursions (we've seen numbers from 30 to 70); in fact, Koh Tao claims to be the second-most popular place in the world for PADI open-water certifications. And finally, all that competition leads to some of the globe's lowest prices. Divers at the 25 local sites might even see spotted eagle rays or grey or bull sharks. Highlights include the Chumphon Pinnacle for batfish and trevally around coral-encrusted pinnacles; Shark Island for wall diving, coral gardens, and scorpionfish; and the HTMS Sattakut, a World War II landing craft wreck rich with blennies and fusiliers.

Crystal Dive (crystaldive.com) is an award-winning 5-Star PADI center with courses at all levels including pro plus eco- and free-drives, as well as technical, navigation, and other specialty courses. It owns its dive boats and has small outings and lodging. **Big Blue Diving Resort** (bigbluediving.com) has grown since 1991 to have certifications from PADI as well as SDI, BSAC, TDI, and SSI. You can learn to take photos and videos underwater and train at any level, plus enroll in instructor, technical, or freediving training. Boats go out three times a day (including nighttime) with two dives each time. You can rent equipment and get discounts by signing up for multiple "fun dives." This outfit also has a hotel and restaurant. The international team at **Roctopus™** (roctopusdive.com) promises four students max per instruction class. The team offers open-water instruction as well as advanced, divemaster, and instructor options (roctopuspro.com). "Fun dives" and Sail Rock Sunday are also available. The fleet includes three boats: a 50-person boat with a canopy, sun deck, and table seating; a similar vessel that accommodates 40; and a free-diving boat, with shade, for 16 people. Roctopus also has its own swimming pool for training, classrooms with custom furniture and flat-screen TVs, 60 full sets of equipment from Aqualung, a wash area, an air compressor, equipment repair services, a separate building for pro training, and a bar. **Pura Vida Diving Koh Tao** (puravidatailandia.com) specializes in Spanish instruction but also teaches in English as well as Catalan, Basque, French, and Portuguese. It has locations in Chalok and Mae Haad, and has SSI courses plus dives and packages.

Goodtime Adventures การผจญภัย Goodtime
Rock Climbing
(goodtimethailand.com; 07745-6941; 14/2 Moo 1)
If you want that surge of adrenaline in Koh Tao, Goodtime has you covered. The company specializes in small group adventure experiences, and rock climbing is a specialty. Expert leaders will bring you to seaside cliffs, mountaintop walls, and lowland boulders, adapting for first-time and seasoned climbers alike. Beginner and advanced courses are offered; they claim to be the only climbing school in the Gulf of Thailand area. Equipment is available. Cliff-jumping, powerboat-handling, diving, and abseiling are other options.

Kitesurfing, Wakeboard, Tubing, Stand-up Paddling ไคท์เซิร์ฟเวคบอร์ดท่อพายเรือเล่นแบบยืน
(evasionkohtao.com; 062665-2860; 9/233 Moo 1; daily 10am-7pm)

You'll be surrounded by stunning, calm water throughout your stay—go enjoy it. Evasion has all kinds of ways to get you going: tubing, waterskiing, kite surfing, knee boarding, and wake boarding. It even has subflying, or subwinging, which lets you see underwater without masks and other gear; you hold onto a specially designed board that is attached to a slowly moving boat. Evasion is a moving target: it operates at Hin Wong Bay from May through October, and from Sairee near Nang Yuan Island the rest of the year.

HIKING AND VIEWPOINTS

Fraggle Rock Viewpoint จุดชมวิว Fraggle Rock

We talk often about the stunning sunset views for Koh Tao's west-facing beaches and the restaurants and bars along the coast. Want more? Head up. Fraggle Rock Viewpoint is an hour uphill, and its vista is vast and beautiful even in the heat of the day—when it is way easier to get down than after dark. You'll see Hin Wong Bay and beyond it the Gulf of Thailand, the stunning clear water, boats in the water, and the tops of houses and businesses nestled into the island's greenery. To get there, walk past Sairee's 7-Eleven to the Tarna Align Resort, then follow the main road until you see the Fraggle Rock sign. Keep going, up the rope ladder or wooden steps that bring you onto the peak of a bald stone. Bring a flashlight if you plan to hike down after sunset.

John Suwan Viewpoint จุดชมวิวจอห์นสุวรรณ

It's only 20 minutes to the top of John Suwan Viewpoint by foot from Sairee Beach, or less if you drive—although either way you'll need to hike the final section and it's not an easy stretch: You'll have to maneuver over stones and such with the help of ropes. Partway up you'll be given a chilled bottle of water; it's in exchange for the $4 entry fee to this site, named for two local men who discovered it, Mr. John and Mr. Suwan. Your goal may be to see the sunrise, and if so, you may be able to scoot in for free. Otherwise, revel in the water and mountain beauty, and, if you're lucky, the chance to see nearby islands in the distance. You'll look over Shark Bay in one direction, Chalok Baan Kao Bay in the other. To find John Suwan Viewpoint, head to the very south of Koh Tao and look for the sign near the Freedom Beach Resort. Follow it to an intersection and choose the center option of three.

John Suwan Viewpoint

Love Koh Tao Viewpoint รักจุดชมวิวเกาะเต่า

If you can handle an early-morning wake-up, be sure to hike to the Love Koh Tao Viewpoint to watch the sun rise. Pack a flashlight if you're walking the hour and a half trek uphill. Or, cheat and drive (a scooter will do nicely) or hop in a taxi: You'll be looking east over Tanote Bay and the Gulf of Thailand—possibly islands beyond too—15 minutes after leaving Sairee Beach. Whether you hike or ride, you'll find decking with netted beds and a café along with the view. Plus there's the lovey-dovey sign that reads "Love Koh Tao"; the first "o" is shaped like a heart. A sole heart symbol is ripe for "say cheese" poses nearby. It costs under a dollar to get in, free if you buy a snack or drink. To find the path up, look for the Tanote Bay sign near the Monsoon Gym.

Mango Viewpoint จุดชมวิวมะม่วง

Your way to Mango Viewpoint is the same as to Fraggle Rock, only you turn at the Mango sign, which you'll see first. From there, you can either hike all the way up, or ride your motorbike partway then hike. The route is three-quarters of a mile (1.2km) in total, but steep. You can also take a four-wheel-drive taxi part-way. It'll take 15 minutes. Your rewards are many: an expansive vista of mountain, valley, Sairee Beach, and Mae Haad Bay, and two viewpoints with different amenities and $4 fees apiece. Between the two, you'll find decks outfitted with traditional and low tables with chairs or seat cushions, plus other seating. You can have a small meal, sip a fresh juice, play a board game, or even swing in a hammock while enjoying the view. Accept the paint and brush given with your order, and use it to paint your names pretty much anywhere you find space at the viewpoint. Keep walking around to find additional viewpoints facing different directions.

BEACHES

Ao Hin Wong Beach หาดอ่าวหินวง

With boulders on either side, you'll feel snuggled into Ao Hin Wong Beach, a serene spot fronting Hin Wong Bay. What a gift. The water is pristine, the snorkeling for coral, anemones and yellowfish is excellent, and the jungle is nearby. People? You'll find few, even during the busiest seasons. If you get bored of the quiet, rent kayaks and paddle into the water.

Chalok Baan Kao Bay อ่าวโฉลกบ้านเก่า

You'll gain quiet but lose the gold-sand advantage at Chalok Baan Kao Bay, a rock-dotted coastline with white sand and stunning clear water. The island's third-largest beach, the southern-facing coastline here is populated with budget hotels, meaning thrifty visitors get ample access to views of the Ang Thong Marine

National Park. You'll find beanbags to plop yourselves into, bars for day drinking and... not so very many people, giving you space to be together.

Jansom Bay อ่าวจันทร์สม
While most Koh Tao beaches are free to all, you might want to shell out the $8 apiece to experience Jansom Bay alongside the lodgers of the hotel that owns the strand. The water has a soft sandy bottom, so swimming and snorkeling are a joy. You might even spy a pufferfish, yellow boxfish, or a blue-spotted ribbon-tailed stingray. Palm trees provide shade over the white sand and huge boulders surrounding quaint bungalows are just begging for photo-sharing snapshots.

Sairee Beach หาดทรายรี
If you like an active scene with your shoreline, Sairee Beach is your prime pick. A crescent with gold sand lapped by ultra-clear waters, this is the main gathering spot for the party crowd—and for everyone, really, because lodging facilities of all price levels hug the coastline. Newbie divers practice their skills; relaxation-seekers nap in hammocks, chill on beanbag chairs, and swing on rope swings with wooden seats; and the assorted restaurants and bars and such are the source of both sustenance and music. Join a volleyball match, rent snorkel gear to see the underwater world from shore, and be sure to catch at least one sunset from here.

Shark Bay อ่าวฉลาม
Worry not about the black-tip reef sharks that circle this scenic bay. They're way out in the water and don't hurt people; in some seasons you can see a shark nursery. There are turtles here, too: You may find them to be scenic companions during your swim. You'll spend time at Shark Bay, aka Thian Og Bay, for the scenery, the silky white sand, the shady Thian trees, and the excellent

snorkeling and diving. Beach hotels are your best bet for meals and drinks.

Tanote Bay อ่าวโตนด

The picturesque beach at quiet Tanote Bay is surrounded by lush green mountains. In front of the wide swaths of sand (with little shade) you'll see a large boulder in the water. Rock on, happy twosome, and take the plunge: Climb to the top and launch yourselves into the water—it's a tradition. Arrive super early to take in a spectacular sunrise over the Gulf of Thailand. If you're snorkelers, expect a win: Coral near the boulders on the beach and in the water house wrasses, moray eels, butterfly fish, and filefish. Take a hiking break into the hills behind you to find several scenic viewpoints.

YOGA

Baan Talay บ้านทะเล

(baantalaykohtao.com; 07745-7049; Moo 3, Aow Leuk Bay)
Baan Talay is a hotel that, among other specialties, hosts yoga classes, courses, and retreats. Practice your lunges and pigeons on an open-air terrace with water and mountain views. Walk-in classes generally last 90 minutes and are held at 12:30pm and 5:30pm daily; they're good for all levels. Retreats are three-day advanced classes that focus on a combination of deep mediation, Raja (eight limbs) yoga, Bhakti (love/devotion) yoga, Karma (action) yoga, self-pacing, and breath.

Ocean Sound Dive + Yoga Ocean Sound Dive + โยคะ

(oceansoundkohtao.com/yoga-classes.html; 080144-6101; 22/22 Moo 3, Koh Tao)
Group and private classes, on-site and off the premises, cater to yogis of all levels at Ocean Sound, and walk-ins are welcome.

Beginners through instructor wannabees can attend all of the 14 sessions held every week. Options include Vinyasa flow, Hatha, Restorative, and Yin & Yin Yang, most in an attractive tile-floor studio. Mats, water, and equipment are provided. Ocean Sound is also a dive outfit.

Shambhala Yoga Centre ศูนย์โยคะชัมบาลา

(shambhalayogakohtao.com; 084440-6755; 4 14/2, Moo 1, Sairee Beach)

Just off Sairee Beach, Shambhala offers Hatha and Restorative yoga classes in a pointed-roof structure with Thai design elements. It accommodates practitioners of all levels, yet never more than ten students participate at a time. Classes start at 10am every morning and 6pm most evenings. The instructors are "seminomadic truth-seekers" to emphasize inclusiveness. Walk-ins are welcome, and private classes are available. You might find meditation, Satsang or Pranayama sessions happening during your stay, too.

ISLAND HOP TO KOH NANG YUAN

As if Koh Tao isn't remote enough, get on a boat: Koh Nang Yuan is a privately owned three-island destination nearby, and it's worth a day trip. The islands form a triangle shape. If you take a longtail boat or ferry over, or kayak (two-seaters are available) from Sairee Beach, you'll get there in 15 minutes. When the water is low, you can walk on sandbars from the center island to the other two. For the ultimate remote romantic rendezvous, stay a night or two in the main island's lodge, Nangyuan Island Dive Resort (nangyuan.com), or in an outer island bungalow; contact the hotel to set you up. If you're not a hotel/bungalow guest, pay the $4 day fee to visit, or just snorkel or dive offshore. You'll find a great viewpoint on the southernmost island, accessed via a 20-minute hike. You can snorkel from shore and dive nearby;

Japanese Gardens is one prime spot. An Easy Divers office is located at the resort (facebook.com/Easy-Divers-at-Nangyuan-Island-Dive-Resort-1404597593093971). The sunbathing is great too, and if you're a hotel/bungalow guest you'll get a seat and shade. Neither cans nor plastic bottles are allowed, so you'll need to buy drinks from the restaurant or bar.

Mountain view of Koh Nang Yuan

KOH LIPE AND
KOH ADANG

Koh Adang

Koh Lipe

WHY GO

If you made a list of the characteristics of a romantic destination, Koh Lipe and Koh Adang would check every box. It may sound cliché, yet these destinations are twin temptresses due to their crystal-clear, aqua waters, powdery white sands, few crowds, good food, and the exotic air of an Asian island—yet with plenty of English-speaking locals and American fare when you want it. Koh Lipe is on the busier side, Koh Adang way quieter, yet the scenery on both: consistently stunning. These islands in the Tarutao National Marine Park, which sits in the Andaman Sea near Malaysia, provide the sea air and sea scenes that so naturally accompany an amorous escape.

Koh Lipe, where you're most likely to stay during your visit, isn't a place for partying—although you'll still find beach bars for day drinking and a few clubs that'll get you dancing into the night. You can stroll barefoot into a local hangout for easy lunches and smooch over candlelit dinners high on a hill; enjoy basic Thai massages on the beach or more pampering ones in a spa. Natural beauty, friendly people, and serene stretches of shoreline will allow the two of you to spend non-tech just-the-two-of-you time together; no pressure, no schedule, no hassle. And touristy? Nuh-uh.

This place is made for couples: here you'll find both a Sunrise Beach, with stunning vistas at daybreak, and a Sunset Beach, where the evening sky show is equally dramatic.

The island is easy to master. It's about 2¼ square miles (5.8km²), and it will rarely take you more than 15 to 20 minutes, 30 absolute tops, to walk from one beach to another, or to Walking Street, the main shopping/dining strip. Most of the island is flat, hence the name Paper Island in the local Chao Ley (Sea Gypsy) tongue.

Getting around offshore is fun, too: you can hop into a kayak to paddle yourself to a nearby island or hire a longtail boat to have a professional bring you around.

If you need a bit more to do than just look at the natural beauty, you can take a hike to a scenic hilltop, dive among the coral, or walk along a deserted stretch of beach at night to see bioluminescent plankton. Charters to these glowing water creatures are on hold for environmental reasons, but with a little splash with an arm or leg and you might discover a group of them on your own.

In this chapter we will firstly discuss Koh Lipe then followed by Koh Adang.

Koh Lipe

KOH LIPE

HOW TO GET TO KOH LIPE

Paradise isn't easy to reach, but we'll get you there.

There is no airport on the island. You can fly to Hat Yai International Airport (HDY) in Southern Thailand, then take a minibus shuttle from there to Pak Bara pier, followed by a ferry or speedboat. The shuttle/ferry combo costs about $21, and the ferry ride takes about 3½ hours. The shuttles leave the airport at 8:30am daily to make the 11:30am speedboats. In low season, get a super-early flight if you want to make the trip in a single day, as there won't be a second boat until the following morning. More shuttles and ferries run during high season. Visit the Transport section of kohlipethailand.com for up-to-date details.

AirAsia sometimes offers flight/shuttle/ferry packages from Bangkok and Chiang Mai. Flights from Bangkok to Hat Yai are a bit over an hour and can be had for under $100, but flights from Phuket and Chiang Mai involve a little more time and money both.

If you're approaching from elsewhere in Thailand, you can take a ferry from Pak Bara, Trang, Phi Phi, and Koh Lanta in high season; it's also possible to get here from Langkawi in Malaysia. In low season (June through September), especially around the time of monsoons, your options are limited. The current ferry and speedboat schedules are online at kohlipethailand.com.

Another option is to take a train ($60 or more) or bus (from $24) from Bangkok to Hat Yai; expect about a 15-hour ride. From there, you take the Pak Bara pier shuttle ($8.50) to the ferry.

As for the ferry dock? Koh Lipe doesn't have one. Actually, it has a floating dock, and sometimes you'll need to use an even smaller floating dock, then wade to shore. Pre-arranged longtail boats, and rogue ones operated by local Sea Gypsies, will pick you up from the ferry, in the water, and bring you to shore.

GETTING AROUND

First off, pack your most comfortable flip-flops or sneakers. Koh Lipe is a small island and it takes a half-hour at most to walk from one place to another (That'll help you work off the fruity cocktails). Otherwise, you can cuddle into the sidebar of a motorbike taxi, always 50 baht (about $1.60), or travel by water: from November through April, you can hop a longtail boat from Pattaya Beach to another point for under $2. The rest of the year, boats line up on Sunrise Beach, as do the motorbike taxis.

WHERE TO STAY

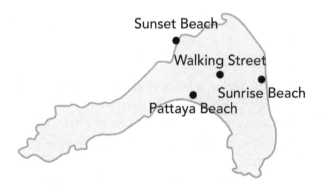

Koh Lipe area map

Most of the accommodations are in four main areas.

Pattaya Beach

Most people stay on Pattaya Beach. It's relatively bustling, not that anything bustles too much on Koh Lipe. You'll be right near Walking Street, plus fire shows and other nightly shenanigans. Oh, and if you want to eat freshly caught fish at a beachfront restaurant, this is your place.

Sunrise Beach

Day will dawn in blooming colors here, and you'll have quick access to a slightly more happening scene. The accommodations here tend to be nestled away from the main drag—this is the place to find romantic lodgings with private plunge pools. When you reach the sand—the longest stretch on Koh Lipe—you'll see places to rent kayaks and more. The water itself is ridiculously rich with sea life, so you can wade right in and snorkel.

Sunset Beach

Sunset Beach is the most intimate of the island's three main strands. It's quiet, lined with mostly bungalows, and, as you'd imagine, has a spectacular sunset. You can stroll over to a few casual restaurants and bars without leaving the area. Walking Street, the main retail area, is a 10-minute walk away.

Walking Street

Generally both more modest and more affordable than other areas on the island, Walking Street is home to small inns offering inexpensive lodgings, some extremely basic, others intriguingly stylish. You'll have to walk a bit to Pattaya Beach. The length of the walk depends on the hotel yet you'll have cafes, food stands, restaurants, boutiques, and nightlife right outside your front door.

ACCOMMODATIONS

Family Song Koh Lipe ครอบครัวสองเกาะหลีเป๊ะ $

(familysongkohlipe.com; 08880-2407; 8 Moo 7, Pattaya Beach)
An Italian investor teamed up with members of a local fishing group and the result is Family Song, a bungalow resort just behind a restaurant on Pattaya Beach. Opened just a few years ago, Family Song features simple wooden bungalows with bamboo furnishings, vividly colored accent pieces, and modern tiled private bathrooms. Wi-Fi, fans, hot water, hammocks, and terraces are standard. Couples relish the quiet setting, with the benefit of an easy five-minute journey by foot to Walking Street. The owners are local fishermen, so treat yourselves to a boating adventure that may reap you grouper, snapper, or cobia.

Idyllic Concept Resort $

(idyllicresort.com; 081802-5453; rsvn@idyllicresort.com; 279 Moo 7, Sunrise Beach)
You want romance? Here it is. The Idyllic Concept Resort is right on the white-sand shore of the Andaman Sea, where the turquoise waters beckon from the beach, restaurant, one of the two swimming pools, and many of the guestrooms. The whole property has a modern look, and many of the 82 rooms—all air-conditioned—have spa tubs and/or private balconies, possibly with a daybed. You'll find key services like a tour desk and fun extras such as kayaks and indoor rock climbing. Situated on mellow Sunrise Beach, it's a quick 10-minute walk to town. The restaurant, The Cove Bistro, is an indoor-outdoor space offering barefoot dining on Thai specialties adapted for Westerners when necessary. For the ultimate privacy, there's the option of in-room dining. Wedding proposal packages, and Thai and Western-style weddings, are also available.

Mali Resort Pattaya Beach มะลิรีสอร์ทพัทยาบีช $

(maliresorts.com/koh-lipe/pattaya-beach; 091979-4600; 306 Moo 7, Pattaya Beach)

Powdery white sand that gently drops into stunning clear Andaman Sea water; massages on the beach; tropical foliage; beachfront cocktails and dinners. This Mali Resort on Pattaya Beach is a natural for couples, whether you stay in the Bali-style rooms with thatched roofs and outdoor showers or the contemporary cottages. Designed with sustainable materials, this resort offers ocean-view and beachfront accommodations, some with wraparound verandas or vaulted ceilings. You'll be far from crowds, yet a quick stroll to Walking Street with its restaurants and such. End each day at the on-site restaurant, dining on grilled seafood by candlelight.

Serendipity Beach Resort เซเรนดิพิตีบีชรีสอร์ท $

(serendipityresort-kohlipe.com; 085080-7197; 140 Moo 9, Sunrise Beach)

Ah, solitude for just the two of you. Serendipity is a small hotel on a secluded stretch of Sunrise Beach. You'll stay in one of 12 wooden villas nestled discretely into nature on the side of a wooded hill. Spend a bit more to get your own plunge pool. Start each day with a hot breakfast delivered to your room, then step right into the water to snorkel (equipment is free), or sign up for a tour. You can have in-room massages and complimentary kayaking too. Will You Marry Me and wedding packages are available.

The Reef Hotel เดอะรีฟโฮเทล $

(kohlipethailand.com/koh-lipe/hotels/The-Reef; 081079-7672; Moo 7, T.Koh Saray a. Muang)

If you'd like easy access to all Koh Lipe has to offer, stay at The Reef. This is a small and simple hotel near Walking Street and the beaches. The space is invitingly light and airy. Rooms vary from a basic space with a fan and shared cold-water shower to more indulgent rooms with air conditioning, TVs, hot showers, and even a balcony. If you're on a tight budget, The Reef provides an affordable way to enjoy this romantic destination.

Wapi Resort วาปีรีสอร์ท $

(wapiresortkohlipe.com; 089464-5854; Ko Tarutao, Sunrise Beach) Cuddle up in your own bungalow or cottage at Wapi Resort, where the sunrise is astounding, the beach awaits, and a free breakfast will help you start each day. A Thai-French family runs this 18-unit hideaway located at the edge of Sunrise Beach. You'll be surrounded by pine trees and other foliage, giving you privacy and shade. You'll have plenty of essentials, including air conditioning, a fridge, and maybe a TV and/or balcony. Ask about massages, bicycle rentals, and boat trips.

BREAKFASTS

Bloom Café and Hostel บลูมคาเฟแอนด์โฮสเทล $

Thai, International

(facebook.com/bloom.cafe.hostel; 097079-9128; 274 Moo 7, T. Koh Sarai; 7am-11:45pm)

You wouldn't expect coffee art on a remote Thai island, yet Bloom Café has all kinds of surprises. Ask the barista to make hearts of your latte foam, then dig into a breakfast of cheesy vegetable omelets, or pancakes topped with mango, roasted almond, cream, and maple syrup. Later in the day, chill out with a fruity iced tea or a cocktail.

Buffalo Thai Cafe & Bistro บัฟฟาโลไทยคาเฟแอนด์บิสโทร $

Thai, International, Vegetarian

(facebook.com/pg/ilovebuffalothai; 083771-3913; 376 Moo 7, Koh Sarai; daily 8am-9pm)

Part of a small guesthouse, Buffalo Thai is a street front café that serves a combo of Thai food and other flavors. Days here begin with freshly brewed coffee as well as French toast, eggs, bacon, and other Western morning staples, including vegetarian options. The café remains open through dinnertime with options from hamburgers to tom yum fried rice.

Café Lipe คาเฟหลีเป๊ะ $

Thai

(cafe-lipe.com; 07472-8036; Bla 457, Pattaya Beach; daily 7am-6pm)

Sip your first morning coffee inside Café Lipe, which brews its own organic house-grown java: that cuppa is worth a trip. Homemade bread, fresh smoothies, and muesli are other day starters, most made with locally raised ingredients, and all with a beach view. Free water refills, and cooking classes for three to five people, are also available. P.S. If you want to win your partner over in the evening, reserve a private candlelight dinner on the sand.

Café Tropical คาเฟทรอปิคอล $

Vegetarian, International

(facebook.com/TropicalKohLipe; 081470-9325; 358 Moo 7 Walking Street, Sunrise Beach; daily 7am-11pm)

Quirky and cheerful, this all-day restaurant features hearty breakfasts—think breakfast burritos and eggs Benedict—plus a good cup of coffee, as well as full meals. Many vegetarian options are available. Smoothie bowls are a hit here, and the menu has gluten-free, low-carb, and vegan menu items.

LUNCHES AND DINNERS

Benny's On The Beach $

Vegetarian, Thai, International

(adangseadivers.com/eat-ko-lipe; 0900700-0233; Adang Sea Divers, Sunrise Beach; daily 9am-7pm)

Clean living and diving clear waters seem to pair well, say the owners, so Adang Sea Divers opened their vegan restaurant, Benny's on the Beach, in 2018. Aiming to be fully earth-friendly, this restaurant's staff buys its produce from farms in Langu, uses solar outdoor lighting and reusable water bottles, and packs to-go items in biodegradable containers. The plant-based menu is Thai and Western, with curry pastes made from scratch and absolutely no fish sauce, shrimp paste, or MSG used. Whether you have a yen for a taco, a burger, a Benny Bowl, or a Thai specialty, it'll be packed with flavor.

Bombay Indian Restaurant ร้านอาหารอินเดียบอมเบย์ $

Indian

(facebook.com/pages/category/Indian-Restaurant/Bombay-Restaurant-400009743668958; 082416-7562; Sunset Road, Changwat Satun; daily 11am-11pm)

With spices imported from India and breads and tikka meats baked in a tandoori oven, you'll get a true taste of the subcontinent at Bombay, tucked away in a spot that's fun to seek out. You can break naan bread over aromatic curries, rice-based biryanis, and a signature butter chicken entrée.

Capriccio $$

Vegetarian, Pizza, Italian

(facebook.com/Capriccio-1424763837757882; 083183-1056; 61 Moo 7, Koh Sarai; daily 5pm-11pm; open November-May)

One day it'll be house-made tagliatelle with mushrooms and eggplant cream, another spaghetti with clams and cherry tomatoes. Italian food plain and fancy—vegan, vegetarian, and for the rest of us—are on offer at this restaurant, along with burgers and pizza. The Australian beef is popular. Split a bottle of wine in the candlelit dining room and let the Latin vibes seep in.

Castaway Restaurant ร้านอาหาร Castaway $

Romantic, Thai, International

(kohlipe.castaway-resorts.com/beachfront-restaurant-and-bar; 083138-7472; Koh Lipe, Sunrise beach; daily 7am-11pm)

Sitting amid the palapa-topped buildings of Castaway Beach Resort, Castaway is a chef-driven beachfront restaurant that plates up Thai and European specialties. Overlook the water as you sip cocktails on the covered deck, at a low table, or on floor cushions if you prefer. For a whole meal, you might request to sit indoors; the seating there is traditional tables with chairs. The menu includes several vegetarian offerings. Happy hour and cooking classes are popular. Pre-plan and request a Romantic Dinner where the two of you will dine solo inside a petite beachfront palapa. P.S. The team will happily help set up your marriage proposal here.

Elephant ช้าง $

American

(elephantkohlipe.com; 089657-2170; 358 Walking Street, Pattaya Beach; daily 7am-1am)

Elephant has been a local institution for years, and that's because it serves so many different purposes. You can get an American-style breakfast, burger, or sandwich here, plus a good cup of coffee. You can have a meal packed up for a beach picnic, or hang around any time of day playing board games, sipping cocktails infused with Thai flavors, reading book-exchange tomes or listening to live music.

Forever Restaurant ร้านอาหาร Forever $

Thai, Burmese

(bit.ly/3a2tKWY; 094590-2859; Main road, just near to Pitiusas resort; Thu-Tues 7am-10pm)

The digs ain't fancy—only one side has a wall—yet you'll be blissfully satisfied with the Thai and Burmese flavors at Forever, an independent restaurant hidden away west of Sunset Beach. For breakfast, try the rice cakes with coconut gravy. Later on, sample tea-leaf salad, tofu curry, or plenty of meat-free dishes including some made with pumpkin. Every dish is presented with a warm smile.

On The Rocks Restaurant at Serendipity $$

Romantic, Thai, International

(serendipityresort-kohlipe.com/bar-and-restaurant; 093581-3741; 276 Moo 7, Sunrise Beach; daily noon-9:30pm)

As if a tranquil Thai island isn't romantic enough, amp up the pucker-up potion by dining nearly 20 feet (6m) above the water at On the Rocks. This three-tier resort restaurant serves Thai, Western, and blended fare, with much of the seafood plucked from local waters. Request the balcony for the ultimate one-on-one dining experience—not that the chefs won't wow you wherever you're seated. Fruit juices, smoothies, and alcoholic drinks are served all day starting at 10am.

Paolo Italian Pizza พิซซ่าอิตาเลียนของเปาโล $

Pizza, Italian

(facebook.com/paoloitalianpizzakohlipe; Walking Street Langu, Satun)

Oversized slices of thin-crust wood-fired pizza—that's the calling card at Paolo, a small stand with counter seating along Walking Street. Order a slice with the topping of your choice, or a whole pie to take back to your bungalow. You'll be shocked at how satisfied you'll be after such an affordable meal or snack.

Ten Moons Restaurant & Cocktail Bar ร้านอาหาร Ten Moons 'และบาร์ค็อกเทล $-$$

Mediterranean, European, Spanish, Asian, International

(tenmoonsliperesort.com/restaurant; 061853-3936; 31 Moo 7, Koh Sarai; 7:30am-9:30pm)

Travel the world, culinarily-speaking, at Ten Moons, a beach-view restaurant within the hotel of the same name. You'll find fresh fish and shellfish from the Andaman Sea and classic Thai dishes, but also Japanese sushi, Spanish hams and paella, pizza, American burgers, Angus steaks and salads, and also many vegetarian and vegan dishes. Make time for a drink or two on the Chill Out Terrace.

The Hill Resort Restaurant by Bayview Sunset Resort $$

Asian, Spanish, Italian

(bayviewsunsetkohlipe.com/thehillresort/bar-and-restaurant; 063448-7485; 145 Moo 7 Bayview, Sunset Beach; daily 5pm-10pm)

Glory be. At The Hill, you'll have dinner facing the sunset over the water. You'll want to start with cocktails—maybe a tangy mojito—then dine slowly, because settings this romantic are hard to find and you'll want the experience to last as long as possible. Share an antipasti platter loaded with imported Spanish sausages and cheeses, enjoy seafood from Thailand's seas, or twirl pasta carbonara around your forks. If you're set to propose, or to celebrate, simply ask in advance. The staff is keen to make your experience extra special.

Tonkow Restaurant ร้านอาหารต้นคาว $

Thai

(facebook.com/tonkowlipe/; 087332-6375; Walking Street, Mueang Satun; daily 8am-11pm)

Slightly more upscale than many Koh Lipe restaurants— but don't let that fool you into thinking you need to dress up, Tonkow has been dishing out Thai cuisine since 2007. It gets consistently high ratings from carnivores and vegans alike, whether for a plateful of local crabs, a bowl of massaman curry, or a classic Pad Thai. You'll have to wait, though. Lines form daily in season.

Thailand's Biggest Buddha

(watmuang.com; 03563-1556; 19 Hua Taphan, Wiset Chai Chan District, Ang Thong; daily 5am-7pm)

You'll find giant Buddha statues throughout Thailand. At 300 feet (92m) tall and 210 feet (63m) wide, this gold beauty is the biggest of all—only eight worldwide are taller. Unveiled in 2008 at the reconstructed temple and monastery of Wat Muang, the Great Buddha (as it's also called) is made of gold-covered cement and seated in the Maravaijaya Attitude position. The $3.75 million statue is in the countryside, just under a two-hour drive from Bangkok. To get there, hop on a van to Ang Thong (ask your hotel desk for details), then drive the remaining 20 minutes via rental motorbike or car. You'll find vendors easily. While you're in the area, visit the unusual Hell Garden.

The Big Buddha at Wat Muang

NIGHTLIFE

Walking Street

You'll visit Koh Lipe for the ridiculously oh-so-lovely beaches, yet you'll spend quite a bit of time roaming around Walking Street. The area looks ramshackle, for the most part, yet you'll find foods to taste (grilled fresh fish! Coconut chicken soup!), drinks to sip, and crafts to ogle every time you show up. In the unpretentious way of island life, Walking Street lures with all kinds of restaurants and drinking holes, shops, and massage parlors. Music tends to waft into the air at every turn, calling you to explore inside yet another door—assuming there is a door. Stalls sell junk and treasures, clubs have live music, and inexpensive hotels are, in some cases, très chic.

BARS

This quiet little island has surprisingly good places to hang out after dinner. Get your Jamaica groove on at **Reggae Bar** (facebook. com/reggaebar.kohlipe), a freestanding, cluttered, nearly hidden bar by Pattaya Beach that's the arch opposite of formal. Grab a colorful drink, watch the fire show, and groove to a "no problem, mon" beat. On Sunrise Beach, **Sea La Vie Beach Bar** (facebook. com/sealaviekohlipe/?_rdc=1&_rdr) has chairs lined up to face the water, a beachfront treehouse loaded with signs like "Happy in Lipe," a hammock, handmade decor accents, and food and drink. This is a classic barefoot beach bar, although the music often gets very loud. **Viewpoint Bar** is small, dark, and mysterious by Sunrise Beach. Its specialty is jelly beer, although margaritas and tequila sunrises are also on offer. Laid back and open late at night, **Rock Stones Bar** (facebook.com/Rockstonebarkohlipe) may become your after-hours go-to. Located in the center of the island, Rock Stones is dark with backlights and random feathers, rocks, and shells. It's quite the joint. In contrast, **OMG! Sports Bar & Restaurant** (facebook.com/OMG-Sports-Bar-Restaurant-227333800616195) by Sunrise Beach is relatively polished—not that you have to wear your best duds. You'll feel almost like you're in, say, Ohio, munching on a burger, watching a sports game, and shooting pool. There's often live music. If you want a true club scene, choose **Art Beach Club** (ananyalipe.com/dining_detail.php?ID_room=1000&type=art_beach_club1) for a hot night on the town. Located at the Ananya Lipe Resort, this Pattaya Beach hot spot has stylish seating, a resident DJ, a pool bar, cocktails, and food like lobster burgers. Jazz and R&B are the main soundtracks, setting the tone for a chill experience.

BEACHES

Pattaya Beach หาดพัทยา

You'll be on Pattaya Beach when you arrive on the island, and will quickly see that this is the hub of Koh Lipe's shore life. Located on the island's southern shore, this is the place to find transportation, excursions, and people-watching—all from powder-soft sand with the enticing backdrop of pristine waters filled with sea life. Keep snorkel goggles handy. The sand is powder-soft. Join a Frisbee game or a volleyball match, hop in a kayak, enjoy the nighttime action at a beach bar... as you wish. Walking Street is very close.

Sanom Beach หาดสนม

West of Pattaya Beach, walk over a wooden path and you'll arrive at Sanom Beach, which still faces south. This has the opposite vibe to Pattaya Beach—it's generally nearly empty, ideal for lounging on the sand in peace. The water varies from aqua to dark turquoise, and large rocks jut out of it—making it so very scenic. The sea here is calm enough for swimming; the two of you could spend hours wading in and out without a care in the world.

This is also a perfect launch spot for diving.

Sunrise Beach หาดซันไรส์

If magical mornings make you smile, be sure to spend at least one sunrise on or overlooking Sunrise Beach. Also known as Hat Chao Ley Beach, Sunrise Beach stretches over the entire eastern side of Koh Lipe. The ritzier resorts tend to be in this area, generally a distance from one another and therefore in peaceful surrounds. You can hang out all day overlooking the water, snorkeling to see clownfish and parrotfish, eyeing remote Koh Kra, Koh Tarutao, and Malaysia's Langkawi in the distance on clear days, and maybe cooling off with a light lunch and a cold beer at a beach bar. Long walks here are lovely, especially given the small amount of intrusive boat traffic. If you get bored, walk a few minutes to Chao Ley, the residential hub for the island's Sea Gypsy population, or hop in a boat taxi to another beach. If you have the budget, take a sunrise yoga class here, doing downward dogs as a duo, or splurge on rooftop massages overlooking the Andaman Sea. Evenings are low-key here.

Sunrise Beach

Sunset Beach ซันเซ็ทบีช

Unsurprisingly, given its name, Sunset Beach (aka Hat Pramong) faces the glowing orb as it descends over the water nightly. Although the beach itself faces west, you'll be on the north part of the island. This is the least busy of Koh Lipe's three main beaches. During the day, you might hang out on the silky white sand, meander in and out of the water, and grab a simple bite to eat at one of the area's no-frills food and drink outlets. To experience a different scene, check out the campground, which has yet more of an anything-goes-if-it's-chill vibe. Once it's time for the sun to set, Sunset Beach is where you want to be. On a clear night, the sky comes alive with vivid colors as the sun slinks down into the water. It's this kind of experience that draws couples to romantic island getaways.

MASSAGES

Heck, one of Thailand's joys is the ability to get a Thai massage at a reasonable price anytime, anywhere. Remote Koh Lipe is no different. Here's where to start. First off, there's Walking Street. Just as you can always find a bite to eat or a cold drink here, you can easily get yourselves side-by-side Thai massages right off the street. Elsewhere on the island, **JK Blue F Health Massage** (facebook.com/jkbluefbestmassagekohlipe) on Sunrise Beach has a row of inviting mats on platforms right inside the storefront. Curtains on both sides provide privacy. **Kamon Puh Massage**, in a strip mall, also by Sunrise Beach, is a simple option filled with colorfully adorned mats on which you receive your treatment. Foot, oil, coconut oil, aloe vera, and aromatherapy massages, plus body scrubs, are offered in addition to a standard Thai massage. There are manis and pedis, too. For a more upscale experience, book a session at the spa within **Pattaya Beach's Bundhaya**

Resort (bundhayaresort.com/bundhaya-resort/facilities-spa. php). This is a full-on spa, with eight treatment rooms and four foot-massage chairs (aaaahh!), and even a couple's whirlpool tub. Choose from a Thai, oil, foot, aromatherapy, coconut oil, head, shoulder, face, or body-scrub massage. You might even be treated under a covered area in the open air. Packages adding on herbal-steam treatments, manicures, and more are available.

YOGA AND DIVING

Keirita's Yoga & Diving โยคะและดำน้ำของ Keirita
(keiritasyoga.com; 087622-5938; 316 Moo 7, Koh Sarai)
Located right on Sunrise Beach, Keirita's wears a few virtual hats. It's a yoga center, offering sunrise classes as well as plenty of others, most of them variants of ashtanga. Keirita's also hosts retreats. And, it's a diving center: scuba enthusiasts can get deep into the water from here. If you like both pursuits, look into yoga-dive packages and mix the two not only technically, but by learning techniques that will improve your scuba experience. And yes, you may find yourself doing yoga twists on a dive boat. Keirita's also supports animals by donating to Help 4 Strays. The studio donates 10 percent of all yoga class profits to the organization, which sterilizes animals and treats them for diseases.

Koh Lipe Diving School โรงเรียนสอนดำน้ำเกาะหลีเป๊ะ
(kohlipediving.com; 087622-6204; 278 Moo 2, Sunrise Beach)
When in paradise... If you're new to diving, let the Koh Lipe Diving School get you started with its 1-Day Try Scuba program. This full-on dive center will start newbies out with a lesson on scuba basics, followed by two dives in up to 40 feet (12m) of water. A buffet-style Thai lunch will be served on the boat. The eight-hour program includes instruction and equipment but not fees for enter the National Marine Park.

ISLAND HOPPING

Considering you can see uninhabited islands from Koh Lipe's beaches, the urge to step foot on those remote, romantic landmasses can be pretty big. Fortunately, that's easily done.

You can rent kayaks on Sunrise Beach (expected around $20 to $30 for a full day). Simply paddle over the placid waters to Koh Usen and Koh Kra (each roughly 15 minutes' away): both, of course, gorgeous and empty of people. Have a restaurant pack you lunches to-go in advance, take plenty of water to stay hydrated, and head out. You'll hike, you'll dig your toes into new-to-you sand, and see yet more fish in crystalline water—how about an orange-spined unicornfish?

Bigger and farther islands beckon—up to about an hour away—and for those you might want someone else to be in charge. Options for single-day boat outings from Koh Lipe include taxi boats from Sunrise Beach that will drop you off where you ask and then pick you up at an agreed-upon time—all for just a few dollars—and charters, where you'll share a longtail boat with other tourists for a half- or full-day tour for about $40. These excursions might include snorkeling, snorkel equipment, and lunch. You can pre-book these with Walking Street vendors.

KOH ADANG

Koh Adang

Hiking, snorkeling, waterfalls... for a getaway from your getaway, head to Koh Adang, the second-largest island in Tarutao National Park at 19 square miles (49km²). This island, about a 10-minute boat ride away from Koh Lipe, has a ranger station, bungalows, and a place for camping, as well as a newish hotel, but mostly it's best for day trips—although the pirates who favored the place way back when may have lingered longer. You'll find forest in the interior and beaches dotting the rim, along with scenic rocky coastline in some parts. There's a black-sand beach on the north end; pay your taxi driver extra to take you there. Bring cash to pay the park entry fee (just a few dollars, but there is no ATM here), pick up a map while at the ranger station, and start your immersion into unadulterated nature. A taxi boat from Koh Lipe will cost under $10 round-trip, a charter about $40 for the whole shebang of services and equipment.

ACCOMMODATIONS

Koh Adang area map

Adang Island Resort เกาะอาดังรีสอร์ท $$

(adangresorts.com; 089654-8888; 30/23 Satunthani Rd, Phiman Muang)

On the southern side, facing the South Andaman Sea, the Koh Adang Resort has about four dozen classic and deluxe garden bungalows, beachfront villas, and a honeymoon suite with glass walls overlooking the water. Hotel guests will be privy to the rare treats of a/c and Wi-Fi, and can use the pool, restaurant, bar, and watersports equipment including paddleboards and snorkel gear. Intimate weddings for up to 90 people will be exceptionally memorable here.

Camping and Bungalow

Koh Adang has one main beach, and, along with the ranger station, this is where you'll find the campground. For about $11 a night, you can camp by the sand or the pine trees which includes a colorful tent and mats to sleep on. You can use the restrooms and shower located near the ranger station. Call 07478-3485 or email reserve@dnp.mail.go.th to reserve your spots.

If you want a little more comfort in the middle of nowhere, upgrade to a bungalow. It's still under $50 a night and comes with a fan and your own bathroom, but nothing beyond a mosquito net. You'll need to reserve these in advance on the park website (nps.dnp.go.th). Try to enlist a Thai speaker to assist if possible. Alternatively, have a local email the park service for you at reserve@dnp.mail.go.th, or call the park service at 07478-3485 to book your stay; you'll need to pre-pay at a bank. Hey, there's no such thing as a free night in paradise.

EATING

In addition to the resort's restaurant, Koh Adang will keep you fueled up at a counter-service eatery nearby. It has a few Thai staples like green curry and a few Western ones including sandwiches. The prices are low and operating hours are from breakfast through a late lunch, and again at 5:30pm through dinnertime.

ADVENTURES

Hiking

If you want to climb any incline you see, you'll be thrilled to view the interior of Koh Adang. Keep your map at hand, wear good footwear, and start on the western side of the beach near the ranger station. You'll see a sign that helpfully says, "Waterfall this way." Head inland to follow the trail through the jungle that leads to Pirate Waterfall. You'll reach the tumbling waters after about 45 minutes. Kinaree Waterfall is another option, but most agree the poorly marked trail isn't worth the hassle for a no-big-deal visual reward. Koh Adang Viewpoint, or Chao Dao, is a worthy destination, about a 45-minute trek up the Chado Cliff. The hike actually has three lookout points, the highest offering the best vistas of the trio. The trailhead is behind the island's sole freestanding restaurant.

Snorkeling

Thanks to rich reef life, snorkeling just beyond the island is exceptional. The ranger station rents not-so-terrible snorkel gear for a low price, or you might want to pick up better rental equipment before leaving Koh Lipe. You needn't travel far to gasp in glee at undersea life. The water right off the ranger station has fish-filled coral. Pufferfish, barracuda... even anemones.

Beaches

You won't be disappointed with Koh Adang's main beach, but if you want to play Robinson Crusoe and sidekick for a bit, you can have a beach to yourself. Head to the aforementioned black-sand strand, to try west coast (and maybe sunset) trips to other remote pockets of sand lapped by stunning waters. Or, have your water taxi driver take you around to check out various beaches until you choose one you like. One beach has a freshwater lagoon, another reachable coral reef. Agree to a pick-up time so you'll have a ride home. Note that drivers charge more as water gets choppy.

Secluded beach on Koh Adang

FESTIVALS

Chiang Mai Flower Festival เทศกาลดอกไม้เชียงใหม่

Blooms aplenty abound at the Chiang Mai Flower Festival, celebrated for three days every February, just before the weather starts turning warmer. The setting is fitting, as the city is known as the "rose of the north." Located primarily at Suan Buak Hat Park, the festivities involve parades with flower-covered floats populated by locals in traditional dress, as well as beauty contests, exhibitions, and retail areas with flower-related merchandise. You may not be able to buy orchids to bring home, but go anyway. The displays are magnificent.

Chinese New Year ปีใหม่จีน

Many Thais have Chinese roots. And so Chinese New Year is celebrated widely, even if the day—in January or February—is not an official holiday. The epicenter for festivities is Bangkok's Chinatown. There and elsewhere, you might happen upon performances, parades involving dragons, and plentiful red lanterns. This is a religious festival, and so observant worshippers can also be seen praying at the Wat Mangkon Kamalawat temple and other Chinese houses of worship. If you visit a temple during this time, show respect: Dress tastefully and be discreet.

Break out the red clothing in your suitcase: Red is a color of celebration for the Chinese, so sporting your cheeriest hues—if not red, other vibrant colors—makes you part of the celebration.

Red is said to bring good fortune and scare away bad spirits. Want more good luck for the year ahead? Dress in new clothing, even new shoes. It is said that those should translate to new good tidings and bundles of hope for the year ahead. If you skip the red, pass on black and white too; they represent mourning, the antithesis of the day's promising spirit. Not that anyone will know, but you're not supposed to wash your hair, talk about dead people, or use cuss words on that day.

Lantern Festivals เทศกาลโคมไฟ

It's a happy time when the rainy season ends. And so the Thais celebrate with two purification rituals. Loy Krathong and Yi Peng take place in late October/early November, each welcoming sunshine in their own ways. (Loy Krathong is on the 12th full moon of the lunar calendar, Yi Peng on the second full moon day of the ancient Lanna lunar calendar.) Loy Krathon involves lanterns: Celebrants place candles and flowers into baskets that are inserted into lanterns, then gently send the items—and ugly feelings—on their way in the local waterway. The baskets are often made of banana leaves. While Loy Krathong is celebrated in Bangkok, Chiang Mai, and Sukhothai, Yi Peng is unique to the north. There, rice paper and bamboo lanterns with candles inside are sent skyward. You're bound to have a lucky year if your lantern stays illuminated until it's out of sight.

Yi Peng festival in Chiang Mai

Vegetarian Festival เทศกาลกินเจ

On the island of Phuket, the Vegetarian Festival is held every fall, principally in September or October—whenever the Chinese lunar calendar's ninth month occurs. It is a tribute to meat-free eating, yet there's more to it than that. Body self-harm, usually while in a trance, is part of the action. That might entail getting a piercing, cutting one's tongue, climbing a ladder with sharp edges, standing too close to active firecrackers, or walking on hot coals. You might see swords—even multiple swords—jutting out of people's cheeks. The acts are seen as a way of cleansing one's soul from the inside out. Participants do this self-harm to usher in good luck and drive away the bad. You'll see barely any blood, and scars are few; that is credited to the Chinese gods who are integral to the reasoning behind this form of worship. —so maybe those Chinese gods are doing their part from the start. The participants doing these self-mutilations are referred to as Ma Song. They congregate at the island's 40 Chinese shrines—which are the festival's hubs—and dress in white for the festival's nine-day duration while eating only vegan foods and abstaining from sex. The principal Chinese shrines involved are Jui Tui, Bang Neow, and Put Jaw, in Phuket Town, as well as Kathu in the Kathu District and Cherng Thalay (Thalang). You can watch processions daily of those partaking of the rituals. Pick up a schedule with the parade routes at the tourist office at 65 Thalang Road in Phuket Town. Oh, and yummy plant-based foods are for sale.

Water Festival (Songkran) เทศกาลเล่นน้ำ (สงกรานต์)

Songkran is Thailand's annual water festival, held throughout the country in mid-April. The holiday has Buddhist roots—it is about sprinkling one another for purity, and in the early days was performed with water used to clean Buddha statues. You'll lose sight of that as you gleefully drenching each other or strangers with huge doses of H20: Buckets, hoses, plastic bazookas. Go for it. Temperatures soar in April, so the timing is just right. Interesting history: Songkran, which means *movement*, was originally the Thai new year and today is officially a national holiday. In 1888, the official new year was moved to April 1. Before that, it fell on whatever spring date the original Buddhist calendar dictated. Then in 1940 it moved again to January 1. That original Buddhist calendar differs from the Gregorian one used in the United States; the actual days are the same, in fact, but the year corresponds to Buddha's birth, not Jesus Christ's. Takeaway: 2021 in the western world is 2564 in Thailand; there is always a 543-year difference. In Central Thailand, residents celebrating Songkran also tidy up their homes in preparation. In the north, men in historical dress join an elephant parade. In other places it's all party, all the time: in Bangkok, the hub is Khao San Road.

ESSENTIAL INFORMATION

CHOOSING WHERE TO STAY

We have recommended hotels we love, in places we love, throughout this book. Each one is a safe bet... but that doesn't mean that every place will be the right place for you.

Whether you're visiting a city, the country, or an island, discuss what matters most to both of you. Consider each of the following:

Location Do you want bustle the second you step out the door, and to be able to get a good cup of coffee a block from your room, or would you rather be in an upscale residential neighborhood? Is being close to fine dining a priority, or would you prefer an easy walk to street-food vendors? Is proximity to nature, or being mere steps from the beach, what your vacation is about? If you're planning to use public transport, consider how easy your accommodations will be to reach from the nearest train, bus, or ferry terminal.

Features Even within the same price range, lodging can vary hugely. One option might have a kitchen or kitchenette—ideal for quiet breakfasts in your room—while another might have an on-site restaurant. Maybe you want somewhere with a bathtub and/or a balcony or terrace with views; perhaps having access to an in-house spa, fitness centre, or concierge desk is important.

Basics If you're traveling on a budget, check in advance that your hotel, inn, apartment, or hostel has air conditioning and Wi-Fi (if those are important to both of you) as they're not always standard at the lower end of the scale.

Decor Some travelers get a true kick out of a hotel that makes a statement, whether the atmosphere says "chic," "colonial," or "traditional Thai." Others just need a clean place to lay their heads at night.

To find the best accommodations for your romantic getaway, hotel websites are a wonderful place to start. Nearly all lodging facilities also have Facebook pages, often detail the latest offers. If the description is in Thai, you can copy and paste it into Google Translate for a translation. Translation is often an issue on websites; some have little information and present it poorly. In that case, it's worth looking at third-party websites like Oyster.com, Hotels.com, and Booking.com: All sometimes mention perks the websites don't, such as free breakfast buffets. Oyster.com is the most straightforward: It lists cons as well as pros, to help you make a wise decision. Google.com, TripAdvisor.com, and Priceline.com are among the other contenders, but their reviews come from regular travelers, not professionals. Taking the opposite approach, the Michelin guide to Thailand lists hotels and restaurants selected by seasoned professionals—but doesn't share much detail or any pictures. Of course, you could also hire a travel agent to find you a hotel: The best ones will take notes of your preferences and tailor an itinerary for you.

When it comes to price, it can be overwhelming to know where to find the best deal. If you've got the time (and the inclination), it's worth checking the hotel's own website as well as a handful of other websites such as hotelscombined.com, kayak.com, agoda. com, skyscanner.com, and hotels.com. While you can often find lower prices on these sites than booking direct, bear in mind that hotels often counteract this by offering special deals for booking direct. Sometimes this might be a special price, other times it's a package that includes, say, a romantic dinner, a spa treatment, and airport transfers. In general, expect more flexibility, as well as loyalty points if it's a chain (although hotels.com has its own loyalty program). If you don't book direct, watch out for "resort fees" (even at hotels that don't label themselves as resorts), and other fees, taxes, and charges that aren't stated up front. These can quickly add up.

If you'd prefer to nestle up in your own little home-away-from-home while in Thailand, or to keep costs down, Airbnb (airbnb. com/thailand/stays) is a good way to do that. It's an American website and app that specializes in short-term accommodation rental, from a room in someone's home to an entire apartment or house.

In Thailand, the options with Airbnb are vast. You might choose an apartment in Bangkok or within a national park, a whole house in a village, a cabin surrounded by rice paddies, a private pool villa near a tribal village, a serviced apartment near the beach, a room in a mansion, or two beds at a hostel. Guests and hosts review one another at the end of the stay and so, together with an array of photographs, you'll have a good idea of what to expect before you book. You'll usually give up the housekeeping services and such that you'd get in a hotel, but you'll gain a more local residential experience and, in most cases, plenty of space. The Airbnb customer service team is responsive when you need assistance.

CREDIT CARDS

You know how your credit card company notices fraudulent activity and jumps in to stop the card until you talk to a representative? That's great at home, but the system occasionally backfires. You might charge one dinner in Thailand and the bank will stop your card because it thinks the card has been stolen. And if the bank can't call you because you have no overseas calling plan, you might not find out until you try to use it again.

There's no simple way around this, but you can make some smart moves. First, call your card provider before you travel to tell a representative where you'll be and when. Sometimes your card will be stopped anyway, but it's much less likely in this scenario. Find out in advance how to contact the issuer if your card is stopped, which will make it much easier to reach someone helpful should you need to. Second, it's worth getting a card that has no foreign transaction fees. (If you already have one, make sure it doesn't expire while you'll be away).

If you're choosing a card, compare other perks: Is there automatic insurance covering your airline ticket? What happens if you lose your card overseas? How is the exchange rate decided? Can you increase or decrease your credit line?

A final option is to use a pre-paid travel card. This will have nothing to do with your bank account. If it's stolen, you'll lose the money you spent to buy it but your other assets will be safe If you use both this and a regular credit card, always keep one in the hotel safe while out-and-about with the other.

Some businesses give the option of charging you in baht or dollars: choose baht. In most instances, the credit card company will give you a better conversion rate than the business owner.

Plus, if you choose dollars over baht, the merchant might add a dynamic currency conversion (DCC) fee of three percent without telling you.

CROSSING THE ROAD

Travel is all about experiences, right? In Thailand, crossing the street is included in that list. In many places, you just have to... cross. Even in Bangkok's trendy Thonglor neighborhood, the main roads have neither traffic lights nor crosswalks for very long stretches. Thankfully, the traffic is usually slow because the roads are packed, but you'll still have to find a sort-of opening between autos, then quickly and carefully maneuver to the other side, hoping eye-contact with drivers plus luck will allow you to arrive safely. So woeful is Thailand's road-safety situation that the World Health Organization reports Thailand has 22,500 fatalities a year—which is high. So look both ways when you're walking, and be ultra-careful for pedestrians when you're driving.

ELECTRICITY

Thailand's electric outlets are for 220V with a 50Hz frequency. Pack O and C plugs, or better yet bring a universal travel adaptor, so you can charge your smartphone and e-reader, and use your hairdryer or electric shaver, without ruining them. Many adaptors include USB ports these days.

EMBASSIES AND CONSULATES

If you need help with a crucial matter, your country's embassy in Thailand might be able to help. Contact your embassy while abroad if you're severely ill, need passport assistance, are dealing with the death of a family member while in Thailand, have been arrested or victimized, or if you need solid advice about transferring money, finding a doctor, or contacting your family. The United States, Canada, and the United Kingdom have embassies in Bangkok and Chiang Mai; Australia has embassies in the same cities and also one in Koh Samui. A full listing is available at embassy-worldwide. com. The U.S. Embassy explains its parameters at th.usembassy. gov/u-s-citizen-services/what-we-can-and-cannot-do.

GETTING CASH

Bring along your bank card for when you need cash, unless you can use your credit card without incurring fees. ATMs tend to have a good conversion rate, and many don't charge large fees like currency exchange businesses do. You may need to exchange enough for at least a cab fare before leaving home—or at an airport currency-exchange counter (unless you can find an airport ATM) when you arrive—but it's generally worth waiting to convert more money at an ATM in your destination. The biggest withdrawal allowed is about 20,000 baht, around $660 at the time of writing. Most cash machines charge a withdrawal fee of 200 baht ($7) or more; some banks will return the fee to you. And, some also bank cards charge foreign exchange fees; see what your bank offers before leaving home. If ATMs ask about choosing a conversion option, say no. You're likely to get a better exchange rate by choosing "Continue Without Conversion." Some will add an "exchange rate market-up" and/or an access fee, so beware. If an ATM charges that once, try a different company's ATM the next time.

Once you're at your destination, you can always trust banks to be honest about conversion, although they do often charge fees. Before leaving home, see if your bank has a no-fee arrangement with a Thai outfit like Bangkok, Kasikorn, Krungthai, or Siam Bank.

If so, try to exchange your money there when possible.

IMPORTANT PHONE NUMBERS

If you don't speak Thai, it may be hard to communicate what your emergency is. Still, it's handy to keep these emergency numbers handy during your visit. There are 100 hotlines in Thailand, so we pared these down to the ones you're most likely to need.

Ambulance: 1554
Car accident: 1146
Car theft: 1192
Crime: 1195
Directory assistance: 1133
Emergency services (with voice prompt): 911
Fire: 199
Highway Police: 1193
Medical emergency: 1669
National Disaster Warning Center: 1860
Police (general emergency call): 191
Taxi driver who refuses your business: 1584
Tourist police: 1155
Tourist Service Center: 1672

INSECT REPELLENT

It's always hot and humid in Thailand—although undoubtedly much more so during the summer. This means you might encounter mosquitos; whose bites are always annoying. In some areas, mosquitos could carry malaria, dengue fever, Japanese encephalitis, or lymphatic filariasis. Use common sense:

- Cover up with lightweight clothing whenever possible, especially at dawn and dusk when mosquitos come out in large numbers. Lightweight long-sleeved tops and pants will keep the bugs off your skin.

- Use spray-on repellent (sold by convenience stores and pharmacies)
- Spray your clothing, not the skin underneath it. Do spray exposed body skin though.
- For the face, it's best to spray the insect repellent onto your hands and gently rub it in.
- If you're also using sunscreen, put that on first, wait half an hour, and then apply the bug spray on top of that.
- Hold off on scented products like perfume and cologne; bugs tend to be attracted to those.

INSURANCE

It might be cheaper to travel without insurance, yet it is highly advisable to buy it for all trips, and especially big ones like a vacation to Thailand. Many insurance options are available, but the basics are this: With the right plan, you'll be covered if you need to cancel for reasons like illness and natural catastrophes. Think of how many people lost pre-paid parts of the trips they'd planned to take during the Covid-19 pandemic, when most travel was halted. Your plan might cover airfare, pre-paid hotel stays, and items like luggage and laptops that are lost or stolen during your trip. Medical plans might cover doctors abroad if your insurance from back home doesn't, and could even pay to have you flown home in a medical crisis. If you book your vacation through a travel agent or tour company, you can usually buy insurance through them. Otherwise, or instead, look at websites like insuremytrip. com, travelinsurance.com, and squaremouth.com.

KNOW THE LAW

It's easy to stay out of trouble in Thailand, as long as you follow the rules: Don't steal, and definitely don't buy drugs (drug offenses can be punishable by execution). Do nothing to show disrespect for the royal family; even a snooty social media post can get you in trouble. Littering is punished fairly harshly, too. Also, wear a shirt while driving. It's illegal.

Be careful what you buy, too. It's illegal to bring the following items out of—or into—Thailand: narcotics, pornography, fake Thai flag designs, phony money or bonds, fake royal or official seals, pirated media, and counterfeit trademark items.

Likewise, many items, especially fine arts, are restricted. That means you need official government permission to bring them in and out of Thailand. Use this general rule: Don't take out a Buddha statue or image, or even parts of one, but trinkets and jewelry are fine. If you have bought—or want to buy—real Buddha art, get a permit. The place you buy it will help. The same goes for antiques.

Another no-no? Going about your business while the Thai National Anthem plays every morning at 8am and in the evening at 6pm. If you hear it over public loudspeakers, in a train station, at a bus station, or while passing a school, stop what you're doing. Stand still, as the locals do, and resume your goings-about when the song ends. It's a matter of respect.

MEDICAL INFORMATION

Every community has its hospitals and pharmacies. Ask at your hotel desk for recommendations, or check online for your nearest options. Most pharmacies are stocked with what you will need, but you may need to seek out an English-speaking employee or fellow shopper for guidance.

The following websites are useful for finding out information, both before you leave home and while you're abroad:

Centers for Disease Control and Prevention (wwwnc.cdc.gov/travel/destinations/traveler/none/thailand?s_cid=ncezid-dgmq-travel-single-001) This well-respected American governmental agency gives trustworthy information on vaccines you must receive, or should consider getting, before traveling to Thailand. We advise also checking with your doctor about vaccinations at least a month before departing.

Thailand Medical News (thailandmedical.news) has English-language articles on the latest medical concerns, though note that it is not run by the Thai government. To find medical assistance near you, either hover over Resources at the top of the home page and choose options like Thailand Hospital Listings or Doctor Listings, or scroll along the home page and click on tabs with the same names.

Travel Health Pro (travelhealthpro.org.uk/country/221/Thailand) is a British resource with information on vaccines, malaria, Covid, and other travel-health information.

PASSPORT

You'll need your passport to get into Thailand. Once there, it's good to carry your passport information with you when out-and-about: That could mean carrying your actual passport, or lock that in the hotel safe and carry around a good-quality copy of the page with your personal information, photograph, and passport number on it. As a couple, you might also put copies of one another's passports in each other's suitcases and backpacks.

Use your smartphones too: Keep pictures of your passports on your phones. If you have the technology, also make scans of your passports before leaving home and back them up with a cloud service you can retrieve from anywhere. You can also set up an app called Mobile Passport, which will save your information. As a bonus, you can also use this for quicker entry through some customs areas when you return home. Warning: Some bike and other rental vendors will ask to hold onto your passport until you return their vehicle. If this happens, go elsewhere. If you do lose your passport, contact the nearest embassy for your country.

SCAMS

Be a cynic. No matter how many hours you've spent sipping champagne at rooftop bars or chugging buckets in island beach bars, kick back into common-sense mode when it comes to transactions. If someone offers too-good-to-be-true prices for jewelry or sim cards, waterpark tickets, or custom-made suits, walk away—they really will be too good to be true. For peace of mind, purchase tickets and services from official or authorized dealers. Be especially wary in densely populated areas like Phuket, Bangkok, and Chiang Mai.

Here's what to watch out for:

Special deals on shopping Your tour guide or tuk-tuk or taxi driver suggests a dip into a jewelry store where he knows the owner. Nope, that special government or wholesale price isn't for real. The jewelry itself may not be made from precious metals or semi-precious stones. Buy from legitimate stores listed with the Thai Gem and Jewelry Association (en.thaigemjewelry.or.th). Your tour guide or driver will also get a cut for bringing you in.

Flat-rate taxi rides Other than from the airport, flat rates aren't trustworthy. Get into a cab that has and uses a meter. For less worry about being ripped off, order your pre-priced ride on an app such as Grab (grab.com) or Navigo (navigothailand.com), both of which work as Uber and Lyft do back home. (Of course, you'll need internet access to use them).

Entry tickets to a theme park or performance A scalper (unauthorized ticket seller) offers you discounted tickets so you can skip the line or get a better price. Another nope. Buy from a hotel concierge, an authorized dealer, or the on-site ticket/ admissions office.

Inflated ticket prices There's no denying that being—not to mention just looking like—a tourist means you might be charged more for some things than locals. This could a Muay Thai match, a palace visit, or a museum entrance fee. You're stuck though: If it's the official pricing policy, not one random crook at the door, pay and enjoy.

Being escorted away from a "closed" attraction Scamsters might try to convince you the attraction you want to visit is closed and insist on driving you to a different one. They'll upcharge you for that entry fee and might also dip into retailers supposedly offering big bargains en route. Walk away from anyone making suggestions like this, and check for yourself if an attraction is open.

Partying with prostitutes' Red-light districts up the scam factor. To avoid this, be sure to stay with the crowds. If you're escorted to an exclusive "ping pong" or other show, you may well end up being charged for a pretty lady's many drinks, and at inflated prices.

Rental motorbikes, bicycles, and watercraft Unfortunately, you can easily end up with junk vehicles, or be falsely accused of damaging them once they've been returned. Go with a legit vendor who has an official storefront or a kiosk related to a hotel. Pay for insurance (don't even consider renting if that's not an option). Snap pics of any dents or scratches beforehand, confirm the vendor has insurance too, and call the Tourist Police if you're being harassed by the vendor. Finally, do not hand over your passport for the vendor to keep while you use the vehicle.

SIM CARDS

If you want your smartphones to work when you're away from Wi-Fi, you'll have to buy a local sim card. Providers include AIS Thailand, China Unicom 4G, ISP Orange, Truemove, and DTAC. If possible, and especially if you're on a budget, be patient and do not purchase your sim card at the airport, even when the cards are presented as part of "tourist packages". Prices are lower in city stores and at major shopping malls. To see what options are best for you, read the pros and cons on websites such as simoptions. com (type "Thailand" into "Enter your destination," then select "Prepaid SIM Card Thailand"), traveltomtom.net (under "site search," type in "11 Best Thailand Tourist SIM Card in 2021"), and thethailandlife.com (run a Google search for "thethailandlife.com sim card" to find "How to Get a Thailand Sim Card & Mobile Data Plan"). Or, just ask your accommodations to point you to the nearest place that sells sim cards or short-use phones, and buy what's available. Try to dig for specifics about the parameters of each choice before you do so.

STREET FOOD

Even if you leave the country vowing only to eat in sterile-looking restaurants, once you inhale the aromas of cooked-to-order Thai street foods, you will no doubt succumb. Some of your tastiest meals in Thailand will be prepared on the spot by vendors who make, say, only crepes, or soups, or noodles, day in and day out. Here's how to stay safe:

- **Choose the busiest vendors** You'll have to wait longer, but you'll know the food is fresh and hasn't been sitting around for hours being pecked by flies.
- **Check out the vendors** Choose those who wash, wipe, or sterilize their hands often. Notice if they clean the spatulas, wipe the grill, and replace cloth towels. If they don't, try another.
- **Avoid raw foods** The ubiquitous, beautifully packaged fresh fruits for sale look mighty appealing, but beware that such delights may have been rinsed with tap water. Since they're uncooked, germs won't have been killed off. Wait for the hotel breakfast buffet to get your fix.
- **Be careful about condiments.** Squeeze bottles are fine, but think twice before scooping up flavor enhancers meant to be pinched between each diner's fingers.

Street food in Bangkok

SUPERMARKETS AND CONVENIENCE STORES

Supermarkets and convenience stores can be found throughout Thailand.

Convenience Stores

Lawson 108 (lawson108.com) is another common option. Based in Japan, this chain specializes in cookies and other baked goods. Its 130 Thai units also tend to have ATMs machines and e-payment machines.

7-Eleven (7eleven.co.th) dominates the landscape, just as it does back home, and branches can even be found on the islands. The stores are filled with the basics: Stop in to pick up a six-pack of beer, an iced coffee, mosquito repellent, a sandwich, or sunscreen.

Supermarkets

Big C (bigc.co.th) has over 150 hypermarkets (i.e. very large stores) in Thailand. Based in Bangkok, this chain is known for competitive pricing on its goods. Seek out regional snacks like dried jackfruit, and potato chips with Thai flavorings such as shrimp tom yum or hot chili squid. Teas are another good find here.

Tesco Lotus (tescolotus.com/en) is an international chain with 2,000 grocery stores and hypermarkets in Thailand. You can stock up on food staples groceries and sundries here, and also on small kitchen electronics, gift baskets, snacks, laundry detergent and, again, Thai spices and curries at prices set for locals, rather than tourists. Some items are sourced from local communities. Many branches are located in malls and have food courts.

Tops (tops.co.th/en) is on the upscale side, stocking everything from bottled water multipacks and pasta to gift baskets and granola. Prices on Thai items like curry powders are better here than in gift stores, and the same goes for cosmetics. The chain has about 120 units altogether, including superstores

TOILETS

You'll find plenty of free, clean, and modern facilities in Thailand—including many with Western-style toilets. You'll also find more basic ones, known as squat toilets—a hole in the ground with spots for each foot on either side, with no flush. You might also come across a hybrid between the two. As toilet paper isn't always supplied, we'd recommend carrying little packs of tissues or travel-size toilet paper rolls with you, especially on long journeys. Pre-moistened wipes like Wet Ones and/or travel-sized bottles of hand sanitizer are also good to tuck into your carryall for keeping your hands clean. Note that not all toilets are free. You may have to pay a nominal fee, say 10 cents, to use town center, park, or beach facilities.

TOURISM AUTHORITY OF THAILAND (TAT)

After this book, the Tourism Authority of Thailand (tourismthailand. org), or TAT, will be the most useful resource for planning your trip. Unlike blogs, tour operator websites, and other informative but unverified sources, TAT is trustworthy. The organization is official, run by the government under its Ministry of Tourism and Sports, and it has the resources to get and share accurate information.

Its website isn't grand. In fact, it's slow and clunky. Not every attraction is featured, and the information is sometimes scant. But you can believe what it says is true, then do further research with what you learn. In addition to facts about places to see, the website has many feature articles about specific topics. Searches for "romance" and "couples" come up blank, so seek out articles like, "Nothing but Chilli in Chiang Khan" and "Escape to Two Unique Hotels in Chiang Rai." You'll also find resources for spa visits, foods, and festivals.

TRANSPORT

Thailand is a modern country, so you can get around the country the same ways as back home. You'll find trains, planes, busses, ferries, and private drivers, many of whom are also guides, to take you between destinations. Some itineraries are simple enough to plan yourselves, others so complex—especially given often-confusing websites and the language barrier—that you'll benefit by having a travel agent step in. One compromise is 12go (12go.asia/en), where the Asia pages recommend travel options for multi-leg routes. For example, if you want to travel from Bangkok to Pattaya, you choose those destinations and a date, then 12go will offer several options. Each option will state what's involved (taxi, train, etc.), how much it will cost, and how long it will take. Then, if you're ready and want to, you can click "Book now". That will reserve all your spots at once so you won't need to take care of each individually. Options for the Bangkok-to-Pattaya trip might range from 1¾-hour taxi ride ($73 total) to a three-hour van ride ($7 per person). Journeys that involve boats, such as Bangkok to Koh Tao, are more complex, with trips ranging from 11½ hours (bus and ferry-$41 per person) to 18 hours (train and ferry-$54 per person).

TRAVEL RESOURCES

TourHQ (tourhq.com/thailand-tours-guide) is a matchmaker between visitors and tourism professionals, it lists tours, itineraries, guides, and tour operators. On its "Marketplace" page (tourhq. com/travelermarketplace), you can type in what you seek and have several guides contact you, decreasing the legwork.

VISA

If your visit will be for 30 days or fewer, you will not need a visa to visit from the United States, although you may need a visa for a 60-day vacation. The same is true for tourists from France, Germany, and the United Kingdom, among others. Residents of many South American countries can stay 90 days without a visa. When you do need a visa, you might need to secure it in advance, and might need to do that upon arrival; that depends on rules specifically for your country of origin. Do the legwork long before leaving home. And, you might need to secure your visa in advance, and might need to do that upon arrival. Rules change, so check via your country's official website and/or Thailand's in advance, or contact the Thai consulate or embassy. In addition, make sure your passport has at least six months left before it expires. The U.S. Department of State (travel.state.gov) has the most reliable information for Americans. To find it, click on International Travel, then type in Thailand under "Learn about your destination." From here, you'll find health alerts, vaccination requirements, passport rules, and embassy and consulate phone numbers, and street and email addresses.

USEFUL PHRASES

Most of the time, a sincere smile and hand gesture or two are all you need to interact with locals. It's always best to be able to start with a greeting in Thai, of course.

Below are common phrases to get you started. Some words change based on the gender of the speaker, with females using *ka* or *kap* at the end of a sentence, males *krap* or *khrup*.

Hello = Sa wat dee
Good bye = La gorn khrup

Thank you [often uttered while taking a deep bow] = Kop koon
Yes = Chai
No = Mai chai
I don't understand = Mai cow jai
How are you = Sa bai dee mai khrup
Not spicy = Mai phet
Delicious = Aroy
Where is the toilet = Hong nam yu nai kha

WATER

Avoid tap water. Your system isn't used to the micro-organisms in it, so it can make you ill. Be safe and use bottled water instead, even for brushing your teeth.

Thank you for reading and we hope this guide has shown you the many great adventures and romantic experiences Thailand has on offer. If you enjoyed this book, we would love if you could take a moment to share your thoughts by leaving a review.

PHOTO CREDITS

Made in United States
North Haven, CT
25 April 2022

18551622R00254